FRANCE AND THE CONSTRUCTION OF EUROPE, 1944–2007

BERGHAHN MONOGRAPHS IN FRENCH STUDIES

FRANCE AND THE CONSTRUCTION OF EUROPE, 1944–2007

THE GEOPOLITICAL IMPERATIVE

Michael Sutton

Berghahn Books
NEW YORK • OXFORD

First published in 2007 by

Berghahn Books

www.berghahnbooks.com

© 2007, 2011 Michael Sutton
First paperback edition published in 2011

Library of Congress Cataloging-in-Publication Data

Sutton, Michael, 1942-

France and the construction of Europe, 1944-2007 : the geopolitical imperative / Michael Sutton.

p. cm. -- (Berghahn monographs in French studies)

Includes bibliographical references and index.

ISBN 978-1-84545-393-0 (hbk) -- ISBN 978-0-85745-290-0 (pbk)

1. France--Foreign relations--1945- 2. France--Politics and government--1945- 3. France--Foreign relations--European Union countries. 4. Europe Union countries--Foreign relations--France. I. Title.

DC404.S87 2007

327.440409'045--dc22   2007044676

British Library Cataloguing in Publication Data

A catalogue record for this book is available from
the British Library.

Printed in the United States on acid-free paper

ISBN: 978-1-84545-393-0 (hardback)
ISBN: 978-0-85745-290-0 (paperback)

In memory of Anthony Hartley and Maurice Larkin

CONTENTS

PREFACE

The general aim of this book is to address the question of the significance of France's role in what the French themselves term '*la construction européenne*'. This French expression, whose literal English translation ('the European construction') does not have the same allusive force, conjures up the element of voluntarism that has been characteristic of France's own role. As is indicated by the book's subtitle, it is a role which, in this author's judgement, has been largely shaped by geopolitical considerations.

The period covered is the past sixty years or so, apart from some setting of the earlier historical background. It starts with the liberation of Paris in August 1944, when Charles de Gaulle assumed power at the head of the new Provisional Government of the French Republic. And, marking perhaps the end of an era in French politics, it concludes with the stepping down from office of Jacques Chirac, the last of the Fifth Republic's presidents to have been a political contemporary of de Gaulle.

The book is proffered to the reader as an exercise in contemporary history, and the author will be rightly satisfied if the story told is judged to be coherent and well founded. As a work of history, the methodological assumptions are Oakeshottian in kind – broadly in keeping, that is, with Michael Oakeshott's reflections on the nature of history. To the extent that it is a study belonging also to the academic discipline of international relations, it lies analytically within the tradition of the 'English School'; this is largely on account of the implicit use of Martin Wight's concept of a 'society of states'. More generally, Elie Kedourie's finely crafted writings on politics and international affairs have provided a model of style and analysis to be aspired to.

Aston University, whose staff I joined in 1995, has provided me with a good academic home and environment for writing a work of this kind. The work's inspiration has also come from questions I have confronted elsewhere, analysing European economic developments during some twenty years spent in Brussels from the early 1970s to the early 1990s, and, overlapping this period, during the course of nearly a quarter century's association with the Economist Intelligence Unit (EIU). Stimulation also came in the first half of the 1990s from teaching international relations, including European integration, at Boston University's London Graduate

Center and at the Maria Curie-Skłodowska University in Lublin, Poland. I am grateful to my colleagues, past and present, in the worlds of praxis and theory for their intellectual liveliness and for what I have learnt from them. And this gratitude extends, of course, to all who have provided library and information support.

The work in its wide sweep is essentially one of synthesis, rather than of narrowly focused scholarship at the academic coalface. It draws heavily on the labours of other scholars whose research has been largely based on the painstaking consultation of unpublished diplomatic and personal archives. Such reliance has been greater for the early part of the period studied, though some excellent works based substantially on archival material have already been published on the recent enough subject of German unification in its international context. On the other hand, extensive use has been made of published official documents and – I hope, not uncritically – memoirs and similar first-hand material. In shaping the broader picture, I am especially indebted to the scholarship of Georges-Henri Soutou, Maurice Vaïsse, and Frédéric Bozo, and, for the pre-war period, Anthony Adamthwaite.

I have drawn in some chapters on my own nonacademic yet research-based published writings, especially those for the EIU's regular quarterly reports on France and, secondly, for *Report from Brussels*, a monthly economics newsletter, now defunct, which I edited during my long stay in 'Europe's capital'. Unless otherwise indicated, the translations of French quotations are mine; exceptions are those drawn from Richard Mayne's translations of Jean Monnet's *Mémoires* and Jean-Baptiste Duroselle's *L'Europe. Histoire de ses peuples*, and also those drawn from A. G. Harryvan and J. van der Harst's *Documents on European Union*.

Charles Jenkins at the EIU heads the list of persons to whom special thanks are due. Without his invitation in 1985 to write regularly on political and economic developments in France, this book would never have materialised. My EIU editor, Philip Whyte, greatly helped me by critically reading the completed manuscript in one fell swoop and commenting upon it. On the academic front, Nicolas Bárdos-Féltoronyi and Rüdiger Görner were assiduous readers from the start, making suggestions and giving constant and much appreciated support. Other willing academic readers, sparing generously of their time, included David Howarth, Jean-Claude Koeune, the late Maurice Larkin, Conrad Reuss, and Georgios Varouxakis. Jacques Prévotat provided strong encouragement as always. Useful books were thrust into my hands by Geneviève Mosseray, Chad Peterson, and (again) Georgios Varouxakis. Other helpers in the field included Rory Clarke, Said Haddadi, Jörg Mathias, Nathalie Mrgudovic, and Anne Stevens. In its last stage, the work benefited considerably from, first, the report of Berghahn's anonymous reader and, secondly, the comments and proposals of Irwin Wall, the series editor. The final improvements, so important for any author, came through the good work of the production and copy editors, Anna Wright and Cecilia Busby respectively. Marion Berghahn has been an attentive, engaged and supportive publisher. For the help, pertinent remarks, criticisms, and suggestions of all involved, I am most grateful. The usual disclaimer applies – mine alone are the faults.

Very special gratitude goes to Agneta Mauléon Sutton for intellectual stimulus, practical support, and long and patient forbearance.

M.S.
May 2007

ABBREVIATIONS AND ACRONYMS

ARRC   Allied Rapid Reaction Corps
BIS   Bank for International Settlements
CAP   Common Agricultural Policy
CEA   Commissariat à l'Energie Atomique
CDU   Christlich Demokratische Union
CFSP   Common Foreign and Security Policy
CINC–AFCENT   Commander-in-Chief of Allied Forces Central Europe
CJTF   Combined Joint Task Force
CSCE   Conference on Security and Cooperation in Europe
CSU   Christlich-Soziale Union
DM   Deutsche Mark
EC   European Communities/European Community
ECB   European Central Bank
ECSC   European Coal and Steel Community
ECU   European Currency Unit
EDC   European Defence Community
EEC   European Economic Community
EFTA   European Free Trade Association
EMA   European Monetary Agreement
EMCF   European Monetary Cooperation Fund
EMS   European Monetary System
EMU   Economic and Monetary Union
EPC   European Political Cooperation
ERM   Exchange Rate Mechanism
ERP   European Recovery Programme (Marshall Plan)
ESCB   European System of Central Banks
ESDP   European Security and Defence Policy
EU   European Union
EUA   European Unit of Account
EURATOM   European Atomic Energy Community
FAR   Force d'Action Rapide
FDP   Freie Demokratische Partei
FRG   Federal Republic of Germany
FTA   Free Trade Area

GATT   General Agreement on Tariffs and Trade
GDP   Gross Domestic Product
GDR   German Democratic Republic
GPRF   Gouvernement Provisoire de la République Française
IGC   Intergovernmental Conference
IMF   International Monetary Fund
INF   Intermediate-range Nuclear Forces
MCA   Monetary Compensatory Amount
MLF   Multilateral Force
MRP   Mouvement Républicain Populaire
NATO   North Atlantic Treaty Organisation
OECD   Organisation for Economic Cooperation and Development
OEEC   Organisation for European Economic Cooperation
OSCE   Organisation for Security and Cooperation in Europe
PCF   Parti Communiste Français
PDS   Partei des Demokratischen Sozialismus
PECO   Pays d'Europe Centrale et Orientale
PR   Parti Républicain
PS   Parti Socialiste
QMV   Qualified Majority Voting
RPF   Rassemblement du Peuple Français
RPR   Rassemblement pour la République
SACEUR   Supreme Allied Commander Europe
SDI   Strategic Defence Initiative
SEA   Single European Act
SFIO   Section Française de l'Internationale Ouvrière
SLBM   Submarine-launched Ballistic Missiles
SPD   Sozialdemokratische Partei Deutschlands
UDC   Union du Centre
UDF   Union pour la Démocratie Française
UDSR   Union Démocratique et Socialiste de la Résistance
VER   Voluntary Export Restraint (Arrangement)
WEU   Western European Union
WTO   World Trade Organisation

INTRODUCTION: DE GAULLE'S SHADOW

As head of France's recently installed Provisional Government, Charles de Gaulle passed an entire week in Moscow in December 1944. Buffeted by four wartime years of political sparring with Winston Churchill and disdained by Franklin Roosevelt up to the time of the Normandy landings, he had travelled to the Soviet capital to negotiate with Josef Stalin in the confidence that he now enjoyed some real international authority. One hope behind the visit was to win the Soviet leader's assent to the principle of French control of the left bank of the Rhine in any post-war German settlement. The Rhine had been seen as one of France's 'natural frontiers' at the time of the French Revolution, and de Gaulle's reflexes were attuned to the preoccupations of Marshal Foch and Raymond Poincaré after the First World War when they had unsuccessfully championed the cause of an independent Rhineland. A bilateral treaty with an initial term of twenty years was signed in Moscow, but without substantive commitments from the Soviet side. De Gaulle thus returned largely empty-handed to France. Fifteen years later his description of this wartime journey to the USSR and the surreal and macabre atmosphere he encountered in the Kremlin were to lie at the heart of one of the celebrated chapters of his elegantly crafted war memoirs – the chapter tellingly entitled '*Le rang*', the author's concern being France's 'rank' in a radically transformed post-war world.[1]

De Gaulle was not invited to the Yalta Conference in February 1945. And nor was he invited to the Potsdam Conference in the summer of 1945. France had therefore little say in what might be termed the Potsdam order for Europe, that is, the shape given to the continent through the arrangements governing Germany's future that were decided by the Big Three in Brandenburg's historic capital. Yet only five years afterwards, by virtue of the Schuman Declaration, France took the lead in initiating a process that would transform the face of the western half of the continent through the setting up of the European Communities (EC). Then four decades later, when the geopolitical divide associated with the Yalta Conference crumbled and German unification took place, France and Germany played the dominant role in the framing of the Treaty on European Union, signed

---

Notes for this introduction begin on page 13.

in Maastricht in 1992. After the fall of the Berlin Wall, the big push for economic and monetary union had come from the French president, François Mitterrand. Furthermore, the Maastricht Treaty's so-called pillar structure accorded with French views of the role of the nation state in the process of European integration. Even if by the start of the twenty-first century France's leadership role – either in its own right or in partnership with Germany – had become less secure, the scale of the achievement could not be doubted. France had emerged from the Second World War in a far weaker diplomatic position than it had come out of the First World War. Yet, in the second half of the twentieth century, France succeeded in restoring a powerful place for itself in Europe, whereas in the 1920s the undisguised ambition to establish and consolidate a position of ascendancy on the continent had singularly failed.

To consider the period of some sixty years since the end of the Second World War, de Gaulle may be seen as the linchpin figure. 'European union' figured highly among his aims. He saw it as consisting essentially in permanently organised close cooperation between Western European states under French leadership. In the late 1940s, under the Fourth Republic, French diplomatic efforts had already been deployed to this end, long before de Gaulle's return to power at the head of the Fifth Republic. Crucially there was the innovative role played at the start of the 1950s by Jean Monnet and Robert Schuman. And much later in the century France was to be at the fore again when Mitterrand did so much to shape the Maastricht Treaty. Through it, the European Economic Community (EEC) and an otherwise inchoate European union were transformed into an integrated international organisation, the officially named European Union (EU). However, de Gaulle's contribution was arguably greater than that of any other of his countrymen, even if none of the major international treaties advancing the political and economic unity of Western Europe was signed when he ruled over France. His achievement was to have put the European integration process securely on the rails for the remainder of the century, after making clear France's conditions for backing it and putting down markers for the process's future development.

This assertion of de Gaulle's significance may appear questionable and, in view of his dislike of supranationalism, something of a paradox. But it is less so when seen from the perspective of the Fifth Republic's beginnings. A telling point in this respect was made by Raymond Aron in his *Mémoires* when he dwelt upon the consequences for future European integration of de Gaulle's resignation as head of government in 1946 and then his return to office twelve years later. Aron pointed out that the succession of regimes – the non-Gaullist Fourth Republic and then the Fifth – made for a quirk of history favouring the successful birth of the EC. 'The politicians of the Fourth Republic', he said, 'had bequeathed a legacy of faits accomplis which the General could not go back on', and so the 'cunning of reason' in history (Hegel's *'die List der Vernunft'*) was favourable, since de Gaulle 'would not have signed the [EC] treaties', whereas 'the Fourth Republic would probably have been incapable of implementing them'.[2]

The pivotal year was indeed 1958. De Gaulle had assumed power in June; and soon afterwards in September the new constitution was approved and in December he was elected President of the Republic. This same year, when the Fifth Republic came into being, was coincidentally the first in the existence of the EEC, which had been established by the Treaty of Rome, signed in March 1957, 'to lay the foundations of an ever closer union among the peoples of Europe' (Preamble). Due to take place at the beginning of 1959 was the first round of tariff cuts by the EEC's six member states, thus starting the progressive establishment of the planned customs union. The incoming French president could well have scuppered this move and the entire EEC project at this particular point in time. Ready support would have been forthcoming in France, since many of the politicians of the erstwhile Fourth Republic remained opposed to the Treaty of Rome for political or economic reasons. Pierre Mendès France, for example, was among their number. Yet de Gaulle chose to stay his hand, notwithstanding his own deep misgivings about the elements of supranationalism in the EEC's design and his lack of sympathy for various ideas of Monnet and Schuman, the two Frenchmen at the origin of the whole EC endeavour in 1950.

Apart from reassuring the heads of government of the other EC member states of France's continued commitment to the treaties, de Gaulle influenced the future development of the EC in various ways. Although his proposals in 1961 for the creation of a 'Union of States' to exist along-side the EC ultimately proved abortive, these same proposals fore-shadowed the 1970s, when there was the setting up of the European Council at the instigation of the then French president, Valéry Giscard d'Estaing, and also the inception of cooperation by EC member states in the sphere of foreign policy. Furthermore, some thirty years later, the 'pillar' structure of the EU, as established by the Maastricht Treaty, echoed de Gaulle's earlier design. This design for a union of European states testified to his resolve that the pursuit of integration in Western Europe should remain firmly in the control of its nation states. Sometimes in opposition to Monnet, he was determined that any ambiguities in the Treaty of Rome about the locus of power should be settled in favour of power at intergovernmental rather than supranational level. And he was equally determined that France's interests should be served by the EC decision-making machinery.

This twin determination was evident in the matter of the EEC's Common Agricultural Policy (CAP), whose shape had been left open by the Treaty of Rome with the consequence that it became an object of negotiation by EC member states in the 1960s. As widely expected, de Gaulle exerted France's weight to ensure that the CAP arrangements served many of the interests of the country's large agricultural sector. Less expected was the diplomatic crisis over the CAP's financing that he provoked in 1965–66; he and Maurice Couve de Murville, the foreign minister, successfully used it to force assent to the principle of unanimous voting by the EC Council of Ministers whenever important national interests were at stake. This principle, as unofficially enshrined in the so-called Luxembourg Compromise, was to be watered down only in 1987 on the coming into force of the Single European Act (SEA), which made qualified majority voting mandatory for matters relating to the completion of the single market. Yet France and other member states, notably the UK, have continued to attach importance to the principle of unanimity, notably in respect of major issues in the sphere of the EU's Common Foreign and Security Policy (CFSP).

Finally, in this enumeration of the ways in which de Gaulle left his imprint on the EC and post-war Europe, there is the forging of France's special relationship with the Federal Republic of Germany (FRG) by virtue of the Elysée Treaty of Franco-German Cooperation which he and Konrad Adenauer signed in 1963. If various events since the middle of the 1950s had helped prepare the ground, the treaty itself marked the formalisation of an alliance that was to shape the future course of France's external relations. Its significance was heightened by the French president's decision to simultaneously blackball the UK's first application for EC membership. Largely because of initial opposition on the German side, the treaty bore fruit only with the passage of time, notably during Giscard's presidency and, more importantly still, Mitterrand's. Yet de Gaulle and Adenauer, through forging this alliance, had indirectly contributed to what later emerged as a union of European states in the shape of the EU.

There have thus been striking continuities in France's approach to European union over the past half century and more. Such continuity marked the passage of the Fourth Republic to the Fifth. And it has also marked the passage of one presidency to another during the Fifth Republic. These continuities have testified to a high degree of constancy in perceptions of national interest. Lying behind the protean enough concept of the national interest have been a variety of considerations that have often meshed uneasily together. Yet if there has been a dominant and persistent idea, it is simply that of its being in France's interest to build and strengthen a union of European states, with France itself holding a privileged place therein.

In this matter of the national interest, more should be said about de Gaulle, especially if he is deemed to have worked for the cause of European union. His ambitions for France on the European stage were not the reflection of any so-called Hobbesian view of international politics – one in which states were implacably locked in continual jealousies and gladiatorial postures of real or virtual war, to borrow imagery from Hobbes's *Leviathan*. Instead, his assumptions about the nature of international politics as practiced within the borders of Western Europe were typical of those who had experienced the old European order prior to the outbreak of the First World War. In particular, there was the assumption that the assurance of peace and security on the continent called for the collective exercise by certain states of a diffused hegemony, with the important rider that, in de Gaulle's mind, there should be a primus inter pares in the exercise of such hegemony and that this role should fall to France. That he could propose a 'Union of States', to be set up alongside the EEC and act as its political framework, marked not only a presumption about France's vocation but also a conviction that this European Union's members would remain bound together by common interests and common values. In short, they would constitute a European 'society of states' – to borrow a term associated with the seventeenth-century diplomat and jurist, Hugo Grotius – albeit in a highly developed and institutionalised form.[3]

De Gaulle's concern with the rank and grandeur of France should be seen in this perspective. Through his conviction, moreover, that the restoration of the French state to a position of preeminence could take place only in the framework of a European society of states, whose leadership lay effectively in the hands of France, not only did he aspire to a recasting of the nineteenth-century European order that had been killed off by the Great War and then partly resurrected in the 1920s, but also he harked back to an earlier period. For – however clichéd the allusion – the founder of the Fifth Republic shared something of the spirit of a Louis XIV in entertaining the aim of a French order for Europe. Or, to borrow a term used by Voltaire, de Gaulle's ambition for continental Western Europe was the creation of an *'espèce de grande république'* ('sort of commonwealth'), with France at its head. However, such ambition was perforce of a quite different and much more modest kind than that pursued a century after Louis XIV by Napoleon. The self-crowned emperor's attempted order had been revolutionary in kind, aimed at the destruction of the existing European society of states, whereas the temper of de Gaulle's thinking about European international statecraft may be judged to have more in common with the frame of mind expressed in, say, the *Regicide Peace* of Edmund Burke or, somewhat differently, Charles Maurras's *Kiel et Tanger*.

It would be anachronistic to look for any precursors prior to the Westphalian settlement of 1648, even in the person of Richelieu, the outstanding French statesman who had marked the Thirty Years War by successfully raising expediency abroad to a fine art in the name of raison d'état. Yet one eminent portraitist of de Gaulle, namely Henry Kissinger, has chosen to identify him above all with the heritage of Richelieu. In *Diplomacy* – a distillation of practical and academic wisdom – the former US Secretary of State and student of Metternich, Castlereagh, and Bismarck opposes two approaches to the pursuit of the national interest, and he identifies them in the American context with the contrasting figures of Theodore Roosevelt and Woodrow Wilson, the two presidents who first brought the US out of isolation in the century of Europe's largely self-inflicted decline. Roosevelt's muscular foreign policy was founded on considerations of balance of power in the European tradition of diplomacy, whereas Wilson's idealism, giving birth to the League of Nations, was quintessentially American in its zeal to equate the national interest with the realisation of a world order founded on moral principle. Such is the diptych which Kissinger places at the beginning of his book. Looking to Europe in the second half of the twentieth century, he portrays de Gaulle as the finest exemplar of the European tradition of diplomacy in the service of old-fashioned national interest; and – alongside Theodore Roosevelt, but in a different way – he is effectively presented as a worthy successor to Richelieu, whom the author of *Diplomacy* credits with the first formulation of the twin concepts of (an amoral) raison d'état and the balance of power.[4]

But it may be wondered, as regards Kissinger's treatment of de Gaulle's place in history, whether the close linking of the concepts of national interest and raison d'état illuminates adequately the reasons that led the French president in the late 1950s and early 1960s to adopt the policies he did in the sphere of European integration. Certainly, balance-of-power considerations entered strongly into play in de Gaulle's forging of the German alliance at the expense of England – his preferred name for France's rival cross-Channel power – and, more globally, in his attempt to create a European 'Union of States' that would pull weight alongside the US and the USSR. On the other hand, in de Gaulle's dealings with other EC heads of government, there was no systematic resort on his part to the practice of raison d'état if by that concept is meant the unprincipled pursuit of interests and power in a Machiavellian mode, without any erosion of the state's independence. If a striking feature of his position on European union building is to be singled out, it is not any evidence that it was all a matter of raison d'état, but rather his acceptance that not only the functioning of the EC but also the pursuit of the national interest through European political cooperation called for some limited but real waiving of the state's powers.

It was thus that de Gaulle accepted, even if sometimes with great reluctance, the role of the EC supranational institutions as established by treaty law and also the joint framing by the Commission and the Council of Ministers of common EC policies. Furthermore, in his never-to-be-implemented design for a 'Union of States', there was provision for additional shared institutional arrangements. Opposed as he was to encroaching supranationalism in those areas of the EC treaties where the apportioning of powers had been left imprecise, he was nonetheless ready to countenance the sacrifice of certain powers. From the bundle of attributions making for statehood, he acknowledged that certain of them could be partially or wholly relinquished, provided the identity and ultimate sovereignty of the nation state was retained.

That France's greatest twentieth-century political figure chose to see matters in this light helps explain why there could be so marked a continuity in French policy towards European unity in the century's second half. De Gaulle was far from totally at odds with Monnet and Schuman. And later Giscard d'Estaing and Mitterrand – not to speak of the two neo-Gaullist presidents, Georges Pompidou and Jacques Chirac – were to be far from being totally at odds with de Gaulle. For the representation of France's role in the early EC years, hagiographical fashion has presumed to dictate that only a Monnet or a Schuman is entitled to the honour of 'father of Europe', but it would be wrong to portray these two figures as championing the cause of idealism for the continent's sake, especially if that same idealism is to be set in stark contrast to the General's crusty realism. No such Manichean divide can be justified, and this holds true too of some of the comparisons drawn between de Gaulle and Mitterrand, especially when the latter has been portrayed, at the expense of the former, as the virtuous heir of both Monnet and Schuman. Mitterrand himself, showing mastery in the display of symbols, laid claim to such a heritage when he decided that it behoved the Republic to have Monnet's and Schuman's remains transferred to the Panthéon in 1988; though since Schuman's family demurred, only Monnet's remains came to be disinterred and civically honoured by being placed in that august place of repose.

This is not to deny that, in the second half of the twentieth century and the first years of the twenty-first, there were sometimes significant differences in the policies adopted on Europe by different French presidents or governments. However, when such differences occurred, they were not usually ones that could be measured in varying degrees of loftiness of motive. They were rather differences in practical judgement about the range of attributions of statehood that could be legitimately delegated or pooled for the purpose of greater European union serving France's interest. No government or statesman in office under the Fourth and Fifth Republics has ever questioned the principle of national sovereignty itself, in the sense that the fount of power has always been seen to reside with the nation state even when the latter has voluntarily ceded certain of its attributions to a wider European body.

It is evident that at the heart of French efforts to construct a European union has been the troubled question of Franco-German relations. 'I love Germany so much that I am thrilled that there are two of them', François Mauriac is famously said to have remarked in 1958.[5] His *boutade* testifies to the trauma wrought on France by three wars with its powerful neighbour in the space of three generations. Even the one victory in 1918 had proved to be of the pyrrhic kind inasmuch as the huge bloodshed did not forestall a further war that ended in national humiliation. Because of this trauma, it is scarcely surprising that France's concern with its German question has lain at the heart of more than half a century's attachment to rebuilding a new European society of states. Expressed crudely, the ambition was, and has remained, to lock (initially) part and (more recently) the whole of Germany into a European union so as to secure French interests, not least peace and cooperation between the two countries.

However, what started as a French initiative was gradually transformed over time into a set of international and supranational arrangements under which Germany came to pull as much weight. Thus, from one Fifth Republic presidency to another, the balance of power has changed. De Gaulle – President of the Republic from 1959 to 1969, after having been the Fourth Republic's last prime minister in 1958 – confidently assumed that France alone could exercise a hegemonic role in continental Western Europe, with the young West Germany kept in a subordinate position. Pompidou (1969–74), fearing correctly that this hegemony was threatened by growing German economic and monetary power, sought anxiously to maintain France's leadership. However, Giscard d'Estaing (1974–81) acquiesced to the establishment of what tended to be a Franco-German diarchy; its modus operandi reflected West Germany's newly acquired leadership role in monetary affairs – both within the EEC and, as the leading European monetary power, in the wider world – and, secondly, the greater political weight which it was acknowledged France could still exert internationally. Mitterrand (1981–95) inherited and sought to consolidate this Franco-German relationship, notwithstanding the emergence of a more confident UK under Margaret Thatcher; and then, when German unification loomed into view, he vigorously accelerated the pace of European integration so as to preserve the special relationship with Germany and lock it more tightly into the union. It was left to Chirac (elected in 1995 and anew in 2002) to look beyond the world of the framing of the Maastricht Treaty and develop relations with the new greater Germany, a state whose European credentials have been impeccable, but whose centre of gravity has moved away from the Rhineland back to Berlin, the capital founded by the Second Reich.

Symbolism has always counted for much in this special relationship. In 1962, half a year before the signing of the Elysée Treaty, de Gaulle and Adenauer had come together for High Mass in Rheims Cathedral, that edifice of High Gothic glory which had been greatly damaged by German artillery fire in the First World War. Two decades later, in 1984, the Chancellor, Helmut Kohl, stood in silence holding hands with Mitterrand on the battlefield of Verdun in a notable gesture of political friendship. Then, in 2003, the German and French parliaments met at the chateau of Versailles to celebrate the fortieth anniversary of the Elysée Treaty and somehow disown earlier awkward memories: the crowning in the Hall of Mirrors of Wilhelm I as Kaiser of the Second Reich in 1871, and the signing in the same place of the punitive Treaty of Versailles in 1919. In 2004 Mitterrand's successor, Chirac, and Kohl's successor, Gerhard Schröder, publicly embraced one another at the War Memorial in Caen on the occasion of the sixtieth anniversary of the Normandy landings.

Yet in the four decades separating the prayers and remembrances of Rheims and Caen, much had changed in the nature of the two countries' relations. The face of Europe had been radically transformed well before the century's end, not only because of German unification but also because of the wider geopolitical upheaval in Central and Eastern Europe in 1989 and the collapse of the USSR in 1991. Until the end of the 1980s successive French presidents had sought to exercise leadership, or a diffused hegemony, over an EC area lying, perforce, largely to the west of the Elbe. Initially, at the time of the EC–6, it was a 'Carolingian Europe', associated geographically and culturally with the lands that had once been Charlemagne's empire, and such coincidence was partly the legacy of the Yalta divide. De Gaulle in his lifetime would have welcomed the restoration of independence to Poland and other Soviet bloc countries, and perhaps also their inclusion in the EC. However, Mitterrand's reaction to these countries' freedom proved ambivalent and almost begrudging, as witness his attitude in the early 1990s once the question of the future EU's enlargement, to include formerly communist countries from Central and Eastern Europe, came to be seriously discussed.

However, by the time of the 1993 legislative elections – which led to the formation of a *cohabitation* government and a waning of Mitterrand's power – the combination of German unification and a new fluidity in international relations in the wider Europe had made politically for a very different continent, which called for a more outward-looking EU. Only then was there the beginning of an adequate perception on the part of France's political establishment that the nature and challenge of continuing European integration had been radically transformed. In particular, the conflicts in former Yugoslavia, marked by so-called ethnic cleansing and even genocidal mass-murder, provided a forceful reminder that politically inspired barbarism was still endemic to the continent at the end of its grim twentieth century. And there was a corresponding recognition in Paris that the EU enlargement process had to continue, perforce prudently.

Swept away by the geopolitical change of the late twentieth century were the conditions under which France had once been able to aspire to the leadership of continental Western Europe. Yet French interests were still being catered for. After the EU's introduction of the euro in 1999, implementing the final stage of economic and monetary union (EMU), France's traditional concern with Germany was freed of many of the fears that had long surrounded the prospect of German unification. Further- more, it was under the firm guidance of the former French president, Giscard d'Estaing, that the Convention for the Future of Europe prepared much of the EU's constitutional treaty, signed in 2004. In the eyes of both Giscard and Chirac, this constitutional treaty appeared to consecrate what had always been the preferred French approach to European integration, an approach encapsulated in the concepts of a 'federation of nation-states' (Chirac's preferred expression) or a 'union of states with federal compet- ences' (Giscard's preference), and allowing for the continued wielding of national power. *Faire l'Europe sans défaire la France*, the felicitous title of a historical work covering the post-war period up to 2003 captures the spirit well – to make Europe, without unmaking France.[6]

The French electorate's rejection of the EU's constitutional treaty in the referendum held in May 2005 was therefore a blow to such assumptions. In France and elsewhere, this rejection was immediately perceived to have been a watershed event for the future course of European integration. Only time will tell whether this judgement was correct, or whether instead the referendum's result was little more than a historical blip, merely delaying the further reshaping of the EU's institutional arrangements by its member states.

This moment of French disenchantment in 2005 and its lingering spell in the remaining two years of the Chirac presidency, constitute an appropriate time for looking back on France's huge role in the process of European integration since the Second World War. Thus, the broad pur- pose of this book is to relate how France came to assume this role, to detail how it exercised its ascendancy, and to show how the geopolitical up- heaval in Europe towards the end of the twentieth century compromised this same ascendancy. A further purpose is to point to the importance of high politics, rather than purely economic considerations, in the conduct of French policy towards what in France is called *la construction européenne* ('the European construction') – a term that catches better the high politics dimension than the equivalent English term, 'European integration'. This approach has often lent a special character to French policy making, especially when framed by the President of the Republic, and it has contrasted with the less lofty goals that have tended to be pursued by most other European states, their horizons primarily set by the prospect of economic gain. The prospect of such gain has, of course, always been greatly important for France too, the most obvious example being the CAP, but it has been associated with, or subordinated to, other considerations relating to the country's security in Europe and its ability to wield power both in Europe and on the wider world stage. De Gaulle's shadow has loomed large.

Yet it has been argued by some scholars, most notably Andrew Moravcsik, that the 'French exception' in this respect is less than meets the eye. Correctly stressing the undiminished centrality of the nation state in the integration process, he has maintained that French policy making in respect of the EC or the EU has been as much dictated by economic con- siderations as anywhere else in Europe, that such considerations have been uppermost for all countries, and that even de Gaulle's motives were more economic in kind than geopolitical.[7] If the focus is strictly on the original EEC, and if, in addition, monetary affairs are lumped together with economic or commercial ones, there is much to be said for this thesis. However, once national foreign policies and matters of security and defence are taken into account, whether before or after the setting up of the EU, the primacy of the economic dimension is not self-evident. Furthermore, and crucially, if monetary integration is considered a matter falling largely under the remit of high politics, the picture changes even more. The strictly economic dimension may then have no claim at all to primacy.

The surrender at national level of what has traditionally been a prime regalian power, namely that of the state's monopoly issue of currency, could never have been a purely economic matter for France. Few would dispute that geopolitical considerations, relating to France's place in Europe, drove Mitterrand's huge, unrelenting effort to secure the implementation of EMU – first in 1989–91, when he forced German assent to the project in the framework of a binding treaty, and, secondly, in 1992–93, when he insisted that the project should not be derailed by any easing of French economic and monetary policy. What has been less widely recognised is the importance of power and security considerations in the leading role earlier played by Giscard d'Estaing, opposite the German Chancellor, Helmut Schmidt, in the planning of the future European Monetary System (EMS) and its Exchange Rate Mechanism (ERM) parity grid. In 1978, behind the jargon-laden Franco-German negotiations concerning symmetrical or asymmetrical burden sharing, lay the deeply political question of the degree to which any French government should be subordinate in the shaping of its economic and monetary policies to decisions taken across the Rhine. The collapse of the Bretton Woods system at the beginning of the 1970s had indirectly led to a change in the relation between the FRG and France in respect of the substance of power wielded in Europe by their respective governments and central banks, and, in this context, Giscard's (ultimately unsuccessful) bid to win German assent for an ERM assuring symmetrical burden sharing was driven even more by high politics than economic calculus.

In brief, therefore, policies pertaining strictly to the EEC as designed by the Treaty of Rome have tended by their very nature to be shaped by economic interests, and France has been no exception to this rule. But once the scope of European integration is viewed more widely, to encompass matters of state and not primarily market arrangements, high politics or geopolitical considerations necessarily intrude, and for no country has this been more evident than for France. In the period between the collapse of the Bretton Woods system and the putting in place in the 1990s of the European Central Bank (ECB), France's subordination to Germany in the exercise of monetary power was a matter of state for Giscard and Mitterrand – and indeed briefly for Chirac as well.

These distinctions make for the absence of a linear structure in the narrative that follows. The tale told in the first and third parts – the first part running up to the end of de Gaulle's presidency in 1969, the third part taking over the story on Pompidou's accession – is essentially one of high or geo-politics. The quest for security, after the trauma of three German invasions within the space of a century, and the related French ambition to exercise a leadership role in the Western half of continental Europe, constitute the dominant theme. French statesmen and governments repeatedly assume that many of the country's external interests are best achieved, through leverage, within the framework of a tightly organised European society of states. Furthermore, the pursuit by France of European monetary integration, to the extent that its rationale is the restraint of German monetary power, is necessarily a highly charged political endeavour. This is strikingly the case once German unification is at hand.

Almost making for a separate tale is how France – initially very reluctantly, and never without second thoughts – adopted progressively the economic liberalism that underlay much of the original Treaty of Rome.[8] Thus, a retreat from the full-blown *dirigisme* of the immediate postwar years started already in the second half of the 1950s, and, at an uneven pace, it continued down to the beginning of the twenty-first century, by which time *mondialisation* ('globalisation') had become established as a catchword denoting the new and sometimes inclement international economic environment. For the French economy, from a business standpoint, it is the tale that really counts. Yet politically speaking and, more particularly, in terms of the initiatives actually taken by France with its partner European states in the second half of the twentieth century, it is a tale that is largely subordinate to the country's wider quest for security and continental influence.

The structuring of the book into three parts, with the first and third parts encasing the second part that deals primarily with the economic (but not the monetary) dimension of European integration, reflects therefore the truth that considerations of power and security have provided much of the wider context for France's concern with European union. If the treatment of France's membership of the EEC – understood in its founding sense as the 'common market' – is confined to only the second part of the book, it is because the pursuit of economic gain as such has not been the prime motivating force for France's leading role, either in its own right or together with Germany, in the post-war European integration process. This is not to say that economic gain has been considered by those who govern France as being in any way unimportant, far from it; rather that the pursuit of economic gain, however vigorous, has often been made subordinate to the pursuit of power and security and the related enhancement of France's place or rank in Europe and the wider world.

On this last point it might even be argued that the French political establishment's often blinkered attitude towards economic matters, especially during the Mitterrand and Chirac years, contributed to the popular vote against the EU's constitutional treaty in May 2005. Widespread incomprehension of the treaty's more arcane aspects was manifest during the referendum campaign period. And there were related worries that incremental treaty change had cumulatively transformed by stealth the locus of sovereignty within the EU. But, equally important, the referendum was seized as an occasion to express a deep-rooted resentment about the state of the French economy, particularly the chronically unsatisfactory employment situation. Arguably, the investment of less high politics into EU affairs by both Mitterrand and Chirac, together with a more consequent approach to the liberalisation of the economy and labour-market reform, would have enabled France to keep better abreast of the changes wrought since the 1980s by the EU's tardy (and still ongoing) completion of its own single market and its insertion as a regional bloc into an ever more global economy.

Be that as it may, Europe in the early years of the twenty-first century had become an utterly transformed continent, compared with the immediate aftermath of the Second World War. For France, the question of how the Gaullist vision of a European 'Union of States' can still influence developments in a greatly enlarged EU remains an open-ended one. Any answer to this question would bring us beyond what Hegel termed the 'grey in grey' world of both philosophy and history – where the 'cunning of reason' might be retrospectively discerned – into the realm of conjecture about an indeterminate future.

Notes

1. Charles de Gaulle, *Mémoires de guerre*, 3 vols, Paris, 1954–59, vol. 3, 54–80. Two days after de Gaulle's return to Paris, the first number of the daily newspaper *Le Monde* appeared, and it welcomed in lyrical terms the 'Franco-Soviet alliance' – see *Le Monde*, 19 December 1944.
2. Raymond Aron, *Mémoires*, Paris, 1983, 229. The paradox is also underlined in Maurice Couve de Murville, *Le Monde en face. Entretiens avec Maurice Delarue*, Paris, 1989, 96–100.
3. For the idea of a 'society of states' or an 'international society' in international relations, see three defining works (listed in the chronological order of their conception): Martin Wight, *International Theory: The Three Traditions*, (eds) Gabriele Wight and Brian Porter, London, 1991; Hedley Bull, *The Anarchical Society: A Study of Order in World Politics*, 2nd edn, London, 1995; Adam Watson, *The Evolution of International Society: A Comparative Historical Analysis*, London, 1992. Arguably, the Gaullist vision of a European union fits in well with what Wight termed the Rationalist or Grotian tradition of international theory, whereas the contrasting vision, in which the emergence of a federal super-state is seen as the final end of the Treaty of Rome's 'ever closer union among the peoples of Europe', belongs to what he termed the Revolutionist or Kantian tradition. Wight's third tradition, the Realist or Machiavellian or Hobbesian one, allows no place, conceptually speaking, for anything that may be meaningfully described as a European union. See Wight, *International Theory*, 30–48, and Bull, *The Anarchical Society*, 24–27, for his reformulation of Wight's threefold division.
4. Henry Kissinger, *Diplomacy*, New York, 1994, 56–67, 575–77, 602–19.

5. The wording is apocryphal. However, this writer and admirer of de Gaulle did clearly express his preference for two Germanys rather than one – see François Mauriac, *Bloc-notes*, 2nd edn, 5 vols, Paris, 1993, vol. 2, 17–18.

6. Gérard Bossuat, *Faire l'Europe sans défaire la France. 60 ans de politique d'unité européenne des gouvernements et des présidents de la République française (1943–2003)*, Brussels, 2005.

7. Andrew Moravcsik, *The Choice for Europe: Social Purpose and State Power from Messina to Maastricht*, Ithaca, 1998. On de Gaulle in particular, see ibid., 83–84, 159–237 (the chapter pointedly entitled 'Grain and Grandeur: Consolidating the Common Market, 1958–1969').

8. The fortunes of the economic liberalism lying at the heart of the EEC Treaty are related in John Gillingham, *European Integration, 1950–2003: Superstate or Market Economy*, Cambridge, 2003. His focus is largely economic integration, and he rightly criticises so-called 'functionalist' theorising, according to which 'spillovers' in the processes of integration drive ever more federalist political agendas and out-turns (the programmed terminus ad quem being the 'super-state' of the book's title). However, Gillingham pays scant attention to much of what is understood in France as belonging to '*la construction européenne*'.

Part I

THE POST-WAR ASSERTION OF LEADERSHIP IN CONTINENTAL WESTERN EUROPE

Chapter 1

BEFORE THE SCHUMAN PLAN

What the French call 'la construction européenne' did not start in 1950, the year of the Schuman Plan. The idea of European union held attraction in the first half of the century. In the late 1940s various initiatives, entailing the setting up of new international institutions, were taken to assure a better future for Western Europe after the ruin of the Second World War. France was to the forefront. Its overriding concern was security, whether of a military, political or economic kind, and much of the background was the 'pax americana' and the onset of the Cold War.

Earlier Calls for European Union

Rathenau, Coudenhove-Kalergi, and Briand

When Schuman, the French foreign minister, proposed in May 1950 that the coal and steel production of Germany and France be placed under a common authority in an organisation whose membership would be open to other European countries, the boldness of the initiative lay partly in its tightly focused nature, namely the linking of the assurance of security in Western Europe to economic integration in the sphere of heavy industry. It was not the first call for European economic or political integration on a Franco-German foundation. Other more lofty or ambitious proposals had long preceded it. Nor did the Schuman Plan represent the start of the European integration process in the post-war period. Various moves, involving notably the UK as well as France, were already afoot to bring about a greater degree of unity among European states.

Notes for this chapter begin on page 40.

The first twentieth-century proposal for European integration around a Franco-German axis was made in late August 1914 at the outset of the tragedy engulfing Europe. Its author was Walter Rathenau, then a leading German industrialist. Already counting on rapid victory, he suggested to the Imperial Chancellor, Theobald von Bethmann-Hollweg, that consideration be given to the idea of a German-led customs union comprising Germany, France, Austria-Hungary, and Belgium, and the term he chose was *Zollunion* rather than the looser one of *Zollverein*. The proposed union would serve to expand German industry's export markets. Yet its essential rationale for Rathenau was geopolitical in kind, to weaken France's ties with both the UK and the US and, to the east, with Russia.[1]

This customs union plan was stillborn as the conflict metamorphosed into the Great War. Rathenau himself was put in charge of the provision of strategic raw materials for the German war effort. Afterwards in 1921–22, serving first as minister of reconstruction and then as foreign minister, he was the leading figure in a government that sought to find a forward-looking compromise with France, in the face of the latter's insistence on the enormous reparations imposed on Germany by the Treaty of Versailles. Rathenau's aim was not just to ease a nigh intolerable financial burden but also to secure a real peace with France in the longer term. However, when Poincaré replaced Aristide Briand as both prime minister and foreign minister in early 1922, the French position on the matter of reparations further hardened. As the international climate in Europe deteriorated, Rathenau was moved to sign the Treaty of Rapallo (April 1922). An apparently insubstantial enough pact between Germany and communist Russia, it included important separate secret agreements for military co-operation. Because of his signing this treaty – thereby associating the Weimar Republic with the Bolshevist state to the east – and also his Jewishness, Rathenau was assassinated later in 1922 by German nationalist zealots.

In the following year the young Austrian, Count Coudenhove-Kalergi, published his most famous book, *Pan-Europa* or *Pan-Europe*, in both German and French editions. This was effectively the manifesto for the movement of the same name which he founded in 1924. His purpose was to promote a confederation of continental European states that would constitute a powerful bloc, alongside the British Empire, the US, and the nascent USSR. For this confederation he proposed a number of names: the Pan-European Union, or the United States of Europe, or, in a more down-to-earth vein, the European Customs Union. Franco-German reconciliation was to lie at the heart of the union, and he was an early advocate of the coordinated exploitation of the coal resources of the Ruhr and the iron ore resources of Lorraine. The first congress of his movement was held in Vienna in 1926, and Briand was elected the movement's honorary president in 1927.

Briand had become foreign minister anew in 1925 and played a large part in the drawing up in October of that year of the Locarno treaties, which led to Germany's being admitted to the League of Nations in 1927. The treaties constituted the Rhine Pact, under which Germany, France, and Belgium recognised the permanence of their existing borders as well as the Rhineland's demilitarised status, while the UK and Italy served as the pact's guarantors. In recognition of the efforts made by Briand and his German counterpart, Gustav Stresemann, to improve Franco-German relations, the two were jointly awarded the Nobel Peace Prize in 1926. In September 1929, Briand went a step further in proposing a form of European union to the Assembly of the League of Nations:

> I believe that among peoples who are geographically close as those of Europe are, there should exist a sort of federal link. These peoples must have the opportunity at any moment to make contact with each other, discuss their common interests, take joint decisions, and establish bonds of solidarity which, when the time comes, will enable them to face any grave situations that may arise. It is these bonds I should like to try to forge. Obviously, such an association will act first and foremost in the economic field, where matters are most urgent. But I am also sure that the federal link can be beneficial in political and social affairs, without affecting the sovereignty of any of the nations that might belong to such an association.[2]

The immediate context for this proposal was the international conference held in The Hague in August 1929, billed as 'the conference on the final liquidation of the war'. The question of German reparations was finally settled there through the adoption of the Young Plan, which fixed German liabilities at only a third of the level originally set in 1921. The UK refused to support France's continuing claims for higher reparations. An incidental fruit of the adoption of the Young Plan was the decision taken at the conference to set up the Bank for International Settlements (BIS), which in the second half of the twentieth century was to play a large role in promoting central-bank cooperation in Europe. The other big question on the conference's agenda was that of fixing a date for ending the military occupation of the Rhineland (a fifteen-year period having been set by the Treaty of Versailles). Briand eventually agreed to bring military withdrawal forward to June 1930, after the British Foreign Secretary, Arthur Henderson, had forced his hand by stating that British troops would be withdrawn anyway before Christmas 1929. Contrary to French wishes, no arrangements for the international verification of the Rhineland's demilitarisation were agreed at The Hague.

The conference marked effectively the end of French hopes in the 1920s to assure the country's long-term security through predominance within Europe. When Briand addressed the League of Nations a month later, he did so from a position of relative weakness. His proposing a federal Europe was motivated primarily by the felt need to tie Germany into new permanent international arrangements, now that the Rhineland was to be relinquished, and at a time when the international negotiations on disarmament were not running in France's favour. The special emphasis put by Briand on the 'economic domain' owed much to anxieties about American economic expansion and his related calculation that Germany might be tempted by the prospect of a Franco-German economic entente to keep American multinationals at bay and also to exclude the UK. However, in his design of tying Germany down, Briand failed to enjoy the success that Mitterrand was to have sixty years later when the fall of the Berlin Wall led to the preparation of the Maastricht Treaty. Stresemann was not tempted. The French foreign minister's proposal included no suggestion of an early return of the Saar (the coal-rich region of Germany contiguous to Lorraine), and, significantly, the feeling in Berlin was that there should be no acceptance of further constraints that would stand in the way of an eventual revision of Germany's eastern borders.[3]

The following month, October 1929, was that of the stock-market crash on Wall Street, the harbinger of the Great Depression; Stresemann died in the same month; and the political mood in Germany was fast changing for the worse. Undaunted, Briand had his proposal transformed at the Quai d'Orsay, the home of France's Ministry of Foreign Affairs, into a detailed memorandum 'on the organisation of a regime of European Federal Union', which was presented to the League of Nations in May 1930. Its author was the foreign minister's *directeur de cabinet*, Alexis Léger, aka the poet Saint-John Perse. In this memorandum the federal dimension was downplayed, and, for the most part, the mooted organisation was simply called the 'European Union'. On the economic front, there would be the 'establishment of a common market to maximise human welfare across the territories of the European community', and this would include freedom of movement not only for goods but also for capital and persons. Yet, stated the memorandum, all progress on the economic front should be made subordinate to considerations of security and political union. Political union itself would be pursued through instituting a 'European Conference' in the form of regular meetings of government representatives of all the Union's member states, and also through setting up a standing 'European Political Committee' (on which would be represented only a limited number of member states, but including always France and Germany).[4]

In May 1930 the memorandum was quickly dropped: only Yugoslavia evinced any interest, while in Germany the salient feature of the Reichstag elections of September 1930 was the breakthrough achieved by the Nazi Party. In 1933 Léger went on to become the secretary general at the Quai d'Orsay – that is, the head of the diplomatic service. He was associated as secretary general with the Munich Agreement of 1938, which may have contributed to his being dismissed from the same post in May 1940 by the prime minister, Paul Reynaud, as part of a last-ditch purge of those in high office whose services were no longer considered best suited to the country's needs in the face of the German invasion. After the fall of

France, Léger repaired to Washington, where between 1942 and 1944 he sustained a whispering campaign against de Gaulle, which helped confirm the US president, Franklin D. Roosevelt, in his conviction that the Free French general was a danger to democracy. Yet the Briand–Léger plan for European union was not out of keeping with de Gaulle's ideas on the same subject, thirty years later, in the guise of the Fouchet proposals for a European 'Union of States'.

Vichy France

Despite the unfavourable international climate in the 1930s for the realisation of the European design contained in Briand's and Léger's memorandum, the idea of European integration, whether political or economic, did not die in France. Among the intelligentsia harbouring fascist leanings and looking forward to France's future as part of an authoritarian European order, Pierre Drieu La Rochelle (*L'Europe contre les patries*, 1931) was to the fore. Furthermore, a younger generation, enamoured by the promise of economic planning, was swayed by a technocratic vision of the continent's future organisation. Bertrand de Jouvenel (*Vers les Etats-Unis d'Europe*, 1930; *Le Réveil de l'Europe*, 1938) was a notable example. During the few years after France's defeat in 1940, when many counted on a long period of German hegemony in Europe, de Jouvenel continued to reflect on the continent's future (*La Décomposition de l'Europe libérale*, 1941; *Après la défaite*, 1941; *Napoléon et l'économie dirigée*, 1942). For his stance not only during the 1930s but also during the Occupation, this economist and political philosopher (most famously, *Du pouvoir*, 1945) was later to be faulted. Yet he was to be defended in his old age by Aron, who had joined the Free French in London early during the war, against the charge of being a 'fascist' and 'pro-Nazi' (Aron's fatal heart attack in 1983 occurring as he left court after testifying in favour of de Jouvenel in a defamation suit against the Israeli historian, Zeev Sternhell). More clearly on the Nazi side during the Occupation was the writer, Alfred Fabre-Luce. His anthology of writings in favour of European unity, published in Paris during the Occupation (*Anthologie de la Nouvelle Europe*, 1942), attracted considerable attention. Like de Jouvenel, Fabre-Luce hailed from the Radical camp; by contrast, the great Radical figure, Edouard Herriot, who had argued for the European cause in the interwar years (notably *Europe*, 1930), turned against the Vichy government's compromise with Germany, after having initially supported Marshal Pétain. Deported in 1944, he was to be President of the National Assembly from 1947 to 1954. Finally, mention may be made of the economist, Francis Delaisi, an elderly man by the time of the Second World War. He had been an economic adviser to Coudenhove-Kalergi in the early years of the Pan-European movement, and he went on to publish an influential plan for

Europe's future (*Les Deux Europes*, 1929) at the time of Briand's League of Nations address. Then, during the years of the Occupation, he felt that a German victory might at least favour European economic unification (*L'Ouvrier européen*, 1942; *La Révolution européenne*, 1942; *Paradoxes économiques*, 1943), thus preferring the Axis cause to that of the 'Anglo-Saxons'.

More generally, during the Vichy years, the question of European unity in a short- or long-term perspective, whether under German rule or else partially or wholly free of it, was often a subject of reflection. Among the Paris-based *collaborationnistes*, Marcel Déat was at the political forefront in attaching importance to the idea of a new European order. A prominent left-wing politician in the 1930s, who had broken with the main socialist party to found the Parti Socialiste de France, Déat headed the collaborationist Rassemblement National Populaire and was editor-in-chief of the newspaper *L'Œuvre*. Drieu la Rochelle, director of the prestigious *Nouvelle Revue Française* from 1940 to 1943, remained the foremost champion in literary circles of a German-led Europe. In non-occupied Vichy France, the Ecole Nationale des Cadres at Uriage (near to Grenoble) was an intellectual hot-house from late 1940 until the end of 1942, when it was closed down on the order of Pierre Laval, whom Pétain had brought back into his government in April of that year. The ethos of this institute was Catholic, reformist and Pétainist – at least until Laval's return to power – and among its instructors were three men who were to influence the French political establishment's attitudes towards Europe in the post-war years, namely Hubert Beuve-Méry, the founder and long-time editor-in-chief of the newspaper *Le Monde*; François Perroux, the economist and author notably of *L'Europe sans rivages* (1954); and Paul Reuter, an expert in international law and later, at a crucial moment, an associate of Monnet. Although their thinking was marked by an aversion to economic liberalism, these and other members of the Uriage group were never in thrall to the Nazi idea of a 'new European order', as Laval knew well. However, the strongest opposition in Vichy France to any idea of European integration under German hegemony came from the conservative camp, notably Lucien Romier and Wladimir d'Ormesson, writing for the newspaper *Le Figaro*, and Maurras, writing for his own newspaper *L'Action française*, the organ of doctrinaire nationalism. Both Romier and d'Ormesson, though not Maurras, had been favourable to the cause of European unity and improved Franco-German understanding in the quite different climate of the 1920s.[5]

Nazi Germany had its theoreticians of European *Raum* ('space'), notably the geopolitics specialist, Karl Haushofer, and, even more importantly, the philosopher and jurist, Carl Schmitt, whose *Grossraum gegen Universalismus* (1939) posited the need for a European 'great space' in which the nation state would become obsolete. Their thinking influenced no doubt some of the papers given at the high-level 'European Economic Community' conference held in Weimar in October 1941. A prominent speaker was Walther Funk, the Reichsminister for Economics and president of the Reichsbank.[6] Proposed in one paper was the setting up of a European currency system at whose heart would be the Reichsmark. The currency area would comprise the greater Germany, the remainder of *Mitteleuropa*, Scandinavia, and the Low Countries, and its anchor, the Reichsmark, would come to rival the dollar and overshadow sterling as an international reserve currency. France was to be left outside this particular 'great space'.[7] Hitler himself had never favoured any idea of Germany's having privileged links with France, and indeed in the 1920s he had been vigorously opposed to the pan-European proposals of Coundenhove-Kalergi, whom he despised.[8] In any case German theorising about a new European order was to suffer a loss of confidence on the entry of the US into the world conflict two months later and, more crucially still, when the military tide turned in Europe at the end of 1942.

Churchill's Call for a Franco-German Partnership

In the aftermath of the Second World War, the successor to Briand among statesmen calling for European union was Churchill. In the speech he made at Zurich University in September 1946, which included a warm reference to Coudenhove-Kalergi, he urged that a 'United States of Europe' be founded on a Franco-German axis. Elevated as was Churchill's tone, the details of his desired organisation of Europe were not spelt out, though his listeners were left in little doubt that he wished the UK to be little more than a benevolent bystander, while France shouldered the immediate responsibility for creating a new continental order in Western Europe:

> We must build a kind of United States of Europe ... If Europe is to be saved from infinite misery, and indeed from final doom, there must be an act of faith in the European family and an act of oblivion against all the crimes and follies of the past ... The first step in the re-creation of the European family must be a partnership between France and Germany. In this way only can France recover the moral leadership of Europe ... Great Britain, the British Commonwealth of Nations, mighty America, and I trust Soviet Russia – for then indeed all would be well – must be the friends and sponsors of the new Europe and must champion its right to live and shine.[9]

No longer prime minister at home, Churchill could speak with the detachment of an international statesman looking beyond the wasteland that was still Europe to the real peace that might eventually emerge after the recent war years. His Zurich speech was a notable gesture in favour of France's exercising a leadership role in continental Europe to the east of the Soviet bloc.

The Quest for Security and the Onset of the Cold War

German Demons and the Iron Curtain

However, the mood in France at the time was scarcely propitious for the sort of reconciliation with Germany that Churchill advocated. Fear still prevailed. In December 1946 Léon Blum, the veteran socialist leader and a survivor of the Buchenwald concentration camp, became briefly prime minister and also foreign minister. Prompted by the UK's independent-minded ambassador, Duff Cooper, he proposed to his fellow socialist head of government, Clement Attlee, on New Year's Day 1947, that the two countries draw up a Treaty of Alliance. The proposal was accepted and the drafting quickly negotiated and executed, though there was a change of government in Paris, with Georges Bidault taking over the foreign-affairs portfolio from Blum. The treaty was signed in Dunkirk in March 1947 by Bidault and the British Foreign Secretary, Ernest Bevin.

If that ardent Francophile, Cooper, had dreamt of a renovated entente cordiale enabling the UK and France to stand together on the world stage as political Siamese twins, equal in might to the US or the USSR, the treaty that materialised proved more pedestrian in import. For it was little more than a defensive pact aimed at preventing Germany from menacing the peace anew. From the French standpoint, the raison d'être of the treaty was to provide the country with credible security arrangements by supplementing the Franco-Soviet Treaty of Alliance, which de Gaulle and Stalin had signed in December 1944 (a treaty also aimed against Germany, but of increasingly doubtful value by 1947), with a British commitment to mutual defence.

But the French obsession with a demonic Germany was to give way in the late 1940s to the ever more widely shared perception in the western half of Europe that the main threat to peace in the continent lay with the USSR. A year to the month before the signing of the Treaty of Dunkirk, Churchill – speaking as Europe's grand old man in Fulton, Missouri, where he was the guest of the US president, Harry Truman – had warned that an 'Iron Curtain', running from Szczecin on the Baltic to Trieste on the Adriatic, had descended across Europe. By 1947 his identification of the Iron Curtain's northernmost point with what had become a Polish city, leaving the Soviet-occupied zone of Germany to the west of the curtain, had begun to seem based on a doubtful reading of Germany's future. For the likelihood of a single German state, even federal in structure, arising from the ashes of the war was now far from assured. Furthermore, in the twelve months following the signing of the Treaty of Dunkirk, the Cold War – whose exact starting date remains a matter of controversy for historians – really took hold. In July 1947 the USSR refused to allow Czechoslovakia and Poland to participate in Marshall Aid. In September the setting up of Kominform, the new communist international, was widely perceived as a defiant gesture to the West. Then, in February 1948, there was the communist coup in Prague:

the mysterious death of the Czech foreign minister, Jan Masaryk, poignantly symbolised the second subjugation of the democratic state his father, Tomáš Masaryk, had founded in 1918. Apart from rebellious communist Yugoslavia, the USSR now enjoyed unbridled hegemony over most of Central and Eastern Europe.

The course of domestic politics in France in 1947 reflected the onset of the Cold War. Sharing or vying for political power after the Liberation had been de Gaulle, as both the President of the Provisional Government (GPRF) and the personal incarnation of a new political legitimacy; and the three main political parties or forces that had contributed to the Resistance; namely, the Communists (PCF), the Socialists (SFIO), and the Christian Democrats (represented by the MRP from November 1944 onwards). What was called tripartism entailed the involvement of all three in the country's government and legislation.

Tripartism was indeed the usual practice in the first two years after the Liberation, and so it outlived de Gaulle's stepping down from power in January 1946 at the time of the first Constituent Assembly. The stopgap government formed by Blum at the end of 1946 – exceptionally, a wholly Socialist one – was the first government to take office under the newly constituted Fourth Republic, and it gave way in late January 1947 to a tripartite government headed by another Socialist, Paul Ramadier. However, already in the months immediately following the Treaty of Dunkirk – and before the announcement of Marshall Aid – there was increasingly less reason for Ramadier and the foreign minister, Bidault, to be beholden to Soviet good will. France's new alliance with the UK was frowned upon by the USSR, and, at the Four-Power Conference held in Moscow in March–April 1947, which marked also a milestone in the onset of the Cold War, the Soviet foreign minister, Vyacheslav Molotov, blankly refused Soviet support for French plans to annex the Saar. In the face of this deterioration in Franco-Soviet relations on top of the rise of working-class discontent at home, Ramadier now found the Moscow-loyal PCF an encumbrance. He accordingly dismissed the Communist ministers from the government in May 1947, bringing an end to tripartism under the Fourth Republic. Thereby too the French prime minister put a further nail in the coffin of the Franco-Soviet Treaty of 1944, even if the time was not yet judged ripe in Moscow to denounce it. As to the French father of the same treaty, de Gaulle had long ceased to believe it had any worth; indeed, already in early 1946, he had feared war with the USSR.

France, the UK, and Western Union

In the fraught months of late 1947 and early 1948 the UK was still by far the most important power in Western Europe and proved itself to be such. A decisive moment occurred in December when the Council of Foreign

Ministers – the allied Four-Power body set up at Potsdam in 1945 to work out a multilateral treaty ending the war – met in London and it became clear that there could no longer be any pretence of a community of interests between, on the one hand, the US, the UK, and France, and, on the other, the USSR. Bevin's reaction in the face of this deterioration was to work closely with his French counterpart, Bidault, in pursuing a twofold course of action: to arrange that the mutual defence commitment of the Treaty of Dunkirk be extended to the Benelux countries – even though the threat to peace was no longer primarily identified with Germany – and to seek a military commitment to Western Europe's security from the US. At the time of the signature of the Treaty of Dunkirk, Belgium had already been pressing the UK for a similar bilateral alliance, and by the end of 1947 there were signs that the Netherlands was interested too. As to an Atlantic dimension, the US Secretary of State, General Marshall, told Bevin that the first step must be the creation of a military alliance within Western Europe; only then would Washington be in a position to consider how it might help.

Such was the background to Bevin's 'Western Union' speech in January 1948 to the House of Commons, where he called for 'the consolidation of Western Europe' around an Anglo-French axis.[10] His initiative led to a flurry of diplomatic negotiations, with the Benelux countries preferring a multilateral regional pact and France holding out for a series of bilateral treaties of the Dunkirk kind. However, the Prague coup in February lent added urgency to the settling of these differences. The outcome was the Western Union Treaty or, to give it its long official title, the Treaty of Economic, Social and Cultural Collaboration and Collective Self-Defence, which was signed in Brussels in March 1948 by the foreign ministers of the UK, France, the Netherlands, Belgium, and Luxembourg.

The new treaty's title bore the promise of providing its five signatories with more than a security alliance. However, a security alliance of half a century's duration – renewed in 1998 and taken over by the EU in 2000 – was essentially what resulted from the Brussels Pact (the simplest designation of the treaty), and it had been Bevin's main intention from the outset. 'If any of the High Contracting Parties should be the object of an armed attack in Europe,' reads the crucial Article IV, 'the other High Contracting Parties will … afford the party so attacked all the military and other aid and assistance in their power'.

To meet French demands, and contrary to the expressed wishes of the Benelux countries, the new treaty respected the fundamental aim of the Treaty of Dunkirk in paying at least lip service to the need to be prepared for a new war against Germany. Thus, figuring in the preamble was the intention 'to take such steps may be held necessary in the event of a renewal by Germany of a policy of aggression'. If France continued to insist on pointing to the German danger, it was partly to assuage Soviet feelings, especially since there were still some in Paris, notably the

President of the Republic, Vincent Auriol, who felt that relations with the USSR were not beyond repair. However, under the Fourth Republic, the president's authority in matters of foreign policy was limited largely to that exercised discretely by persuasion; actual policy was made by the government, with the foreign minister often enjoying a very large degree of independence (partly because of the expert advice at his disposal), and the then master at the Quai d'Orsay, Bidault, was under no illusion that the main threat to the continent's security now came from the USSR.[11]

The hopes of both Bevin and Bidault to involve the US in Western Europe's security arrangements were to be fulfilled. Although Article IX of the Western Union Treaty allowed for other states to adhere to the alliance, and purposefully did not specify that any new member state should be European, there was the constitutional impediment in the US that no government in Washington was empowered to commit the country to an alliance in time of peace. But in June 1948 the Senate acting on the 'Vandenberg resolution' lifted this obstacle to the participation of the US in the Brussels Pact or any other alliance that might supplement or replace it. Later that same month the USSR began its blockade of West Berlin. The blockade, albeit relieved by the airlift run mainly by the American and British air forces using military and civilian planes, was to be kept in place for nearly a year. The fears raised by this aggravation of the Cold War encouraged a greater urgency in the diplomatic talks between the UK, France, and the US concerning the future alliance.

In July 1948, at the start of the Berlin crisis, Schuman replaced Bidault at the Quai d'Orsay; they were both from the MRP and, on the question of the desirability and urgency of new security ties with the US, the new foreign minister took broadly the position of his predecessor. Although France would have preferred a simple widening of the Western Union Treaty to include the US, it soon became clear that the US Congress's jealously guarded right to declare war – a right that was not the president's – precluded an American acceptance of the automatic nature of the mutual military-assistance pledge under the treaty's Article IV. Hence another treaty, providing for somewhat different alliance arrangements under American leadership, had to be negotiated. This was the North Atlantic Treaty, establishing the North Atlantic Treaty Organisation (NATO), signed in Washington in April 1949.

NATO's mutual assistance pledge comes under the treaty's famous Article 5. 'Each of [the Parties] … will assist the Party or Parties so attacked by taking forthwith, individually and collectively and in concert with the other Parties, such action as it deems necessary, including the use of armed force, to restore and maintain the security of the North Atlantic area.' The deliberate looseness of the carefully crafted wording (notably the clause 'such action as it deems necessary') was scarcely welcome on the European side. And doubts about the strength of the American commitment were later to trouble de Gaulle in particular.

However, in the negotiation of the treaty, France won at least one victory. Its insistence that Italy be admitted as a founding NATO member state gave the new alliance more of a Mediterranean dimension; the inclusion of this southern neighbour of France balanced that of Denmark, Norway, and Iceland – a northern bloc whose membership was more in British interests – and it made the treaty's name something of a misnomer from the start.

Western Union in its first year of existence had established, with some difficulty, an embryonic military organisation. Although a Military Committee was set up at the outset, it was only in July 1948 that there was an agreement to establish a command structure. A few months later Field-Marshal Montgomery was appointed Commander-in-Chief of the Western Union forces and General de Lattre de Tassigny its Army Commander; this was after a refusal of the latter post by General Juin, France's most distinguished serving army officer, having headed the French expeditionary force in the Allied Forces' Italian campaign of 1943–44. Even then the organisation had little worth in operational terms. The North Atlantic Treaty led to its being considered henceforth part of the wider Atlantic Alliance and to its being subsumed at the end of 1950 into NATO's new integrated military command.

The Treaty of Dunkirk and the Western Union Treaty had provided France with what was essentially a British defence guarantee; this was now effectively supplemented and indeed largely replaced by a security commitment from the US. The time of the special relationship between France and the UK, dating from the renewal of the entente cordiale in 1904, was virtually over.

Western European Economic and Political Cooperation

The American Contribution to Economic Recovery

The influence of the US on France's fortunes in the middle of the twentieth century was indeed huge.[12] On the economic front, decisive American intervention in Europe had already taken place in 1947, nearly two years before the signing of the North Atlantic Treaty. The reason for the decision taken in Washington to extend its pax americana to Europe's economic affairs was the perception of the still abysmal state of the continent's economies, especially to the west, and of the social unrest to which it was giving rise – notably in France and Italy, with the two countries' communist trade unions playing the leading role. Six years of war had wrought economic havoc across Europe, and, even if more physical capital was left standing than many supposed, the rebuilding of roads, railways, and factories was taking time. Two exceptionally bitter winters after the end of the war had, moreover, played a part in slowing down the pace of recovery and reconstruction. Very crucially, reconstruction efforts entailing the purchase of capital goods were being seriously hindered by balance-of-payments constraints. In France, where the war had reduced economic output by about a half, there was still very little to export at the beginning of 1947, and so imports of vital machinery and equipment were largely unaffordable, unless backed by American loans. The twin fear in Washington was that peace in Europe would fail to be adequately secured and that the ambitious plans for a properly functioning international economy, which had been drawn up at Bretton Woods in 1944, would come to naught.

The decisive step forward occurred in early June 1947 when General Marshall proposed the aid to which his name would soon be given. Receiving an honorary degree of Doctor of Laws at Harvard University early that month, the Secretary of State declared that it was his government's plan to provide major financial assistance to the whole of Europe in the framework of a recovery programme that would be worked out with the beneficiary countries, provided they themselves took the first step. 'It is logical that the United States should do whatever it is able to do to assist in the return of normal economic health', said Marshall, but 'the initiative ... must come from Europe'.[13] Accordingly, several weeks later, Bevin, Bidault, and Molotov met in Paris to discuss Marshall's proposals. It was in the course of this tripartite meeting that Molotov was instructed from Moscow that the offer of American largesse should be refused by the USSR and therefore also by the European countries held in Stalin's sway. It was left to Bevin and Bidault to invite to Paris those European countries – excepting Franco's Spain – which were glad and ready to take up the offer of an American-financed recovery programme. And so when the representatives of sixteen countries met in the French capital in mid July the European economic cooperation called for by Marshall at Harvard was born.[14] However, the Soviet refusal, which had not been unexpected in Washington, had made the divide of the Iron Curtain in Europe an economic reality as well as a political one.

Marshall Aid was a great boon for the French economy. Under the US Foreign Assistance Act of April 1948, $12.9 billion, largely in the form of grant aid for investment purposes, was channelled through the European Recovery Programme (ERP) to all recipients during a period of nearly four years. By the standards of the day, it was an enormous sum, representing an annual average 1.2 percent of American GNP from 1948 to 1951. And France received as much as a fifth ($2.7 billion) of the total, most of which ($2.4 billion) was in the form of grants. Without this financial assistance, France's first post-war economic plan, which initially covered the period 1947 to 1950 and was subsequently extended to 1952, would never have met with success. This was the Monnet Plan, taking its name from Monnet, then head of the Commissariat Général du Plan.

Nearly half of the plan's investments financed through the Fonds de Modernisation et d'Equipement in 1948–51 drew on ERP funds.[15]

The American design for restoring health to Western Europe's economies was not limited to raising investment levels and remedying shortages of essential goods. There was also the desire on the part of policy makers in Washington that a sustained economic recovery should lead to the progressive liberalisation of trade and payments. For bilateral trade – virtually barter – and currency inconvertibility had persisted as striking features of the economic situation in Europe, not only when Marshall made his Harvard speech, but also a year later when the ERP was launched. Much in mind was the lesson of the early 1930s when trade protectionism practised by both the US (through the Smoot–Hawley Tariff Act of 1930) and the UK (through the raising of Imperial Preferences in 1932), coupled to the disorderly end to the gold standard, had contributed to the breakdown of the international economy, thereby aggravating the situation in Europe and facilitating Hitler's rise to power.

To foster a gradual move to free trade and currency convertibility in Western Europe, the Truman administration, in requesting Congress to authorise the ERP, asked also that a permanent European organisation be established so that the recipient countries could cooperate in an appropriate institutional framework. This was the origin of the Organisation for European Economic Cooperation (OEEC), which was set up in Paris in the summer of 1948, with the sixteen countries that had met in the French capital a year earlier acting as its founding members. The first secretary general was the French economist and civil servant, Robert Marjolin, plucked from Monnet's team at the Commissariat Général du Plan. More than a decade later, in 1961, partly through Monnet's efforts to bring about institutionalised cooperation between the US, the EEC, and the UK in the domain of economic policy, the OEEC was transformed into the geographically more widely-based Organisation for Economic Cooperation and Development (OECD).

Advancing beyond Western Union

In early 1948 the US Foreign Assistance Act had followed on the heels of the signing of the Western Union Treaty, so that by the spring of the same year there were grounds for more hope for the future of Western Europe. It was in this improved climate that a congress, organised by the International Committee of Movements for European Unity, took place in May 1948 at the Binnenhof in The Hague. The assembled politicians and other notables approved a political resolution which welcomed the first steps in European political and economic cooperation, stated that the cooperation in question remained insufficient, insisted that the German problem could be satisfactorily resolved only in the framework of

European economic and political union, and called for the creation of a 'European Union' or 'European Federation'. Presiding over the congress was Churchill. Yet the British Labour Party, then in power, was scarcely represented. From Germany the still stateless Adenauer came in his capacity as president of the young CDU party. The French delegation was the largest, and it included a sprinkling of Gaullists.[16] Also present was the rapidly rising star among the younger politicians of the Fourth Republic, Mitterrand.[17]

Most of the text of the political resolution passed by this congress in The Hague was of little practical import. Yet it did contain one concrete proposal, namely that a European Assembly should be set up, bringing together national parliamentarians, and that this European Assembly should recommend economic and political measures to further European union and that it should also take the initiative in creating a Court of Justice whose remit would be defined by a Charter of Human Rights.

In Paris the idea of a European Assembly was favourably received by Bidault. Attracted also by the idea of economic integration, he used a meeting in The Hague of the skeletal Western Union's Consultative Council in July 1948 to bring the two ideas together, proposing to his fellow foreign ministers that such an assembly be set up, and that it should draw up plans for an economic and customs union between the states concerned. This was effectively Bidault's swansong as foreign minister in the immediate post-war years, after having headed the Quai d'Orsay ever since September 1944, save for a six-week interruption at the very beginning of the Fourth Republic. On the same day Bidault made his 'European declaration' in the Dutch capital, the government in Paris fell, and a week later it was the outgoing prime minister, Schuman, who was entrusted with the foreign-affairs portfolio. Schuman took over and further developed his predecessor's proposal. However, Bevin was reticent, being averse to anything that might be prejudicial to the prerogatives of the Westminster Parliament. The Foreign Secretary proposed therefore the setting up of a European Council in the form of a ministerial standing committee. Compromise had to be sought. Thus, the five Brussels Pact countries making up the Western Union agreed in February 1949 to the creation of a Council of Europe consisting of both a Committee of Ministers and a Consultative Assembly. France and Italy had wanted the new organisation to be called the European Union, but British objections prevailed. In London in May 1949, a month after the North Atlantic Treaty's signing, the treaty establishing the Council of Europe was signed. Its initial membership was decided by the Western Union's Consultative Council. Apart from the Brussels Pact Five, it included Italy, the three Scandinavian countries – Denmark, Norway, and Sweden – and Ireland.[18]

Under the auspices of the Council of Europe, the European Convention for the Protection of Human Rights and Fundamental Freedoms was signed in November 1950, a year and a half later. A leading part in the convention's drafting was played by the MRP's Pierre-Henri Teitgen.[19] A law professor, he had served as justice minister in the GPRF, succeeding François de Menthon, also a law professor belonging to the MRP, when the latter became France's chief prosecutor at Nuremberg. Teitgen and de Menthon had taken part in the Resistance together (in Henri Frenay's *Combat* movement), an experience that no doubt tempered their broadly similar views on Europe in the late 1940s and early 1950s when the MRP certainly counted.[20] As to the European Convention, France was to ratify the human-rights convention only in 1973, towards the end of the Pompidou presidency.

Wariness about the New West Germany

The Creation of the FRG and Schuman's Succession to Bidault

Yet the setting up of the Council of Europe was not the most important event for Europe in May 1949. Just a day after the signing of the treaty establishing the new Strasbourg-based organisation, the Basic Law – the constitution of the future Federal Republic of Germany – was approved by the constitutional convention of the Länder in the Western zones of occupation. Elections were held in August, and Adenauer took office as Chancellor in September as the new West German state was born. In the absence of a peace treaty between the victors of 1945 and the defeated Third Reich, the decision to create the FRG had been taken, formally speaking, by the US and the Brussels Pact Five in June 1948 at the conclusion of the Three-Power London Conference held in February–March and April–June of that year. However, the collective form of these decisions notwithstanding, the real creator was the American superpower; the FRG was above all a fruit of the pax americana in post-war Europe.

The French reaction was not unbridled joy. Although 1948 and 1949 were marked by a remarkable advance in inter-state cooperation in Western Europe – Western Union, the OEEC, the Council of Europe, and NATO – and by a widespread perception that the USSR had replaced Germany as the main threat to international peace, the general attitude of France's political establishment towards the future of its neighbour and near-century-old hereditary enemy remained one of wariness and per-sisting apprehension. The FRG's creation, however peaceable, could not lead to a sudden change in attitude. And the proclamation in October 1949 of the communist German Democratic Republic (GDR), which consecrated the division of Germany into two, was not to change matters. Prussian militarism, that longstanding object of French fears, might exist no longer. But the new East Germany was unlikely to be forever abandoned by the economically stronger and more populous Germany lying to the west.

Particularly worrying for any French government was the prospect of the eventual emergence of a powerful FRG no longer acting as beholden to the West. It could be tempted by neutrality as the price to be paid for the recovery of the East German territories (lying to the centre rather than the east of the old pre-war Germany – East Prussia, Pomerania, and Silesia having been transferred to the westward-shifted Poland in 1945). Such worries were to persist, with fluctuating degrees of intensity, up to the time of the fall of the Berlin Wall in 1989 and its immediate aftermath.

The worries were, moreover, evident from the start. Schuman's taking charge of foreign policy at the Quai d'Orsay in from July 1948 did make for some difference in France's approach to the German question, especially in tone. Yet the difference between him and his predecessor, Bidault, has often been exaggerated, for there was a real element of continuity between the two. Certainly, Schuman desired improved relations between the two peoples and also wider unity in Western Europe; this ambition was infused with a positive feeling towards Germany that was not shared to the same extent, if at all, by Bidault. Yet it had been Bidault, in the course of the Three-Power London Conference that ran from February to June 1948, who had bowed to American and British pressures to adopt a more positive policy towards Germany and to accept the creation of the FRG. This London agreement in June had been the decisive moment, and it was the very lukewarm nature of the National Assembly's support for this inflexion of French policy that led so soon afterwards to Bidault's departure from the Quai d'Orsay. Already in April 1948 Bidault had written to his American counterpart, General Marshall, indicating that he was amenable to the creation of a West German state, provided it took place under the umbrella of new Atlantic-wide security arrangements. Furthermore, when in July he made his 'European declaration' to his fellow Western Union foreign ministers, he effectively linked his proposed pursuit of European integration to the German question by saying that 'a lasting and durable settlement of the essential problem posed by Germany cannot be found outside the European framework'.[21]

Schuman quickly reassured the Americans and the British that France would honour its commitments under the London Accords. However, at least until 1950, Schuman, reflecting the mood of the National Assembly, often showed himself to be hesitant or wary in the face of the state the Americans had decided to create. It was as if the new foreign minister were still partly shackled to the frame of mind that had marked France's hardline foreign policy towards Germany in the first three years after the war. Although the wisdom of the American approach was quietly acknowledged within the Quai d'Orsay already during the Bidault years, such recognition was not evident in the actual conduct of foreign policy, even after Bidault's turnaround in 1948 and his replacement by Schuman shortly afterwards.[22]

However, progressively during his four-and-a-half years as foreign minister, Schuman's personal background was to prove important in transforming attitudes. Identifying strongly with his family roots in Lorraine, he was predisposed to the cause of better Franco-German relations by a natural inclination to reconcile the differing strands of his own life. Born in Luxembourg, yet accorded German nationality – which was that of his parents by virtue of the annexation of Alsace-Lorraine to the Second Reich in 1871 – Schuman had studied law at the universities of Bonn, Munich, Berlin, and, finally, Strasbourg, in what was then Reichsland Lothringen. This led to his entering legal practice in Metz in 1912. He served very briefly as a noncombatant soldier in the German army in the First World War, before starting life afresh as a French citizen in 1918. He was elected to the Chamber of Deputies, representing the Moselle, in 1919, and he was repeatedly reelected Deputy of the Moselle up to the end of the Third Republic, and anew, to the National Assembly, under the Fourth. In 1932 he joined the Parti Démocrate Populaire, the Christian Democrat party created towards the end of the Third Republic. For several months in 1940, prior to the fall of France, he served as a junior minister in the government headed by Reynaud (as did, even more briefly, de Gaulle). Then in late 1944, after having spent some of the war under house arrest by the Germans, he joined the MRP. Schuman was an ardent Roman Catholic, and his views about the desirability of political unity in Western Europe owed much to the idea that it was above all the continent's Christian heritage which gave consistence and meaning to the identity of European civilisation. And the Europe he knew and loved best was the Carolingian Europe that accorded with his religious faith and his experience of French and German cultures.

Schuman did not turn his back on Germany. In 1948 he entered into contact with leading German figures from political, trade union and church circles, and in 1949 he played a major role in the setting up of the Council of Europe. But his handling of France's interests in these two years tended to be as hard-nosed and calculating as that of his predecessor. In the matter of Germany's future, there was a real wariness on his part. If he felt a real spiritual and even political affinity with Adenauer and certain other Catholic members of the CDU, he was apprehensive, on the other hand, about the designs that Kurt Schumacher, the leader of the socialist SPD, might entertain for Germany's longer-term future.

So France's guard was not to be dropped. In November 1948 Schuman protested against the decision taken by the American and British authorities in the Bizone (the United Economic Area, bringing together their respective two zones of occupation) to put, albeit provisionally, the management of mines in the Ruhr back into German hands. This protest led to a compromise agreement by the three Western occupying powers to the effect that the question of ownership would not be finally settled until the long awaited peace treaty – a treaty that was never to materialise. In

December 1948, during the Berlin airlift, Schuman protested against ideas emanating from Washington in favour of some rearmament of the future West Germany; and he protested too against the US policy of seeking in the Bizone to slow down the dismantling of factories for reparation purposes. Then in November 1949, when the Western occupying powers drew up the Petersberg Agreement establishing the conditions to govern the FRG's external relations (effectively the first international treaty signed by the new government in Bonn), he was still not quite ready to abandon what had become France's established policy of seeking to act as a brake on any steps favourable to German reconstruction and independence. On the one hand, Schuman advocated West Germany's integration into the wider Western Europe; on the other, even if he personally questioned the value of the continued dismantling of factories, he required persuasion from Dean Acheson (Marshall's successor as Secretary of State) to soften France's hardline position on the matter, and he was anyway adamant that the ceiling on West Germany's steel production should remain unchanged at 11 million tonnes.[23]

The Saar in French Hands

Yet it was above all over the future of the Saar that Schuman and other leading French politicians dug in their heels. Already in 1945 at the Potsdam Conference, the US, the USSR, and the UK had decided against any radical dismembering of the defunct Third Reich, which would have led to a multiplicity of states and the absence of any political entity worthy of the name of Germany. On the French side this had been the policy initially pressed by de Gaulle and the Quai d'Orsay. After their early disappointment on this score, hopes were still entertained for a while of France's gaining some sort of effective control over all of the German left bank of the Rhine through setting up a number of small states partly or wholly separate from the rest of Germany. But these hopes too were dashed. On the signing of the London Accords in 1948, de Gaulle denounced them for their giving birth to a new 'Reich', which, he said, would prompt the Soviet Union to create in Berlin or Leipzig another 'Reich', before one eventually devoured the other.[24] Whatever the General's position, all that remained by that year for France was the Saar. With a population of about 900,000, it was economically important because of its coal mines and steel industry. At the end of 1946 the Blum government, carrying out French plans in preparation since the beginning of that year, established a customs union between France and the Saar. The latter was thereby completely detached from rest of the French zone. It reverted to being de facto a French protectorate, a status that it had held under international law from 1919 to 1935 by virtue of the Treaty of Versailles. No change of policy occurred when Schuman became foreign minister in mid 1948.

A year and a half later Schuman conceived the idea of coupling the FRG's entry to the Council of Europe as an associate member with the simultaneous entry into the same body of the Saar, also as an associate member. In this way the FRG would be obliged to recognise diplomatically the Saar's separate existence. He proposed such a linkage in November 1949 at the Three-Power Paris Conference sealing the Petersberg Agreement. The nascent West German state had been permitted to join the OEEC in the previous month without any strings attached; indeed it had simply taken over the Bizone's effective membership of the American-sponsored organisation. That Adenauer now, in the closing months of 1949, should come to be concerned with an impending invitation to join the Council of Europe, rather than positively welcome it, testified to the troubled climate of the time. It was, moreover, in this same climate that Schuman's first official visit to the FRG in January 1950 proved a diplomatic disaster. The considerable strains over the Saar contributed to the sour mood of the public on the occasion of the French foreign minister's visit to Mainz, to the difficult nature of the talks he had in Bonn with the leaders of the political parties, to the frosty reception he received in public from Adenauer, and to the open criticisms of the justice minister, Thomas Dehler, who deemed that Schuman's visit was an opportune moment for him, Dehler, to assert that French foreign policy towards Germany in the 1920s had served as a catalyst for the rise of Nazism (a diplomatic lapsus that led to an apology from Bonn to Paris).

The Council of Europe's invitation, in parallel with a like invitation addressed to the puppet government of the Saar, was eventually issued from Strasbourg at the end of March 1950. There was no prompt reply. Earlier in March conventions had been signed at the Quai d'Orsay between the French and Saar governments with a view to bolstering France's position under international law. Adenauer reacted by holding a press conference to denounce the conventions, and he ordered that a White Paper refuting their validity be quickly published. He took a different tack later that same month in associating the return of the Saar with a surprising call for Franco-German union in the framework of a United States of Europe. Nonetheless, relations between the Chancellor and the French foreign minister were at their nadir at the time of the invitation from the Council of Europe. Little could it have been imagined then that only two months later the course of Franco-German relations would be suddenly and radically transformed for the better.[25]

The Coal and Steel Conundrum

If during the immediate post-war period successive French governments attached importance to exercising control over the Saar's coal mines and steel industry, it was because of a perceived need to redress significantly the imbalance between France and Germany in the sphere of heavy industry. Prior to the introduction into Europe of nuclear weaponry in the 1950s and 1960s, steel was the vital economic resource for military strength. Equally importantly, it was also a time, in the aftermath of the destruction wrought by the war, when greatly increased domestic steel production was seen as essential to economic reconstruction and modernisation. Such was certainly the view held in France. And steel figured prominently in the priorities adopted by the national economic planning office, the Commissariat Général du Plan, headed by Monnet.

It was de Gaulle, partly with an eye to the prospect of American financial assistance, who had asked Monnet in August 1945 to plan the economic modernisation of post-war France. A unique type of planning was then conceived and practised by Monnet and his small team at the Commissariat Général du Plan. Drawing on the experience he had gained in both world wars in the organisation and coordination of allied supplies, Monnet orchestrated the setting of production and investment priorities for both public and private sectors on the basis of concertation between government, business, and trade unions. The first plan – the commonly called Monnet Plan – gave priority to the development of heavy industry, energy, and transport infrastructure, and, with the help of Marshall Aid, as has already been pointed out, it was to make a fundamental contribution to France's economic growth in the late 1940s and early 1950s.

The plan's steel production targets were especially ambitious. Thus, the annual target for 1950, as presented by France in 1947 to the Committee on European Economic Cooperation (the embryonic OEEC), was 11.7 million tonnes of crude and semi-finished steel, as compared with an actual output of 5.8 million tonnes attained in 1947 and 9.7 million tonnes in 1929, the peak interwar year.[26] However, the doubling of French steel production in the first four years of the plan was predicated on the assumption that the French steel industry, then mainly located in Lorraine, would be helped by the supply of coking coal from the Ruhr. The nationalised coalfields in the north of France, the heart of the French coal industry, produced insufficient coking coal for the steel industry's rising requirements.

In 1947 steel production in the Ruhr was allowed by the Bizone authorities to rise faster than originally envisaged, thereby increasing German industrial demand for coking coal and calling into question the Monnet Plan's assumptions about the availability of coal for export to Lorraine. But there was no readiness on the French side to admit that its domestic steel production targets should be lowered. Instead France's claims on Ruhr coal continued to be vigorously insisted upon.

This insistence had the full backing of the Elysée, which reinforced the French government's stance. From the beginning of his seven-year term as President of the Republic in January 1947, Auriol was greatly concerned with France's entitlement to coal from the Ruhr. Already in February and

March 1947 he was disturbed by the Bizone plans then afoot.[27] Their implications, as he recorded in his diary in March, were worrisome for the Commissariat Général du Plan:

> France will be able to reconstruct its destroyed towns and villages only if it increases its production. The Monnet Plan will enable it to acquire anew plant and equipment, but the need is for the driving force, namely coal. Germany can supply it, since its mining output is on the increase. Molotov and the United States now acknowledge this claim after earlier having been hostile to it. Bevin finally recognised yesterday ... that the reconstruction of German industry must be carried out gradually, with account being taken of the imperative of allotting the coal by priority to the countries that have been liberated.[28]

To strengthen its position, France won an agreement in August 1947 from the US for the setting up of an international board with powers to allocate the Ruhr's output of coal and steel between domestic consumption and exports. Sitting on the board were to be representatives of the three Western occupying powers, the three Benelux countries, and, last and perhaps least, Germany itself. This was the origin of the International Authority for the Ruhr, which was not, however, to be established immediately. When Schuman became foreign minister in 1948, Germany's considerable coal-mining capacity was still far from being fully utilised. However, since output was rapidly rising, there was apparently confidence at the Quai d'Orsay that France's longer-term economic interests in the Ruhr could be preserved, initially with the good will of the Bizone authorities, the US and the UK, but later, more importantly, through the planned International Authority.

But soon affecting the Quai d'Orsay's calculations was the speed of recovery of not only German coal output but also steel production. In conjunction with the question of the Saar, it came to confront Schuman with his biggest foreign-policy challenge. In 1948 coal output totalled 88.4 million tonnes in the Western-occupied zones of Germany, far ahead of 12.6 million tonnes in the Saar and 43.3 million tonnes in France. West German output (excluding that of the Saar) rose to 104.8 million tonnes in 1949 and to 112.3 million tonnes in 1950. These increases went hand in hand with rising steel production, which mopped up much of the additional coking coal production. However, even without the additional output from the Saar, France was still producing more steel in 1948 than Germany. In the latter's Western-occupied zones, output of crude steel amounted then to 5.6 million tonnes, as compared with 7.2 million tonnes in France and 1.2 million tonnes in the Saar. But in 1949 output in the newly created West Germany rose to 9.2 million tonnes, slightly more than in France. And by 1950 Germany's role as continental Western Europe's leading steel producer was clearly reestablished. West German output of crude steel in that year surged to 12.1 million tonnes, still considerably less than British output, but well above the 8.7 million tonnes produced in

France, even if there was a supplement from the Saar of 1.9 million tonnes.[29]

Such was the economic background to the setting up of the International Authority for the Ruhr and the subsequent launching of the Schuman Plan. The treaty establishing this body was signed only in April 1949, more than a year and a half after the Franco-American agreement that marked its conception. Designed to become operational at the same time as West Germany became a political state, it assumed responsibility in May 1949 for the control of the production, distribution, and pricing of coal and iron and steel products from the Ruhr area. But it was not until November of the same year, when the Petersberg Agreement was signed, that West German representatives joined the International Authority to sit alongside representatives from the three occupying powers and the Benelux countries. For Adenauer, its existence represented a most regrettable constraint, both politically and economically, on the fledgling state.

Attempts had been made to head off the creation of the International Authority for the Ruhr. On New Year's Day 1949 Karl Arnold, the Minister–President of North Rhine–Westphalia, had proposed a new organisation providing for the international control of the coal resources of the Ruhr, the iron-ore resources of Lorraine, and the heavy industries of France, West Germany, the Saar, Luxembourg, and Belgium. It was a proposal without immediate echo. Then in August of the same year, just after the first elections to the Bundestag, Adenauer wrote to Schuman calling for international cooperation in the sphere of coal and steel around a Franco-German axis. This was in the context of an attempt to prevent the dismantling of the Thyssen steelworks at Hamborn in the former Bizone, which was one of the biggest and most modern steelworks in Europe, since the surrender of economic assets by way of international reparations had not yet been brought to an end. However, there was no response from the French foreign minister.[30]

The Paris Conference of November 1949 put a final end to reparations. But Adenauer had to accept the humiliation of the FRG's being obliged to be represented on the foreign-controlled board of the International Authority for the Ruhr. Yet in American eyes the International Authority's days were already numbered. At the Paris Conference Acheson, to his satisfaction, found Bevin tired of the issue of West German steel capacity and willing to admit an increase in the annual ceiling on crude steel production from 11 million tonnes to as much as 16 or 17 million tonnes (roughly the same level as the UK's production at the time). Schuman was less enamoured with the idea.[31] However, in the face of a request from Bonn for a ceiling of 14 million tonnes, the US was determined to ease the economic straitjacket binding West Germany. One reason was the doubts being expressed in the US Congress about the effectiveness of Marshall Aid's contribution to German economic recovery. In early March 1950

Acheson wrote to Schuman to make clear that France's foot-dragging was no longer acceptable and that, at the next Three-Power meeting planned for May in London, a more cooperative attitude would be expected.[32]

This signal from Washington proved to be the catalyst of future EC integration. It put the French foreign minister in a serious quandary, especially since Acheson had requested him, half a year earlier, to prepare proposals on how best the Three Powers might constructively address the German problem. It was out of this same quandary that the bold approach represented by the Schuman Plan emerged.

Notes

1. Walther Rathenau, *Tagebuch 1907–1922*, (ed.) Hartmut Pogge von Strandmann, Düsseldorf, 1967, 185–86.
2. Jean-Baptiste Duroselle, *Europe: A History of its Peoples*, London, 1990, 358–59.
3. For Briand's proposal and its background, see Anthony Adamthwaite, *Grandeur and Misery: France's Bid for Power in Europe, 1914–1940*, London, 1995, 110–39. Summarising the French approach to the peace settlement of 1919, Adamthwaite says pithily that 'for the French, security and hegemony were synonymous' (ibid., 91). See also Elisabeth du Réau, *L'Idée d'Europe au XXe siècle. Des mythes aux réalités*, Brussels, 2001, 97–123.
4. For the text of the 'European Federal Union' memorandum, see Charles Zorgbibe, *Histoire de la construction européenne*, Paris, 1993, 8–14.
5. On the intelligentsia, see Bernard Bruneteau, *'L'Europe nouvelle de Hitler'. Une illusion des intellectuels de la France de Vichy*, Paris, 2003. The role played by the Ecole Nationale des Cadres has been a controversial subject for more than two decades – see John Hellman, *The Knight-Monks of Vichy France: Uriage, 1940–1945*, 2nd edn, Montreal, 1997; as well as the debate in Michael Sutton and John Hellman, 'Distinguishing between anti-liberals', *Modern and Contemporary France*, 7(4), 1999, 520–24.
6. For Funk's ideas already in July 1940 on the economic reorganisation of Europe, see Walter Lipgens (ed.), *Documents on the History of European Integration*, vol. 1: *Continental Plans for European Union, 1939–1945*, Berlin, 1985, 65–71.
7. Bernard Connolly, *The Rotten Heart of Europe: The Dirty War for Europe's Money*, 2nd edn, London, 1996, 230–32; John Laughland, *The Tainted Source: The Undemocratic Origins of the European Idea*, London, 1997, 30–32, 36, 39–43. The proposed exclusion of France from the Reichsmark currency area was in keeping with German Foreign Office plans – see Robert O. Paxton, *Vichy France: Old Guard and New Order, 1940–1944*, 2nd edn, New York, 2001, 67–68, 363.
8. See Gerhard L. Weinberg (ed.), *Hitler's Second Book: The Unpublished Sequel to Mein Kampf by Adolf Hitler*, New York, 2003, 116–17.
9. For the text of the speech, see A.G. Harryvan and J. van der Harst (eds), *Documents on European Union*, London, 1997, 38–42.
10. Harryvan and van der Harst (eds), *Documents on European Union*, 45–47; Alan Bullock, *Ernest Bevin: Foreign Secretary, 1945–1951*, London, 1983, 519–20.
11. Georges-Henri Soutou, 'Georges Bidault et la construction européenne, 1944–1954', in Serge Berstein, Jean-Marie Mayeur, and Pierre Milza (eds), *Le MRP et la construction européenne*, Brussels, 1993, 198–211.
12. See especially Irwin M. Wall, *The United States and the Making of Postwar France, 1945–1954*, Cambridge, 1991.

13. Harryvan and van der Harst (eds), *Documents on European Union*, 43–45.
14. Austria, Belgium, Denmark, France, Greece, Iceland, Ireland, Italy, Luxembourg, Netherlands, Norway, Portugal, Sweden, Switzerland, Turkey, UK.
15. These ERP figures are taken from Gérard Bossuat, *L'Europe occidentale à l'heure américaine. Le plan Marshall et l'unité européenne (1945–1952)*, Brussels, 1992, 138–39. For the view that this aid was of immense importance for the realisation of the Monnet Plan, of someone very well positioned to judge, see Robert Marjolin, *Le Travail d'une vie. Mémoires 1911–1986*, Paris, 1986, 168–70, 177–84, 224–29.
16. René Capitant and Jacques Chaban-Delmas were among the Gaullists. Leading MRP figures were François de Menthon, Maurice Schumann, and Pierre-Henri Teitgen. Schuman and Bidault, also from the MRP but then respectively prime minister and foreign minister, were absent. The most prominent French Socialist was Ramadier. Edouard Daladier and Paul Reynaud attended as luminaries of the defunct Third Republic. Other Frenchmen included Raymond Aron and Jacques Rueff. The PCF was not represented. See 'Les congrès de l'Europe, 1948–1998', *Commentaire* 21(82), 1998, 532.
17. Mitterrand recalled in 1986 that 'it was the beginning of the great adventure that will remain the major achievement of our generation' – François Mitterrand, *Réflexions sur la politique extérieure de la France. Introduction à vingt-cinq discours (1981–1985)*, Paris, 1986, 67–68, 267–68. Coincidentally, it was on 8 May 1988, exactly forty years to the day of the close of the congress in The Hague, that he was reelected President of the Republic and embarked upon a second seven-year term, during which his focus was to be much more on Europe's future than on the furtherance of socialism in France.
18. On the creation of the Council of Europe and the respective roles of the French and British foreign ministers, see John W. Young, *Britain, France and the Unity of Europe, 1945–51*, Leicester, 1984, 108–17.
19. Pierre-Henri Teitgen, *«Faites enter le témoin suivant». 1940–1958, de la Résistance à la Ve République*, Rennes, 1988, 479–93.
20. Already in September 1940 de Menthon and Teitgen, as well as the future Gaullists, Capitant and Marcel Prelot, decided to launch a clandestine paper *Liberté*. Ten numbers were printed in 1941 and distributed across southern parts of France. One called for a more integrated Europe, compared with the interwar years, once France had regained her freedom. See Lipgens (ed.), *Continental Plans for European Union*, 285–86; Teitgen, *«Faites enter le témoin suivant»*, 24–25, 31–34, 41.
21. Soutou, 'Georges Bidault et la construction européenne', 210–16; see Young, *Britain, France and the Unity of Europe*, 92–95. For a detailed treatment of Bidault's approach to the question of Europe in 1947–48, see Jean-Rémy Bézias, *Georges Bidault et la politique étrangère de la France (Europe, Etats-Unis, Proche-Orient), 1944–1948*, Paris, 2006, 311–474.
22. For elements of the revisionist view that French foreign policy towards Germany in the late 1940s was not greatly at odds in general with positions taken in Washington and London, see Geneviève Maelstaf, *Que faire de l'Allemagne? Les responsables français, le statut international de l'Allemagne et le problème de l'unité allemande (1945–1955)*, Paris, 1999; M. Creswell and M. Trachtenberg, 'France and the German Question, 1945–1955', plus responses (C. Cogan, W. I. Hitchcock, M. S. Sheetz) and a rejoinder, *Journal of Cold War Studies* 5(3), 2003, 5–53.
23. Raymond Poidevin, *Robert Schuman. Homme d'État, 1886–1963*, Paris, 1986, 210–14.
24. Declaration on 9 June 1948 – see Charles de Gaulle, *Discours et messages*, 5 vols, Paris, 1970, vol. 2, 188–93.
25. Poidevin, *Robert Schuman*, 213–14, 216–18, 224–28; Hans-Peter Schwarz, *Konrad Adenauer: A German Politician and Statesman in a Period of War, Revolution and Reconstruction*, 2 vols, Providence, 1995–97, vol. 1, 488–503.
26. Alan S. Milward, *The Reconstruction of Western Europe, 1945–51*, London, 1987, 363.
27. Vincent Auriol, *Journal du septennat, 1947–1954*, (eds) Pierre Nora et al., 7 vols, Paris, 1970–80, vol. 1, 78–79, 138–39.

28. Ibid., 167–68.

29. Data drawn from André Piettre, *L'Economie allemande contemporaine (Allemagne occidentale), 1945–1952*, Paris, 1952. French imports of coking coal from the Ruhr rose from 748,000 tonnes in 1947 to 2.4 million tonnes in 1948 and to 3.3 million tonnes in 1949, before falling back to 1.9 million tonnes in 1950.

30. Poidevin, *Robert Schuman*, 251.

31. Dean Acheson, *Present at the Creation: My Years in the State Department*, New York, 1969, 339.

32. Poidevin, *Robert Schuman*, 272.

Chapter 2

POOLING COAL AND STEEL

The Schuman Plan for the pooling of coal and steel was the decisive French initiative in the establishment of closer unity between European states in the post-war period. Conceived by Monnet, adopted by Schuman who was then foreign minister, and proposed by the French government to the rest of Western Europe, it gave rise to the ECSC, the first of the ECs. At the heart of the plan was France's concern for its own security in the face of the rising economic power of the nascent FRG.

The Monnet Initiative

The Man from Cognac

Notwithstanding its name, the Schuman Plan was conceived primarily by Monnet – rather than the foreign minister – between late March and early May 1950. No one else in France was better suited to the task than the head of the Commissariat Général du Plan. Benefiting from an insider's knowledge of government in Washington and, in particular, enjoying the friendship of a number of key officials in the Truman administration – notably Acheson, the Secretary of State, and John McCloy, the US High Commissioner for Germany – Monnet was able, with considerable flair, to measure how hitherto conflicting American and French interests could best be reconciled.

An extraordinary life had placed him in this position. Born in the town of Cognac in the Charente, Monnet came from a part of France oriented towards the Atlantic and the wider world. Before the First World War, as a very young man, he had represented his family's cognac firm overseas, and, in particular, he had become familiar with England, especially London, and afterwards with North America. The leading customer in Canada of Monnet cognac was the financially powerful Hudson Bay Company, which had its head office in the City of London and was to build up considerable shipping interests during the war. Monnet's personal link with the Hudson Bay Company, combined with the patronage in Paris of Etienne Clémentel (a government minister and friend of his father), led to his serving as the French representative on the Wheat Executive – a body set up in London in 1916 to coordinate the purchase and shipping of wheat for the UK, France, and Italy. And, once the US entered the war, he became the French representative on the Allied Maritime Transport Council. During the interwar years, in the course of a spectacularly varied career, he was deputy secretary general of the League of Nations in Geneva (1920–22) and later, during the Depression, vice-chairman of Transamerica in San Francisco (1930–32) – the holding company controlling the large Californian-based Bank of America. In the Second World War Monnet became a major figure in the allied war effort, first during the 'phoney war' as chairman of the London-based Anglo-French Coordinating Committee (AFCOC) for joint purchases (1939–40), then, despite his French nationality, as a member of the British Supply Council in Washington (1940–42), and, lastly, as commissioner for arma-ments, supply and reconstruction on de Gaulle's Comité Français de Libération Nationale (CFLN) in Algiers (1943–44).[1]

An imaginative pragmatism and a detached understanding of the ways of the Anglo-Saxon world were two of Monnet's evident qualities. By the end of the Second World War he was much closer in spirit to policy makers in Washington than in London, enjoying a large circle of influential friends in the American capital. So when Acheson's pointed request in early March 1950 to Schuman was made known to Monnet – to return the reader to the subject of the Three Powers and the nascent FRG – he, Monnet, clearly realised that the US was bound to have its way in the vexed matter of the lifting of restrictions on German steel production, and sooner rather than later. He also knew that the State Department was much in favour of further integration in Western Europe. Some bold arrangement had therefore to be found to reconcile France's interests with the fact of American benevolence towards West Germany. A walking holiday in the Swiss Alps allowed Monnet two weeks of uninterrupted reflection on the French government's predicament, and it resulted in his returning to Paris in early April with a clear view of the issues at stake and of the best strategy for moving forward.

Monnet committed his reflections to paper during the course of the walk, as he was later to recount and detail in his memoirs. To simply acquiesce to American pressure in the matter of German steel restrictions, with no proper account being taken of France's own economic and political concerns, would spell disaster. West Germany, he thought, in rebuilding its heavy industry, might well profit from a new found strength to weaken abusively France's own heavy industry and so encourage French protectionism. Partly by sapping France's position, it might even be tempted in the longer term by a political rapprochement with East Germany and the USSR: '[West] Germany expanding; German dumping on export markets; a call for the protection of French industry; an end to trade liberalisation; the re-establishment of pre-war cartels; perhaps, eastward outlets for German expansion, a prelude to political agreements; and France back in the old rut of limited, protected production'. To 'solve the German problem' and to avoid another war, the parameters shaping the situation had to be radically and imaginatively altered. Therefore the way forward was to abolish the International Authority for the Ruhr, and provide instead for the joint organisation by France and West Germany, on an equal footing, of the two countries' entire coal and steel production.[2]

Monnet's idea of pooling coal and steel resources was not a novel one.[3] For instance, back in the 1920s Coudenhove-Kalergi had entertained the same sort of ambition. And ideas in a similar vein to Monnet's had been mooted by others in France in 1948 and 1949 – and in Germany too, as witness the proposals of Arnold and Adenauer (see the previous chapter). Indeed Monnet himself, in the course of his work for the CFLN in 1943 as he looked to the war's end, had mulled over the idea of separating off Lorraine and the Ruhr from France and Germany and uniting the two regions together in a kind of latter-day Lotharingia, which would have deprived the two countries of the economic resources required for yet another war with one another. But this imaginative redrawing of the map of Europe had been only a pipe dream. By contrast, his musings now had a directly practical focus. And their practicality lay, almost paradoxically, in the reach of their ambition. For he had come to the conviction that the joint organisation of the two countries' coal and steel production would prove unworkable on a purely intergovernmental basis; the practical way forward had to entail some degree of sacrifice of national power.

Not that Monnet advocated unreservedly supranationalism. In his account of the genesis in the spring of 1950 of the Schuman Plan, he declared that the use of the adjective 'supranational' to qualify the new authority he envisaged had never really pleased him. To explain the nature of the relative loss of national power in question, Monnet preferred to emphasise what would normally be the binding quality of the authority's decisions, a quality expressed, he said, by the adjective '*exécutoire*' (mandatorily binding). It was an emphasis with a Saint-Simonian or technocratic edge. What was true was that his proposed authority, as an executive power, was in no way set to constitute a sovereign political entity, and the interests of the nation states that agreed to be subject to it – in its own particular limited sphere – were to be secured by various international treaty guarantees and safeguards.[4]

Monnet's Men

Monnet had no direct practical experience of heavy industry. However, Etienne Hirsch, who was his closest colleague and deputy at the Commissariat Général du Plan (after having worked for him already in Algiers) and later his successor, did have such competence. He had been trained as a young man at the prestigious Ecole des Mines, and practical vacation work had included a month's study visit in 1921 to a Saar coal mine. More importantly, from 1924 to 1940 he had worked for Etablissements Kuhlmann, then France's second largest chemicals group, as a chemical engineer and senior manager. He had no illusions about the competitiveness of the French steel sector – for instance, at the outset of his work for the Commissariat Général du Plan, he drew Monnet's attention to the startling fact that France's most modern steelworks had been built in 1906 by Thyssen in Lorraine, at the time part of Reichsland Lothringen.[5] It was Hirsch who helped put meat on the bones of Monnet's initial ideas in respect of such matters as pricing, quotas, taxes, social security, and transport.

If Hirsch's commitment to public service in the post-war period was driven by a desire to serve France's interests through increasing the country's economic strength and security, it was also effectively a commitment to the fostering of peace in Europe and a political rapprochement with the new FRG. This commitment came after tragic personal loss. A Jew of partly German and Austro-Hungarian origin, who was distantly related to Arthur Koestler, Hirsch had been among the first to answer de Gaulle's call of 18 June 1940 by immediately leaving for London, where he became second-in-charge of armaments supply for the Comité National Français (CNF). Retaining this responsibility, he moved to Algiers in 1943. During his absence from France at the time of the Shoah, members of his own family and close friends were arrested and deported in the convoys from Drancy – the concentration camp at the edge of Paris – to meet their death at Auschwitz, if not on the journey there.[6] He was to admit that his work from 1950 onwards for improved Franco-German relations, and so for greater European unity, necessitated overcoming feelings of repugnance towards the people at whose hands his family had so suffered. His work's justification, he thought, could lie only in the securing of a better future for those who had survived and their posterity. From 1959 to 1961 Hirsch was president of the Euratom Commission, this being prior to the setting up of a single Commission for all three ECs; and it was by virtue of Article 9 in the Treaty establishing Euratom – the second of the two treaties signed in Rome in March 1957 – that he drew up the first plan for what was later to be the European University Institute in Florence.

In early April 1950 Monnet had also required expertise in the field of international law and, in particular, on the question of how to define the powers of a joint coal and steel authority that would be independent of national governments and yet ultimately beholden to the nation states that were party to its purpose. Luck had it that, shortly after his return from the Alps, Monnet was visited at the Commissariat Général du Plan on quite different business by Reuter, who had become professor of international law at Aix-en-Provence and was also a legal adviser (*jurisconsulte*) to the Quai d'Orsay. This led to further discussions on the following weekend in mid April – between just the two of them on the Saturday, and involving Hirsch as well on the Sunday. Not only was the industrial side of the plan thought through, but the three agreed on how the basic institutional arrangements might be best spelt out in a treaty.

Reuter was a native of Metz, Schuman's beloved city in Lorraine. Only thirty-nine at the time of this meeting with Monnet, he was of a new generation anxious to give France a fresh start after the public dispiritedness of the 1930s and the ignominy of the defeat of May 1940. Serving as an army captain, he had been wounded during the German invasion and taken prisoner. But he escaped to become one of the main figures at the Ecole Nationale des Cadres, the Uriage-based institute that dispensed leadership courses and Catholic social philosophy under Vichy auspices (see previous chapter). By the time this institute was closed down at the end of 1942 by Laval, Reuter was engaged in the Resistance, which led after the Liberation to his serving as *directeur de cabinet* for Teitgen, the GPRF's information minister and afterwards justice minister. At the end of 1944 Reuter played a large part in Teitgen's decision to call upon another of Uriage's instructors, Beuve-Méry, to establish the newspaper *Le Monde*. If Hirsch's commitment to a more united Europe was driven by personal grief, Reuter's own commitment drew on strong Christian convictions.[7]

The text – taking the form of a government declaration – that Monnet recast through successive drafts on Sunday, 16 April, with the help of Reuter and Hirsch, was essentially the text Schuman was to use just over three weeks later. An important change made by Monnet in the course of that day was to allow for the possibility that other European countries would wish immediately to participate in the setting up of the coal and steel authority, and there was accordingly an invitation for them to do so. What he had initially conceived as a matter for France and West Germany became thus a project with a wider European dimension. In the following week some further improvements were to be made to the text by Pierre Uri, another of Monnet's colleagues at the small Commissariat Général du Plan; he was of the same young generation and indeed the exact same age as Reuter, and in 1955–56 he was to be the main drafter of the Spaak Report, which paved the way for the EEC Treaty.

The Schuman Declaration

The Lot of the Foreign Minister

Immediately after Reuter's initial visit, Monnet had contacted Schuman's *directeur de cabinet*, Bernard Clappier, to say that he might be able to help the foreign minister resolve his difficulty over the American demands. However, on 28 April Monnet finally addressed the proposed government declaration, under confused circumstances, to both Bidault and Schuman. It was sent to Bidault, by way of his *directeur de cabinet*, partly because the Commissariat Général du Plan reported directly to the prime minister's office, and it was also sent later the same day to Schuman through Clappier. This was on the eve of a weekend. When the foreign minister returned to Paris from Metz on Monday morning, 1 May, he signalled his approval, whereas the identical text on the prime minister's desk was still unread. However, Monnet lunched with Bidault on Friday, 5 May, after having addressed a memorandum (dated 3 May) to him a day earlier.[8] This memorandum was effectively a document containing the fruits of Monnet's earlier reflections in the Swiss Alps – small parts of it were to be used for the writing of his memoirs a quarter of a century later (notably the section raising the twin spectre of West German economic expansionism and French protectionism), and it also included some brief words pointing to the danger that Washington might come to prefer the FRG over France as the US's privileged partner in continental Western Europe.[9] Bidault, apparently, did not substantially dissent from the analysis and its conclusions. On Tuesday, 9 May, the final version of the text that had been sent by Monnet to Schuman was approved by the Council of Ministers, whose regular Wednesday weekly meeting was brought forward a day because of the foreign minister's upcoming talks with Acheson and Bevin; these were scheduled to start on 10 May in London.

At the Quai d'Orsay, on the evening of 9 May, Schuman read his declaration to a hastily convened press conference, and it revealed the boldness of Monnet's design. Almost at the outset there was a rhetorical doff of the hat to the memory of Briand, but it was followed immediately by its quite practical focus:

> France, by advocating for more than twenty years the idea of a united Europe, has always regarded it as an essential objective to serve the purpose of peace. Because a united Europe was not achieved, we had war. Europe will not be made all at once, nor according to a single, general plan. It will be formed by taking measures which work primarily to bring about real solidarity. The gathering of the European nations requires the elimination of the age-old opposition of France and Germany. The action to be taken must first of all concern these two countries.
>
> With this aim in view, the French government proposes to take immediate action on one limited but very decisive point. The French government proposes

that Franco-German production of coal and steel be placed under a common 'High Authority', within an organisation open to the participation of other European countries. The pooling of coal and steel production will immediately ensure the establishment of common bases for economic development as a first step in the federation of Europe, and will change the destinies of those regions which have long been devoted to the manufacture of arms, to which they themselves were the constant victims. The common production thus established will make it plain that any war between France and Germany becomes not only unthinkable, but materially impossible. The establishment of this powerful entity, open to all countries willing to take part, and eventually capable of making available on equal terms the fundamental elements of industrial production, will give a real foundation to their economic unification …

The tasks entrusted to the common 'High Authority' will be to ensure in the shortest possible time: the modernisation of production and the improvement of its quality; the supply of coal and steel on equal terms to the French and German markets, as well as to those of any other participating countries; the development of joint exports to other countries; and the equalisation as well as improvement of the living standards and working conditions in these industries.[10]

If a single moment is to be privileged as marking the start of France's post-war endeavour to lead the Western half of the continent in some form of European union, then it is this declaration made by Schuman in the Salon de l'Horloge at the Quai d'Orsay in May 1950.

German Assent

Adenauer gave his assent to the Schuman Plan on 9 May, just in advance of its approval the same day by France's Council of Ministers. For the French foreign minister had secretly sent his own emissary to Bonn to enquire of the German Chancellor's opinion; this was to bypass André François-Poncet, the French High Commissioner, whose relations with the Chancellor were far from good. Adenauer's immediate reaction was positive, and it was only after this news was signalled by telephone to Clappier, when the meeting of the Council of Ministers had already started, that Schuman unveiled his proposal to the prime minister and others around the table.

From Adenauer's standpoint, the Schuman Plan offered the prospect of a new form of international organisation that would allow West Germany to be integrated – quickly and, at least in principle, on an equal footing – into a post-war concert of Western European states. More particularly, it promised implicitly the abolition of the International Authority for the Ruhr, and it also transformed the question of the future of the Saar, for the territory's main economic activities would come under the control of the planned European High Authority, and would therefore no longer be exclusively a matter for the French government. Since the question of the future of the Saar was transformed, so too was the hitherto vexed question of West Germany's associate membership of the Council of Europe. Coincidentally, on 9 May the West German cabinet was meeting to discuss it anew. After having received with satisfaction Schuman's urgent and surprising message, Adenauer was able to convince the majority of his cabinet that the invitation for entry into the Council of Europe should now be accepted. After the Bundestag's approval – despite the opposition of the SPD – the FRG became an associate member in July 1950, with full membership of the Council of Europe following in May 1951.[11]

Acheson had been informed by Schuman of the plan even before Adenauer. The US Secretary of State arrived in Paris on 7 May for a few days' rest, in advance of going to London for the Three-Power talks and the related meeting of the NATO Council. At the American Embassy, the French foreign minister let him into the secret and spoke of Monnet's role. Once disabused of an initial suspicion that a giant steel cartel was being planned, Acheson warmed to a design that seemed fully in keeping with the American ambitions entertained for Western Europe's economic recovery ever since the announcement of the Marshall Plan three years earlier.[12]

The British Refusal

One consequence of Schuman's handling of events and Monnet's assertiveness was the isolation of the UK. On 9 May, Bevin, the Foreign Secretary, was aggrieved when he learnt that he had been kept in the dark by both his French and American counterparts. Irascible by nature and already handicapped by grave illness – death awaited less than a year later – Bevin gave vent to his fury, for which he had some cause.[13] He was in a minority of one, and, though Acheson had much personal affection for Bevin, there was perhaps a whiff of condescension on the US Secretary of State's part in the face of the British refusal to play ball. In any case, the American's view was that there was no 'special relationship' between the two Anglo-Saxon powers, and that 'Britain made her great mistake of the post-war period by refusing to join in negotiating the Schuman Plan'.[14]

If Bevin's personal anger was soon spent, the substantive issue of whether the UK could be tempted to participate in the proposed European coal and steel pool was left unresolved. The Three-Power talks brought no answer. Monnet paid a visit to London in mid May to explain the advantages of the Schuman Plan, to no avail.

Schuman was concerned that British objections should not derail the proposals that Monnet and his collaborators had concocted. In February 1950 an unconvincing plan for a customs union between France, Italy, and the Benelux countries – initially labelled Fritalux (raising subliminally the image of high-quality pommes frites), and then, less ludicrously, Finabel –

had finally run into the sands, partly because of British reservations. Neither Schuman nor Monnet greatly believed in the plan, which had started life in July 1947 at the first meeting of the Western European countries to discuss Marshall Aid, on which occasion Count Sforza, the Italian foreign minister, had proposed a Franco-Italian customs union (obtaining a positive response from Bidault, his Italophile counterpart). However, Finabel's fate did bring home to Schuman the danger of the UK's spoiling role. To prevent a repetition now, Schuman set a deadline for the British response. And so the French invitation to participate in the coal and steel pool was declined at the beginning of June 1950.

Fears in London about supranationalism and related losses of sovereignty counted for much, but not quite to the extent that has sometimes been assumed. Attlee, the prime minister, was to make clear in June both to the House of Commons and privately to René Massigli, France's ambassador to the Court of Saint James since September 1944, that the UK was not opposed in principle to surrendering certain powers of decision to international bodies, even in respect of sectors of the economy that were as important then as coal and steel. However, there was a real uncertainty in London about what actually were the powers that would have to be surrendered to the proposed High Authority. This was because Monnet, the key player in the whole affair, had never put into writing the details of what exactly would be involved. For Adenauer, it had been sufficient that the FRG would be admitted as an equal partner into a new European organisation that would replace the loathed International Authority for the Ruhr. From the quite different vantage point of London, there were understandably serious reservations about being embarked by France on an uncharted voyage with no clear destination. In Massigli's judgement the culprit was Monnet: not only had he been allowed by a weak foreign minister to usurp responsibilities that should have been those of the Quai d'Orsay, but his bulldozer approach, that of the fait accompli, should never – Massigli thought – have been allowed to govern relations between France and the UK at such a critical juncture.

The French ambassador's views in May and June 1950 were largely disregarded by Schuman. Yet they were not the views of a run-of-the-mill career diplomat. Massigli had joined de Gaulle in London in January 1943. He had become successively the CNF's commissioner for foreign affairs, the CNLF's commissioner exercising the same responsibility from Algiers, and very briefly the first foreign minister in the GPRF – being succeeded by Bidault – before taking up his ambassadorial post in London. Belonging to the Anglophile breed of Gaullist – Debré was another – Massigli viewed with dismay the turn of events associated with the Schuman Declaration.[15]

Mistake or not, the Schuman Declaration proved to have momentous consequences. France's security was further loosened from the UK's. The creation of NATO had placed the US at the apex of a military-security framework for the West as a whole, and now the Schuman Plan was pairing off France with Germany in what was effectively a supplementary international security scheme founded apparently on economics, but essentially on a new type of political partnership.

Forging the ECSC Treaty

Fortuna and Ministerial Change

The proposed Schuman Plan did not, of course, establish mutually confident relations between France and West Germany overnight. Such a transformation was beyond the powers of a Monnet or a Schuman. On the French side, some of the most senior diplomats at the Quai d'Orsay, in addition to Massigli, showed a distinct lack of enthusiasm, which encouraged the foreign minister to continue to rely heavily on Monnet and his colleagues at the Commissariat Général du Plan. In the National Assembly, few were the politicians who had Schuman's qualified readiness to push openly aside earlier fears or suspicions about the direction of future German policies. To the (limited) extent that it had a collective position independent of its members, even Schuman's own party, the MRP, did not provide wholehearted backing for his plan. Bidault, for one, despite his acceptance of the plan, had reservations about the powers that might be given to the proposed 'common authority'. The MRP's subsequent reputation for its commitment to the cause of a supranational Europe was to be acquired only gradually in the first half of the 1950s, and more because of its support for the EDC than for the ECSC.

The Bidault government fell towards the end of June 1950. Henri Queuille and René Pleven then alternated twice as prime minister, in a pas de deux that was exceptional enough even by the musical-chair standards of the Fourth Republic. First, Queuille – a wily old Radical, who impressed the young Mitterrand and later the young Chirac – took over from Bidault, after having preceded him in the same office from September 1948 to October 1949. But he had less luck with his second government since it lasted only four days. Replaced in July 1950 by Pleven, the latter gave proof of greater longevity, his government not being brought down until February 1951 on a question of electoral reform prior to the June 1951 legislative elections. Queuille then bounced back for a third term. In the run-up to these elections, he had more success than Pleven, inasmuch as he won support for major electoral law changes prejudicial to the National Assembly's two trouble-makers, the PCF and the RPF, both hostile to the supranationalism of the Schuman Plan. The RPF – the first Gaullist party, even if de Gaulle preferred to regard it as a 'movement' – had seriously frightened the Fourth Republic's political establishment by taking more than a third of the vote in the 1947 municipal elections. The new law served its intended purpose: the PCF lost many seats; and the RPF's breakthrough was far less pronounced than would otherwise have been the case. Yet the Gaullists' still not inconsiderable gains in 1951 were mainly at the expense of the MRP. The Christian Democrat party lost even more seats than did the Communists, and if Schuman survived as a Deputy of the Moselle, it was only after considerable uncertainty about his fate beforehand, which was a source of worry for Adenauer. Following the legislative elections, Queuille's government soon fell, and so Pleven returned in August 1951 at the head of his second government, which lasted until January 1952.

Hence, for reasons having no direct connection with foreign policy, Pleven's first period as prime minister covered most of the negotiations between France, West Germany, Italy, and the three Benelux countries to draw up the Treaty establishing the ECSC; and his second period covered the same treaty's approval by the National Assembly. Fortune had smiled, for Pleven was better disposed than either Bidault or Queuille to the Schuman Plan. Yet, although a Catholic and a Breton, he was not a member of the MRP, having declined to join it in 1944. Strongly Republican – a so-called *Bleu de Bretagne* – and suspicious of Catholic clericalism, he had been one of the founders in 1945 of the UDSR, a small party identifying with the Resistance. He was its president from 1947 to 1953, when Mitterrand, with whom he was never personally close, took over.

However, the UDSR had no clear stance on Europe. In the early 1950s, what counted more than any party programme was that Pleven was a longstanding friend and former associate of Monnet. More than two decades earlier, he had served as Monnet's chief assistant in Poland; this was in 1927 when the Blair and Company Foreign Corporation – a New York investment bank's Paris-based affiliate, headed by Monnet – was advising the Polish government on an international bond issue. He was subsequently general manager of the European operations of the Automatic Telephone Company (later AT&T). During the 'phoney war' Pleven moved to London to join AFCOC and serve anew under Monnet. Both were involved in the drafting of the quixotic proposal of 16 June 1940 for Anglo-French Union, which Churchill agreed to put to the French government, then in Bordeaux, in a doomed last-ditch attempt to forestall France's surrender. However, after de Gaulle's appeal of 18 June, Pleven joined the Free French and came during the next four years to be someone whose services the General prized most highly. From 1941 to 1943 Pleven was the CNF's commissioner for finance, economics, and the colonies (and, for some months for foreign affairs as well); he was then commissioner for the colonies in the more broadly based CFLN in Algiers. After the Liberation he was successively colonial minister and finance minister, and when, in 1945, Pierre Mendès France eventually stood down as economics minister, having failed to win de Gaulle's support for an austerity programme, this portfolio was added to Pleven's responsibilities. Although he followed de Gaulle in resigning from the GPRF in January

1946, he subsequently made his peace with the Fourth Republic and became defence minister in the Bidault government of 1949–50. It was in this function, in early May 1950, that he was admitted by Monnet to the tiny circle who knew of the Schuman Plan before it was unveiled at the Council of Ministers.

Fortune also smiled inasmuch as Schuman himself remained foreign minister. Indeed it was a post that he was to hold in eight successive governments from July 1948 to December 1952, thereby making for a large element of continuity in foreign policy in what were momentous enough times at a height of the Cold War and during the intensification of France's colonial war in Indochina. To ensure a successful outcome to the inter-governmental conference (IGC) on the proposed coal and steel pool, Pleven could have had no better partner at the Quai d'Orsay. This conference had opened just three weeks before Pleven took office, and when his government fell seven and a half months later on a question of electoral reform, the initialling of the treaty establishing the ECSC was almost at hand.

Yet, curiously, even if he backed Monnet's and Schuman's initiative, Pleven may not have been altogether convinced by the logic of the design. The French steelmakers, fearing for their lack of competitiveness compared with German steelmakers and jealously possessive of Lorraine's iron ore resources, sought to persuade the prime minister of the dangers of the Schuman Plan. Pleven summoned Hirsch, whom he knew from the Algiers days of the CFLN, and quizzed him about the reasoning that underlay the Schuman Plan. 'I understand', he allegedly said, 'why coal is being shared, since we are short of it. But why are we sharing the iron ore that we ourselves possess?'[16]

Monnet in Control

Pleven and Schuman had fresh concerns over Germany in the summer of 1950. Towards the end of June war had broken out in Korea as the army from the Soviet-backed communist regime in the North crossed the 38th parallel to attack the American-backed regime in the South. The Cold War had taken another turn for the worse. The spectre of even worse still, in the shape of Soviet aggression against Western Europe, loomed on the horizon. The reaction from Washington was to insist that the young German state should contribute militarily to the security of Western Europe, especially since a large part of the French army was mired in Indochina where France was waging a losing fight to preserve its colonial protectorates. For some years the US Defence Department had been in favour of a military contribution from Western-occupied Germany, but it was only after the outbreak of the Korean War that the State Department came round to the same view. In early September President Truman approved the American position that any substantial increase in the strength of US ground forces in Europe, to meet the heightened Soviet threat, must be matched by major increases in French and British forces on the continent; that they should be joined by army contingents raised in West Germany at divisional level (though without the creation of a German General Staff); and that all should be combined in a European defence force headed by an American supreme commander (foreshadowing NATO's integrated command).

The American position was most unwelcome in Paris inasmuch as it appeared as a willingness to accept a partial recreation of the Wehrmacht. Besides, Monnet himself feared that if West Germany were granted the right to rearm in this way, the Schuman Plan might unravel before it was worked out in treaty form. For to confer upon the FRG the most important of the traditional attributions of statehood, that of the right to a standing army, would be to lessen the new state's essentially political interest in the proposed coal and steel pool. Eventually too, it might lead to a loosening of ties with the rest of Western Europe. These forebodings were voiced by Monnet to Schuman as the foreign minister was about to embark for New York, where, besides taking part in the UN General Assembly's annual meeting, he was to address the rearmament issue at Three-Power talks and at a meeting of the NATO Council. 'If the Germans', said Monnet, 'get what the Schuman Plan offers them, but without the Plan itself, we shall run the risk of their turning their backs on us. If they were rearmed on a national basis, and thereby recovered their freedom of action, they would be able – and tempted – to strike a balance between East and West.'[17]

Schuman, duly forewarned, was to be successful in New York in stalling the talks on German rearmament. And soon an alternative approach to this defence quandary was being prepared in Paris as the result of yet another Monnet initiative (see next chapter). However, this diversion of Monnet's energies did not prevent him from continuing to mastermind the implementation of the Schuman Plan, notably with Pleven's support.

The coal and steel IGC had already opened in Paris in late June, shortly before Pleven became prime minister. Monnet was France's chief negotiator and, to allow him full scope, the government made him, formally speaking, France's only delegate. Quite exceptionally for the preparation of a major international treaty, the Quai d'Orsay's negotiating expertise was not greatly resorted to. However, Schuman did have Clappier, his own *directeur de cabinet*, included in Monnet's team, as well as Hervé Alphand, the head of the foreign ministry's economic-affairs section, who had championed the Finabel plan in 1949, partly because it would have allowed France to put a brake on American pressures to liberalise trade and payments on a multilateral basis. Like Pleven, Alphand had a Free French background. Figuring prominently at Monnet's side were both Hirsch and Uri from the Commissariat Général du Plan. The drafting of the treaty was in the hands of Uri and Maurice Lagrange, a jurist on loan from France's Conseil d'Etat, and there was also some help from Reuter who served effectively as an external adviser.

The enormous influence wielded by Monnet over the course of the negotiations derived not only from his formal powers but also from his having been the author of the Schuman Plan. And there was a further reason too. He had quickly won the trust of Adenauer. This was on the occasion of a meeting between the two men in Bonn already in May, a fortnight after Schuman's declaration and a month before the start of the actual negotiations. Furthermore, as a result of this meeting, Monnet was allowed by Adenauer to vet names for the head of the West German delegation, and so the Frenchman came to play a part in the choice of Walter Hallstein, a law professor and former rector of Frankfurt University. The choice proved of consequence: Hallstein later headed the German delegation at the IGC preparing the EDC; he was the German representative at the Messina Conference, where the EEC project was born; and afterwards he became the first president of the EC Commission (1958–67), in which office he was a fervent supporter of supranationalism, thereby provoking de Gaulle's deep ire.

Notwithstanding the misgivings of the Lorraine steelmakers, and also various reservations in the other countries party to the IGC, the negotiations were conducted with a speed that resulted in most of the design of the Schuman Plan being detailed out and agreed by December 1950. Narrowly defined sectoral interests were not allowed to stand in the way of Monnet's overall purpose, namely that of promoting arrangements conducive to France's security interests, political as well as economic, under the auspices of the planned High Authority. Perhaps the greatest practical challenge was raised by the patent lack of competitiveness of Belgium's coal industry, then so vital to the economy in the Walloon south of that country; to meet it, a system of cross-subsidies, financed by the more efficient German and Dutch coal industries, was negotiated by Hirsch.

In the Schuman Declaration, the economic-policy framework for the planned pooling of coal and steel had not been spelt out. What was decided in the second half of 1950 at the IGC was that a common market would be set up for both coal and steel. There would be the setting of maximum and minimum tariffs in respect of imports from third countries, and, within the common market, the abolition of all import and export duties and government subsidies, as well as the elimination of discriminatory and restrictive practices. But the functioning of this common market would not be purely market driven. Like France's Commissariat Général du Plan, the High Authority would engage in the sort of 'indicative planning' pioneered by Monnet for the post-war reconstruction of the French economy. In particular, the High Authority would seek to co-ordinate investment plans by securing the agreement of the interested parties to long-term general objectives for modernisation and capacity expansion.

On the political side, the term 'European Community' was absent from the declaration penned for Schuman by Monnet and his close collaborators. But, during the course of the negotiations, it was either Hirsch or Monnet who successfully suggested that this term be used for the name of the new organisation – both were later to claim paternity, the former confidently so, and the latter with a touch of hesitation.[18] The negotiations led, moreover, to agreement that the ECSC should embody institutions of a political and not just technocratic character. The only institution mentioned in the Schuman Declaration had been the High Authority, an executive body responsive to the needs of both government and economic enterprise. The inspiration for this High Authority was not purely that of traditional French *dirigisme*. Monnet was at least as much influenced by the spirit of Rooseveltian America – Franklin's rather than Theodore's – where in the New Deal the worlds of government and business could join forces in bold ventures, as, for example, the creation of the Tennessee Valley Authority. But since Monnet's High Authority was not to be set up in Europe in the framework of a duly constituted federal state, the question of the new international body's accountability was tricky and had to be attended to. The negotiations led to the provision for a permanent Consultative Committee – including, importantly, trade union representatives – attached to the High Authority, which was fully in keeping with Monnet's approach to policy management. Yet it was not enough. By the end of 1950 it was settled that the High Authority should be answerable to national governments, not only by virtue of obligations written into the ECSC treaty but also on an ongoing institutionalised basis, and, secondly, that there should be a token involvement of national parliaments too.

The issue of a role for national governments was raised above all by the head of the Dutch delegation, Dirk Spierenburg, who made clear that the High Authority as conceived by Monnet would be virtually unanswerable to a smaller country such as the Netherlands, never mind even smaller Belgium or tiny Luxembourg. This was all the more unacceptable inasmuch as the High Authority's remit concerned not just the coal and steel sectors but impinged more widely on overall national economic policies. Spierenburg therefore proposed that there should be a body bringing together ministers from the national governments to give assent to the decisions taken by the High Authority. This proved acceptable to Monnet, provided the ministers' own decision making was by majority voting and not by unanimity. Such was the origin of the Council, which was to be established for all three ECs and soon become known in common parlance as the Council of Ministers, with its powers being different and greater under the EEC and Euratom treaties than those originally allowed for the ECSC.

The idea that an element of parliamentary democracy should be associated with the functioning of the ECSC came from the French Socialist politician, André Philip, who suggested it to Hirsch.[19] The two had known one another since their participation in a socialist student discussion group thirty years earlier. Philip combined the moral rigour of French Protestantism with a keen Europeanism, and also enjoyed much political respect in France. He had been the most prominent figure from the SFIO to join de Gaulle in London during the war; he became the CFLN's commissioner for the interior and was afterwards interior minister in the GPRF. But then, as president of the drafting committee for the new constitution in the first Constituent Assembly (1945–46), he and de Gaulle broke bitterly with one another over the question of parliamentary control of the executive. Monnet's initial reaction to the suggestion relayed by Hirsch was negative. Yet a few days later he changed his mind. It was accordingly agreed that there should be an Assembly comprising delegations from national parliaments and sitting in ordinary session just one day a year, essentially just to approve the High Authority's annual report; and this was the forerunner of the present European Parliament.

Even if the bulk of the ECSC treaty was agreed before the end of 1950, its signature did not take place until several months later. The delay was due to difficulties that arose in West Germany over a matter in which French interests had American backing, namely competition policy and industrial decartelisation. There had been a considerable American involvement in the drafting of the treaty. The US State Department and the office of the US High Commissioner for Germany exerted, secretly, more influence over the proceedings of the coal and steel intergovernmental conference than did the Quai d'Orsay.[20] Largely as a result of this influence, the ECSC treaty was made to embody strong rules on competition, reflecting the American anti-trust tradition. To legally enforce these competition rules, there was need for a court: hence the treaty provided for a Court of Justice, which became the EC Court of Justice once the EEC and Euratom were set up. The provisions in the competition rules against cartels suited French interests, inasmuch as there was a strong concern in Paris to put an end to the cartelisation that had characterised the Ruhr's coal and steel industries in the past, especially under the Third Reich.

The persistent fear of the industrial power of the Ruhr had been apparent in the second half of May 1950 when Schuman sought unrealistically to reassure the foreign-affairs standing committees of the National Assembly and the Council of the Republic – the Fourth Republic's name for the Senate – that the coal and steel pool would involve no relaxation of the controls exercised by the International Authority for the Ruhr, even in the event of that body's abolition. Later that year, over the issue of decartelisation, the ECSC negotiations became entangled with the work of the Allied High Commission. Since the Allied Occupation Statute (as revised by the Petersberg Agreement) was still in force in West Germany, so too were the powers of the High Commission, which, under American leadership, had decided to decartelise the heavy industries of the Ruhr. In particular, the High Commission wished to break up the giant steel combine, Vereinigte Stahlwerke, to drastically curtail the ties between the steel and coal industries, and to dissolve the monopoly coal sales agency, Deutscher Kohlenverkauf (DKV). The prospect of such change gladdened France but not West Germany. And it seemed for a while that the German objections might torpedo the treaty. However, Adenauer eventually persuaded the Ruhr industrialists and trade unions that ground had to be ceded. This was announced by the Chancellor in a letter to McCloy, the US High Commissioner, in March 1951. A last stumbling block had been removed.

Ratification and Implementation

The French Parliament's Hesitations and the High Authority's Creation

Hence the Treaty of Paris establishing the ECSC was signed on 18 April 1951. It brought together France and West Germany, the three Benelux countries whose coal and steel industries were already partly integrated with those of their two big neighbouring countries, and Italy, whose interest was above all political – as witness the initial enthusiasm for the Schuman Plan of the Italian prime minister, Alcide De Gasperi, and the foreign minister, Sforza. Fourteen months elapsed before the ECSC Treaty was ratified by the parliaments of all signatory states. Despite France's leading role, the approval of the French parliament had not been a foregone conclusion.

The vital debate took place in December 1951 in the National Assembly, where Gaullists and Communists in opposition to the treaty accounted for more than a third of all Deputies and where there were also anti-treaty Deputies representing the interests of the Lorraine steelmakers. The question of sovereignty had to be addressed. 'Provided there is reciprocity', read the preamble of the Fourth Republic's constitution, 'France consents to the limitations of sovereignty necessary for the organisation and defence of peace.' This wording allowed those in favour of the treaty to justify it for reasons of high politics and, in particular, security. The defence of the treaty was led by Pleven, who tied the ratification debate to the future of his government, and by Schuman, who spoke persuasively several times and at length. They were backed by the justice minister and Radical politician, René Mayer, another of the tiny circle to whom the Schuman Plan had first been secretly divulged.[21] On 13 December 1951 the National Assembly finally approved the treaty with 337 votes for and 233 against. The debate in the Council of the Republic opened towards the end of March. Michel Debré – de Gaulle's ardent follower – strongly denounced the treaty. But other Gaullist senators were more favourably disposed. Most of them abstained when the vote was finally taken on 1 April 1952, which left the Communist senators as the sole bloc in the second chamber opposing the treaty (177 for, 31 against, and as many as 87 abstentions).

A week after the National Assembly approved the treaty, the Ruhr statute establishing the International Authority and providing for ceilings on German output of coal and steel was terminated. The ECSC Treaty itself entered into force on 25 July 1952 following a meeting in Paris of the six foreign ministers to launch the new organisation. The same meeting had also to decide upon the location of the ECSC's institutions, the use of languages, and the composition of the High Authority. The question of location led to long and acrimonious discussions, and eventually, more out of ministerial fatigue than for any reason of obvious suitability, Luxembourg was chosen as the temporary home of both the High Authority and the Court of Justice. This temporariness for the High Authority lasted until its demise in 1967, while the Court of Justice was still ensconced in the Grand Duchy's capital more than half a century later. Strasbourg was chosen for the Assembly by virtue of its being already the seat of the Council of Europe. On the question of working languages, Schuman proposed that French be used alone, an instance of an attempted exercise of 'soft power'; but because of an objection from Adenauer, who represented the FRG by virtue of being foreign minister as well as Chancellor at the time, it was decided that German, Italian, and Dutch should be used too. What was uncontroversial was the invitation extended to Monnet to become president of the High Authority, and so he moved to Luxembourg in August. Uri remained at his side, becoming head of the High Authority's economics division.[22]

Monnet stepped down from the presidency of the High Authority in June 1955, by which time the influence he exerted in Paris on European policy had greatly waned. This was partly because Schuman had ceased to be foreign minister, having been replaced in January 1953 by Bidault. The latter was succeeded in June 1954 by Mendès France, combining the posts of prime minister and foreign minister, thereby bringing to an end the MRP's virtually uninterrupted run of almost ten years in providing the head of the Quai d'Orsay, in the person of either Bidault or Schuman. René Mayer became Monnet's successor in Luxembourg, and so the presidency of the High Authority remained in French hands.

Mayer had been the incoming prime minister when Schuman and Bidault switched places for the last time as foreign minister. Because of the need for RPF support in the National Assembly, Mayer had considered it necessary in 1953 to call Bidault back to the post he had held almost constantly for several years after the Liberation. Crucially, Bidault was reputed for his wariness of supranationalism, and his successor as foreign minister, Mendès France, proved more wary still. By 1955, when Mayer moved to Luxembourg, the glory days of the Schuman Declaration were truly over.

The Coal and Steel Pool in Operation

As an organisation, the ECSC fulfilled its design in providing for the pooling of coal and steel resources. Thus, a common market for coal and steel existed by the end of the transitional period in February 1958, though it was a far from perfect one. Tariffs within the ECSC were abolished, many restrictive practices were eliminated, and rail freight rates were harmonised on a non-discriminatory Community-wide basis. On the other hand, there were crying anomalies. For instance, in the case of France's nationalised coal industry, state subsidies were not discontinued; further help to poorly performing coal mines was maintained in the form of cross-subsidisation; and coal imports from elsewhere in the ECSC were discouraged by a licensing system that remained in force until 1961. Furthermore, through an irony of history, the spectre that had given rise to Monnet's initiative – that of a shortage of German coal for the French economy, especially coking coal – had simply disappeared by 1958. Falling transatlantic freight rates and high productivity in the American coalfields led to an abundant supply of coal to Western Europe at prices cheaper than for Ruhr coal. Technological advances in the steel industry had, moreover, lessened the amount of coking coal required for a given quantity of steel production. More generally, the importance of coal was on the decline, and, even if steel remained essential for the modern economy, the role traditionally played by heavy industry in both conferring national economic strength and underpinning military potential was already in decline by the end of the 1950s.

The High Authority proved to be not so much an independent supranational body as an effective international management committee representing national interests. However, in the face of the crisis in 1958–59 resulting from the overproduction of coal, it failed to be even that, and temporarily the ECSC virtually collapsed.[23] Later, in 1967, when the Treaty establishing a Single Council and a Single Commission of the European Communities (1965) came into effect, the High Authority was replaced by the EC Commission. The Commission was subsequently to enjoy better fortune in confronting the ECSC's second major crisis – that resulting from steel overcapacity after economic growth in Western Europe turned for the worse in the mid-1970s – though by then the relative role of heavy industry had greatly declined.

If in the longer term the ECSC had not the narrowly defined economic importance that Monnet had imagined, it served nonetheless in the 1950s to foster close ties between France and the new West Germany, thereby, in French eyes, reducing the risk of any return to conflict. François Duchêne was Monnet's assistant in 1958–63 before becoming much later his biographer. In this latter capacity, speaking of the ECSC and the failed EDC, he wrote appositely that 'the first Europe was in many ways a security Europe, not an economic one'.[24] Attention may now be paid to the EDC saga – like the ECSC project, it did indeed testify to France's understandable obsession with security, and also, in the first half of the 1950s, to growing French reservations about Monnet-type supranationalism.

Notes

1. For Monnet's multifaceted life or career up to the end of the Second World War, see François Duchêne, *Jean Monnet: The First Statesman of Interdependence*, New York, 1994, 27–146. The influence of Clémentel on the young Monnet is highlighted in John Gillingham, *Coal, Steel, and the Rebirth of Europe, 1945–1955: The Germans and French from Ruhr Conflict to Economic Community*, Cambridge, 1991, 2–6 ('Along with Walther Rathenau and V.I. Lenin, Clémentel was among the first to recognise that the organisations set up to administer industry, agriculture, and trade during the war could serve as the basis of a peacetime economy whose priorities would be determined by the state rather than the marketplace.').
2. Jean Monnet, *Memoirs*, London, 1978, 288–93 [*Mémoires*, Paris, 1976, 415–24].
3. William Diebold, *The Schuman Plan: A Study in Economic Cooperation, 1950–1959*, New York, 1959, 21–46.
4. Ibid., 297 [*Mémoires*, 430].
5. Etienne Hirsch, *Ainsi va la vie*, Lausanne, 1988, 89.
6. Among those deported to their deaths were one of Hirsch's sisters and her four children in September 1942, his father-in-law and brother-in-law in September 1943, Raymond Berr – Kuhlmann's general manager – with his wife and daughter in March 1944, and then Hirsch's own parents at the end of July 1944, only three weeks before the liberation of Paris.
7. Reuter's importance in the genesis of the Schuman Plan has often been overlooked. In 1951 he moved from Aix to Paris, where he taught international law and European law at the Faculté de Droit. See Georges Vedel's obituary notice in *Le Monde*, 4 May 1990.
8. For this detail, see Soutou, 'Georges Bidault et la construction européenne', 216–17; Jacques Dalloz, *Georges Bidault. Biographie politique*, Paris, 1992, 305–6. It serves to correct any mistaken belief that could easily arise from a reading of Monnet's memoirs, where Bidault is virtually airbrushed out of the picture – the prime minister doing nothing other than giving Monnet a peeved dressing-down on account of the latter's having short-circuited him (*Memoirs*, 299–300 [*Mémoires*, 433–34]).
9. For the entire text of this memorandum, see Bossuat, *Faire l'Europe sans défaire la France*, 287–90.
10. Harryvan and van der Harst (eds), *Documents on European Union*, 61–63.
11. Schwarz, *Konrad Adenauer*, vol. 1, 503–7.
12. Acheson, *Present at the Creation*, 382–84.
13. Bullock, *Ernest Bevin*, 766–75.
14. Acheson, *Present at the Creation*, 384–88.

15. For the Schuman Plan and its attendant diplomacy (or lack thereof), see René Massigli, *Une comédie des erreurs, 1943–1956. Souvenirs et réflexions sur une étape de la construction européenne*, Paris, 1978, 185–235.

16. Hirsch, *Ainsi va la vie*, 107–8.

17. Monnet, *Memoirs*, 341 [*Mémoires*, 495–96].

18. Cf. Hirsch, *Ainsi va la vie*, 109; Monnet, *Memoirs*, 323 [*Mémoires*, 467].

19. Hirsch, *Ainsi va la vie*, 107.

20. Duchêne, *Jean Monnet*, 212–15; Gillingham, *Coal, Steel, and the Rebirth of Europe*, 254–62, 266–80.

21. Like Pleven, Mayer had worked under Monnet on AFCOC in London during the 'phoney war', before joining the Resistance and then becoming the CFLN's commissioner for transport, thus teaming up anew with Monnet in Algiers in 1943.

22. On this meeting, see Poidevin, *Robert Schuman*, 295–96.

23. See Alan S. Milward, *The European Rescue of the Nation-State*, 2nd edn, London, 2000, 106–13.

24. Duchêne, *Jean Monnet*, 256.

Chapter 3

GERMAN REARMAMENT AND MILITARY SECURITY

French fears of Germany were not immediately dispelled by the Schuman Plan and the negotiation of the ECSC Treaty. The Pleven Plan, leading to the EDC Treaty, was designed to limit the scope of West German rearmament. Two consequences of France's failure to ratify the same treaty were German membership of NATO and a settlement of the conflict over the Saar. By the time of the signing of the Treaty of Rome setting up the EEC, in the traumatic aftermath of the Suez crisis, proof had been given of a readiness in Paris to privilege ties with Bonn.

The Pleven Plan

The Refusal of a German Army

When Schuman went to New York in September 1950 for the Three-Power talks and the NATO Council meeting, his determination to refuse in New York anything resembling the reemergence of a German national army was fortified by the presence at his side of the resolutely anti-German defence minister, Jules Moch. A Socialist, Moch had lost during the war a son, garrotted by the Gestapo for belonging – like himself – to the Resistance. Because of French opposition to Acheson's request that ten German army divisions be formed, the NATO Council meeting ended without any agreement on the contentious question of an eventual German military contribution to the West's defence, save that the question should be reopened at the end of October at a meeting of the NATO Defence Committee (the defence ministers' forum). However, agreement was won for the creation of NATO's integrated military command structure.

The indefatigable Monnet had a solution of his own for the new German problem. It mirrored the solution he had hit upon in April 1950 to Schuman's dilemma about the future of coal production in the Ruhr: the broad American aim had to be accepted, but not the means proposed; instead of allowing West Germany to regain military strength as a nation state, the framework for a German military contribution should be a supranational European one. On this occasion, Monnet sought to influence the prime minister – now his friend, Pleven – rather than to rely anew on the foreign minister. He had broached the problem in general terms with Pleven already in August. By October he had persuaded the prime minister to propose to the National Assembly that France, on top of the arrangements for the coal and steel pool, should take the lead in creating a European army that would include West German troops but no separate German divisions. Thus, the Pleven Plan came to be launched alongside the Schuman Plan.

The way was paved by Monnet and the small team he had formed for the coal and steel IGC, notably Alphand, Clappier, Hirsch, Reuter, and Uri. Following Schuman's return from New York in late September 1950, they found time in the first half of October, alongside their other work, to flesh out the idea of creating a European army to resolve the question of a German military contribution to the West's defences.[1] The crisis atmosphere was heightened in October by a series of adverse developments in the Far East: the fall of the garrison at Cao Bang early in the month, the most serious reversal suffered up to then by the French army in Indochina; more importantly from an international standpoint, communist China's dramatic intervention in the Korean War in the middle of the month; and, only a few days later, the fall of another French garrison in Indochina, at Lang Son. Any proposal put to NATO's Defence Committee at the end of the same month would have to take account of the deepening challenge facing the army pinned down in Indochina (a French overseas commitment that added to the need for a German military contribution in Western Europe) and, also, of the increased sense of urgency in Washington as the Korean War itself escalated. As Monnet and his collaborators worked out their new design and drafted a text for Pleven, they did so in the knowledge that time was short and that the French proposal had to be at least credible even if it did not immediately attract widespread support.

Of help to Pleven and his government was the congruity between Monnet's defence initiative and a resolution of the Council of Europe's Consultative Assembly, voted in August of the same year, which had called for the creation of a European army under the authority of a European Defence Minister. The author of the motion in favour of the resolution was no less a person than Churchill, though in his own speech he had spoken of a unified command rather than of a supranational defence minister, the text of the resolution being subsequently changed in the course of the debate.[2] Even if Churchill had been studiously vague about the desirability of the UK's involvement in such a venture, not deigning to admit in Strasbourg that it was a proposal meant exclusively for the countries of continental Western Europe, his association with the resolution gave it a certain force and international respectability. So when Pleven addressed the National Assembly on 24 October 1950, and announced as government policy the plan that was to bear his name, it was politic to claim, as he did, that it had sprung directly from recommendations adopted by the Assembly of the Council of Europe.

At the heart of Pleven's declaration was the recognition that West Germany should contribute to the defence of Western Europe and, yet, the insistence that this contribution should not entail the rebuilding of a German army:

> Germany, not being a party to the Atlantic Treaty, is nevertheless also destined to enjoy the benefits of the security system resulting from the latter. It is therefore right that it should contribute towards setting up a defence system for Western Europe ... [But] any system that would lead, immediately or in due course, directly or indirectly, subject to conditions or not, to the creation of a German army, would cause mistrust and suspicion again. The creation of German divisions, of a German ministry of defence, would inevitably lead, sooner or later, to the reconstitution of a national army and, thereby, to the resurrection of German militarism.

The solution, continued Pleven, was the setting up of a European army in which there would be no contributions, German or otherwise, at divisional level – though only once the ECSC treaty was signed (a precondition insisted upon by Monnet, marking his fear that West Germany might still abandon the coal and steel negotiations):

> The signing of the coal and steel plan will very shortly, we hope, set a seal on the agreement of the six participating countries, guaranteeing to all the peoples of Europe that the steel and coal industries of Western Europe will no longer be used for aggressive purposes. As soon as the treaty is signed, the French government will ask for a solution to the problem of the German contribution to the creation of a European force, taking into account the cruel lessons of the past as well as the direction which so many Europeans in all countries would like to see Europe take. It proposes the creation, for our common defence, of a European army under the political institutions of a united Europe ... A Minister of Defence would be nominated by the participating governments and would be responsible, under conditions to be determined, to those appointing him and to a European assembly ... The contingents provided by the participating states would be included in the European army on the level of the smallest possible unit.[3]

In this declaration to the National Assembly, Pleven took care to indicate that much of the French army would continue to have a life of its own, independently of the European army: 'the participating states which currently have national forces at their disposal', he asserted, 'would retain their own authority over that part of their existing forces which was not integrated into the European army'. On the other hand, the requirement that national contingents in the European army be 'at the level of the smallest possible unit' (this being understood as battalion level) testified to the French government's determination in 1950 to rule out even the makings of an embryonic German army. The FRG was to be kept to the status of a political dwarf by being refused one of the leading, if not the foremost, attributions of statehood, that of maintaining a standing army. Such an attitude on the part of France only five years after the Second World War was scarcely surprising. It was anyway the essence of the somewhat unusual realpolitik to which Monnet and Pleven were resorting. As Acheson remarked years afterwards, 'the second-class accorded Germany was all too plain'.[4]

After a debate, the government declaration was approved by the National Assembly. But the majority in favour of it was not overwhelming (349 votes for, 235 against). A separate vote was taken on the government's determination to head off the creation of a German army and general staff. Tellingly, the majority greatly increased (402 for, 168 against). A final vote on the order of the day gave the government the go-ahead (343 for, 225 against). Among Deputies opposed to the Pleven Plan, many were concerned about its implications for the independence of the French army, notwithstanding the reassurance about nonintegrated national forces. The PCF's opposition was total; since the purpose of the proposed European army was to defend the Western half of the continent against the USSR, it could only deny the assumed need. In general, the mood of this first debate in the National Assembly on the Monnet-inspired defence initiative presaged difficulties ahead.

At the NATO Defence Committee meeting held in Washington on 28 October, just four days later, Moch presented the Pleven Plan. If the plan passed, only barely, the test of credibility, it was not liked. All the other NATO defence ministers preferred the simpler American option, which was that of admitting West Germany to NATO itself (though without the creation of a German army general staff). But Moch stood his ground, and it was decided that the best way forward was to seek some sort of compromise, even if there was no obvious one in sight.

German and American Changes of Mind

The long and difficult negotiations between the initial negative reactions from France's NATO partners and the eventual signing of the EDC Treaty took place in a variety of forums. NATO itself was the initial one and remained central throughout. Key talks with Adenauer or his defence delegate, Theodor Blank, were arranged by the Three Powers at foreign-minister level or through the offices of the Allied High Commissioners. Among the latter McCloy was particularly influential.

The Conférence pour l'Organisation de l'Armée Européenne – the intergovernmental conference launched on the back of the Pleven Plan – opened in Paris in February 1951. Delegates from only five of the states negotiating the ECSC treaty turned up. The Netherlands initially preferred observer status, in the company of all other NATO member states (apart from the five). This lack of a Dutch commitment to the Paris talks was to end in October 1951; the turnaround came after the failure of a drawn-out conference held at Petersberg, near to Bonn, from January to June 1951, at which the three Allied High Commissions and a German delegation fruitlessly explored the possibility of an agreement to resolve the German rearmament problem in a purely NATO framework. At the Paris inter-governmental conference, Alphand, as the chairman of a powerful steering committee, directed its proceedings. In addition, all the confer-ence's standing committees were chaired by Frenchmen, with Hirsch, for example, at the head of the armaments committee.[5]

In the face of France's persistent refusal to allow West German forces to be directly integrated into NATO, the two parties other than France with the highest stakes at play, namely West Germany itself and the US, began to adopt more accommodating or flexible positions. By June 1951 Adenauer had overcome his initial strong hostility to the Pleven Plan. Once it became clear that the principle of contingents 'at the level of the smallest possible unit' – at least when the principle meant the provision of contingents at battalion level – was quite impractical and would therefore have to be abandoned, Adenauer swung to the view that a European army need not be militarily a farce from Germany's standpoint. Furthermore, he felt that the formation of a European army, even if a second-best solution compared with the NATO one, would head off his greatest fear of all, which was that Four-Power negotiations over Germany might lead – despite the Cold War – to the country's too precipitate unification on the basis of demilitarisation, and ultimately to Soviet control. It was better therefore to act on the Pleven Plan and have it modified by pressing determinedly for equality of treatment for West Germany.[6]

On the American side, General Eisenhower, after having been appointed NATO's first Supreme Allied Commander Europe (SACEUR) in December 1950, was converted to the French cause in June 1951, effectively in step with the FRG's Chancellor. The agent of his conversion was the ever active Monnet. Acheson swung the State Department behind Eisen-hower's position a month later. The ground had been prepared for the American shift of stance by McCloy, who had been invited to Monnet's home near to Paris already at the end of October 1950 for a day's briefing from both Pleven and Schuman. Yet again Monnet's transatlantic connections had paid off, as he enjoyed a friendship of twenty years' standing with the US High Commissioner.[7]

Eisenhower resolved the question of the size of contingent by proposing a *groupement* (grouping), supposedly a new level of military formation, but in reality a division by another name. It was eventually agreed that West Germany would contribute twelve out of a total of forty-three. French fears about German rearmament – the latter now more substantive than allowed originally by the Pleven Plan – were partly assuaged by a British commitment in February 1952 from the Foreign Secretary, Anthony Eden, to keep armed forces on the European continent as long as was necessary, which was followed in April by a draft treaty agreement between the UK and the EDC providing for mutual military assistance.[8]

The Rejection of the EDC Treaty

Opposition from within France

The treaty establishing the EDC was signed in Paris on 27 May 1952; on the previous day, France, the UK, and the US had signed the so-called General Treaty with the FRG, which abolished the Allied Occupation Statute and recognised German sovereignty in international affairs. However, the ratification process, ultimately abortive, for the EDC Treaty was to drag on for more than two years, and this held up the implementation of the Contractual Agreements forming the General Treaty, to the exasperation of Adenauer and others. During this period a paradoxical situation developed: the US – in the person of Eisenhower, who had been elected US president in November 1952, and, more keenly still, his Secretary of State, John Foster Dulles (yet another of Monnet's old Washington friends) – became the treaty's impatient champion; whereas the treaty's begetter, France, was prey to a growing reluctance to approve a treaty accepted by its five ECSC partners.

In his occasional political pronouncements, when he sallied forth from his small manor house in the Haute-Marne village of Colombey-les-Deux-Eglises, de Gaulle was the most forceful critic of the EDC's implications for France's sovereignty and the independence of its army. Not that he denied the need for some form of German rearmament, for the international situation, in his eyes, was now a far different one from that in 1948 when he had rejected the London Accords. Already in August 1950 – several days after Churchill had made his proposal at the Council of Europe for the creation of a European army – de Gaulle had called for a 'Franco-German practical entente'. In the spheres of economics and defence, it would entail the creation of new European institutions 'to which participating states would delegate part of their sovereignty', with a 'system of common defence' led by France.[9] A return was made to this theme in June 1952 when de Gaulle made a formal declaration denouncing the freshly signed EDC Treaty. The 'Soviet menace', he said, could be met only by forging the 'unity of Europe', and what should have been established, rather than the treaty, was a 'confederation of Europe' organised by virtue of powers 'proceeding directly from its peoples' and 'encompassing and binding Germany' with a view to the creation of a continental 'community of interests'.[10]

Later, at a press conference in February 1953, the General described the EDC's Board of Commissioners as a 'technocracy', yet one that was largely powerless, since under the treaty SACEUR would exercise quasi-discretionary rights over the European defence forces. Rather than such an artificial creation, there should be an 'alliance of the free states of Europe', headed by a 'council of the heads of government, meeting in a regular and organised manner', and under whose auspices a joint army general staff could be set up. This alliance, he continued, would include West Germany, and it would lead to the building of a 'confederation' whose member states 'without losing their body, soul, or form' would 'delegate part of their sovereignty in strategic, economic and cultural matters'.[11]

At another press conference in November 1953 de Gaulle entered into a long analysis of France's interests and the EDC Treaty. He expressed satisfaction that the Atlantic Alliance had been brought into being. But he added that, under the alliance, the Fourth Republic's 'inconsistency' had resulted in France being reduced to a US protectorate, and he questioned American motives in putting such pressure on France for ratification. To explain the genesis of 'Frankenstein' – his sobriquet for the EDC – de Gaulle pointed to the malfeasant force of 'the Inspirer', who was none other than Monnet, and at whose expense the General's redoubtable sarcasm was allowed full play. For instance, in attributing naïvety to Monnet, de Gaulle said that he himself had considered Churchill's use in June 1940 of the idea of Anglo-French Union to be no more than a psychological ploy of last resort, whereas 'the Inspirer' had been deadly serious, believing that 'one could integrate King George VI with President Lebrun, the House of Lords with the Senate, and the Home Guard with the Garde Républicaine'. Instead of the approach of 'the Inspirer', there had to be recourse in Europe to 'an association of nations in a confederation of states'.[12]

De Gaulle's protest was a far from solitary one. For instance, Herriot – the aged Radical politician and illustrious throwback to the Third Republic, who presided over the National Assembly from 1947 to 1954 – was scathing in his condemnation of the EDC and declared it unconstitutional. Another influential opponent was Auriol, whose seven-year term as President of the Republic came to end in December 1953. Like de Gaulle, he would have preferred a confederal European solution. Noteworthy too was the opposition from the army in the person of Marshal Juin, who had been elevated to the rank of Marshal of France in 1952. He was to be relieved of his command in April 1954 by the government headed by Joseph Laniel because of his expressed conviction that the EDC would be unworkable and unacceptable to the French army. Prominent on the other side of the debate were Schuman and other MRP luminaries, with the exception of Bidault, who as foreign minister between January 1953 and June 1954 was sometimes reserved or ambivalent in his support of the treaty – though without ever actually turning against it.[13] In favour of the EDC was the SFIO's secretary general (the party's leader), Guy Mollet, though the SFIO's large parliamentary group in the National Assembly was deeply divided on the matter. The controversy in France over the treaty's ratification turned out from 1952 onwards to be an impassioned one, so much so that de Gaulle's pugnacious lieutenant in the Council of the Republic, Debré, who led the Gaullist campaign against the EDC, referred to it famously as a 'new Dreyfus affair'.[14]

If justification existed for talking of a 'new Dreyfus affair', it owed something to the way in which the EDC Treaty had become entangled with ambitions for European federalism. The trigger had been the IGC's decision to abandon the idea of a European Defence Minister in favour of a Board of Commissioners modelled on the ECSC's High Authority. In the debate in France, this raised the question of whether national sovereignty could be meaningfully retained once an ECSC type of political structure had been extended to the realm of defence. The question assumed an added importance because of the treaty's Article 38, which provided for the eventual setting up of a federal or confederal European Political Community, encompassing both the EDC and the ECSC.

This provision had not been the result of a French initiative. It had come rather from De Gasperi, Italy's Christian Democrat prime minister, who had taken charge of the foreign ministry on Sforza's retirement (1951). For he had successfully pushed forward a proposal made by Altiero Spinelli – the Italian reformist communist – in the name of the European Federalist Movement. In September 1952 the EDC Treaty's Article 38 led to a resolution from the ECSC's Council, at its very first meeting, which invited the ECSC's Assembly to transform itself into an 'ad hoc Assembly' and prepare a draft treaty for establishing the envisaged European Political Community. This draft treaty was published in March 1953, and it signalled inter alia the goal of a common market.[15] However, as an extension to the EDC treaty, it found singularly little favour in France and prejudiced the chance of the treaty's ratification.

Year of Climax, Year of Dien Bien Phu

Also complicating matters was a certain lingering for the entente cordiale. For there was a reluctance in Paris to exchange the UK for West Germany as France's privileged military partner in Western Europe. Even those in favour of the treaty wanted an additional commitment from London on top of that already given in 1952. In January 1954 Alphand picturesquely expressed this desire to the Parliamentary Under-Secretary of State for Foreign Affairs, Anthony Nutting: 'if the French are to go to bed with the German tiger, it is essential that the British be the bolster down the middle of the bed'.[16] Eden obliged with a cooperation agreement between the UK and the EDC, which was signed in Paris in April 1954.

By that month the FRG and the Benelux countries had ratified the treaty. Italy's ratification was set to follow France's automatically. But French procrastination persisted. Matters were not helped for the EDC's supporters by international developments. For the situation that had given rise to the Pleven Plan nearly four years earlier had considerably changed. Stalin had died in March 1953. And an armistice put an end to the Korean War only four months later. The Soviet bloc was accordingly no longer perceived in the West as quite so threatening. For France, on the other hand, the war in Indochina intensified. In May 1954 the French army's most traumatic defeat occurred when the besieged, hill-surrounded base at Dien Bien Phu, garrisoned by some of the best troops of the French expeditionary corps, finally fell to the Vietnamese forces of General Giap. There was a huge loss of life (some seven thousand dead on the French side by the time the base fell; still more among the Vietminh) and the humiliating capture of the remaining French soldiers (eleven thousand or so). Against the background of the war in Indochina, many now considered the quarrel over the EDC to be a paltry squabble, with little to be said in favour of a European army.

Already before the fall of Dien Bien Phu a Five-Power Conference (China, France, UK, US, USSR) had been convened in Geneva, and Indochina was at the top of its agenda. In France the Laniel government fell in June; this was a delayed effect of the dramatic military setback a month earlier. On accepting in mid June to serve as both prime minister and foreign minister, Mendès France – the National Assembly's great political loner, as de Gaulle was the great loner outside it – pledged that within the space of a little more than four weeks he would win honourable terms in Geneva for terminating France's unhappy involvement in Indochina, or else he would resign. The pledge was kept. The outcome on 20 July 1954 – the deadline Mendès France had set himself – was a Five-Power agreement to a North-South partition of Vietnam and guaranteed independence for Laos and Cambodia.

It was only in late August that Mendès France set aside time for the long awaited ratification debate. Prior to that moment he had attended a last-ditch meeting of the foreign ministers of the EDC signatory states, organised in Brussels by the Belgian foreign minister, Paul-Henri Spaak. Mendès France made proposals for a protocol that would have substantially modified the treaty's implementation. For instance, the Board of

Commissioners would have been allowed lesser powers, especially during the EDC's first eight years. Also the integration of ground force units would have been limited to those in the forward zone (that is, all the German forces and the other member states' forces stationed in West Germany, but not elsewhere). However, these proposals were rejected out of hand by Adenauer, Spaak, and the other foreign ministers.

The debate itself took place in the National Assembly on the last three days of August 1954. Mendès France had decided not to make the question of ratification a matter of confidence in his government. On 30 August General Aumeran – a vociferous Deputy in foreign-affairs debates, who was opposed to any German rearmament – proposed, for a second time in the three days, a procedural guillotine motion (*motion préalable*); its passing would result in the ratification bill's being definitively withdrawn. On this occasion he was successful. Herriot spoke in favour of Aumeran's motion and thus against the EDC. Speaking against the motion and in favour of the EDC was the SFIO's Christian Pineau, who was to become foreign minister in 1956. When the vote was taken, the government ministers, including Mitterrand, abstained. There were 319 Deputies in favour of the motion and 264 against it. The EDC was dead.

The Communists and the Gaullists provided slightly over half of the votes for the guillotine motion. Most of the rest came from the Fourth Republic's mainstream parties. Roughly equally divided on the motion were Deputies from the SFIO (53 in favour, including Moch, thereby defying the party line; 50 against), the Radicals (34 in favour, 33 against), and the UDSR (10 in favour, 8 against). Only the MRP voted in majority against the motion, indeed overwhelmingly so (80 against, 2 for).[17]

The National Assembly's vote at the end of August 1954 proved a defining moment, inasmuch as it made clear that there were definite limits to any French surrenders of independence in the cause of European integration. Both the ECSC and the stillborn EDC were essentially French creations. The two treaties were negotiated in Paris in the wake of French initiatives and at IGCs chaired by, respectively, a great French maverick and a senior French diplomat. A small but telling token of the strength of the French imprint in the case of the EDC treaty was its ordaining that French should be the exclusive language of the Board of Commissioners. Yet, for the majority of politicians of a still proud nation state, the EDC proved ultimately a step too far.

The Paris Accords

British Intervention, WEU, and an Enlarged NATO

Eden picked up the pieces with alacrity. An international conference was organised in London on 28 September 1954. Invited by the Foreign

Secretary were the other Brussels Pact member states, the US and Canada, and West Germany and Italy. Eden himself served as chairman and proposed that West Germany be brought directly into NATO, and also that it become a member of an enlarged Brussels Pact, with safeguards limiting future German military might. The Brussels Treaty itself would be modified, first, to remove from the preamble the mention of countering potential German aggression, and, secondly, to provide for a new organisational structure in parallel to NATO's. Joining this organisation would be not only West Germany but also Italy (the latter's membership of the Brussels Pact never having been considered in 1948, though it joined NATO a year later). The two-track approach would respect the sovereignty of nation states, while the new Brussels Treaty framework would result in the formation within the Atlantic Alliance of an institutionalised sub-group comprising the stillborn EDC's aspirant member states and also the UK. So, to return to Alphand's imagery, the UK would after all act as 'the bolster down the middle of the bed' and give reassurance to France.

Compared with almost four years between Pleven's declaration and the National Assembly's discarding the EDC treaty, the London Conference was brought to a successful conclusion in just one day. The ground had been carefully prepared beforehand. The key figures were Dulles, Adenauer, and Mendès France. The first of them posed the most difficulty for Eden. An angry US Secretary of State was initially loath to relinquish all hope of a European supranational defence organisation, a project to which American policy makers had become progressively attached since 1951. Yet he bowed to the force of adverse circumstances. More positive was the German Chancellor. Even if there were strings attached, what was now being proposed was West Germany's admission to the Atlantic Alliance on an essentially equal footing with the majority of NATO member states. And Adenauer felt strong enough to insist that this should be coupled with the FRG's rapidly acquiring full sovereignty, by virtue of the Contractual Agreements of the General Treaty (1952). As to Mendès France, he approved of the Eden initiative in respect of the Brussels Pact and, at a later date, he was even to claim that this part of the proposed remedy to the EDC debacle had been largely his conception. The French prime minister had to be persuaded, however, of the desirability of West Germany's actually joining NATO.

Of decisive importance at the London Conference was the commitment given by Eden that the UK would keep in place its existing forces assigned in continental Europe to SACEUR – that is, four army divisions and a tactical air force – as long as the majority of its Brussels Pact partners so desired. Among the agreements contained in the London Conference's Final Act was a Declaration by the Three Powers that the Allied Occupation Statute in the FRG would be revoked as soon as possible. Attached to the part of the Final Act dealing with the modifications to be made to the Brussels Treaty was a Declaration from the German Chancellor that the

FRG would not manufacture nuclear, biological or chemical weapons, or, for that matter, strategic missiles, large warships, or bomber aircraft. To allay French fears, the Final Act provided for the setting up of an armaments agency to control levels and kinds of armaments, notably those held by West Germany. In addition, the NATO member states party to the Final Act declared that the North Atlantic Treaty should be considered of indefinite duration.[18]

One satisfied person present at the conference in London was the French ambassador, Massigli. Still convinced in 1954 of the desirability of a confederal Europe constructed around a Franco-British axis, he had viewed with dismay the course of the two countries' bilateral relations ever since the launching of the Schuman Plan more than four years earlier. However, his satisfaction was partly based on what was to be the unrealised hope that the (modified) Brussels Treaty would at last serve as a framework for economic cooperation, as originally intended, and not just mutual defence.[19]

The content of the London Conference's Final Act had now to be put into the form of a series of accords for submission to the NATO Council meeting to be held several weeks later in Paris. So what took place in the French capital from 20 to 23 October 1954 was a three-day IGC followed by the NATO Council meeting.

Between the London and Paris Conferences two events of note occurred. On 13 October Mendès France called on de Gaulle at the Paris hotel used by the latter for his periodic visits to the capital. The Mendès France government was the first (and only) government of the Fourth Republic for which the General showed some respect, especially in the sphere of foreign policy, and this publicised meeting lent added authority to the prime minister as he faced the challenge of winning French approval for Eden's alternative to the EDC. Then on 19 October, the day before the Paris Conference, Mendès France and Adenauer met at the chateau of La Celle-Saint-Cloud – once Madame de Pompadour's residence – on the outskirts of Paris. On the subject of the next day's conference, the two heads of government came to an understanding on the question of a linkage between the changes to the Brussels Treaty and the future of the Saar. Other matters were dealt with too. There were agreements on sensitive issues relating to the aftermath of the Second World War (for instance, the care of German war cemeteries in France). Important for the future were decisions on economic matters. Long-term bilateral trade agreements – including agreements for the sale of French agricultural produce to West Germany – were to be negotiated, and there was to be institutionalised bilateral economic cooperation in the form of a Franco-German Economic Committee (eventually set up in 1956). More generally, the French prime minister reassured Adenauer that in no time in the future would West Germany's interests be sacrificed in any effort to improve Franco-Soviet relations. The meeting at La Celle-Saint-Cloud represented a decisive step forward in the post-war rapprochement between France and West Germany.[20]

The Paris Accords took mainly the form of declarations and new protocols to existing treaties. Some of the accords were limited to the Three Powers and the FRG. This was the case of those implementing the abrogation of the Allied Occupation Statute. Another accord – concerning the Saar – was a purely bilateral one between France and the FRG. The remainder involved the original Brussels Pact Five, the new Brussels Pact Seven, or all fourteen NATO member states. The NATO Council duly gave its blessing to everything. Thus, pending ratification of treaty changes, the FRG – five years after its birth – won international sovereignty and was admitted to both NATO and the Brussels Pact. Furthermore, a new international organisation had been brought into being, namely Western European Union (WEU), the name given to the more extensive and ambitious organisational structures for which the modified Brussels Treaty provided.

A Close-run Ratification

The National Assembly debated the ratification of the Paris Accords towards the end of December 1954. Mendès France defended the accords at length and was backed by the chairman of the foreign-affairs standing committee, Daniel Mayer, who had led the SFIO as a group in the Resistance during Blum's captivity in Germany. Speaking in favour of ratification was Schuman. However, other Deputies from the MRP spoke against it. De Menthon, for instance, underlined his party's constant opposition to any German rearmament in the form of a national army, and he denied that the WEU-NATO formula could be an acceptable substitute for the defunct EDC. On Christmas Eve votes began to be cast. The first vote was on the first article of the ratification bill which allowed for both the establishment of WEU and the FRG's becoming a member of NATO. Since the PCF's parliamentary group was joined in opposition by the vast majority of the MRP's Deputies, and since this bloc was increased by a sizeable leavening from the SFIO and also about a third of those identifiable as Gaullists, the article was rejected (259 for, 280 against). Yet the articles of the bill allowing for the abrogation of the Allied Occupation Statute and for a new policy towards the Saar were comfortably passed.

The response of Mendès France, before the brief Christmas recess, was to turn subsequent votes on the ratification bill into a matter of confidence in the government, and to resort to a procedural device so as to be able to put the content of the key first article before the National Assembly anew. Help came from across the Channel. Eden made clear that, in the event of a French rejection of the Paris Accords, there would be no further question of a British military commitment to continental Western Europe of the kind given at the London Conference. The combination of Mendès France's resolve and the Foreign Secretary's threat turned the tide. On 29 December the National Assembly approved of the FRG's joining NATO (287 for, 256 against). On 30 December, in a near identical split, it approved of WEU (287 for, 260 against).[21]

Because the RPF had disappeared from the parliamentary scene, there was no official Gaullist voice in the National Assembly for the debate on the ratification of the Paris Accords. The large fraction of Gaullists who voted against the accords was headed by Jacques Soustelle who had played a decisive role in the RPF's creation in 1947. However, he was no longer close to de Gaulle, largely because, in the latter's eyes, he had been overly keen some two years earlier to compromise himself with the Fourth Republic by angling for the post of prime minister. Before the French parliament's ratification process was completed, with the passage of the bill from National Assembly to the Council of the Republic, Soustelle was indeed gone, having been appointed governor of Algeria in January 1955.

The bill providing for the ratification of the Paris Accords came before the Council of the Republic in March 1955. Debré, the leading Gaullist senator, had some title to represent there the General's views. Not only had he distinguished himself in the campaign against the EDC, but he had a conception of Europe that largely corresponded to de Gaulle's, the one noteworthy difference being his more favourable attitude towards the UK. On the question of German rearmament, Debré had long argued that the FRG should be integrated militarily into NATO under certain restrictions, and that not only France and West Germany but also the UK should closely cooperate in defence matters. Debré did give his approval to the Paris Accords and a majority of Gaullist senators followed his lead, thereby contributing importantly to the positive vote of the Council of the Republic (184 for, 110 against), which brought the ratification process in France to a positive conclusion.[22]

Following ratification by all the states concerned, the Paris Accords came into force on 5 May 1955. This month marked a milestone in the Cold War. In the previous December, prior to the National Assembly debate, the USSR had warned France that ratification would rule out any international agreement settling Germany's future – that is, a long delayed Second World War peace treaty providing at last for German unification and demilitarisation. Such a prospect still exerted an attraction among some French politicians, especially in the relative thaw that followed Stalin's death. In the same month a further Soviet note warned that ratification would lead to Moscow's denouncing the Franco-Soviet Treaty of Alliance of 1944. The threat was duly carried out on 7 May 1955. And the same fate befell the Anglo-Soviet Treaty signed in 1942. On 14 May the Warsaw Pact was established when, in the Polish capital, a treaty of mutual assistance was signed by the USSR and its European satellite states, including the GDR.

Settlement of the Future of the Saar

The bilateral accord concerning the Saar's future, which Mendès France and Adenauer signed at the Paris Conference, was an agreement to compromise over the issue that had deeply divided France and the FRG ever since the latter state's creation five years earlier. It was a diplomatic achievement. The Franco-Saar Conventions of 1950 had bedevilled the ECSC treaty negotiations, and Adenauer had finally to resign himself to France's signing the 1951 treaty on behalf of the Saar. However, by the middle of 1952 when the ECSC became operational, there was no longer the earlier confidence in Paris that the Saar could remain permanently in union with France. The new tack followed by Schuman was that the territory should be accorded a special European statute. For instance, he angled for such a solution during the row that broke out between the foreign ministers of the Six in July 1952, at the launching of the ECSC, about the location of its institutions. The French foreign minister's unsuccessful proposal was that they should be located in Saarbrücken and that the Saar itself should be governed under a permanent European statute. During the negotiations of the EDC treaty and the long process of its ultimately unsuccessful ratification, the question of the Saar's future was often raised but only to complicate matters; there was certainly no willingness on the French side to move towards an acceptance of German territorial claims.

Adenauer and Schuman had continued to clash over the Saar up to the end of the latter's long period as foreign minister. Yet the German Chancellor did not turn his back on a European solution. He simply did not accept Schuman's idea of what such a solution might entail. On Bidault's return to the Quai d'Orsay no further progress was made, save for a bid made by Teitgen in May 1954 to secure a compromise under the auspices of the Council of Europe, which the French foreign minister himself soon disavowed. Only with Mendès France was there a breakthrough. Adenauer's concession at La Celle-Saint-Cloud was that the Saar's future might be resolved – at least until a German peace treaty – by a European statute, provided it were implemented under WEU auspices, with the effect that a European commissioner acting in WEU's name would be responsible for the Saar's external relations. An agreement to the principle of a referendum on such a statute was accordingly built into the Paris Accords.

The referendum was set for October 1955. Since the previous February, when Edgar Faure had succeeded Mendès France as prime minister, the Quai d'Orsay was in the hands of Antoine Pinay. His maladroit efforts to secure continuing French control of the Saar steel industry, by inviting French steelmakers to make a bid for the sequestrated Völklingen steelworks, raised serious doubts about French intentions. Although Adenauer subsequently persuaded Pinay that ownership of the steelworks had to be split equally between France and West Germany, the views of local trade unions about the future of the Saar steel industry, under the proposed European statute, became distinctly jaundiced, and this proved to be one of the factors influencing the referendum's results. In October, to the surprise of Adenauer, and also his delight, the statute was rejected by two-thirds of the Saar's voters. Since France could no longer impose its protectorate, the way was opened for the Saar's integration into the FRG. Political unification took place at the beginning of 1957, and economic unification followed in July 1959, when the Franco-Saar customs and monetary union was dissolved.[23]

The Suez Crisis and its Aftermath

A Divided West

If the infant WEU was undoubtedly a success by virtue of its having served as the vehicle for West Germany's joining the Atlantic Alliance, its functioning as an international organisation quickly proved disappointing for those in France – led by Mendès France – who had hoped that it would be a more constructive framework for European union than the model of organisation favoured by Monnet. Contributing in 1955 and 1956 to this failure of the modified Brussels Pact arrangements were a variety of factors, which were observed with melancholy by Massigli during the year and a half he was secretary general at the Quai d'Orsay – a post he took up in January 1955 just before the fall of the Mendès France government. The US Secretary of State, Dulles, never cared for WEU; it complicated the exercise of American hegemony and added nothing militarily to NATO. As to the UK, while it stood to gain politically from WEU, there was parsimony on the part of Harold Macmillan – then Foreign Secretary – when key budget decisions were taken about resources for the new organisation. The Benelux countries were concerned that WEU should not stand in the way of their own important initiative, the Messina Conference of June 1955. Spaak was very much of this view. Finally, in France, the Faure government paid little attention to WEU, partly because Pinay had the immediately pressing task of handling the demands for independence of Morocco and Tunisia. Furthermore, the leading French Socialist, Mollet, who was a leading figure in the Council of Europe's Consultative Assembly, won Macmillan's agreement for reducing the range of subjects to be debated by WEU's Consultative Assembly – a potential rival. They were henceforth limited to defence matters and the Saar. The result of the Saar referendum tarnished, moreover, WEU's name in France.

So WEU never got far off the ground. Nonetheless, international developments in late 1956 served to advance the rapprochement between France and West Germany initiated by Mendès France and Adenauer at La

Celle-Saint-Cloud. At the beginning of November the Soviet armed intervention in Budapest, to put down the Hungarian revolution, dispelled many an illusion in the West about Soviet intentions and, in particular, about any readiness in Moscow to allow eventually a unification of Germany on terms that could be acceptable to both the FRG and France, not to speak of the US and the UK. Mollet, who had succeeded Faure as prime minister in February, abandoned any hope he had entertained of a new Franco-Soviet entente.

More traumatic still, just two days later, was the sudden, externally imposed halt to the joint military operation carried out by France and the UK, in collusion with Israel, to gain control of the Suez Canal. The vital international waterway had been owned by Franco-British interests before its nationalisation earlier in the year by Colonel Nasser, who was not only Egypt's charismatic dictator but also the leading voice of Arab nationalism in North Africa and the Near East. The Suez climbdown was forced on the two countries by an effective alliance between the US and the USSR. The humiliation felt personally by Mollet was intense. Yet far more than personal feelings were at stake, since the action of Dulles, the leading figure on the American side, threw massively into question the scope and meaning of the Atlantic Alliance from a French standpoint. Indeed, the Suez crisis was France's first great moment of disenchantment with the US in the post-war period, and, as such, it was the harbinger of repeated strains to come in the next half century, both big and small.

This disenchantment owed much to the close link in French eyes between the aborted military operation's ultimate aim, the toppling of Nasser, and halting the worsening crisis in Algeria. The help received by France from the US in putting down the rebellion had been at best hesitant or lukewarm, though the North Atlantic Treaty included an article stipulating inter alia that an armed attack against the French *départements* in Algeria would activate the provision for NATO mutual assistance. Even if the hypothetical armed attack referred to external aggression rather than internal rebellion, a widespread feeling existed in French political circles that a claim on unqualified American assistance was in order. To justify the claim, the Mollet government pointed to Soviet military assistance to the rebel Front de Libération Nationale (FLN), much of it passing through Nasser's Egypt, as was increasingly evident from the summer of 1956.[24]

Adenauer, as the head of the government of the Western European state that depended most on American support, was appalled by the turn of events representing the Suez crisis. He looked upon Nasser as an 'ill-mannered Hitler'. More importantly, his earlier occasional fears about the strength of the Eisenhower administration's military commitment to the FRG, in the face of Soviet aggression or because of an agreement between the two superpowers to carve up the world, seemed to have gained an added justification. At the height of the crisis he decided to proceed with a planned official visit to France, and it was actually when he was travelling overnight by rail to Paris that the USSR threatened both France and the UK with nuclear missile attacks. After consultation with Paris the train continued forward, and so on the morning of 6 November 1956, at the gravest moment for France since the end of the Second World War, the German Chancellor and the French prime minister stood together at the Gare du Nord as the Garde Républicaine played the two countries' national anthems. They stood together in a mood of shared, profound disappointment with the US.[25]

It would be hard to overemphasise the significance of the Suez crisis for future relations between the four leading powers of the Atlantic Alliance. It made for a shift in the nature of France's post-war relations with the US – the essence of the shift being revealed gradually, especially under de Gaulle, as a refusal of any subordination – and also to a further shift in the nature of its relations with the FRG. Furthermore, it transformed the nature of future Franco-British relations, because of the quite different response in London to Washington's call to order.

A New Phase of Franco-German Rapprochement

The tightening of ties with West Germany started instantaneously. For Adenauer's talks with Mollet on 6 November 1956 marked a new phase in the Franco-German rapprochement that had started three years earlier with Mendès France at La Celle-Saint-Cloud. It was agreed now that the Saar should be simply returned to Germany. Furthermore, after the Spaak Report (March 1956) that had paved the way for the joint IGC for the EEC and Euratom, the two heads of government approved the lines of a compromise on the future shape of the common market. At work on this compromise were Marjolin – the right-hand man of Maurice Faure, the minister leading the French delegation at the IGC – and Karl Carstens of the German Foreign Office. In addition, Adenauer conceded that Euratom should not stand in the way of France's acquiring an independent military nuclear capacity. These agreements were vital for the negotiations that resulted in the EEC and Euratom treaties of March 1957. Finally, in the sphere of military security, the perceptions of British pusillanimity in the face of American pressures over Suez encouraged a readiness on Mollet's part to give greater priority to France's relations with West Germany. To Adenauer he presented a package of proposals, prepared by the French foreign and defence ministries, for Franco-German cooperation 'in the domain of military concepts and armaments'. These proposals met with a positive response from Adenauer and also Franz Josef Strauss – belonging to the CDU's smaller Bavarian sister party, the CSU – who had recently become the FRG's new defence minister.

One reason for the Chancellor's being open to the idea of defence cooperation with France was his concern for West Germany's long-term military strength in a nuclear age. On the question of the use or acquisition of nuclear weapons, his position in 1956 appears to have been changing. In July, in a long personal letter to Dulles, he had scolded the Secretary of State in arguing that the deployment of nuclear weapons was at odds with Christian principles. Yet after Suez he was convinced that it could be in West Germany's interest to have nuclear weapons at its disposal – the Paris Accords having banned only their manufacture in Germany. In the absence of American help, France might well be the best partner to this end, since it was already embarked upon efforts to develop an atomic bomb – the initial decision having been taken, secretly, by Mendès France in December 1954. Adenauer was strongly backed by Strauss, who was much in favour of an independent German nuclear capability. The two men were therefore susceptible to the overture made by Mollet.

The first fruit was an ambitious agreement in January 1957 for cooperation 'in the domain of military concepts and armaments', a repeat of the terminology used in the document proffered by the French prime minister. The protocol was signed by Strauss and the French defence minister, Maurice Bourgès-Maunoury, in the Algerian town of Colomb-Béchar, near to a major missiles testing centre in the Sahara, and also the nearest town to the future nuclear testing site of Reggan, a site to be chosen by the government half a year later when Bourgès-Maunoury himself was prime minister. Although the protocol made no mention of nuclear weapons, it put an emphasis on the development of sophisticated weaponry in general. And Strauss, on the occasion of his visit to Colomb-Béchar, made no secret of his desire that the Bundeswehr should not be excluded from the nuclear club. However, the Mollet government fell in May, essentially because of divisions in the National Assembly over the handling of the Algerian crisis. It was also over Algeria that the Bourgès-Maunoury government fell in September.

Taking over in early November 1957 as prime minister was Félix Gaillard, another Radical, and the new defence minister was the Gaullist, Jacques Chaban-Delmas. As the Algerian crisis further deepened, the USSR surprised the world with the launching of its Sputnik satellite. In the wake of this demonstrated prowess in rocketry, which appeared to threaten the balance between the superpowers, the Gaillard government sought to strengthen the recently agreed military cooperation between France and West Germany and to extend it to Italy. The result was a protocol signed in Rome in late November by the three countries' defence ministers. The protocol gave priority to the development of military aircraft, missiles, and 'military applications of nuclear energy'. It was envisaged in Rome that an annex to the protocol would detail nuclear cooperation in the form of joint research centres and production facilities. At a further meeting in April 1958 of the three defence ministers, they came to a verbal agreement that the FRG and, to a lesser extent, Italy would participate financially in the construction of the Pierrelatte nuclear plant for producing enriched uranium. This plant would be needed by France for the future development of thermonuclear weapons – the UK's explosion of its first hydrogen bomb in May 1957 acting as a spur for such plans. The verbal agreement was struck a week before the fall of the Gaillard government, the Fourth Republic's penultimate government before the return of de Gaulle.

The interests of France in signing the two protocols of Colomb-Béchar and Rome overlapped with German ones. Military cooperation was genuinely desired. On both sides there was also the idea that such agreements, worthwhile as they were in their own right, might prompt the US to share some of its nuclear weaponry and related scientific and technological expertise with its NATO partners in continental Europe. In November 1957 neither Gaillard, the new prime minister, nor Pineau, the new foreign minister, saw any incompatibility in seeking increased cooperation with simultaneously the US and West Germany, not to speak of Italy. Indeed, the Colomb-Béchar and Rome protocols made clear that the planned military cooperation was to take place in a NATO as well as a WEU framework. Some satisfaction was indeed given to both France and West Germany in December 1957 when, at a meeting of the NATO Council, Eisenhower announced that the US would make intermediate-range ballistic missiles available to its European allies, with dual-key control of the nuclear warheads.

However, France's position clearly differed from West Germany's, inasmuch as it had started upon a programme of nuclear armament and its hands were not tied by the Paris Accords. When those in power in France in 1957 and early 1958 signalled to Adenauer and Strauss that they wished for military cooperation between the two countries, they were looking above all for the contributions West Germany could make, in both expertise and finance, to France's efforts to join quickly the military nuclear club. And there was the additional consideration in Paris that Germany's own nuclear ambitions could be better controlled if there were formalised cooperation. The Rome protocol, by bringing in Italy as well, gave a European veneer to the endeavour. In 1950 France had initiated a process of European integration so as to have a real measure of control over economic developments in the nascent German state and also to benefit from its coal resources; in the twilight of the Fourth Republic, similar motives were at play mutatis mutandis in the sphere of nuclear weaponry.[26]

The limits of such nuclear cooperation with West Germany were to be clearly laid down by de Gaulle after he returned to power in mid 1958. By the early 1960s he was to show that his own plans for France and its place in Europe were designed on an entitlement to continental leadership, not least in the military sphere.

Notes

1. Monnet, *Memoirs*, 343–47 [*Mémoires*, 498–505].
2. Edward Fursdon, *The European Defence Community: A History*, London, 1980, 74–77.
3. Text of declaration in Harryvan and van der Harst (eds), *Documents on European Union*, 65–69.
4. Acheson, *Present at the Creation*, 458.
5. For the French-controlled committee structure of the Paris intergovernmental conference, see Fursdon, *The European Defence Community*, 111–14.
6. Adenauer's change of mind was linked to the failure of the Petersberg talks – see Fursdon, *The European Defence Community*, 107–8, 110–11, 114–16. For Adenauer's handling of the question of West Germany's defence and security in the period from September 1950 to May 1952, when the EDC Treaty was signed, see notably Schwarz, *Konrad Adenauer*, vol. 1, 589–687.
7. Fursdon, *The European Defence Community*, 117–19; Monnet, *Memoirs*, 348–49 [*Mémoires*, 507, 509]; Duchêne, *Jean Monnet*, 63.
8. Fursdon, *The European Defence Community*, 123–24, 135, 138–41, 169.
9. De Gaulle, *Discours et messages*, vol. 2, 379–83.
10. Ibid., 523–26.
11. Ibid., 564–75.
12. Ibid., 586–600.
13. Dalloz, *Georges Bidault*, 308–34, 381–82.
14. Michel Debré, *Trois Républiques pour une France. Mémoires*, 5 vols, Paris, 1984–94, vol. 2, 161–256.
15. For selected articles of the draft treaty, see Harryvan and van der Harst (eds), *Documents on European Union*, 75–79.
16. Fursdon, *The European Defence Community*, 243.
17. For the death of the EDC at the hands of Mendès France and the National Assembly, see Alfred Grosser, *La IVe République et sa politique extérieure*, 3rd edn, Paris 1972, 312–20.
18. For Eden's diplomacy, the London Conference, and the subsequent Paris Conference, see notably Fursdon, *The European Defence Community*, 303–33.
19. Massigli, *Une comédie des erreurs*, 457–519.
20. Georges-Henri Soutou, *L'Alliance incertaine. Les rapports politico-stratégiques franco-allemands, 1954–1996*, Paris, 1996, 27–30.
21. Grosser, *La IVe République et sa politique extérieure*, 324–26; Fursdon, *The European Defence Community*, 333–36; Guy de Carmoy, *Les Politiques étrangères de la France*, Paris, 1967, 45–46.
22. Debré, *Trois républiques pour une France*, vol. 2, 225–33; Grosser, *La IVe République et sa politique extérieure*, 338.
23. Georges Goriely, 'Il y a trente ans : La Sarre dit non au « statut européen »', *Le Monde*, November 1985, 3–4.
24. For the Suez crisis and the tensions between France and the United States over Algeria in the closing years of the Fourth Republic, see Irwin M. Wall, *France, the United States, and the Algerian War*, Berkeley, 2001, 9–133.
25. For Adenauer's view that the Suez crisis made imperative closer European integration (through the future EEC and Euratom) and closer, privileged links between the FRG and France, see Schwarz, *Konrad Adenauer*, vol. 2, 228–45.
26. On the innovative period in Franco-German relations from the talks between Mollet and Adenauer in November 1956 to the signing of the tripartite Rome protocol of November 1957, see Soutou, *L'Alliance incertaine*, 55–121.

Chapter 4

THE GAULLIST VISION OF THE ATLANTIC ALLIANCE AND EUROPEAN UNION

Against the background of the Berlin crisis, de Gaulle and Adenauer pushed further the rapprochement between their two states. Internationally, the Frenchman's ambitions were twice frustrated, first with his failed proposal for a reorganised Atlantic Alliance and secondly with his failed attempt to create a European union of states under French leadership. Serving as pis aller was the Franco-German Elysée Treaty. Although even this treaty had little strategic significance after Adenauer's retirement and de Gaulle's withdrawing France from NATO's integrated command, it remained the framework for a bilateral partnership that would eventually lead to the EU's creation.

Adenauer, the US, and the Berlin Crisis

The Advent of the Fifth Republic

The Fourth Republic came effectively to an end on 29 May 1958 – only five months after the EEC's inception – when René Coty, the President of the Republic, officially called upon de Gaulle to form a government to save the Republic itself. The immediate background was dramatic: near anarchy in Algiers, where the settler community had raised the French Revolution's cry of *salut public* to justify the setting up in Paris of a dictatorial government (Gaullist or otherwise); the virtual rebellion in Algeria of the army general staff, siding with the settlers; the rallying of the army's paratrooper units in Corsica to the army in Algeria; and the imminent threat of a coup d'état through an army airborne operation launched against the

---

French capital. On 1 June the National Assembly gave its approval to a broadly based government led by de Gaulle, and on 3 June it authorised constitutional change to be approved by referendum. The way was open for the drafting of the constitution of the Fifth Republic, duly approved in September, and for de Gaulle's election in December as head of the new Republic. Yet the Algerian crisis was not to be resolved until March 1962, when, under the Evian Agreements, Algeria was accorded its independence, making for an outcome totally at variance with the aspirations of those whose actions had precipitated de Gaulle's return to power four years earlier.

By the time of the signing of the Evian Agreements, the rapprochement between France and West Germany had advanced a stage further, and it was less than a year later that the Elysée Treaty of Franco-German Cooperation was signed by de Gaulle and Adenauer. However, it was not the case that relations between the two men flourished without fail. Indeed, the Chancellor's initial view of France's new leader in 1958 was marked by circumspection if not downright suspicion. De Gaulle, after all, had sought Stalin's support at the end of 1944 for a radical dismembering of Germany. On the other hand, the Frenchman did show a different attitude towards Germany from 1949 onwards; for it was in Bordeaux in September of that year that he had first called, in the face of the Soviet menace, for a European confederation built on a Franco-German entente.[1] Even so, Adenauer feared that the change of regime in France would be favourable neither to NATO nor to European integration in the Western half of the continent. There was, moreover, an inauspicious start when Strauss visited Paris in July 1958. There he was informed, much to his displeasure, that de Gaulle had decided to suspend the implementation of the provisions for nuclear cooperation contained in the tripartite protocol of November 1957.

The Colombey Meeting

Nonetheless, in September 1958, Adenauer accepted an invitation to visit de Gaulle at his home at Colombey-les-Deux-Eglises and to stay overnight. Such an invitation to a major political figure, on the part of the de Gaulles, was unprecedented and never to be repeated. The meeting, in the simple surroundings of the old house at Colombey, proved a success. A real rapport was created between the two men, who were marked by none too dissimilar Catholic educations, by the experience of the century's two wars between their peoples, and by their opposition in different ways to Hitler. They conversed at length about the state and future of Europe, and much of Adenauer's earlier unease about French intentions was put to rest.

The account of the meeting between 'this old Frenchman' and 'this very old German', which de Gaulle was to give in 1970 in the first volume of his

Mémoires d'espoir, bears some relating. His purpose, he told Adenauer, was that he, de Gaulle, had judged that the time was now ripe for France to embark upon a new policy towards Germany. His perspective was that of France's interest in 'the union of Europe, a union that required above all cooperation between Paris and Bonn'. There was thus a readiness on France's side to help Germany regain its 'rank' internationally; to 'contribute to its security in the face of the Soviet camp, notably in respect of the threat hanging over Berlin'; and to 'admit its right to reunification'. On the last point, France's preconditions were 'the acceptance of faits accomplis in the matter of borders, an attitude of good will in dealings with the East, a complete renunciation of nuclear weapons, and a boundless patience in awaiting reunification'. In the pursuit of European union, supranationalism was to be eschewed. And this too was the view of Adenauer. 'There could be no question', for either of them, said de Gaulle, 'of making our peoples, with their states and their laws, disappear into some sort of stateless edifice, even if [Adenauer] admits to have gained substantial advantages for Germany from the mystique of integration, and so remains grateful to those at the fore on the French side, notably Jean Monnet and Robert Schuman, for what they gave gratuitously.'

France for its part, continued de Gaulle, would seek to implement the EEC Treaty to the extent that 'its personality was not compromised'. As to the treaty, the CAP should be put in place, and 'as long as Great Britain remains economically and politically in its present state', it should be excluded from EC membership. To judge by the *Mémoires d'espoir*, Adenauer's guarded response to the French prime minister's privileging of these two practical objectives was to indicate that he himself would not stand in the way of French interests, even if some ministers in his government might think differently. He readily agreed with de Gaulle's proposal that there should be regular meetings between the EEC's six member states, with a view to their acting in concert on matters of foreign policy.

The discussions at Colombey focused also on the two countries' respective roles in the Atlantic Alliance. The security logic of the FRG's full participation in NATO was acknowledged by the General. Not that Adenauer was vaunting the advantages of American ties. He complained to de Gaulle about the neglect of NATO by the US. De Gaulle, for his part, expressed his opposition to the American monopoly over NATO's integrated military command. After reasserting France's commitment to the North Atlantic Treaty and, in particular, to the principle of mutual assistance in the face of aggression, he told his guest that France was set 'to leave, one day or the other, the NATO system, especially since it was about to equip itself with nuclear weapons which could not be brought under the umbrella of integration'.[2]

The NATO Memorandum

What de Gaulle did not mention to Adenauer was that he was seeking to actually change the NATO system – to France's advantage, but not West Germany's. Only two days after the satisfied Chancellor left Colombey, the head of the French government dispatched a memorandum to President Eisenhower and the British prime minister, Macmillan, proposing a radical restructuring of the Atlantic Alliance and NATO's integrated command, with the effect that the US, the UK, and France would constitute a ruling directorate. The directorate idea had already been put forward by Mendès France in 1954, and, earlier still, repeatedly by Bidault as from 1948 onwards, even prior to the creation of NATO; indeed, in 1952, Bidault secretly pressed the idea on de Gaulle himself.[3] One development prompting now de Gaulle's memorandum was the unilateral decision in July 1958 of Eisenhower and his Secretary of State, Dulles, to send US marines into Lebanon to prop up the presidency of Camille Chamoun at a time of crisis in the Middle East. If there was one country in the region which France could still claim to lie in its zone of influence, it was the Lebanon, and de Gaulle was angered by the American decision, especially since he had personally warned Dulles beforehand against taking any action in which France would not be invited to participate. De Gaulle's reaction to this Lebanese affair, his responsibilities for Algeria and the still extensive French Empire, and his fundamental and ongoing concern with the place of the Western European powers in a bipolar world dominated by the US and the USSR, were all reflected in the memorandum's central passages:

> It was the prospect of action within a particular area that led to the birth of the Atlantic Alliance and the arrangements for giving it practical effect. Political and strategic realities have changed, however. The world being what it is, an organisation such as NATO, which limits itself to security in the North Atlantic area, can no longer be considered adapted to its purpose. For example, it is as if what happens in the Middle East or in Africa, were not of immediate and direct interest to Europe, and as if the indivisible responsibilities of France did not extend to Africa, the Indian Ocean, and the Pacific. Furthermore, so confined a system has been rendered militarily out-of-date by the radius of action of warships and aircraft and also by the range of missiles. Admittedly, it was accepted at the outset that nuclear weapons – clearly of capital importance – would remain for a long time the monopoly of the United States, which might appear to justify that decisions concerning defence on a world scale should effectively be delegated to the government in Washington. But, here again, it must be recognised that such a state of affairs, once assumed to be permanent, no longer corresponds to reality.
>
> France is not therefore ready to judge that NATO in its present form meets the requirements of the security of the free world and, in particular, its own security. It seems necessary that an organisation should be set up at world level, treating of political and strategic affairs, to which France would be directly party [together with the US and the UK]. This organisation would, on the one hand, take joint decisions on political questions relating to world security, and, on the

other, establish, and implement, as necessary, strategic plans of action, notably as regards the use of nuclear weapons.[4]

De Gaulle's proposal for a transformation of the Atlantic Alliance's structures met with a mixed response on its reception in Washington. There was certainly no American assent, rather an evasive response showing no enthusiasm for the proposal. Yet it was not rejected out of hand, for the principle of Anglo-American-French tripartism was not entirely anathema to Eisenhower.[5] Several weeks after his visit to Colombey, Adenauer learnt to his ire of the content of the supposedly strictly confidential memorandum. It had been divulged by Spaak to Herbert Blankenhorn, the German ambassador to both France and NATO, then headquartered in Paris. The former Belgian foreign minister, after playing a prominent role in setting up the EEC, was now NATO's secretary general. His reaction to the memorandum had been particularly negative, which explained no doubt the leak. Although the German Chancellor cannot have been totally surprised at the news relayed by Blankenhorn, having had some inkling of de Gaulle's idea for a tripartite directorate prior to going to Colombey, he still felt that the confidence he had accorded there to de Gaulle had been partly betrayed. Their relationship was to be marked thereafter by its ups and downs; real as were their personal affinities and their shared desire for concert in Europe, the vagaries of differing national interests precluded any constantly idyllic political partnership.

Yet there was no essential incompatibility between the content of de Gaulle's memorandum to Eisenhower and Macmillan and his Colombey musings on France, Germany, and Europe. His commitment to the Atlantic Alliance was never feigned, neither then nor later, notwithstanding his readiness in the second half of the 1960s to seek better relations with the USSR (or Russia, as he always preferred to call it), until the brutal putting down of the 'Prague Spring' restored a sterner sense of reality. What the memorandum at least implied was the abandoning of NATO's existing integrated military command, an aim that he had conveyed to Adenauer. Also implied, by the idea of the directorate, was that France would assume a leading role in the defence of continental Western Europe. And this was perfectly compatible with his advocacy of privileged Franco-German links. For France was on the way to becoming a nuclear power, while the FRG, he deemed, should never become one – hence his rebuff to Strauss before the Colombey meeting.

Khrushchev, the Berlin Wall, and the West

Between October 1958 and July 1960, when Adenauer was officially welcomed at the chateau of Rambouillet – the official summer residence of the President of the Republic – relations between Paris and Bonn were not particularly close, at least when compared with their flourishing in the closing two years of the Fourth Republic under successively the Mollet, Bourgès-Maunoury and Gaillard governments. In 1958 and 1959 de Gaulle was as much concerned with good Franco-Italian relations. Thus, if the Colombey meeting was to prove the harbinger of reinvigorated Franco-German relations, these days were not immediately coming, partly because of de Gaulle's high-handedness over France and the Atlantic Alliance.

However, what did arrive almost immediately was a new conflictual phase in the Cold War. The first such phase had come to an end with the death of Stalin. Now, in early November 1958, Nikita Khrushchev, the Soviet leader, stoked up tension by announcing in Moscow that the Four-Power military occupation of Berlin had to be terminated, especially since the city served as the capital of the GDR. This was followed in late November by an ultimatum from the USSR to the US, the UK, France, and the FRG. They were requested to agree to a German peace treaty, one that recognised the existence of two German states. As to Berlin, the treaty had to provide for a demilitarised 'free city'. Otherwise, in the absence of a positive response from the West within six months, the USSR would invest the GDR with all the rights over Berlin and East Germany that it, the USSR, had held since the Potsdam Conference in 1945. This was therefore a threat to put the security of West Berlin in the hands of a state denied recognition until then, not only by the three Western Powers, but also, uncompromisingly, by West Germany. For since 1956, under the so-called Hallstein Doctrine, the FRG held that it would treat any state's opening of diplomatic relations with the GDR as an unfriendly act. Thus did the Berlin crisis open, and, once the Soviet bluff had been called, it dragged on for some four years. It was during this crisis that in August 1961 the GDR authorities erected their fortified wall on the western side of East Berlin, so as to block the movement of their own citizens to the West; and, additionally, a system of watch towers and barbed-wire fencing was built around the outer perimeter of West Berlin.

During the first Berlin crisis, that of the blockade a decade earlier, the US, backed by the UK, had brooked no compromise. However, during this crisis – especially after Dulles's death in May 1959 and then the change of administration in January 1961 when John F. Kennedy succeeded Dwight Eisenhower at the White House – there was a wavering in American policy, particularly since the Soviet leader's toughness on Berlin was accompanied by the advocacy of détente on a wider front. For instance, shortly after the Geneva Four-Power Conference of May–June 1959, which looked fruitlessly at the question of a peace treaty, the new US Secretary of State, Christian Herter, indicated that some agreement with the USSR, setting constraints on the independence of West Berlin, might well be in order. On the British side, in the person of Macmillan, there was a patent desire for compromise with the USSR. But all such wavering was deeply worrying for Adenauer, who feared that the road of compromise could eventually lead to the sacrifice of the FRG on the altar of a neutralised, unified and potentially Communist-dominated Germany.

The one Western leader to stand rock firm was de Gaulle. Already in November 1958, on the occasion of his unofficial visit to Adenauer at Bad Kreuznach two months after the Colombey meeting and only two weeks after Khrushchev's first broadside, he reassured the German Chancellor that France was totally opposed to any change in Berlin's statute. This opposition was to be firmly expressed in 1960. At the instigation of Macmillan, a Four-Power Conference – bringing together the Second World War's victorious powers – took place in Paris in May 1960, with the question of Berlin to top the agenda. Just before this conference an American U-2 spy plane was shot down over Soviet territory, and, once in the French capital, the Soviet leader used the incident to refuse serious negotiations. Khrushchev's motives in effectively stalling over Berlin were varied. He needed to deflect criticisms from within the Communist world, both at home, where hardline elements within the Soviet Politiburo were opposed to allowing the GDR any real independence, and also in Beijing, where his policy of détente with the West was radically contested. There was probably the further calculation on Khrushchev's part that it was in his interest to delay serious negotiation of Berlin's future until after the US presidential elections, when there could be a more compliant American attitude if Kennedy were elected. Before the conference, de Gaulle had met with Adenauer to coordinate their positions on the Berlin question. At the botched Four-Power talks, France spoke in the FRG's name, as witness de Gaulle's mixture of imperturbability and intransigence in the face of Khrushchev's diplomatic histrionics, and also his pressing Eisenhower not to heed Macmillan's argument for a more conciliatory stance on the part of the West.

The Proposed Organisation of Western Europe

When de Gaulle and Adenauer met anew for two days of talks at Rambouillet in late July 1960, it was to discuss Europe's future. Partly because of the festering Berlin crisis and doubts about the degree of determination shown by Washington and London, new European defence arrangements were very much in the mind of the host. Already at the end of May 1960, in the course of an address on French television, de Gaulle had advocated 'organised cooperation' between Western European states and had raised the possibility of this cooperation's leading eventually to an 'imposing confederation'; and, for the first time, speaking in his capacity as President of the Republic, he had included a defence dimension in this design, albeit vaguely, by referring to the building up in Western Europe of a 'political, economic, cultural and human grouping organised for action, progress, and defence'.[6] This was the theme to which he now returned in his talks with Adenauer. What he stressed was that moves towards European political union and radical reform of the Atlantic Alliance were fundamentally related and must go hand in hand. On the second day de Gaulle presented the Chancellor with a nine-point handwritten note. Not only did the nine points summarise the ideas he had developed with his guest on the first day, they also went to the heart of his thinking about continental Western Europe's future:

I. If one believes that it is necessary for Europe to become a real entity, exercising a role in its own right in world affairs, then one must wish that it be organised by itself and for its own purposes in the political, economic and cultural domains and also in the domain of defence.

II. 'Europe' at the present time can consist only in an organised cooperation of states; such is the case if it to be effective, if it is to draw on the feeling and support of its peoples, and if it is to avoid losing itself in vaporous theories. Everything dictates that it be based on an agreement between France and Germany, to be joined in the first instance by Italy, Holland, Belgium, and Luxembourg.

III. To adopt this conception is to admit that the 'supranational' bodies, which have been set up between the Six and tend inevitably and improperly to become irresponsible super-states, will have to be reformed, made subordinate to governments, and harnessed to advisory and technical tasks.

IV. To adopt this conception is also to put an end to the American-style 'integration' that constitutes at present the Atlantic Alliance and that is in contradiction with the existence of a Europe having, from an international standpoint, its own personality and responsibility. The Atlantic Alliance should be founded on new bases. It is incumbent upon Europe to propose them.

V. In practice, to put the beginning of organised cooperation between states on a sound footing, those holding supreme responsibility ought to meet periodically and regularly and to concert their joint action in various domains, with the meetings themselves followed and preceded by ministerial meetings to prepare and implement decisions.

VI. Joint standing committees comprising civil servants and experts would bring together the materials for the governments' decisions and monitor their implementation. Four committees would seem required for, respectively, the following domains: the political, the economic, the cultural, and that of defence.

VII. Later it could be worthwhile for delegations from the different national parliaments to constitute an assembly. A consultative body, it would debate questions of common interest at regular intervals.

VIII. At the appropriate moment, the European peoples themselves should confer legitimacy upon the organisation of Europe through a general and solemn referendum. If, as is likely, the result of such a sounding is overwhelmingly positive, Europe will unambiguously be the creation of its peoples.

IX. The conjunction of present circumstances provides an exceptional opportunity for the organisation of Europe. The President of the French Republic and the Chancellor of Federal Germany should take the required initiatives by way of obligation to Europe, their two countries, and themselves.[7]

It was in 1959 – the previous year – that *Le Salut*, the third and last volume of de Gaulle's *Mémoires de guerre*, had been published. He wrote therein of the goals he had set himself after the cessation of hostilities in 1945, goals which he would seek anew to realise now that France was on its feet again. Placing France at the head of the Western half of continental Europe figured high. What was required was 'to bring the states close to the Rhine, the Alps, and the Pyrenees in a group together for political, economic and strategic purposes', and 'to make this organisation into one of the three global powers and, if necessary one day, the arbiter between the Soviet and Anglo-Saxon camps'.[8] It was this ambition that had now become embodied in the nine-point Rambouillet note.

Its recipient was not necessarily to be persuaded. For constancy was not a hallmark of Adenauer's attitude towards de Gaulle. The uncertainty engendered by the deception he had felt in the wake of their earlier meeting at Colombey never quite left him. And, before coming to Rambouillet, he had been beset afresh by doubts about the views of the French president, despite the latter's hardline stance over Berlin at the Paris Four-Power Conference in May 1960. One incident troubling the Chancellor was the conceit of Debré when, as de Gaulle's prime minister, he had told the National Assembly's standing committee for finance earlier in July that states without nuclear weapons could be no more than satellite states. This utterance was made in connection with a new government bill providing for five years' military expenditure, most of it designed to capitalise on France's success in exploding its first atomic bomb at Reggan in February of the same year. Debré's words were consonant with his master's declared ambition that France should assume the leading role in assuring the security of continental Western Europe. Adenauer himself was adamantly opposed to the FRG's becoming independently a military nuclear power. However, he still felt that Debré's dismissive tone threw into question all hopes that Germany be treated as an equal partner by France, and that it also ran in the face of the FRG's participation as a full member in NATO. But, once engaged in the talks at Rambouillet, the old statesman appeared to fall anew under the spell of the visionary general with his nine-point plan for Europe.

That was anyway de Gaulle's impression when, immediately after the meeting, he wrote to his foreign minister, Couve de Murville, to say that they had now 'to strike the iron of the organisation of Europe, for the iron is hot'. Since the realisation of the goal of European political union also entailed a radical reform of the Atlantic Alliance, the French president dispatched a long letter a week later to Eisenhower. In keeping with his 1958 memorandum, he urged the US president to reconsider the idea of a tripartite directorate, with a view to providing the Alliance with a global reach (the case then in point being the chaos in the Belgian Congo) and rectifying what had become an increasing anomaly, namely the American-led integrated command structure in Europe.[9]

Yet Adenauer's backing was far from total. At Rambouillet the Chancellor had been careful not to express clear agreement to all that was proposed in the nine-point note. Even so, some of what he did concede, notably on the need for new European confederal arrangements and for the dilution of the supranationalism of the EC treaties, dismayed members of the German delegation, notably Heinrich von Brentano, the foreign minister, and Blankenhorn, the ambassador to Paris, who, like their French counterparts, were held at a distance so that the two great men could concentrate on their one-to-one talks. On returning to Bonn, Adenauer was confronted with expressions of dissatisfaction from within his government – von Brentano not being alone in protesting – and also from the CDU. His reaction was to temporise in the diplomatic follow-up to Rambouillet, notably in the matter of EC treaty revision, which annoyed de Gaulle. Furthermore, in September, Adenauer signalled to the Americans a continuing interest in West Germany's being allowed to acquire the (dual-key) use of tactical nuclear weapons in the framework of NATO's integrated military command; this was in response to proposals put forward by SACEUR, General Norstad, for a NATO multilateral nuclear force (MLF). Thus, while Adenauer was sympathetic to de Gaulle's views on Europe, not only did he have to take account of the opposing views of German politicians, particularly those from within his own party, but also, despite his disappointment about the American stance on Berlin, he himself still deemed it in Germany's interest to be a deferential ally of the US, and, correspondingly, he was deeply ambivalent about de Gaulle's thinking on European defence.

So neither the initial meeting of de Gaulle and Adenauer at Colombey in September 1958 nor that nearly two years later at Rambouillet bore fruit in a permanent meeting of minds between these two statesmen. Indeed, the last five months of 1960 were marked by a new frostiness in Franco-German relations, which a visit by Debré and Couve de Murville to Bonn in October did little to dissipate. The only tangible but limited progress was on the military front, since agreements were signed later that month allowing the Bundeswehr to train and keep depots in France, and providing facilities to the Luftwaffe at French aerodromes. Encouraged by Monnet, Adenauer did agree at the end of December to a future meeting in Paris of EC heads of government (in the case of France, the President of the Republic rather than the prime minister), together with their foreign ministers, to discuss the French proposals for European political union. But, in the absence of solid German backing for what had been put forward at Rambouillet, the chance of any agreement to de Gaulle's grander design for Europe and, related to it, a revamped Atlantic Alliance appeared slim.

The Failure of the Fouchet Committee

Seeking Agreement among the Six

Two important political changes occurred in January 1961: de Gaulle's position at the head of the Fifth Republic was greatly strengthened as a result of the successful referendum on self-determination for Algeria (a majority voting in favour, thereby opening the way for the Evian negotiations later that year); and, on the other side of the Atlantic, power passed from Eisenhower to Kennedy. The first change enhanced de Gaulle's stature as a statesman, not least in the eyes of Adenauer. As to the change in Washington, which was also a change of generation, it heralded a more optimistic and confident approach by the US to foreign policy, in which even greater priority would be given to the assertion of American might and to the securing of peace through dealing directly, whenever possible, with the USSR. The urbane East Coast style of the young Kennedy administration appealed to many in Western Europe, but such felt affinity was certainly no guarantee that either the susceptibilities or the interests of Western Europe's leading states would be carefully catered for. Apprehensions on this score were quickly felt in West Germany. For instance, at the first regular meeting of a newly established Franco-German standing group bringing together senior officers from the general staffs of the two countries' armies, which was held in January, the Bundeswehr's Inspector General, General Heusinger, warned that Western Europe might soon have to count upon its own strength in the face of continuing Soviet threats. Such apprehension, coupled with the realisation that the albatross of Algeria might really be cast from France's neck, would seem to have encouraged Adenauer afresh to cooperate positively on European matters with his sometimes difficult French partner.[10]

On the eve of the EC summit held in Paris in February 1961, the French and German leaders met to coordinate their positions. De Gaulle made two concessions. First, there would be no mention in the French proposals of the word 'confederation', an unloved word in Bonn; used instead would be the term 'organised cooperation' that had figured in the Rambouillet note. The second concession was that defence questions would not be raised. Hence, when the summit opened under French presidency, there were jointly agreed Franco-German proposals for launching political cooperation in the form of meetings every three months of the heads of government of the Six – meaning again, in the case of France, the President of the Republic – and also regular meetings of their foreign ministers, education ministers, and ministers responsible for culture. Italy, Belgium, and Luxembourg showed themselves ready to engage in such cooperation, provided it was not to the detriment of either NATO or the existing EC treaties. However, the reaction of the Netherlands, as voiced by its foreign minister, Joseph Luns, was categorically negative. Not only did he subscribe to the caveats about NATO and the EC treaties, but he refused the very principle of such political cooperation in the absence of the UK. Because of this Dutch obstruction, no agreement was possible in Paris. The proposals were not buried, however. It was agreed to allow the subject to be further considered by a committee (*commission d'études*) of senior diplomats from the Six under the chairmanship of Christian Fouchet, France's ambassador to Denmark.

The choice of chairman testified to the French president's concern to steer the committee's work. Fouchet had been a Gaullist from the outset. As a young army officer, he had been among the very first to join the General in London in June 1940. He was later entrusted with the politically delicate task of acting as the GPRF's representative in Poland in 1944–5, and his subsequent career included a stint as minister responsible for Moroccan and Tunisian affairs in the Mendès France government. He was not to chair the committee set up in February 1961 throughout its relatively short existence, for, after the Evian Agreements in March 1962, he was appointed France's High Commissioner in Algeria to oversee the vital months of disengagement prior to independence, after which time he became a government minister again. However, he was a safe pair of hands for de Gaulle during all the time the committee counted – that is, up to January 1962.

By April 1961 the Fouchet Committee had produced its preliminary report, but its further work appeared blocked by continuing Dutch objections. Only further talks between Adenauer and de Gaulle in Bonn in May kept the project alive. The two men succeeded not only in winning assent to a further meeting in July of EC heads of government and foreign ministers, but also in setting an agenda that included defence, even if only peripherally. At the ensuing summit, held at Bad Godesberg in July, a declaration was cobbled together which satisfied all the Six. Although defence was not explicitly mentioned in the declaration, a link was drawn between the promotion of European political union and the reinforcement of the Atlantic Alliance. De Gaulle himself called for the setting up of a European defence force within NATO.

At Bad Godesberg the Fouchet Committee was instructed to prepare the statutes of this new European Union. The Quai d'Orsay accordingly drew up a draft treaty establishing a 'Union of States'. It was submitted in France's name to the French-headed committee in October 1961. Position papers prepared by other foreign ministries were also tabled. Dated 2 November, the French-proposed treaty became effectively the first Fouchet Plan. It specified in its first article that the object was indeed a 'Union of States'; earlier, to fudge the issue of supranationalism, use had been made in the Bad Godesberg declaration of the term 'Union of Peoples'. The key provisions concerned the setting up of a Council, which would meet regularly at the levels of both heads of government and foreign ministers.

Its decisions would be taken on the basis of unanimity. Four objectives would be pursued: the adoption of a common foreign policy whenever a common interest prevailed; the promotion and safeguarding of the heritage and values of European civilisation, through cooperation in the domain of science and culture; the defence of human rights and democracy; and, lastly and controversially, reinforced security cooperation through the adoption of a common defence policy. The Council would not be concerned with economic matters, these remaining the exclusive preserve of the EC treaties. Bringing together the heads of government, the Council would meet every four months; and, in its alternative incarnation, comprising foreign ministers, it would meet halfway through the intervening periods and so also thrice yearly. Matters relating to the Union would fall within the purview of the existing parliamentary Assembly, as established by the EC treaties, but this body's role would be no more than deliberative. More significantly, reflecting the importance attached to foreign-policy cooperation, a European Political Commission would be set up in Paris; composed of high-ranking civil servants from the ministries of foreign affairs of the Six, its role would be to assist the Council in the preparation and execution of its decisions. In general, the spirit of the plan corresponded to de Gaulle's own ideas – and, it might be added, there were certain affinities with the vision for Europe of Coudenhove-Kalergi.[11]

At the level of the foreign ministers, these proposals were deemed acceptable as a basis of discussion by West Germany, Italy, and Luxembourg. On the other hand, there were new Dutch and Belgian objections relating not only to defence matters but also to worries about France's intentions towards the UK, which had applied for EC membership in August, and, secondly, about the possible emergence of a Paris–Bonn–Rome axis. Luns was now abetted by Spaak, who had stepped down as NATO secretary general to become Belgian foreign minister again. Yet there was still agreement on the part of the Six to strive for compromise, and the Quai d'Orsay set to work anew, by including, for instance, a positive mention of the Atlantic Alliance in connection with defence cooperation (thus, the wording 'the adoption of a common defence policy that would contribute to the reinforcement of the Atlantic Alliance').

The Death of the Fouchet Proposals

At this juncture the affair took an unexpected turn. Just prior to France's formal submission of the new version of the draft treaty to the Fouchet Committee in January 1962, de Gaulle reviewed his diplomats' handiwork, which had already been approved by Couve de Murville. The search for compromise by the French foreign ministry was abruptly cast aside, and, through a limited number of textual changes, the spirit of the proposed treaty was partly transformed and brought more in line with the proposals the French president had made to Adenauer at Rambouillet a year and a half earlier, notably as encapsulated in the nine-point note. Not only was the mention of the Atlantic Alliance summarily crossed out, but economic matters were brought into the purview of the 'Union of States', which was coupled with the suppression of a phrase stipulating that any subsequent treaty revision must leave untouched the structures established by the EC treaties. The result was that this second Fouchet Plan, dated 18 January, was even more in tune with de Gaulle's views than the first version and, as such, unacceptable to his EC partners, including a sadly bemused Adenauer.

A further attempt was made at compromise on the basis of a new Quai d'Orsay draft close in content to its previous one – that is, before it was radically amended by de Gaulle. This third Fouchet Plan and a variant, in the form of proposed alterations agreed by the 'Five', were discussed fruitlessly at a meeting of EC foreign ministers in March, and anew in April when the Plan was finally buried. The refusal came again from the Netherlands and Belgium on the grounds that the proposed treaty was inimical to the UK's quest for EC membership and also to EC supranationalism. Couve was not slow to point out to Spaak that there was a certain incongruity between the two grievances.[12]

De Gaulle had overplayed his hand, deliberately or otherwise. Various factors have been adduced to explain the sudden hardening of his position in mid January 1962. The fundamental one was the increasing confirmation of his fear that Kennedy was even less willing than Eisenhower to accept any dilution of American hegemony within NATO. In particular, he had received a letter from Kennedy only two weeks earlier, in which the US president objected in principle to a 'specifically French nuclear capability', and also cast doubts on whether France (or the UK) had the technical means to develop and maintain a 'truly effective deterrent'.[13] In pursuing his own twin-track policy of seeking to put France at the head of a European political union, as well as winning a place for it alongside the US and the UK in a revamped, more globally orientated Atlantic Alliance, de Gaulle must have realised that attaining the former aim, but not the latter, risked to be no success at all. Furthermore, if the political union of European states for the purpose of moving towards a common foreign policy were to have sense and credibility, such a confederation would need to have appropriate military force directly at its disposal. As he himself had written just before the Bad Godesberg summit, 'there can be no political identity for Europe, if Europe does not have an identity from the standpoint of defence'.[14] This was the truism that dogged de Gaulle, as it was later to dog his successors, especially Mitterrand and Chirac in the post-Maastricht era.

As the Fouchet Committee had proceeded with its work, it had become increasingly clear to the French president that the prospect was slight of winning any meaningful agreement to the principle of a common European defence in view of the attachment of other EC member states to existing NATO structures. Not only was this attachment vigorously insisted upon by the Netherlands and Belgium, but it was real also on the part of West Germany, and even more so after the Bundestag elections of September 1961. These brought the liberal FDP into the ruling coalition, as well as a promise from the 85-year-old Adenauer that he would stand down in two years' time. The strongly committed Atlanticists included Gerhard Schröder, the leader of the northern Protestant wing of the CDU. His replacing von Brentano as foreign minister had been forced upon Adenauer because of the election results.

In short, because of the strength of commitment to NATO elsewhere in Western Europe and his own heightened perception of the Kennedy administration's deep-rooted hostility to his geopolitical designs, de Gaulle had lost interest by the middle of 1962 in any quick resurrection of the Fouchet Plan. Yet the Italian government, headed by Amintore Fanfani, continued to deploy efforts, quixotically, to that end.

Heightened Concerns about the Kennedy Administration

The discontent of de Gaulle with the approach of the Kennedy administration was shared to a large extent by Adenauer, even if only partially for the same reasons. The handling of the ongoing Berlin crisis was one bone of contention, the other the far-reaching revision of US defence policy undertaken by Kennedy's Secretary of Defence, Robert McNamara. Thus, after the construction of the Berlin Wall in August 1961, serious differences emerged between Washington and, on the other hand, Paris and Bonn. Kennedy made clear that he had no time for the Four-Power conference method of resolving Cold War conflicts. On Berlin, as on other matters, he preferred dealings restricted to the two superpowers. In 1961 and 1962, moreover, the US president, backed by Macmillan, responded to the Soviet and East German provocation in a consistently more conciliatory way than that favoured by either Adenauer or de Gaulle. Matters came to a head in April 1962 – the month the Fouchet proposals finally died – when an American plan was leaked for the setting up of an International Access Authority for Berlin. The thirteen parties represented on this planned body – consisting of five Western, five Eastern and three 'neutral' states – would have included both the FRG and the GDR. The latter would thereby have acquired some sort of official recognition from the West, while, in the event of a stand-off between East and West, the final say over access to the city would have belonged to the three neutrals, Austria, Sweden, and Switzerland. The plan was totally rejected by Adenauer who, for the first time, publicly criticised America. French support of the German Chancellor went without saying. In line with the stance he had adopted at the outset of the crisis in 1958, de Gaulle maintained his position of refusing any change to the statute providing for the Four-Power control of Berlin.

As to the Kennedy administration's revision of US defence policy, which so worried both de Gaulle and Adenauer, it was designed to increase the military clout of the US through continually improved nuclear weaponry and stronger conventional forces. It was also designed to establish new policy parameters for a more discriminatory use of the American nuclear arsenal, which would allow the arms race with the USSR to be brought under better control. This last aim lent a premium to nuclear non-proliferation. Regret tempered by some indulgence marked Washington's view of the UK's attachment to an independent nuclear deterrent; the attitude towards France's efforts to put such a deterrent in place was largely negative; and there was the firm resolve that West Germany should never acquire the independent use of any nuclear weapons. The desire to exercise an effective monopoly over the West's nuclear fire power and establish what would effectively be a US–Soviet condominium was accompanied by the change in nuclear strategy pushed by McNamara. The deterrence represented by 'massive retaliation' – the strategy adopted by NATO in 1954 – was to give way to one of 'flexible response'.

De Gaulle's and Adenauer's readings of these developments were essentially the same. It led them to question the degree of American commitment to Western Europe, especially in the event of a land battle, which they feared would be allowed to range extensively before any deployment of nuclear weapons. The lesson of Suez had not been forgotten, and nor had the memory of weak American support for France over Algeria prior to the fall of the Fourth Republic, even if Algeria was now being given its independence.

Although the new doctrine of 'flexible response' had already been in the making in 1961, it was only in May 1962 that it was publicly announced and explained by McNamara. The leaking of the American plan for the creation of an International Access Authority for Berlin had come only four days after the EC foreign ministers had buried the third Fouchet Plan, and this unwrapping of the McNamara doctrine took place less than three weeks later. The cluster of events partly explains why the defunct plan for a European 'Union of States' was soon to be transmuted into a bilateral alliance between France and West Germany. Heightened Franco-German security worries were opening the way to the Elysée Treaty.

A Rose and a Rose Garden

Adenauer's and de Gaulle's Official Visits

In April 1962 Adenauer accepted de Gaulle's invitation to pay an official visit to France. The close of this visit in July 1962 was the occasion of the charged symbolic event, the two statesmen attending together High Mass in Rheims Cathedral. Also symbolic was the parade earlier the same day at the nearby Mourmelon military camp, a camp dating from before the Franco-Prussian War. There the two leaders reviewed French and German troops and took the salute in a march past, during which units from the two armies alternated with one another. De Gaulle paid great attention to ensuring that the entire official visit passed well, even to the point of underlining in his farewell speech the popular acclaim received by Adenauer in the streets of Paris and elsewhere. However, such acclaim had been virtually nonexistent – 'I have always acted imaginatively, *comme si*; and often what is supposed to have happened eventually becomes the reality', he explained to a surprised Alain Peyrefitte, who held the twin responsibility of information minister and government spokesman.[15]

Defence matters were discussed during the July visit. The focus was on the unwelcome shape of the policy change in Washington. And de Gaulle spoke to Adenauer of France's future nuclear force as if it might be some substitute in Western Europe for the American deterrent. However, it was on political union that they agreed to move forward. De Gaulle asked Adenauer whether 'the Federal Republic would accept to conclude a political union with France, which in fact and by force of circumstances would be limited to the two?' 'I would say definitely yes', replied the Chancellor; 'we would be ready to accept this restricted union while leaving the door open to other members.'[16]

In September it was de Gaulle's turn to make an official visit to the FRG. He arrived with the credit of having recently honoured the Chancellor in France; and his international reputation was riding high, thanks to the Evian agreements signed in March, which had brought the Algerian crisis to an end. Speaking in German before large crowds, notably in Bonn, Cologne, and Düsseldorf, the French president enjoyed a huge success. Never in the twentieth century was a French leader to be greeted so warmly on German soil. Not only was the sight of Adenauer and de Gaulle a tangible public sign of the reconciliation between the two countries, but there was also the welcome insistence on the General's part that Germany was still a great nation. Addressing Bundeswehr officers at the Führungsakademie in Hamburg, he was not shy in associating this greatness, and the greatness of France too, with military prowess. Looking to the future, he called at the military academy for 'organic cooperation' between the two countries' armies with a view to a single defence.[17]

The Elysée Treaty and the International Background

Later in September 1962 – after de Gaulle's return from Germany – a French memorandum containing detailed proposals for cooperation was sent to Bonn. The intention was to prepare the details of a joint declaration on political union on the occasion of Adenauer's next visit to Paris, a visit already planned for early 1963. The proposals were largely in keeping with the Fouchet Committee's earlier endeavour, even if now only two countries were concerned. The subjects of the regular meetings, at summit and ministerial level, would be foreign affairs, defence, and education. Economic matters were not mentioned. The most delicate of the three subjects was defence. According to the memorandum, cooperation would be extensive, both operationally and in the matter of armaments production. The German response in early November was broadly positive, but without any clear commitment to details, since there was a concern that any defence cooperation should be compatible with existing NATO obligations. There was anyway sufficient agreement for the two foreign ministers, Couve de Murville and Schröder, to meet in mid December to finalise the content of the joint declaration. Adenauer's visit to the French capital had been set for 21–22 January. Only on 16 January came a German request that, instead of the planned declaration, a treaty be signed. The treaty, still largely based on the Quai d'Orsay's September memorandum, had therefore to be drafted in haste. Providing for the 'organisation and principles of cooperation between the two states', it was duly signed at the Elysée on 22 January by de Gaulle, Pompidou, and Couve de Murville for France, and by Adenauer and Schröder for the FRG.

The German request for a treaty owed much to political divisions in Bonn. They were related in turn to an interplay of international events starting with the Cuban missile crisis in October and culminating in de Gaulle's memorable press conference on 16 January, when he announced that he was blocking the UK's application for EC membership.

The USSR's decision to begin work in October 1962 on the construction of sites in Cuba for medium-range and intermediate-range ballistic missiles, in striking distance of much of the US, was essentially a geographical displacement of the still rumbling Berlin crisis. Kennedy's show of resolve in the face of Khrushchev's threat won de Gaulle's immediate support. Yet this same resolve – both the naval blockade of Cuba and the threat to unleash nuclear war against the USSR if the sites were used against any target in the Western hemisphere – confirmed de Gaulle in his opinion that the degree of 'flexible response' chosen by Washington would always be a function of the immediacy of the danger to the US itself. The General thought, as did Adenauer, that Berlin and Cuba had not been weighed on the same scales.

In this trial of strength between the two superpowers, Kennedy's successful facing down of Khrushchev bestowed a new international stature on the American president, and also served to rein in the Soviet leader's impetuousness. Consequently, the Berlin crisis finally petered out. In January 1963 Khrushchev renounced further recourse to pressure in declaring that the 'success' of the Berlin Wall obviated any need for new treaty arrangements that would give the GDR an official say over the city's future. It marked the start of a period of relative détente between the two superpowers.

A quite different effect of the Cuban missiles crisis was to reinforce the personal political relationship between Kennedy and Macmillan. Not only had the British prime minister promptly proffered his country's backing – as de Gaulle had proffered France's – but he had also served as an appreciated confidant to Kennedy during the tense October days. In the second half of December he was rewarded when he met Kennedy in Nassau in the Bahamas to determine the future of the UK's independent nuclear deterrent. In 1960, because of a failure on the British side to develop an up-to-date delivery system, Eisenhower had promised to Macmillan that the Skybolt cruise missile – then in the course of development in the US – could be sold to the UK as a vector for its nuclear warheads. However, just prior to the Nassau Conference, all work on the missile was stopped. The American decision to bury Skybolt was driven by technical reasons and a growing awareness of the vulnerability of manned aircraft for the purpose of delivery. In addition, a strong view in the Kennedy administration was that short shrift should anyway be given to the UK: its presumption of continued nuclear independence accorded ill with US defence strategy and complicated Washington's task of handling NATO's continental European members, especially France with its own ambition for independence and West Germany with its desire not to be excluded from the nuclear club. This view was pressed above all by the so-called 'Europeanists' in the State Department. They were led by the Under-Secretary of State, George Ball, yet another longstanding American friend of Monnet. Nonetheless, at the Nassau Conference, Macmillan prevailed upon Kennedy to allow the UK to purchase Polaris submarine-launched ballistic missiles, and it was agreed that the Royal Navy's future Polaris submarine fleet would be assigned to NATO's integrated military command, save on occasions when 'superior national interests' were at stake.

The Nassau Agreement on 21 December provided de Gaulle with what he could flaunt as a clinching argument for refusing the British application for EC membership. 'England', he told Peyrefitte at the time, 'is no more than a satellite of the US. If it were to enter into the common market, it would be solely as a Trojan horse for the Americans. That would mean Europe's renouncing its independence.'[18] However, what the agreement afforded was an additional pretext, since the French president had already decided to block the UK's accession.

Kennedy, for his part, wrote to de Gaulle on 24 December to offer Polaris missiles to France on what he called 'similar' terms to those agreed with Macmillan. The offer was declined. Unlike the UK, France did not have the miniaturised thermonuclear warheads needed for Polaris, and nor was it then in a position to construct the type of nuclear submarines required. Although the US president expressed a certain willingness to help, de Gaulle was not interested. He was determined that the control of France's future *force de frappe* should lie totally outside NATO's American-led command structure. It could perhaps be the case that de Gaulle miscalculated, inasmuch as there is evidence to suggest that the opportunity had arisen for some sort of discussion about the idea of a nuclear tripartite directorate and a related reorganisation of the Atlantic Alliance, and that Kennedy, despite the State Department 'Europeanists', was prepared to move towards the somewhat more amenable position that had once been Eisenhower's – a marked change from his position a year earlier. However, as regards conventional forces, there was no sign from Washington of any readiness to reconsider NATO's integrated command structure.[19]

Adenauer's immediate reaction to the Nassau Conference was negative. Not only was he piqued by the FRG's having been kept in the dark, but he also feared – until de Gaulle provided reassurance to the contrary – that the Anglo-American agreement might be the harbinger of a two-tier NATO structure, with France joining the UK in the Polaris arrangements. Yet much as he shared many of de Gaulle's doubts about the Kennedy administration, he still did not lose hope of gaining some satisfaction from Washington in his quest for a German nuclear capability within NATO. Indeed, at the end of 1962 Washington appeared the only avenue open. De Gaulle, for all his eagerness for a Franco-German security partnership, had never allowed that future French-manufactured nuclear weapons might be made available to West Germany. Strauss had variously tried but failed on this front, his last initiative having been taken in January 1962 when he proposed to his French counterpart, Pierre Messmer, that the two countries embark upon a common defence policy, giving West Germany access to French nuclear weaponry in time of war. And in any case Strauss was now no longer defence minister. Less than two weeks before the Nassau Conference, the Chancellor had been obliged to replace this proponent of the French connection with a less controversial and more Atlanticist figure, Kai-Uwe von Hassel (CDU); this was because of an embarrassing quarrel pitching Strauss against the weekly newspaper, *Der Spiegel*.

On 16 January – the day de Gaulle issued his veto against the UK, partly on the ground that its EC membership would lead to a mammoth Atlantic Community under American domination – Adenauer received Ball in Bonn. He was informed about the state of plans afoot since May 1961, which was when Kennedy resuscitated the earlier Norstad proposal for a multilateral force – MLF – of nuclear armed submarines. These were to be provided by the US and kept under American control, but manned by contingents from other NATO members. Additionally, as an outcome of the Nassau Conference, a place was to be reserved in the MLF for the UK's Polaris submarines. Ball was assured of Germany's keen willingness to participate. Yet, typically, this did not prevent Adenauer a week later from seeking to ascertain from de Gaulle, for a last time, whether the defence cooperation promised by the new treaty might eventually extend to the sharing of nuclear weaponry.[20]

As to the Elysée Treaty, this cascade of international change between October 1962 and January 1963 helps explain the nature of the last-minute request from Bonn that the new Franco-German cooperation agreement be put in treaty form. It was not a sign of heightened German enthusiasm, rather the opposite. De Gaulle's interests and even Adenauer's were not necessarily those of most of the political class in the West German capital. The French president's overriding interest lay in a security alliance that would serve his twofold ambition of asserting France's leadership in continental Western Europe and putting an end to the American monopoly over NATO's military command. Adenauer's overriding interest, as he looked towards his impending political retirement, was to set a seal on a historically momentous Franco-German reconciliation. On the other hand, the leanings of the majority within Adenauer's own ruling CDU party – shared in varying degrees by the FDP and the new pragmatic generation of SPD politicians – were straightforwardly Atlanticist. Adenauer's acceptance in principle of the American MLF proposal had reassured them. But de Gaulle's refusal of the UK's application for EC membership provoked widespread discontent. At the forefront in expressing this discontent were Schröder and the powerful economics minister, Ludwig Erhard. It was partly to appease them that Adenauer agreed to ask for a treaty. A treaty, they knew, would be subject to the double control of the Constitutional Court and the Federal Parliament, particularly the Bundestag. So there would be a limit to what the old Chancellor might choose to sacrifice on the altar of French friendship.

The treaty that was hastily drafted and agreed in Paris provided inter alia for meetings at least twice a year between the German Chancellor and, on the other hand, both the French president and prime minister, and for meetings at least every three months of the countries' foreign ministers and defence ministers. Under the treaty's programme for cooperation in the sphere of foreign affairs, the first area specified for mutual consultation was 'problems relating to the European Communities and European political cooperation' – the latter being the essence of political union from a French standpoint. Three aims were set for cooperation in the sphere of defence: 'in strategy and tactics, the competent authorities in the two countries shall seek to reconcile their [military] doctrines with a view to arriving at common conceptions [an echo of the Colomb-Béchar and Rome protocols of 1958]'; 'the exchanges of military personnel shall be multiplied'; and 'in the matter of armaments, the two governments shall strive to organise work in common as from the stage of project design for suitable armaments and the preparation of their financing'. Finally, under the heading of education and youth, the emphasis for cooperation was put on the learning in schools of the other country's language and on the organisation of youth exchanges.[21]

The Bundestag's Preamble

'The substance of the treaty', Kissinger has written, 'was not remarkable. Indeed, it was an empty vessel which could be filled with whatever French and German leaders might put in it in the years ahead.'[22]   In any case, during the ratification process, the substance was diminished. In France ratification was completed quickly, without any serious difficulty raised in the National Assembly, though the SFIO and the PCF voted en bloc against it. But the Bundestag, acting effectively on a cross-party basis, engineered a radical change. Thus, in April 1963 the first chamber of the Federal Parliament voted unanimously a preamble whose content and tenor were at odds with the inspiration of the main body of the treaty; and this preamble was adopted by the Federal Parliament in May. According to the preamble, the treaty was to serve the FRG's longstanding foreign-policy aims rather than to establish new ones. The principle of 'particularly close cooperation between Europe and the United States of America' was stressed, as was the commitment to 'common defence in the framework of the North Atlantic Alliance and the integration of the forces of the countries belonging to this alliance'. Another specified aim was 'the unification of Europe, continuing along the path started by the creation of the European Communities, with Great Britain included'. Before the Bundestag's vote, de Gaulle ruminated bitterly about the already announced changes. 'The Americans', he told Peyrefitte, 'are trying to rid our treaty of its content. They want to turn it into an empty shell.'[23]

On the French side, Monnet was widely suspected to have had a hand in the drafting of this preamble. This was to exaggerate his reach and capacity for involvement in the affairs of other states. Since 1955 Monnet was at the head of the Action Committee for the United States of Europe, and it had proved an influential pressure group. But, after the treaty's signature, what Monnet canvassed was the Bundestag's outright rejection of it. The more astute device of a unilateral preamble to a bilateral international treaty was conceived by politicians and constitutional lawyers on the German side.

Monnet's more personal efforts had been deployed earlier. When Adenauer arrived in Paris on 20 January for the two-day visit culminating in the treaty's signature at the Elysée, he was visited at the German embassy by Monnet, who made a last-minute bid to restrain the Chancellor. The Frenchman's plea was that Adenauer should sign the treaty only if de Gaulle agreed to change his stance on the question of the UK's EC membership.[24] In taking a positive attitude initially towards the work of the Fouchet Committee, Monnet had shown that he was not fundamentally opposed to de Gaulle's idea of political union, provided the existing ECs were left in place; and nor could he have been averse in principle to a privileged partnership between France and West Germany, since he himself had been its advocate in 1950. However, he disagreed with de Gaulle's blackballing of the UK, having vigorously backed the Macmillan government's EC application from the outset. But Adenauer, unlike most other leading German politicians, was unsympathetic to the same application – and so Monnet's plea fell on deaf ears.

In the Bundestag, the parliamentarians who looked askance at the new treaty needed little prompting from French quarters. The dominant figure in the CDU proved to be Erhard rather than Schröder. The preamble's stress on the importance of the suppression of tariff barriers between the EEC, the UK, and the US – in the framework of the GATT – testified to the economic minister's Atlanticist conviction that international free trade was very much in West Germany's interest. Willy Brandt from the SPD also played a major role in shaping the preamble. Becoming the mayor of West Berlin in 1958, he had won the effective backing of both Adenauer and de Gaulle for his own uncompromising stance on the city's future. On a visit to Paris shortly before the Bundestag debate, Brandt spoke with the French president. But he was not swayed by the General's objections to the moves afoot in Bonn.

In July, on the eve of his departure to Germany for his first meeting with Adenauer as ordained by the Elysée Treaty, de Gaulle wryly remarked that the life of a treaty could be as transitory as the beauty of either a young woman or a rose, and he added – quoting Victor Hugo – '*Hélas! Que j'en ai vu mourir de jeunes filles*'. A connoisseur of roses, the old Chancellor responded in kind. Whatever the ephemeral quality of a young woman's beauty, he told the French president a few days later, the roses in his own garden at Rhöndorf were hardy and survived the winters; this would be the case with Franco-German friendship. Yes, admitted de Gaulle without conviction, their treaty was to be compared to a rose garden rather than the passing beauty of a single rose – a rose garden could last for a long time with care.[25]

Failed Geopolitical Ambition

The rose garden simile was to set a good face on what was really a failure, at least from de Gaulle's standpoint. The preamble's immediate effect was a stymieing of Adenauer's and de Gaulle's hopes to develop a special partnership between their two countries; and it was not until eleven years later, when Giscard d'Estaing and Schmidt came to power in the same year, that close bilateral cooperation was to be vigorously fostered in keeping with the spirit of the original treaty. In particular, the preamble immediately put paid to de Gaulle's design of drawing on the support of Germany to establish defence arrangements in Western Europe under French rather than American leadership. This failure became soon apparent as foreign policy in Bonn swung in a more resolutely Atlanticist direction.

One sign was Kennedy's visit to Berlin in June 1963. It was intended in Washington that the visit should be seen to be even more successful than that paid by de Gaulle in 1962 to West Germany, when Berlin had not been on the General's itinerary. Successful the visit certainly was. In particular, the acclaim given to Kennedy, after he pronounced his 'Ich bin ein Berliner' address to several hundred thousand West Berliners, meant that any perceived American weakness during the Berlin crisis – which had done so much to bring Adenauer and de Gaulle together – was now forgotten, the crisis itself being over. For the visit's purpose was to persuade Bonn that the FRG's interests were best served by their holding firm to the Atlantic Alliance, by their resisting the siren calls of France, and by their raising their nuclear ambitions no higher than participation in the proposed MLF.

The real transition to a new era took place in October 1963 when Adenauer finally stepped down as Chancellor, to be replaced by Erhard at the head of a government based on the same coalition of the CDU–CSU and the FDP. No personal affinity drew Erhard and de Gaulle together. Partly reflecting their different attitudes towards the US, the two countries' perceived interests in security and defence matters widened, and hence a cooling in relations occurred during the three years Erhard served as Chancellor.

French defence policy became ever more centred on the nuclear *force de frappe*, which became operational in October 1964 with initially just four Mirage IV long-range aircraft to deliver their nuclear payload. Beforehand there had been signs of de Gaulle's ever increasing determination that France be militarily independent of the US. In August 1963, France had refused to join the US and the UK in signing with the USSR a treaty banning nuclear tests in the atmosphere and under the sea, and in November 1963 de Gaulle put an end to talks with Washington on nuclear strategy – thereby blocking any formal agreement by the NATO Council on substituting 'flexible response' for 'massive retaliation'.

By 1964, however, not only was there a political consensus in West Germany in favour of the MLF – with the SPD's defence experts, Fritz Erler and Schmidt, being strongly of this view – but participation in the MLF had come to be seen as incompatible with support for France's independent nuclear option. Once it boiled down to a choice between military allies, there could be no doubt for Germany's leaders: the might of American power spoke for itself, and a further factor was that the Bundeswehr's general staff had become persuaded by 1964 of the benefits of McNamara's 'flexible response' strategy.

None of this was to France's satisfaction. In early November 1964 the French prime minister, Pompidou, publicly asserted that an MLF agreement between the FRG and the US would constitute an infringement of the Elysée Treaty. Later the same month de Gaulle visited Strasbourg for the twentieth anniversary of the city's liberation by French forces under the command of General Leclerc, and he used the commemoration in the Alsatian capital to call for the 'construction of a European Europe'. What this meant was that 'in the political domain at the forefront of which lies defence, [the EC Six] should set up and put into operation an organisation, allied indeed to the New World, but which belongs to them alone, with its own objectives, resources, and obligations'.[26]

The MLF project was to die at American hands. Lyndon B. Johnson – Kennedy's successor – was not firmly wedded to it, and at the end of December 1964, bowing to arguments from Paris and London (where a Labour government was now in power), he effectively killed it off. Nonetheless, on the German side, hopes of the MLF lingered on; they were to be finally renounced only in December 1966, with the coming to power of a 'grand coalition' government of Christian and Social Democrats (the CDU–CSU and the SPD).

The Erhard years were marked by no advance in Franco-German cooperation in defence. Earlier plans, dating from 1961, to engage France's 1st armoured division in the FRG's forward defence – by stationing the division near to the Czechoslovak border – came to naught. Instead the French government made no exception to its established policy of keeping all its forces in West Germany near to the Rhine. For their part, Erhard and Schröder persisted in believing that West Germany's fundamental loyalty should lie with the US, in particular in the domain of defence.

In the face of their position, the Elysée Treaty must have appeared to de Gaulle as a rose garden of singularly little promise. His 'European Europe' was rejected in Bonn. 'The Germans', de Gaulle sighed in November 1965, 'had been my great hope, [but] they are my great disappointment.'[27]

'Tous Azimuts' and the Limits of Détente

NATO Withdrawal, Nuclear Deterrence, and West Germany's Defence

In 1965 de Gaulle's European ambitions appeared to have come to naught. The adoption that year of a policy of détente with the USSR entailed an element of reorientation of foreign policy; it followed the burial of the Fouchet proposals in 1962, the Bundestag's thwarting of the design of the Elysée Treaty in 1963, and, finally, the further deterioration in Franco-German relations during the Erhard years. Then, in 1966, relations with the FRG and the rest of the Atlantic Alliance took a further knock when France withdrew altogether from NATO's integrated military command.

Announced in March 1966, the final withdrawal from the integrated command had been long in coming and indeed long announced; it was only indirectly related to the rapprochement with the USSR, which was a rapprochement that never amounted to a reversal of alliance. Already in March 1959 France's Mediterranean fleet had been withdrawn from NATO command. The request was then made in the following month that US bomber aircraft with a nuclear capability be removed from French bases.

In June 1963 it was the turn of the North Atlantic fleet to be withdrawn from NATO's naval forces. Also, prior to 1966, there had been some reduction in the US military presence in France, partly in anticipation of France's final withdrawal. Nonetheless, the timing of the letter of de Gaulle to Johnson announcing the change was unexpected; less brusque would have been a decision to the same effect in 1969 on the occasion of the renewal of the North Atlantic Treaty, whose initial duration was twenty years. An ineluctable consequence of the March 1966 decision was that various of NATO's key decision-making centres were removed from France: the NATO Council's headquarters and SHAPE (Supreme Headquarters Allied Powers Europe) were transferred to Belgium, while the headquarters of Allied Forces Central Europe – operationally responsible for NATO forces in West Germany and the Benelux countries (and until then also in France) – was transferred to the Netherlands.

Part of the background to this staggered withdrawal from NATO's integrated command in 1959–66 was the concentration of France's military effort on rapidly building up its independent nuclear force. Apart from the expansion of the Mirage IV striking force after 1964, work had started at the beginning of the 1960s on designing and building a small fleet of nuclear-propelled submarines (the first, the *Redoubtable*, being launched in 1967) and on developing the submarine-launched ballistic missiles (SLBMs) with which they were to be equipped. There was also work on developing short and medium-range surface-to-surface missiles. Great priority was accorded to acquiring a thermonuclear capability, and the breakthrough came eventually in August 1968 with the explosion of two hydrogen bombs at the Mururoa atoll in the Pacific.

In line with these efforts, and in the wake of the NATO withdrawal, there was the much remarked upon formulation of French defence strategy in December 1967 when the Chief of Staff of the Armed Forces, General Ailleret, published the article 'Défense dirigée ou défense tous azimuts' in the quasi-official *Revue de défense nationale*. It was essential, ran the article, that France dispose of a 'thermonuclear force of global reach and capable of striking in all directions (*tous azimuts*)'. De Gaulle gave his public blessing in a speech he made at the Institut des Hautes Etudes Militaires in January 1968, as well he might since Ailleret had based his article on a confidential directive from the president. Following the Soviet invasion of Czechoslovakia in August 1968, Ailleret's successor, General Fourquet, appeared to qualify the *tous azimuts* principle by letting it be known that France's strategic weapons would serve to defend the country from a threat from the East. Nonetheless, the principle itself was far removed from the spirit of the talks on security and defence, however ambivalent, between de Gaulle and Adenauer in 1958–63. And it was even further removed from the spirit of the proposal for a NATO tripartite directorate that de Gaulle had made on returning to power and still entertained at the time of the Fouchet Committee's launching in 1961.[28]

Yet neither the NATO withdrawal nor the provocative enunciation of strategy altered significantly France's contribution in conventional forces to West Germany's defence. In December 1966, after months of diplomatic negotiations, the two governments – through an exchange of letters between the foreign ministers – agreed new terms for the maintenance of French forces in Germany. Such an agreement was necessary inasmuch as the withdrawal from the integrated command had rendered inapplicable various provisions of the Paris Accords. On the military side, arrangements were eventually agreed in August 1967 – again in the form of an exchange of letters, though secret in this instance – between the Chief of Staff of the Armed Forces, General Ailleret, and SACEUR, General Lemnitzer. Under this agreement, in the event of war in Europe involving the Atlantic Alliance and subject to an affirmative decision of the French president, the French army corps stationed in Germany on the Rhine would be put under the command of NATO's Commander-in-Chief of Allied Forces Central Europe (CINC-AFCENT).[29]

Détente and the Close of the 'Prague Spring'

France's withdrawal from NATO's integrated military command was preceded by the shift in French foreign policy that became discernable in 1965. Instead of the priority attached in 1958–63 to establishing France's leadership on its own continent by means of a meaningful European political union, the effort towards asserting France's role as an independent power on the wider world stage was stepped up. Notable already at the beginning of 1964 had been France's decision to accord diplomatic recognition to the People's Republic of China, and later the same year de Gaulle undertook a long voyage in Latin America. It was in 1965, moreover, that the rapprochement with the USSR was prepared, giving rise in 1966–68 to a number of visits by de Gaulle to the Soviet bloc, starting with the USSR itself. Also in 1965 France was alone among the Western powers in withholding support from the US as the Johnson administration escalated the war in Vietnam. De Gaulle, who could refer to the bitter experience of the French war in Indochina in 1946–54 and to his own handling of the Algerian crisis, considered American policy to be foolhardy and dangerous for world peace. Yet opposition to the US in the matter of the Vietnam war and closer ties with the USSR did not amount to an abandoning of the Atlantic Alliance. Unaltered were France's stance on Berlin and its refusal to recognize the GDR. But what was new was the calculation that France could draw considerable advantage from enhancing vigorously its role as an actor in an increasingly multipolar world.

In this context, there was a displacement in the focus of de Gaulle's approach to the German question: when Adenauer had been Chancellor, the emphasis had been on building up a Franco-German partnership in the face of perceived Soviet danger and inadequate American support; now the French president deemed that the resolution of the German problem hung upon finding an entente between all the European peoples, including Russia once it had thrown off the shackles of totalitarianism. Such a view was expressed in the course of his press conference in February 1965. De Gaulle indicated his hope that détente would open the way to radical political change in communist Central and Eastern Europe. His aim of a political union on the basis of the existing EC was not dropped. In particular, he called upon the six states to organise themselves 'in the political domain and in the domain of the defence, so as to make a new balance of power (*équilbre*) possible on our continent'. However, he chose to put most emphasis on his conviction that a settlement of the German question, with agreed frontiers and arms limitations, could be eventually achieved – with the backing of the US – only through some kind of pan-European concert established 'from the Atlantic to the Urals'.[30]

Some affinity existed between these ideas and those of Brandt, the future architect of the FRG's *Ostpolitik*. The mayor of West Berlin became foreign minister – and also Vice-Chancellor – in December 1966 when the CDU/CSU-SPD 'grand coalition' was formed and Kurt Georg Kiesinger (CDU) replaced Erhard as Chancellor. Brandt largely shared the Atlanticist sympathies of Schröder, his predecessor at the Foreign Office. He had, moreover, greatly admired Kennedy, being struck by the late president's 'strategy of peace' speech – delivered shortly before his 1963 visit to Berlin – in which the US president had argued for coexistence between the superpowers. However, unlike his predecessor, Brandt also admired de Gaulle: not only did he accord credit to de Gaulle for his robust stance over West Berlin in 1958–62, but he also believed that the General's policy of détente was the correct one in the changed circumstances of the mid-1960s. De Gaulle, for his own part, had approved of Brandt's policy, as West Berlin's mayor, of seeking limited accommodation through 'small steps' with East Germany's Soviet masters.[31]

De Gaulle's use of the expression 'from the Atlantic to the Urals' in 1965 was far from new. When he had first called in 1950 for a 'Franco-German practical entente' aimed at creating something more substantial than the Council of Europe, he had allowed himself the rhetorical flourish of wishing for the rebirth of a Europe defined in such geographical terms. The expression, which came to be used more frequently at this time of rapprochement with the USSR, reflected his belief that political ideologies were essentially transitory, whereas nations had a perennial quality and drew in Europe upon values issuing from a common civilisation. This belief was publicly voiced during his official visit to Poland in September 1967. But the hopes de Gaulle entertained for a Europe more at peace with itself, and so for a climate more conducive to an acceptable long-term settlement of the German question, were to be dashed in August 1968 when the USSR put a brutal end to the 'Prague Spring' by the invasion of

Czechoslovakia with Warsaw Pact troops. To Couve de Murville and Debré, he made the disabused remark that it was 'Yalta again'.[32] It followed on the heels of France's own insurrectionary domestic turmoil, the events of May 1968. Much of de Gaulle's grand design for France and its place in Europe must have appeared to him as fragile or even in tatters.

Yet in a different sphere of European endeavour, that of the creation of the common market and the latter's special provisions for agriculture, de Gaulle had proved very successful during his presidency in furthering French interests. It is to that tale, which shows also continuities between the Fourth and Fifth Republics, that the reader's attention is now directed.

Notes

1. De Gaulle, *Discours et messages*, vol. 2, 307–10.
2. Charles de Gaulle, *Mémoires d'espoir*, 2 vols, Paris, 1970–71, vol. 1, 184–90.
3. Georgette Elgey, *Histoire de la IVe République*, vol. 2: *La République des contradictions, 1951–1954*, Paris, 1968, 286–87; Wall, *The United States and the Making of Postwar France*, 193; Dalloz, *Georges Bidault*, 302–5; Soutou, *L'Alliance incertaine*, 33.
4. Charles de Gaulle, *Lettres, notes et carnets*, 12 vols, Paris, 1980–86, vol. 8, 82–84.
5. Eisenhower – with the backing of Macmillan – sought some accommodation in 1959 and 1960 with de Gaulle over the tripartite issue, albeit without success. The refusal of tripartism by the succeeding Kennedy administration marked therefore an inflexion of US policy. See Constantine A. Pagedas, *Anglo-American Strategic Relations and the French Problem, 1960–1963: A Troubled Partnership*, London, 2000, 10–91, 129–75. However, in terms of the policy climate in Washington below the level of the president, there was less of a break between the two administrations. 'President Eisenhower's attempt to bring about Anglo-American-French tripartism in 1959 and 1960', writes Pagedas, 'was in stark contrast to the ideas of his closest advisors' (69). See also Frédéric Bozo, *Two Strategies for Europe: De Gaulle, the United States, and the Atlantic Alliance*, Lanham, 2001, 9–23, 36–37.
6. De Gaulle, *Discours et messages*, vol. 3, 220.
7. De Gaulle, *Lettres, notes et carnets*, vol. 8, 382–83. Cf. Soutou, *L'Alliance incertaine*, 159–61, where the author argues that the nine-point note represents the most authoritative statement by de Gaulle of his project for European political union. See also Jacques Bariéty, 'Les entretiens de Gaulle–Adenauer de juillet 1960 à Rambouillet. Prélude au plan Fouchet et au traité de l'Elysée', *Revue d'Allemagne et des pays de langue allemande* 29(2), 1997, 167–76.
8. De Gaulle, *Mémoires de guerre*, vol. 3, 179–80.
9. For the letters to Couve de Murville and Eisenhower, see de Gaulle, *Lettres, notes et carnets*, vol. 8, 383–84, 388–90.
10. Soutou, *L'Alliance incertaine*, 177–78.
11. Like Churchill, de Gaulle showed some favour to Coudenhove-Kalergi's Pan-European movement. In 1947 the movement took the form of the European Parliamentary Union, and Coudenhove-Kalergi, who died in 1972, was its secretary general. De Gaulle wrote to him in 1948, speaking of 'France's destiny … to promote the European Union' – see the letter in Georges Pompidou, *Pour rétablir une vérité*, Paris, 1982, 106. Two decades later, in August 1960, a confidential paper on the stymieing of supranationalism was

prepared for de Gaulle by Alain Peyrefitte, then a budding Gaullist politician sitting in the National Assembly, who had earlier served as a young diplomat in the French delegation at the IGC preparing the EEC and Euratom treaties. Because of a mistake by Peyrefitte's secretary, the content of the paper quickly became public. It was apparently also in 1960 that de Gaulle asked Peyrefitte to assemble a collection of his writings and speeches, so as to demonstrate his longstanding attachment to a confederal idea of Europe. The result of this enterprise would have been a book entitled *Charles de Gaulle : L'Europe des nations.* Peyrefitte, whose name would have figured in small letters on the title page, was to be identified as representing the Comité Français pour l'Union Paneuropéenne, a Gaullist association sympathetic to Coudenhove-Kalergi's ideas. De Gaulle eventually decided that the book's publication was inopportune – see Alain Peyrefitte, *C'était de Gaulle*, 3 vols, Paris, 1994–2000, vol. 1, 60–70. In 1965, at the time of the EEC's 'empty chair' crisis, Coudenhove-Kalergi defended de Gaulle's stance in the columns of *Le Monde*, taking issue with the former British ambassador to Paris, Gladwyn Jebb, and Maurice Faure – see Edmond Jouve, *Le Général de Gaulle et la construction de l'Europe (1940–1966)*, 2 vols, Paris, 1967, vol. 1, 684–86, 707–9.

12.   For details of the three Fouchet Plans, reactions, and sequels, see Jouve, *Le Général de Gaulle et la construction de l'Europe*, vol.1, 316–44; vol. 2, 441–58. For an account of the strategic dimension of the Fouchet proposals, especially as envisaged by de Gaulle, see Soutou, *L'Alliance incertaine*, 149–201. See also Maurice Couve de Murville, *Une politique étrangère, 1958–1969*, Paris, 1971, 347–84.

13.   Pagedas, *Anglo-American Strategic Relations and the French Problem*, 186–87.

14.   De Gaulle, *Lettres, notes et carnets*, vol. 9, 107–8.

15.   Peyrefitte, *C'était de Gaulle*, vol. 1, 155–56.

16.   Quai d'Orsay archives, as quoted in Maurice Vaïsse, *La Grandeur. Politique étrangère du général de Gaulle, 1958–1969*, Paris, 1998, 251.

17.   For the text of the Führungsakademie speech and its significance, see Pierre Maillard, *De Gaulle et l'Allemagne. Le rêve inachevé*, Paris, 1990, 177–78, 292–93.

18.   Peyrefitte, *C'était de Gaulle*, vol. 1, 348.

19.   On France and the Nassau Agreement, see Soutou, *L'Alliance incertaine*, 233–39; Pagedas, *Anglo-American Strategic Relations and the French Problem*, 225–73; Bozo, *Two Strategies for Europe*, 87–94. It is Soutou who argues that there was a willingness on the American side in January 1963, prior to de Gaulle's famous press conference, to engage in meaningful discussions about a nuclear tripartite directorate and, to some extent, the shape of the Atlantic Alliance itself; on the other hand, Bozo judges that that there was no fundamental policy change in Washington.

20.   Vaïsse, *La Grandeur*, 255–57.

21.   For the text of the treaty, including the preamble added by the Bundestag, see Soutou, *L'Alliance incertaine*, 445–51. For the genesis and fate of the treaty, see ibid., 241–49; Vaïsse, *La Grandeur*, 253–62; Schwarz, *Konrad Adenauer*, vol. 2, 662–76.

22.   Kissinger, *Diplomacy*, 615.

23.   Peyrefitte, *C'était de Gaulle*, vol. 2, 228.

24.   Duchêne, *Jean Monnet*, 330.

25.   Jean Lacouture, *De Gaulle*, 3 vols, Paris, 1984–86, vol. 3, 308–9.

26.   De Gaulle, *Discours et messages*, vol. 4, 314–16.

27.   Peyrefitte, *C'était de Gaulle*, vol. 2, 305 (see also 295–96, 303–4).

28.   Lacouture, *De Gaulle*, vol. 3, 476–83.

29.   Soutou, *L'Alliance incertaine*, 293–301; Vaïsse, *La Grandeur*, 392–94; Bozo, *Two Strategies for Europe*, 210–13.

30.   De Gaulle, *Discours et messages*, vol. 4, 337–42.

31.   Brandt's political memoirs give a perceptive view of de Gaulle's policies in respect of Germany, Europe, and the Atlantic Alliance – see Willy Brandt, *People and Politics: The Years 1960–1975*, London, 1978, 114–37.

32.   Lacouture, *De Gaulle*, vol. 3, 547.

Part II

THE COMMON MARKET AND THE INTERNATIONAL ECONOMY

Chapter 5

THE BENELUX INITIATIVE AND THE FORMATION OF THE COMMON MARKET

If Euratom was yet another Monnet brainchild, the EEC was the fruit not of a French initiative but rather a Dutch one. Of the six states embarking upon the venture of the common market, France was initially the most hesitant. However, when the EEC Treaty was signed in the penultimate year of the Fourth Republic's existence, major French interests were catered for. Subsequently, de Gaulle's decision to turn France away from industrial protectionism was the key to the EEC's successful transition period and assured future. His hardline stance in the CAP negotiations secured long-term price arrangements favourable to French agriculture.

Messina to Venice

Combining Beyen and Monnet

De Gaulle, of course, inherited the 'common market', which, unlike the ECSC and the EDC, had not been launched as part of France's design for mid-twentieth-century Europe. This launching effectively took place in June 1955, when the foreign ministers of the ECSC's member states met in the Sicilian town of Messina to appoint a successor to Monnet at the head of the High Authority and to consider, after the previous year's EDC fiasco, new approaches to European integration. Neither France nor West Germany expected that the meeting would be of watershed importance. Adenauer – still foreign minister as well as Chancellor – sent Hallstein, now his secretary of state at the German Foreign Office. Yet the Messina

Conference proved to be the start of a diplomatic process that led to the Treaties of Rome establishing the EEC and Euratom.

The initiative leading eventually to the EEC's creation came in Messina from the Benelux countries. It originated in a plan for a customs union, organised on a supranational basis, which had been conceived in 1952 by the Dutch foreign minister, Johan Willem Beyen.[1] Known therefore as the Beyen Plan, it was a contribution to the preparation of the (abortive) draft treaty establishing a European Political Community, which itself was linked to the (failed) ratification of the EDC Treaty. Beyen was thus the father of the same draft treaty's provision for 'the progressive establishment of a common market'. Still Dutch foreign minister at the time of the run-up to the Messina Conference, he advocated his plan anew, and it came to be adopted by all three Benelux foreign ministers as one of two sets of proposals put forward in their joint memorandum of May 1955 in preparation for the conference. The raison d'être of the resuscitated Beyen Plan lay not in security, save in the loosest of senses, but rather in the concern to consolidate and further develop the foreign-trade dynamic that had gathered pace in Western Europe since the beginning of the 1950s, and very strikingly so in trade between West Germany and the Benelux countries.

The main locomotive of this fast foreign-trade growth was certainly the German economy. Already making for the German 'economic miracle' (*Wirtschaftswunder*), the country's rapid post-war economic reconstruction had had its beginnings in the radical currency reform of 1948. The latter had been drawn up by Erhard – then working for the US military government – and implemented in the American, British and French occupation zones. Contributing to the 'economic miracle' in the 1950s, as Marshall Aid to Western Europe tapered off, was the switch of much of the high demand in the OEEC area for investment goods (notably machine tools and other mechanical engineering products) to West German suppliers at the expense of US ones. Trade creation in Western Europe was, moreover, fostered by the removal of quantitative restrictions agreed within the OEEC, even if the continued pursuit of such liberalisation was meeting with resistance on the part of different national governments. Growth in trade was helped too by the functioning of the European Payments Union (EPU); set up by the OEEC in 1950, it was a multilateral clearing arrangement, including the provision of credit facilities, which served to improve the external convertibility of currencies.

In this context, the purpose of the Benelux-proposed common market – consisting of a customs union and common economic policies – was to maximise the benefits that could be derived in the long term from the German-led trade creation in Western Europe. Primarily in mind were the perceived interests of the Benelux countries themselves, though it was assumed that these interests were complementary to those of other ECSC member states. But, as Erhard was to insist, the assumption was questionable in the case of West Germany: it would depend upon the degree to which its important trade elsewhere was adversely affected by the setting up of the customs union – in particular, German trade with the UK and the Scandinavian countries. As to the potential interest of Italy and France in a customs union, their economies had received a strong lift in the first half of the 1950s from booming German demand and its wider ripple effects. France was to prove the less easily persuadable of the two, however. Industrial protectionism was deeply entrenched, and, in the face of the faster than expected reemergence of German economic power, the time when Bidault, as foreign minister in 1948, could push forward the idea of a customs union belonged already to another era.[2]

However, the second of the two sets of proposals contained in the Benelux memorandum was more attuned to French perceptions of where their interests lay. Proposed was further sectoral integration, so as to cover all energy and transport, and, in particular, the setting up of a new 'community' for the development of the peaceful use of atomic energy. The author of this plan, notwithstanding its Benelux provenance, was none other than the man de Gaulle had nicknamed the 'Inspirer', Monnet. In the closing phase of the EDC saga, the Belgian foreign minister, Spaak, had been at the forefront of those striving to save the doomed treaty, and, after the battle was lost, he turned in September 1954 to Monnet to work out new ways of relaunching supranational integration. A fruit of this unusual partnership between Belgium's leading francophone socialist politician and the French head of the ECSC High Authority was Monnet's preparation in January 1955 of a draft proposal for the aforementioned atomic energy community, a proposal which was to be polished up in the few months that followed. Spaak had thus succeeded Schuman and Pleven as the political sponsor of Monnet's repeated efforts.

Monnet's enthusiasm for harnessing atomic energy to the European cause derived from a number of considerations. He remained convinced of the effectiveness of sectoral integration, at least when the sector in question was economically a key one and induced spillover effects that called for additional coordinated action at European level. As to the choice of atomic energy, he subscribed to the growing belief that it was set to be by far the cheapest form of primary energy for electricity production, and that it would also open up wide fields for technological development. A sign of the times had been President Eisenhower's 'Atoms for Peace' address to the UN General Assembly in December 1953. A different consideration reflected Monnet's agreement with the thrust of US policy concerning European security. In view of the dangerous potential for diverting civil applications of atomic energy to military ends, he thought that the sector was ideally suited for some form of supranational control – a control to be exercised in cooperation with the Americans in return for technological assistance.[3]

That the Benelux foreign ministers chose to put forward simultaneously two quite different sets of proposals in preparation for the Messina Conference was a quirk of fate. Spaak, playing the leading role among the three, had written in early April to the French, German and Italian foreign ministers to propose Monnet's new plan. The Belgian foreign minister also suggested that Monnet might be ready to postpone his stepping down from the presidency of the High Authority. It would allow him to borrow the prestige of that position to take charge of yet another IGC. But there was a relative lack of German interest in an ECSC-type arrangement for the civil development of atomic energy. This feeling was conveyed to Monnet, almost immediately after Spaak had sent his letter, by the new German Foreign Office's Political Department. Fortuitously, at the same moment, Beyen wrote to Spaak to resurrect his own plan. The upshot in May was that the Benelux foreign ministers effectively hedged their bets by proposing both renewed sectoral integration – privileging atomic energy – and 'general' integration in the shape of a common market.

In Paris the moderately 'pro-European' government of Edgar Faure – a government including both MRP and Gaullist ministers – was ready to entertain the idea of further integration in the energy sector, including atomic energy, provided it was not organised with a pronounced supranational bias. Partly because of this precondition, there was no question of Monnet being invited to stay on in Luxembourg or even of his being invited to Messina. Already before the end of May Faure had obtained the agreement of his partners in the Six that Monnet would be replaced by René Mayer. The foreign minister, Pinay, then embarked for Messina with apparently the thought that France could choose to consider the energy proposals, yet reject the idea of a common market. If this really was his conviction, he found himself representing a minority of one. Not only Hallstein but also the Italian foreign minister, Gaetano Martino, as well as the Benelux trio, were more interested in a common market than an atomic energy pool. With no real consensus possible in Messina, the foreign ministers adopted a resolution whose effect was to shunt the Benelux memorandum's proposals, for further study, into the hands of a committee of national representatives and experts chaired by Spaak.[4]

The Spaak Report

Boldly, Spaak decided to prepare separate blueprints for two treaties, one establishing what was to be the future EEC and the other the future Euratom. Even if Monnet – now actively leading his Action Committee for the United States of Europe – was kept at arm's length from the committee's work, he enjoyed a vicarious presence. For France's delegation was led by the Radical politician and future prime minister, Gaillard, who had been Monnet's *directeur de cabinet* at the Commissariat Général du

Plan in the immediate post-war years. Furthermore, the chairman of the working group on atomic energy was Louis Armand – the executive head of the SNCF (Société Nationale des Chemins de fer Français) and chairman of the supervisory board of France's own atomic energy authority, the Commissariat à l'Energie Atomique (CEA). He shared the enthusiasm of his friend, Monnet, for the development of this new form of energy. Armand indeed coined the name Euratom and was later to be the first president of the Euratom Commission. Most important of all, the foremost expert on the Spaak Committee was Uri, Monnet's long-term associate, who, after participating in the working group on the common market, served as rapporteur. Much of the committee's report was dictated by Uri during an intense fortnight at a hotel on the French Riviera, where he and a small staff had secluded themselves in March 1956. For Euratom he drew on the working-group report that had been prepared almost entirely by Armand. The one other person who contributed substantially to the final shape of the Spaak Report and assisted Uri in his work was Hans von der Groeben, the head of the ECSC section in the German economics ministry and later an EEC commissioner; unlike his free-market orientated minister, Erhard, he was well disposed to the idea of a regional common market and, therefore, effectively closer to Adenauer.

Late in April 1956 the completed Spaak Report was submitted to the foreign ministers of the Six. And at the end of May they met in Venice to decide whether to move ahead on its basis. On the French side there was less reticence than there had been in Messina. One reason was the largely reassuring nature of the Spaak Report's proposed institutional arrangements, with intergovernmentalism appearing to have largely triumphed over supranationalism. Also entering into play were the sympathies of the prime minister and foreign minister, Mollet and Pineau, who had won their European spurs in the battle over the EDC, both within their own divided Socialist party and in the National Assembly. This past European commitment had been reaffirmed by Mollet when, on taking office as prime minister, he accepted the goal of a common market. There was accordingly a minimum of good will and confluence of perceived interests. On this basis, the Six agreed in Venice to transform the Spaak Committee into an IGC in Brussels under the Belgian foreign minister's continued chairmanship.

Negotiating the EEC and Euratom

The French Government Memorandum

Mollet's stance, however, was far from fully backed by France's administrative elite. And, largely because of French demands, the negotiations were to prove far from straightforward. Just after the Spaak Report had been unveiled, a first meeting was held in Paris of a national committee bringing together high-ranking civil servants holding responsibilities for economic matters affected by the proposed common market. Their virtually unanimous opinion of the resuscitated Beyen Plan was negative. In May 1956, at the committee's behest, a lengthy memorandum was prepared in the name of the French government to show under what modified or alternative conditions a common market might be acceptable, and it was submitted to the other governments in time for the Venice Conference.

The main point advanced in this French memorandum was that a common market could not be expected to function properly in the absence of harmonisation of the conditions of competition. In particular, social legislation – governing hours of work, pay conditions, and social-security arrangements – had to be harmonised if France were not to suffer. Other major requirements were set: the duplication of French-style indicative economic planning at European level; the setting up of a common agricultural policy (a matter not mentioned in the Messina Resolution and scarcely tackled in the Spaak Report); and the introduction of special agreements under which the other members of the future common market would provide financial assistance to the overseas countries and territories linked to France, in exchange for access to these overseas countries' and territories' markets. As to the dismantlement of tariffs and quotas, the memorandum argued for a trial experimental period of four years during which the first reductions would be made, after which France and the other member states would decide whether it was worthwhile to proceed further with the common market. Notice was given in advance of the rejection of the one obvious measure that could smooth the economy's adjustment during the creation of the customs union, namely a substantial devaluation of the French franc. Beneficial as might be its effects on the price competitiveness of the economy, it had to be ruled out because of its effects on the population's living standards. Finally, any progressive implementation of freedom of movement for workers had to be limited to the extent that structural unemployment still prevailed, while the implementation of freedom of movement for capital had to remain at the discretion of individual governments.[5]

France and the Common-Market Negotiations

Especially in view of the demands made in the French government memorandum, the successful negotiation of a treaty establishing a common market was not a foregone conclusion. That the IGC nonetheless advanced forward, with a constructive role played by France, owed much to Maurice Faure, the secretary of state responsible for European affairs (subordinate to the foreign minister), who headed the French delegation, and, more importantly still, his chief adviser, Marjolin, who took charge of the day-to-day negotiations concerning the common market.[6]

Marjolin's teaming up with Faure was the result of his having joined Pineau's staff in February 1956 to advise the new foreign minister on European affairs. He had stepped down from his post as secretary general of the OEEC a year earlier, partly because he felt that there was no longer any hope of that organisation's serving as the midwife for a customs union that covered most of Western Europe, including the UK. Marjolin was to become an EEC commissioner in 1958–67, but he was not in the Monnet mould. Although he admired Monnet from the days they had worked together at the Commissariat Général du Plan, he differed in his views of the politics and economics of international relations. He believed much more strongly than Monnet in the perennial quality of the nation state. Although of socialist political persuasion, he was not an advocate of technocratic economic management and was averse to the sectoral approach to European integration. Indeed, as an economist, he was convinced of the merits of an essentially liberal international economic order, in which the price mechanism and market forces governed trade flows and related economic activity. Because of his own economic philosophy, Marjolin was well suited for negotiations and compromise with his German and Dutch counterparts at the IGC, and this was a factor contributing to a softening of the French line on social harmonisation and hence to eventual agreement on the treaty. On the question of agriculture he argued the French case for a policy of non-discrimination between national producers within the common market, and, back in France, he succeeded in convincing the main agricultural organisations that they would be assured adequate export outlets, especially for the growing surpluses of wheat and sugar beet.

The question of France's overseas countries and territories proved to be the most delicate issue in the common-market negotiations. The French empire remained vast in size even after the relinquishing of Indochina and the termination of the protectorates in Morocco and Tunisia – both accorded independence in March 1956, shortly before the release of the Spaak Report. Few could have imagined as the negotiations started in earnest that all of France's colonies in West and Equatorial Africa, as well as the Algerian *départements*, would no longer be ruled from Paris only some six years later. Making the implicit assumption that the empire was set to be long-lived, Schuman in his famous declaration of 1950 had asserted that increased coal and steel resources would enable Europe 'to pursue one of its essential tasks: the development of the African continent'. Monnet had inserted these words in the Schuman Declaration at the behest of René Mayer, then justice minister and one of the Deputies representing Algeria in the National Assembly.[7] They testified to a real concern, namely that of squaring France's interest in Western European economic integration with the maintenance of its special links with large parts of the world beyond Europe. That concern became much more acute once there was question of a European customs union.

How to associate overseas countries and territories with the planned common market was indeed the most important matter that had not been tackled by the Spaak Report. The French government memorandum of May 1956 set the base for the negotiations, and, on this matter, the main input into the memorandum had come from the minister responsible for Overseas France, Gaston Defferre, who had been quick to see the potential advantages for France of a common market extended to the colonies ('*marché commun eurafricain*').[8] The amount of financial assistance to be provided to overseas countries and territories by all the Six, in exchange for the markets of the former being opened on an equal footing to exports from all of the Six, became the key practical question. France, of course, was not alone in holding colonies. Yet it counted most. The Belgian state's interests in the huge Belgian Congo (to which Ruanda–Urundi was effectively joined) were not comparable to those of the French state elsewhere in Africa. Not only was Belgian industry proportionally less engaged than French industry in exporting to colonial markets, but also less was demanded of the Belgian Treasury, since the heart of the Belgian Congo's economic development – the exploitation of industrial raw materials – was in the hands of Belgium's most powerful private-sector industrial and financial conglomerate, while much of the colony's social infrastructure – in the form of schools and hospitals – was provided directly by the Catholic Church. Whether the Belgian Congo should be associated with the common market was not perceived by Belgium as a question of vital national interest. This was even more true of the Netherlands, whose remaining colonial territories were of little consequence after Indonesia's achievement of full independence in 1950. Against this background it was largely left to France to push for the provision of substantial financial assistance to the Six's overseas countries and territories. Considerable German reluctance had to be overcome, and it was only in February 1957, when the IGC negotiations moved exceptionally from Brussels to Paris, with Adenauer taking part in the meeting only three months after the worst of the Suez crisis, that the matter was finally settled.

This last-minute agreement was the origin of the Treaty of Rome's fourth part, entitled 'Association of the Overseas Countries and Territories'. The 'economic and social development' of these countries and the establishing of 'close economic relations between them and the Community as a whole' were declared the purpose of the association (Article 131). By virtue of the 'Implementing Convention on the Association of the Overseas Countries and Territories with the Community', the European Development Fund (EDF) was set up. Algeria was covered by this fourth part of the treaty and the related convention, but, being independent, Morocco and Tunisia were not. Instead, in their favour, a 'Declaration of Intent on the Association of the Independent Countries of the Franc Area with the European Economic Community' was annexed to the treaty. Declared therein was a concern on the part of the Six to 'maintain and intensify the traditional trade flows' and to 'contribute to the economic and social development [of the franc area's independent countries]'. To this end, a readiness was expressed to open negotiations with Morocco and Tunisia 'with a view to concluding conventions for economic association with the Community'; in the meantime, France was allowed by the provisions of a treaty protocol to maintain its existing preferential trade arrangements.

All the difficulties raised by the French government memorandum of May 1956 were not ironed out during the IGC. Hence annexed to the treaty was a 'Protocol relating to Certain Provisions of Concern to France'. The first of two concessions was that France would be allowed to maintain its system of export subsidies and import surcharges under certain conditions. The second concession – an extraordinary one – allowed France to introduce industrial safeguard measures at the end of the first four-year stage of the transitional period, if by that time the other member states had not aligned their rules for the remuneration of overtime work on those applying in France.

Crucial as was the role played by Faure and Marjolin for the success of the common-market negotiations, the Mollet government's overriding objective remained that of steering an initiative, which France would never have proposed, in a direction that brought national advantage. Yet in no way could it be pretended that France recovered a clear leadership role of the kind exercised for the ECSC and EDC Treaties by the time the Rome Treaties were signed in March 1957.

Under these circumstances, it might be thought strange that a Frenchman could describe himself as the 'father of the common market'. Such a claim, however, was made years later by Uri, when he very legitimately associated himself with Monnet, whom he described as the (overarching) 'father of Europe'. That this brilliant French economist and technocrat was the 'inspirer' – de Gaulle's word for Monnet – of much of the detail of the Treaty of Rome establishing the EEC, there can be little doubt. In that limited sense, Uri's claim of his own importance was no doubt correct. He also claimed that he had the informal backing of Gaillard, the head of the French delegation at the time of the preparation of the Spaak Report. But he had been seconded to the Spaak Committee in his capacity as a high-ranking ECSC official, not as a representative of the French government. Indeed, in May 1956 when the foreign ministers of the Six and their accompanying officials met in Venice, at the former monastery of San Giorgio Maggiore, to discuss the Report, Uri found that no place had been set for him. His difficulty was resolved by Spaak's inviting him to join the Belgian delegation, and not long afterwards he was invited by the Belgian foreign minister to serve as his right-hand man during the IGC. Uri's adoption by Belgium signalled the truth that

Monnet-type European integration was no longer politically fashionable in Paris. Compared with the ECSC and EDC negotiations, the negotiations were now being handled on the French side by a national delegation acting on more classical diplomatic lines and through the more traditional channels of authority.[9]

Cross Purposes over Euratom

In the French delegation Marjolin's counterpart in the parallel negotiations for the future Euratom was not Monnet's fellow enthusiast, Armand, but Pierre Guillaumat, the Gaullist-inclined executive head of the CEA – he was to be de Gaulle's defence minister from 1958 to 1961. Mollet had felt that it was better to have Guillaumat directly involved in the negotiations rather than carping from outside. The prime minister knew, moreover, that France's interests would be pushed at all costs. Varied considerations underlay the priority given to atomic energy in Paris. Besides the belief in the high economic promise of this form of energy, there were, yet again, French motives relating to national security. One aim was to benefit from the expertise and finance of other countries, notably West Germany, for the development of uranium processing and, in particular, isotope separation. Another aim was that France alone in continental Western Europe should have the atomic bomb, and this aim, it was thought, could be furthered by the institution of a Euratom that would not only regulate the use of nuclear energy but also confine the use of fissionable materials outside France to strictly non-military purposes.

On the issue of atomic energy, France and West Germany were on a collision course. Although Adenauer was partial to the Euratom project, both Erhard and Strauss, the nuclear energy minister until October 1956, were strongly opposed to it. Their reason was that Euratom would be prejudicial to the nascent German civil nuclear industry, since it would stand in the way of its profiting directly from American and British technology. With German and French aims at odds with one another, the Euratom Treaty that finally emerged provided for little of substance when measured against the earlier hopes of Monnet and Armand. And de Gaulle, for one, was apparently surprised when Guillaumat demonstrated to him the treaty's flimsiness.[10]

That France would anyway continue to pursue largely its own path was evident in April 1957 – a month after the treaty was signed – when the Mollet government announced the country's second five-year civil nuclear programme, which was drawn up in a purely national framework. Later, in the 1960s, both France and West Germany were to develop their own different types of fast-breeder reactors. This sounded the knell of Euratom as an organisation of any great substance. By 1967, when the Euratom Commission was absorbed into the EEC Commission, all three of the

Euratom Commission's successive presidents had been French. But this symbolic privileging of France's place in this particular Community had led to little advantage.

De Gaulle's 'Practising the Common Market'

Mollet's Resolve and Treaty Ratification

Despite Mollet's commitment as prime minister to the idea of a common market, he had initially kept his options open. As late as September 1956, against the background of Anglo-French preparations for the Suez venture, he was toying with the idea of a radically different alternative in the shape of reviving the 1940 idea of a union between France and the UK, even bringing together somehow the French Union and its equivalent, the Commonwealth. But this idea – secretly communicated to his British counterpart, Eden – met with no favourable response in London.[11]

The decisive turning point for Mollet was the result of the Suez fiasco two months later. The prospect of a major and rapid advance in European economic integration now came to be seen as a means of overcoming the humiliation that had been inflicted upon France by the American-enforced climbdown. That the UK had been the one to bow to American pressure encouraged the French prime minister to put aside lingering desires to explore the British connection and opt instead for an endeavour confined to the Six. The months following Adenauer's November visit were a period of intense diplomatic activity. And so on 25 March 1957 France signed in Rome the two treaties establishing the EEC and Euratom.

The EEC and Euratom Treaties were ratified by the French parliament soon afterwards. The National Assembly approved them on 10 July 1957 with 342 votes for and 239 against (almost the same numbers as for the approval of the ECSC Treaty in 1951). The Council of the Republic followed on 23 July with 222 votes for and 70 against. By that time the Mollet government had fallen, but the new prime minister, Bourgès-Maunoury, kept both Pineau and Maurice Faure at the Quai d'Orsay, and the latter especially proved a persuasive orator in the National Assembly. A salient feature of the National Assembly vote, compared with the final debate over the EDC Treaty in 1954, was that the SFIO maintained party discipline and held together. The effective alliance between Socialists and the MRP provided well over half of the support for ratification. Support also came from the small UDSR, now headed by Mitterrand. The bulk of the opposition came from the PCF, abetted by the much reduced number of Gaullists left in the National Assembly after the legislative elections of January 1956. The Radical party was badly split.

In the National Assembly, Mendès France led the Radicals who voted against the treaties. Already in a preliminary debate in January 1957 he had spoken at length against the EEC, arguing largely on economic and social grounds. In July in the ratification debate he warned that premature accession would result in Germany's exercising economic hegemony over France. If the positive role he had played three years earlier in improving Franco-German relations was dictated by political or security considerations, his negative stance now was based mainly on economics.[12] Such economic pessimism was more widespread in ruling circles than the ratification vote in the National Assembly might suggest. It was not altogether without reason. Later in 1957, because of the financial strains engendered by the Algerian War, the country's economic difficulties had become so severe that Gaillard, first as finance minister and then as prime minister, introduced restrictive economic measures, including the suspension of the liberalisation of trade quotas within the framework of the OEEC. Official reserves were so depleted in January 1958 – the first month of the EEC's formal existence – that Gaillard called on Monnet to use his good offices in Washington to raise a substantial loan for the Fourth Republic. Although such a loan was secured by Monnet, there were still fears that France would not be able to participate in the first step of EEC tariff reduction and quota liberalisation at the beginning of 1959.

De Gaulle's Option

De Gaulle's coming to power later in 1958 raised the question of whether he would use the crisis conditions as a reason for effectively withdrawing France from the common market. He certainly would not have signed the EEC Treaty in the form it was finally agreed. In particular, he would not have accepted the basic rule that 'save as otherwise provided in this Treaty, the Council [of Ministers] shall act by a majority of its members' (Article 148). Nor would he have accepted the degree of initiative allowed to the Commission. He would, moreover, have insisted that the common agricultural policy be accorded more substance before the treaty's signature in March 1957, rather than being left for subsequent negotiation between member states during the transition period. Yet he was not opposed in principle to certain sacrifices of national independence to promote sensible confederal arrangements; for instance, this had already been his position in September 1952, when tentative talks were held between the RPF and the MRP in view of a rapprochement between the two parties.[13]

Faced indeed with the fait accompli of the EEC, de Gaulle decided to draw maximum advantage from it, rather than to torpedo it. His reasoning was essentially economic. He was convinced that it was in France's interest that its industry be more exposed to international competition, at least within the Europe of the Six. He also knew that French industry had considerably benefited from the real if imperfect trade liberalisation that had occurred in Europe since the beginning of the 1950s, especially through exporting to West Germany and the Benelux countries. For these reasons, as he expressed it in his *Mémoires d'espoir*, he was resolved on regaining power 'to practise' the common market:

> What counts is international competition, because it is the lever which can raise the horizons of our enterprises, compel them to pursue greater productivity, induce them to merge with one another, and gird them to fight for foreign markets; hence my resolution to practise the common market, which was then no more than a [treaty] document, by proceeding to the elimination of customs duties between the Six and by liberalising widely our trade with the rest of the world.[14]

If de Gaulle's ambitions for France on the international stage were very much shaped by geopolitical considerations, he was keenly aware that the pursuit of these ambitions depended on a strong, growing economy. But the latter could be only partly in his gift to France, for markets had their role to play.

A First Rebuff for the UK

Towards the end of 1958 two far-reaching steps were taken by de Gaulle and his government. First, in November it was announced that France no longer found it useful to pursue negotiations over the UK's plan for the creation of a free trade area (FTA) in industrial goods. It would have comprised the EEC, the UK, and other Western European states remaining outside the common market. This plan had first been proposed in February 1957, shortly before the signing of the Treaty of Rome, in the form of a British government memorandum addressed to other OEEC member states. It had led in October 1957 to the creation within that organisation of the Maudling Committee – taking its name from Reginald Maudling, the minister in the Macmillan government who headed the British delegation. The plan was formally buried in December 1958 by the French foreign minister, Couve de Murville, at what turned out to be the committee's last meeting.

The main reason for France's refusal of the British proposal, which had at least the merit of heading off Western Europe's impending internal economic division, was a fear that it could eventually lead to West Germany's abandoning the EEC and the promised common agricultural policy. There was a keen awareness in Paris that an FTA extending to most of Western Europe had long been favoured by Erhard, the German economics minister, in preference to a common market limited to the Six. As a result of Couve's veto, the UK took the lead in the setting up in January 1960 of the European Free Trade Association (EFTA), whose founding member states included also Denmark, Norway, Portugal,

Sweden, and Switzerland. EFTA was destined to a slow death, which began in 1973 when the UK and Denmark joined the EEC. By that time, the CAP had been launched, without, crucially, British participation in its shaping.

Rueff's Medicine

The second far-reaching step was taken in December 1958 and consisted of the adoption of a series of measures giving effect to a radical currency reform. Although the package came to be known as the Pinay-Rueff Plan, an entirely negative role had been played in its launching by the finance minister, the prudent Pinay, who had been appointed to his post by de Gaulle to reassure the more timorous of the saving and business classes. For Pinay ferociously opposed the controversial measures that had been planned by Jacques Rueff, de Gaulle's preferred economist and a liberal one to boot. Still acting as prime minister under the Fourth Republic, de Gaulle had to throw all his weight into the balance to push through Rueff's measures. This was in the face of the opposition of not only Pinay but also most of the rest of his government, with the exception of the ever faithful pair, Couve and Debré.

A new French franc was introduced – the *franc lourd* (worth domestically a hundred times the old one) – to convey the impression of a more solid currency. But it was set at a parity against the US dollar that represented a hefty devaluation of 17.5 per cent. The devaluation proved a success in boosting in a sustained fashion the price competitiveness of French goods abroad. Since the domestic prices of imports of foreign goods were also raised, it was to the twofold benefit of the trade balance. Because the devaluation was accompanied by a massive squeeze on domestic demand, with public expenditure slashed and taxes considerably raised, the induced gains in price competitiveness were not eroded by inflationary pressures generated by higher import prices. This had been the fate of the franc's previous devaluation in August 1957; a disguised one amounting to 20 per cent, it had been carried out by applying surcharges or premiums on, respectively, the purchase or sale of foreign exchange.

Accompanying measures included the discarding of the system of export subsidies and import surcharges, thus rendering already redundant half of the Treaty of Rome's 'Protocol relating to Certain Provisions of Concern to France'. In addition, the commitment was given that by 1 January 1960 the freeing of imports from quantitative restrictions would apply to 90 per cent of France's imports from other Western European countries, and to 50 per cent of imports from the dollar zone. This was on top of France's commitment to respect the EEC timetable for the elimination of intra-EEC customs duties in the first stage of the transitional period.

As recently as May 1958, the short-lived Pflimlin government had informed its EEC partners that France would not be in a position to implement the first round of reduction of customs duties on 1 January 1959. And in June 1957, prior to the franc's disguised devaluation, it had been decided to suspend the staged liberalisation of imports from quantitative restrictions, to which France was committed under an OEEC code. So the situation changed radically with the Pinay-Rueff Plan.

Its medium-term effect, at a time of strong economic growth across continental Western Europe, was a surge in French exports and a much improved trade balance. Before the end of the first four-year period of transition for the elimination of customs duties on intra-EEC trade, the majority of French industrialists had become persuaded of the advantages of the common market. The currency reform concocted by Rueff at de Gaulle's behest enabled France to benefit considerably from the initial trade creation generated by the progressive setting up of the customs union. Consequently, the same currency reform contributed to the firming up of France's political commitment to the EEC, and hence to the securing and consolidation of the latter's future.[15]

Securing Agricultural Interests

Pflimlin and the Green Pool

Hirsch related in his memoirs how once when he told Queuille, then prime minister, that the French agricultural sector could become a net exporting one, the venerable politician stared at him as if he were an utter fool. This meeting took place probably in the autumn of 1948.[16] Queuille had been agricultural minister in the 1930s and had held fast to the legacy of agricultural protectionism associated with the name and action of Jules Méline, a leading figure in the Third Republic. Méline's career had included periods as agricultural minister – during the 1880s and again during the First World War – and as prime minister during the Dreyfus Affair, and he was the instigator of the highly protectionist tariff law passed in 1892 which was to be long associated with his name. His legacy ran deep in the first half of the twentieth century.

The occasion of Hirsch's meeting with Queuille was connected to the revision of the Monnet Plan in 1948 and its extension by a further two years. When the modernisation plan had first been drawn up at the Commissariat Général du Plan in 1946 for the years 1947–50, Monnet had largely neglected agriculture. For developing the economy's export capacity, he had placed more hope in the raising of sales abroad of French-manufactured tractors than of agricultural produce. However, under the Schuman government, which held office between November 1947 and July 1948, certain priorities were changed. This was notably the case for agriculture, largely through the efforts of Hirsch and the MRP's Pierre Pflimlin.

Pflimlin was agricultural minister in the Schuman government, a post he kept in three further successive governments up to December 1949 and held anew, in four more governments, between June 1950 and July 1951. In 1947–48 he was instrumental in convincing Monnet of the need to channel more public investment into the sector. Linked to this adjustment of priorities was the revised plan's target for stepping up considerably agricultural exports, so as to contribute by 1952 to the elimination of the country's trade deficit. As Pflimlin put it, when speaking of his first spell as agricultural minister in 1947–49, 'exports became ... the keyword of the policy I was trying to implement'. Production of wheat, sugar beet, and dairy products was stimulated by guaranteed prices. However, there remained the problem of securing export markets. In March 1951, as a result of Pflimlin's efforts, Schuman – now foreign minister – proposed to the Council of Europe that a conference bringing together virtually all of the countries of Western Europe be convened, with a view to the setting up of a High Authority modelled on the ECSC's. The aim of the French government was that, under the tutelage of this new High Authority, European countries should extend export preferences to one another – at the expense of North America and Australasia – in respect of a limited number of products, including notably wheat.[17]

In 1950, before Schuman's proposal to the Council of Europe, the long-standing Dutch agricultural minister, Sicco Mansholt, had been floating proposals of his own for a European Board for Agriculture and Food. Some liaison took place between Mansholt and Pflimlin. The essential difference between their proposals, as Pflimlin acknowledged, was that the Dutch ones were designed to remove all barriers to intra-European agricultural trade on a level-playing-field basis, whereas the French aim was simply to assure the profitable disposal through export of national surpluses. An outcome of their two initiatives was an unsuccessful exploratory conference held in Paris in March 1952, presided over by Pflimlin, and attended by representatives of fifteen countries, including the UK. Further discussions and soundings bumbled along for a few years inconclusively, until the proposed European Agricultural Community (Pflimlin's coined name for the enterprise) or 'Green Pool' was finally abandoned as a practical project.

French Interests after Stresa

At the end of the 1950s the problems that had given rise to the Pflimlin and Mansholt proposals had not gone away. On the contrary, especially from a French standpoint, they had been seriously aggravated by the underlying trend of ever rising agricultural output, which was a quasi-automatic effect of continuing gains in agricultural productivity – a particularly striking phenomenon in the case of wheat yields.

Against this background it fell to the EEC Commission, once the Treaty of Rome entered into force, to convene a conference of member states before making its own detailed proposals for the future CAP to the Council of Ministers. The conference, held in Stresa in July 1958, proved inconclusive, which lent even more power of initiative to the agricultural commissioner, who was none other than Mansholt. Although the treaty provided for a choice between three types of common organisation of agricultural markets – the weakest consisting of no more than common rules on competition – the fact that Mansholt was at the helm, with Dutch interests in mind, increased the likelihood that the CAP would be of an ambitious kind, entailing a truly European market organisation.

This then was the situation de Gaulle inherited when he assumed the reins of power in the second half of 1958. He could see that the EEC Treaty's skeleton provisions for the setting up of a CAP offered an opportunity for France to create a more viable and prosperous future for its agricultural sector. The largest in Western Europe in terms of output, the sector still accounted for a quarter of total employment in the late 1950s. A CAP serving French interests could resolve the problem posed by growing surpluses of wheat and sugar beet and the high cost to the French Treasury of subsidising their export. For the financial burden, as he intimated in *Mémoires d'espoir*, could be placed on the shoulders of all the member states of the common market, rather than on France's alone:

> It is therefore necessary for us to export. In a world where there are large supplies of agricultural surpluses, we must do it at prices that match the needs of our producers, yet without the state being obliged to provide subsidies on a scale that would ruin its finances. I must admit that if I accepted straightaway the common market when I assumed anew control of our affairs, it was because of our condition as an agricultural country, as well as the imperative of progress for our industry.[18]

The progressive establishment of the CAP in the early years of the EEC's existence owed much to the vigorous pursuit of French interests.[19] During these years there was an effective linkage between progress in fleshing out the CAP and establishing the customs union for trade in industrial goods. By 1 July 1968 the customs union was fully in place, a year and a half ahead of schedule, and a series of single market organisations had been set up to cover practically all the agricultural products in which member states had substantial interests, the main exception being wine, for which an agreement on market organisation had to await April 1970.

However, negotiating the CAP proved an arduous and fraught affair. As to France's role, there were a number of occasions between 1961 and 1966 when de Gaulle – abetted by Couve de Murville and the agricultural minister, Edgard Pisani – exerted considerable diplomatic pressure and sometimes muscularly so. The first such occasion was at the threshold of the transitional period's second stage of tariff dismantlement, in December 1961 and January 1962, when negotiations came to a head on the question of the shape of the CAP's price-guarantee mechanisms. A second occasion was in 1964 when the level of the price of wheat (the key cereal) had to be determined by the Six for the first time. Lastly, at the threshold of the transitional period's third and final stage, the 'empty chair' crisis broke out in the second half of 1965 and spilled over into January 1966; this was when the question of the CAP's future financing arrangements became entangled with the all-important political question for de Gaulle of whether the EEC was going to be run on an essentially intergovernmental basis or a supranational one.

The Market-Organisation Agreement

The crucial package on market organisation was struck by the EEC Council of Ministers on 14 January 1962, following the procedural device of 'stopping the clock' in the diplomatic pretence that the date was still 31 December 1961. Its central feature was the interrelated price mechanisms for the organisation of the market in cereals, which was also designed to serve in varying degrees as the model for the market organisation of the other products covered by the CAP. This was the case for the market-organisation agreements for the three 'cereal-based' products – pigmeat, poultry, and eggs – which were part of the same package. Also, as part of the same package, the Council agreed to set up the European Agricultural Guidance and Guarantee Fund (best known by the acronym of its French name, FEOGA), which was to prove to be the giant devourer of EC budget funds, for agricultural price support, once it became fully independent of member states' direct contributions – that is, from 1971 onwards.

For cereals, the Six decided that the market organisation for cereals would consist of a system of 'target' and guaranteed 'intervention' prices applying to trade in cereals produced within the EEC. These prices would be internationally protected by a system of variable import levies, applied at the borders of the customs union, so as to prevent the prices of EEC-grown cereals being undercut by low-cost cereals from abroad. Of particular interest to France's wheat growers, surpluses sold outside the customs union at lower than prevailing EEC prices would be entitled to export price 'restitutions' (that is, subsidies).

What had held the cereals agreement up in 1961 was German hesitation, initially because of the Bundestag elections in September. There was the fear that import levies would be insufficient to protect Germany's own high-cost wheat producers, especially against competition from France (the lowest-cost wheat producer of the Six). De Gaulle's reaction was simple: he made clear to Adenauer in December that, in the absence of a satisfactory agreement, France would exercise its right to block the EEC's moving forward to the second four-year period of transition (by virtue of Article 8 of the Treaty). The combination of this threat with the offer to Germany of a temporary national safeguard clause opened the way to the January 1962 agreement.

The Wheat Price Agreement

The transformation of national support mechanisms into EEC ones, under the FEOGA umbrella, started at the end of July 1962 in the case of cereals and 'cereal-related' products. However, in the absence of intra-EEC price harmonisation, which required a prior agreement on the level of support and protection, single markets for the different products did not yet become operational. Initially it had been planned that common cereals prices would be fixed in time for the 1963/4 agricultural year; but, because of political delays, it was not until the 1967/8 agricultural year that common cereals prices came to be applied. The origin of these delays lay again mainly in German foot-dragging.

In January 1962 Germany had clashed with France and the Netherlands over the urgency of price harmonisation for cereals. The compromise was to freeze national price guarantees at their existing levels, to request the Commission to establish criteria for harmonisation, and to actually begin harmonisation in 1963. In the event only a small first alignment was made. In November 1963 Mansholt presented a new plan aimed at the introduction of common prices for the 1964/5 agricultural year, with the pill being sweetened for the three high-cost wheat producers – Germany, Italy and Luxembourg – by temporary compensation. But considerable disquiet prevailed in German farm circles about any plan that led to German wheat prices being substantially lowered towards the levels prevailing in the Netherlands or Belgium and a fortiori in France. In early 1964, as the government headed by Erhard began to worry about the Bundestag elections of September 1965, the word from Bonn was that there could be no cuts in farm prices before that date. A decision by the Six on harmonisation was accordingly postponed anew to the end of 1964. However, at last, in December 1964, another major CAP package agreement was struck. Germany accepted that the future EEC 'target' price for wheat should be some 10 per cent lower than the then ruling guaranteed national price. As a sop to Germany, it was agreed that the future 'target' prices for barley and rye, as well as maize, should be set relatively close to the wheat price. And it was further agreed that the introduction of the common cereals prices would not take place until 1 July 1967.

The December 1964 agreement on the future level of the price of wheat brought considerable relief to de Gaulle and his government. It followed more than a year of frictions and ill feeling between Paris and Bonn on the matter – a period that had started shortly after Erhard became Chancellor. One lever used during this period was to make clear that, as long as the wheat price question was unresolved, France would use its position in the EEC Council of Ministers to block all moves in the Kennedy Round towards the further liberalisation of international trade in industrial goods. This round of multilateral trade negotiations, held in the framework of the GATT, opened in May 1964. Its trigger was the US Trade Expansion Act of June 1962, initiated by the late American president. The French threat carried weight since a successful Kennedy Round was (correctly) perceived, especially by the free-trade Chancellor, as being very much in the interest of German industry. There was a still greater French threat, however, which was to bring the EEC to a standstill, if not to sink it altogether. The threat was hinted at by de Gaulle in his press conference of July 1964. In October, following two fruitless meetings of the Six's agricultural ministers, the other member states were informed that France would 'cease to participate in the EEC if the agricultural common market were not organised as it had been agreed it would be organised'. In this diplomatic leverage, de Gaulle had the backing of Spaak, the Belgian foreign minister. In the relative privacy of France's Council of Ministers or in his tête-à-tête conversations with Peyrefitte, the French president made no bones about his determination to force the issue to breaking point – but Erhard eventually gave way.[20]

From a French standpoint, what had been secured for the foreseeable future was a CAP that would meet the problem of rising wheat surpluses, to the advantage of the country's public finances and its balance of payments. But de Gaulle had no particular sympathy for the main beneficiaries, the big wheat growers of the Paris Basin – the vast area, including the country's largest farms, extending from the great plain of Beauce around Chartres in the south-west to Picardy in the north and to Champagne and the edge of Burgundy in the east. In his opinion, these wheat growers, as well as the sugar-beet growers in the north of France, were all too ready to use the FNSEA (Fédération Nationale des Syndicats d'Exploitants Agricoles) – the powerful national farming umbrella association – as a pressure group for their own particular interests; while they disregarded the needs of the country's economically disadvantaged small farmers, especially to the south of the Loire.[21]

The 'Empty Chair' Crisis and the Luxembourg Compromise

The last of the three major occasions on which de Gaulle intervened personally over the shaping of the CAP was of a quite different nature from the first two. Economic considerations were no longer to the fore, and the conflict of interests was no longer one that put primarily France and

Germany at loggerheads with one another. The immediate cause of what came to be called the 'empty chair' crisis was the Commission's tabling of its proposals for implementing the CAP's new financing arrangements from 1 July 1967. The Commission made its move in May 1965 when France held the half-year presidency of the EEC Council of Ministers. That the source of the financing of CAP expenditure should be the EEC's 'own resources' – initially the proceeds of customs duties and agricultural import levies – was quite acceptable to France. But what was not acceptable was that the EEC Commission had presented its proposals earlier to the Assembly in Strasbourg, rather than to the Council of Ministers, and had included among these proposals an increase in the Assembly's powers, so as to give it a share of control over the use of the EEC's 'own resources'.

At the beginning of 1965 de Gaulle had already been expressing disquiet about what he took to be the pretensions of the Commission's president, Hallstein, to transform the EEC into a supranational federation, with the Commission as its putative government. And he foretold that Hallstein would use the CAP financing issue to advance this cause, especially since 1965 was a year of presidential elections in France and French farmers were pushing for the launching of the CAP. However, seeking to turn a difficulty to his advantage, the French president chose not only to refuse the Commission's proposals, but also to engineer a full-blown crisis over the EEC's modus operandi as an international institution. According to the Treaty of Rome, the basis of the decision making of the Council of Ministers in a number of policy areas was to due to change from unanimity to qualified majority voting (QMV) at the beginning of the third stage of the transitional period (that is, on 1 January 1966). This was notably the case for the CAP (Article 43). Gaulle's resolve was now to block this change.

To this end, all compromise was rejected on the CAP financing issue, and in Brussels in the early hours of the morning on 1 July 1965, at the very end of the French presidency, Couve de Murville informed the Council of Ministers that any further discussions were pointless. Later that day Peyrefitte announced that, because of the 'serious crisis', France would no longer be represented at any meeting of the Council of Ministers, and that its Permanent Representative in Brussels was being withdrawn. So began the 'empty chair' crisis.[22]

It was resolved only in late January 1966 at a special meeting of the foreign ministers of the Six held in Luxembourg. A compromise of sorts was agreed. The key words in the agreement gave official recognition to a difference of position between France and the other Five:

> Where, in the case of decisions which may be taken by majority vote on a pro-
> posal of the Commission, very important interests of one or more partners are
> at stake, the members of the Council will endeavour, within a reasonable time,

to reach solutions which can be adopted by all the members of the Council while respecting their mutual interests and those of the Community ... [though] the French delegation considers that where very important interests are at stake the discussions must be continued until unanimous agreement is reached.

The foreign ministers openly acknowledged that such words could not prevent new difficulties arising at a later date. Yet they agreed that the EEC's work would be 'resumed in accordance with the normal procedure'.[23]

Instead of a protocol modifying the treaty's provisions for the use of QMV, for which no unanimous agreement would have been forthcoming on the part of the Six, what was decided in Luxembourg was no more than a fudge. But it was a long-lasting one, since voting on the basis of unanimity remained the normal practice of the Council of Ministers for a further two decades. By thwarting Hallstein's political ambitions and successfully defending the cause of intergovernmentalism, de Gaulle was the victor in the 1965–66 diplomatic crisis.

The Luxembourg Compromise was to be watered down when the SEA came into effect in 1987. QMV then became mandatory for measures bringing about 'the completion of the internal market' – a long overdue task, so the European Council had decided by the 1980s, in view of the failure after so many years to implement fully the EEC Treaty's original design for a properly functioning common market.

De Gaulle – apart from his determination in the 1960s to secure a special, highly interventionist regime for agriculture – had shown some favour for the common market design as originally laid out in the 1957 treaty. This was marked by his rejection of any policy of defensive industrial protectionism for France. The injection in the closing decades of the century of a new breath of economic liberalism into the common market, which was made possible by the SEA's watering down of the Luxembourg Compromise, figures in the next chapter, and it was at least in the spirit of the sort of economic policies championed under de Gaulle by the independent-minded Rueff.

Notes

1. For the Beyen Plan, see Harryvan and van der Harst (eds), *Documents on European Union*, 71–74.
2. For the Beyan Plan in the context of foreign-trade trends in Western Europe in the first half of the 1950s, see especially Milward, *The European Rescue of the Nation-State*, 119–96.
3. The start of Monnet's captivation with the idea of a new European Community for the regulation of civil nuclear power may be precisely dated to January 1955 – see Duchêne, *Jean Monnet*, 264–66.
4. For the text of the Messina Resolution, see Harryvan and van der Harst (eds), *Documents on European Union*, 92–94. Edgar Faure claimed in his memoirs that he was favourable

to the Benelux memorandum, and that Pinay's conduct of negotiations in Messina matched his own position. However, he made no distinction between the memorandum's two elements: the one from Beyen and the other from Monnet. As to Monnet's staying on as president of the ECSC High Authority, Faure asserted that Adenauer was opposed to such an extension, having come to be disenchanted with the Frenchman's idiosyncratic style of heading an international organisation. See Edgar Faure, *Mémoires*, 2 vols, Paris, 1982–84, vol. 2, 204–17.

5. For the French government memorandum, see Marjolin, *Le Travail d'une vie*, 283–86; Bossuat, *Faire l'Europe sans défaire la France*, 60–65. Hostility to the Spaak Report was clearly manifest among senior civil servants at the ministry for economic and financial affairs, particularly on the economic side, and also in the person of the minister himself, Ramadier – see the documents published in Bossuat, *Faire l'Europe sans défaire la France*, 328–33, 338–40, 348–51.

6. For Marjolin's own account of the negotiations, see *Le Travail d'une vie*, 294–303.

7. Monnet, *Memoirs*, 300 [*Mémoires*, 434–35]. In September 1943, serving as commissioner for communications and the merchant navy on the Algiers-based CFLN, Mayer had put to paper extended reflections on Europe's post-war future. His central proposal was the creation of a Western European federation comprising France, the Benelux countries, and a new Rhineland state (including the Ruhr), and one of its advantages would be that the financial burden of developing infrastructure in France's colonies could be shared out – for Mayer's 1943 document, see Bossuat, *Faire l'Europe sans défaire la France*, 233–37.

8. See Defferre's letter to Mollet, dated 17 May 1956, in Bossuat, *Faire l'Europe sans défaire la France*, 341–47.

9. Pierre Uri, *Penser pour l'action. Un fondateur de l'Europe*, Paris, 1991, 112–37. He claimed paternity for the following: the original Benelux memorandum (bringing together his own improved version of the Beyen Plan and Monnet's atomic energy proposals, the latter embodied in a memorandum he, Uri, had written); essentially all of the Spaak Report; and many of the provisions of the EEC Treaty, including the formula for setting up the common external tariff, the formula for the elimination of trade quotas, the arrangements for the association of overseas countries and territories, and the rules for qualified majority voting (QMV) by the Council of Ministers. Uri also prided himself in having invented the concept of the value added tax (VAT) – ibid., 48–51.

10. Duchêne, *Jean Monnet*, 299.

11. P.M.H. Bell, *France and Britain 1940–1994: The Long Separation*, Harlow, 1997, 155–58; Francis M.B. Lynch, *France and the International Economy: From Vichy to the Treaty of Rome*, London, 1997, 178–80.

12. Marjolin, *Le Travail d'une vie*, 286–91.

13. Lacouture, *De Gaulle*, vol. 2, 389–92.

14. De Gaulle, *Mémoires d'espoir*, vol. 1, 143.

15. Lacouture, *De Gaulle*, vol. 2, 665–78. See also Leland B. Yeager, *International Monetary Relations: Theory, History, and Policy*, New York, 1966, 398–401.

16. Hirsch, *Ainsi va la vie*, 98, 122.

17. Pierre Pflimlin, *Mémoires d'un Européen. De la IVe à la Ve République*, Paris, 1991, 30–51; Milward, *The European Rescue of the Nation-State*, 242–48, 251–53, 265–78, 284–308; Lynch, *France and the International Economy*, 146–68. Pflimlin was briefly prime minister in May 1958, before handing over to de Gaulle. In May 1962, by which time he had become mayor of Strasbourg as well as overseas cooperation minister, Pflimlin led the resignation from the government of five MRP ministers. It was in protest against de Gaulle's public mocking of a supranational Europe and, more pointedly, of the two European parliamentary assemblies based in Strasbourg. The French president had spoken of the largely meaningless existence of the Consultative Assembly of the Council of Europe, borrowing sardonically a line from Racine's *Phèdre*, in which Phèdre herself tells of her sister, Ariadne: '*qui, me dit-on, se meurt aux bords où elle fut laissée*' ('who, I am

told, is at the point of death on the shores where she was abandoned'); derided by him was what he perceived as the pretensions of the EC's Assembly to turn itself into a proper parliament – see de Gaulle, *Discours et messages*, vol. 3, 406–9. In March 1958 the EC's Assembly had decided to call itself the European Parliamentary Assembly; then in March 1962 it renamed itself as simply the European Parliament, though it was not until the SEA, quarter of a century later, that it was recognised as such under treaty law. The incident marked the MRP's demise as a party of government – see Pflimlin, *Mémoires d'un Européen*, 210–20.

18. De Gaulle, *Mémoires d'espoir*, vol. 1, 167.

19. 'Un jeune exportateur aux dents longues' ('A young exporter with high ambitions') was a subheading denoting France's rising agricultural ambitions in Pierre Drouin, *L'Europe du Marché commun*, Paris, 1963, 98–101 – coming from the pen of an influential *Le Monde* journalist, it said something about the spirit of the times.

20. On this diplomatic forcing, see de Gaulle, *Discours et messages*, vol. 4, 230; Peyrefitte, *C'était de Gaulle*, vol. 2, 231–32, 237, 248–49, 250–56, 263–64, 265–70, 271–74; Vaïsse, *La Grandeur*, 551–53.

21. Peyrefitte, *C'était de Gaulle*, vol. 2, 298, 300–1, 356–59, 373–74.

22. De Gaulle, *Discours et messages*, vol. 4, 377–81; Peyrefitte, *C'était de Gaulle*, vol. 2, 281–301; Vaïsse, *La Grandeur*, 553–60.

23. Harryvan and van der Harst (eds), *Documents on European Union*, 151–52.

Chapter 6

Moving from Dirigisme to Qualified Economic Liberalism

As from the second half of the 1970s, the thrust of economic policy making in France became less dirigiste, though there was certainly never any question of the state's self-effacement before the dictates of the market. The EC internal-market programme, launched in 1985, accorded with the general direction of such policy and, for the greater part, with French interests. Not only EC membership but also the forces of globalisation contributed to a far-reaching reorientation of foreign trade. Yet doubts about the virtues of economic liberalism persisted, and these were to surface spectacularly in France's rejection of the EU's constitutional treaty in 2005.

The Watering Down of Post-war Dirigisme

Economic Liberalism and the 'Social Market Economy'

The framers of the EEC Treaty, when they carried out their negotiations in 1956–57, did not have an economic 'fortress Europe' in mind – even if, in the case of agriculture, the CAP turned out in the 1960s to be built on fortress lines. Under the rules of the GATT (specifically its Article XXIV treating of customs unions and free trade areas), it was incumbent upon EEC member states to ensure that the trade barriers facing third countries, after the transitional period, were not 'on the whole' higher than those previously in effect. And the treaty's signatories averred, in the rhetoric of the Preamble, that the EEC should 'contribute, by means of a common commercial policy, to the progressive abolition of restrictions on international trade'.

This ambition for international trade was one to which France formally subscribed. Intra-OEEC trade liberalisation in the late 1940s and 1950s had gone hand in hand with tariff cutting by the industrial countries of the West in the framework of GATT multilateral trade negotiations. Now, in the 1960s, the establishment of the EEC's customs union was to be accompanied by further steps in the liberalisation of international trade under GATT auspices, first through the Dillon Round (1960–61) and then, more importantly, the Kennedy Round (1963–67). The progress achieved in the 1960s – and subsequently through the Tokyo Round (1973–79) and then the Uruguay Round (1986–94) – was facilitated by the centralisation of diplomacy on the European side, by virtue of the Treaty of Rome's 'common commercial policy', under the authority of the EC Council of Ministers. Leaving aside agriculture, the French voice on the Council tended to be a positive one. Under the Fifth Republic, from the time of de Gaulle, successive French governments were little tempted to turn their back on the benefits of international trade.[1]

As to the design of a common market, the heart of the EEC Treaty lay from the outset in its provisions for free movement of goods, services, persons, and capital, and in its rules on competition. The spirit of these provisions and rules was a tempered economic liberalism, and their framework was a well defined legal order. The treaty had also a social dimension, even if its social policy provisions fell far short of the initial French demands for social harmonisation. These social provisions were not intended to nullify the active play of market forces, but rather to set certain limits and correct their play. If the economic philosophy underlying the earlier design of the ECSC might be alternatively described as Saint-Simonian or Rooseveltian in the 'New Deal' mode, the implicit economic philosophy of the EEC was above all that of the German 'social market economy' (*Soziale Marktwirtschaft*). Some of the leading 'social market economy' theorists, notably Wilhelm Röpke and Erhard himself, belonged to the so-called *Ordo* school of liberal thought.[2] They would have preferred a wider European free trade area or customs union, instead of the common market comprising the Six alone. Their thinking marked, nonetheless, the EEC Treaty. Close in spirit to the *Ordo* theorists on the French side was Rueff, the economist called upon by de Gaulle in 1958 to recommend, successfully, the appropriate policy mix enabling France to benefit from EEC tariff dismantlement.

Yet after 1958 de Gaulle remained convinced that the type of indicative economic planning pioneered by Monnet in the immediate post-war period could still serve France well. It had been at his personal behest that Monnet had set up the Commissariat Général du Plan, and, during the few years when the GPRF was in place, economic and administrative reform – highly dirigiste in nature – had borne real fruit. Hence it was scarcely surprising that the General should hark back to the practice of this earlier time. In his *Mémoires d'espoir*, he declared grandiloquently that the preparation and implementation of the five-year plan had become on his return to power an 'ardent obligation'.[3]

However, during de Gaulle's years at the head of the Fifth Republic, which largely overlapped with the EEC's transitional period, the French economy became progressively more open. Quasi-autarky had been abandoned towards the end of the 1940s through France's participation in the ERP and OEEC trade liberalisation, and, already in the 1950s, France's foreign trade had grown very rapidly. The trade creation resulting from the establishment of the customs union led to a still more open economy in the course of the 1960s. In 1958, the year before the start to the abolition of intra-EEC customs duties, France's exports of goods and services had been the equivalent of just over 11 per cent of GDP. In the next eleven years, as the EEC became a reality, the average annual increase in the volume of exports lay between 9 and 10 per cent, well above the (impressively high) average annual increase in GDP of between 5 and 6 per cent in the same period. By 1970 exports of goods and services amounted to the equivalent of nearly 16 per cent of GDP.[4]

As external trade became ever more important, indicative economic planning became an ever more difficult task. Already in 1965 the head of the Commissariat Général du Plan, Pierre Massé, had pointed to the need for a rethinking of French planning methods because of the much more open nature of the economy.[5] Whereas the centralised coordination of production and investment decisions in a largely closed economy recovering from the aftermath of war could make strong practical sense, it became less so to the extent that economic decision making was increasingly shaped by external demand over which no French government or planning body could exercise control.

Dirigisme was not just the national economic plan. During his five years as President of the Republic – and earlier as prime minister – Pompidou attached great importance to government intervention in the industrial sector, so as to modernise further the economy and enhance its international competitiveness. At the start of his presidency in 1969, he aimed to double France's industrial output within the space of ten years, and to bring the country level with West Germany as an industrial power. Although some of the policies were pursued in the framework of the VIth Plan (1971–75), the sort of planning involved was quite different from that practised by Monnet and Hirsch under the Fourth Republic. The locus of policy decision making was no longer the Commissariat Général du Plan but rather the Elysée, where Pompidou drew on the expertise of his industrial-affairs adviser, Bernard Esambert, as well as on his own past professional experience in the service of the Paris house of Rothschilds. Pompidou also relied on an active industry minister, François-Xavier Ortoli, until the latter became president of the EC Commission in 1973 – the first of the two Frenchmen to have held this post, the second being Jacques Delors. The fruits of Pompidou's interventionism included the successful encouragement of a wave of mergers, helped by tax incentives and interest-rate subsidies, which rationalised in varying degrees the structures of major industries including steel, non-ferrous metals, chemicals, glass, and mechanical and electrical engineering.

Yet the Fifth Republic's second president believed in giving the market economy more of a free rein than did the first. 'For Pompidou', wrote a perceptive observer, 'the state should not protect the economy from the market. For de Gaulle, the state should take charge of both the one and the other.'[6] Peyrefitte's witticism was a little exaggerated, since the Fifth Republic's founder had prescribed EEC competition as a bracing remedy for French industrial lethargy, and, under both presidents, the French economy continued to be run largely on dirigiste lines. Yet it was true that Pompidou was better disposed to the private-sector world of business and finance than was his predecessor, and such a disposition fitted well with the continued and rapid opening of the French economy (exports of goods and services rising to the equivalent of 21 per cent of GDP in 1974; by 2000, at the turn of the century, the figure was to be 29 per cent).

The Giscard–Barre Tandem

Pompidou's life was cut short by cancer, and his sudden death in April 1974 coincided with the end of an economic era. The 1973–74 international oil price shock, resulting from a quintupling of the dollar-denominated price of crude oil, contributed to a major change in economic conditions. It marked the end of continental Western Europe's long post-war period of fast economic growth – '*les trente glorieuses*' years in French parlance. Any person elected at this particular juncture was therefore bound for a difficult time, and so it proved for Giscard d'Estaing.

The second round of the May 1974 presidential elections, which pitted him against Mitterrand, resulted in a narrow victory for Giscard. The new President of the Republic had served as finance and economic-affairs minister in 1962–66, when still in his thirties, and again in 1969–74 (as economics and finance minister, a slight change of title). Yet he was not a Gaullist. By family background he belonged to that part of the French establishment best described as the moneyed Orleanist aristocracy; rooted in the nineteenth century, they cultivated a liberalism in economic as well as in political matters. Obliged because of the need for broad parliamentary backing to appoint a Gaullist as prime minister, Giscard opted for Chirac. Having made this choice, he tended initially to put his economic liberalism on hold, seeking to prove his liberal credentials instead on the social front – for instance, liberalising abortion. But the changed economic conditions in the first two years of his presidency called for a bolder approach to economic policy. The post-1974 slowdown in economic growth and the attendant sharp rise in unemployment resulted in a deterioration in the country's public finances, limiting the state's capacity for intervention; and double-digit inflation was calling for more fundamental remedies than those afforded by administrative price controls. Furthermore, the constraints on domestic demand heightened the need to promote France's international competitiveness and make it the leading economic-policy aim; and this entailed a more extensive acceptance of market principles.

The change came in September 1976. Following Chirac's resignation – a tempestuous affair – Giscard called upon Raymond Barre to take over. The new prime minister also assumed the post of economics and finance minister. He had served beforehand as foreign trade minister, and had given proof of a technical competence and a measured liberalism that accorded well with the president's own economic views. At Matignon – the town mansion harbouring the office of prime minister – he was now responsible for a concerted effort to swing economic policy in a more market-oriented and less dirigiste direction.

Barre, indeed, turned out to be a pivotal figure for the course of French economic policy making in the last quarter of the twentieth century. His liberalism marked a real break with the strong leaning towards state interventionism, so characteristic of the post-war period until then. Yet his liberalism was neither that of the unbridled free marketeer nor that of the *Ordo* school. As a university professor of political economy, he considered that his masters were John Maynard Keynes, Joseph Schumpeter, and François Perroux. He acknowledged a further debt, for his political thought, to Alexis de Tocqueville and Alexandre Kojève – the latter's disquisitions between 1933 and 1939 on Hegel's philosophy before a small regular audience, including Aron and Marjolin, had been an unusual, rich feature of pre-war Parisian intellectual life. Barre's intellectual convictions included a belief in the fundamental importance of the state in its provision of the legal and administrative framework for economic activity and, more generally, for civil society.

This was a belief that Barre brought to Matignon after considerable experience of public service. In the 1950s he had worked in the economic and finance ministry's external economic relations division alongside Kojève, who by then had forsaken the teaching of Hegel to become the ministry's leading adviser on GATT matters. In 1959–62 Barre entered the political domain, serving as *directeur de cabinet* for the industry minister, Jean-Marcel Jeanneney. In 1967 he was dispatched by de Gaulle to Brussels to become EC commissioner for economic and financial affairs, effectively in succession to Marjolin, where he stayed for four years. At the Commission he was influenced by German economic thinking. In particular, he was persuaded of the benefits of liberalising international payments through the abolition of exchange controls. If Barre was not a convert to the German *Ordo* school of economic liberals – which had links with France through Rueff and the Mont Pèlerin Society – he was certainly a subscriber to the idea, loosely defined, of a 'social market economy'.[7]

In the five years of Barre's premiership, the measured economic liberalism he espoused was manifest in the measures introduced by the government to improve the functioning of price mechanisms and hence the play of market forces across the economy. All remaining price controls on industrial products were abolished in 1978, and some price deregulation took place in the services sector. Public-sector enterprises were encouraged to adopt a more market-oriented approach. Thus, they were allowed more independence, and a stricter attitude was taken towards the disbursement of government subsidies. To foster competitive and non-inflationary price-setting, new powers were introduced to prevent the abuse of monopoly or oligopoly power; this was a deliberate move towards the spirit of the German economic model, with its strong anti-cartel bias, which had influenced the drafting of the EEC Treaty's rules on competition.

Another area for reform when Barre entered Matignon was monetary policy. In line with similar developments in the UK, Germany, and Italy in the second half of the 1970s, the targeting of aggregate money supply was introduced as a key instrument for reducing inflation. Furthermore, exchange-control restrictions were eased, even if to a very limited extent compared with the situation across the Channel, where Margaret Thatcher's radical dismantling of exchange controls in 1979 aligned the UK with Germany. In a longer-term perspective, Barre's goal was the realisation of freedom for capital movements and the related lifting of virtually all French exchange-control restrictions – formally within the EEC, effectively *erga omnes*. With this aim, he strongly backed Giscard d'Estaing's partnership with the German Chancellor, Schmidt, for the launching of the EMS in 1978–79. And Schmidt himself attached considerable importance to Barre's support.[8]

Yet such economic policy was bearing little political fruit as the 1981 presidential elections loomed into view. Although economic growth recovered in 1976–80, albeit modestly, the second oil shock occurred in 1979–80. It led to renewed inflationary pressures. A tightening of both fiscal and monetary policies then contributed to a sharp economic slowdown. If one feature of Giscard d'Estaing's defeat by Mitterrand in May 1981 was the outgoing president's hauteur in the face of alleged scandal (notably the affair of the Bokassa diamonds), another was the economy's renewed sluggishness and a surge in unemployment. Nonetheless, despite Giscard's defeat, a direction had been set for economic liberalisation. It was abandoned by the Socialist-led government at the beginning of Mitterrand's first seven-year term, but that proved only a pause.

Further Economic Liberalisation under Fabius, Chirac, and Rocard

The foolhardy turn given to economic policy in 1981–82 was in fulfilment of pledges made in the *Cent dix propositions*, the presidential-election campaign programme. With its vein of neo-Marxism in the matter of economic analysis, which owed much to the faction within the PS led by Jean-Pierre Chevènement, the programme was far removed in inspiration from the 'social market economy' policies pursued in West Germany by Schmidt, then at the head of an increasingly fragile SPD–FDP coalition government. A policy of vigorous fiscal expansion was aimed to stimulate economic growth, almost regardless of the consequences for the foreign balance. To transform economic structures and to raise the long-term level of fixed investment, the Nationalisation Act of February 1982 brought into public ownership five large industrial groups, a host of banks, and the country's two powerful financial holding companies, Compagnie Financière de Suez and Compagnie Financière de Paribas. This was to add to the wide-ranging nationalisations carried out in 1944–46 by the GPRF under very different political and economic circumstances.

Apart from some worthwhile industrial restructuring in the framework of the nationalisations, the Socialist economic strategy did not meet with success. By the middle of 1982 the prime minister, Pierre Mauroy, and the economics and finance minister, Delors, had begun to question the strategy because of its adverse short-term effects, including a marked deterioration in the balance-of-payments current account. However, the President of the Republic still remained to be persuaded of the necessity of a change of course. And it was only in March 1983, at a moment of foreign-exchange crisis, that Mitterrand acknowledged that an expansionary economic policy could not be pursued in France if it were out of line with the broad thrust of macroeconomic policy elsewhere in the EEC and, in particular, in West Germany. French economic and monetary policies became henceforth systematically geared to an EMS exchange-rate target. Delors had now more scope to rein in inflation and encourage a more export-led pattern of growth on Barre-like lines. But he had little more than a year left in office as economics and finance minister before being appointed president of the EC Commission.

When Laurent Fabius became prime minister in July 1984, with a government that no longer included any ministers from the PCF, economic liberalisation benefited from an unexpected lease of life. He and the new economics and finance minister, Pierre Bérégovoy, had been among the leading opponents of the Delors–Mauroy line prior to March 1983. Indeed until then Fabius had been the confidently expansionist budget minister – in principle, but not in practice, subordinate to Delors – after which he was elevated by Mitterrand to the post of industry minister, to be again at odds with Delors. Now, in the changing climate of the mid-1980s, Fabius and

Bérégovoy paid a tribute of sorts to their Brussels-bound former colleague by effectively renouncing the spirit of their earlier ambitions for the economy.

Thus, partly on German prompting, the new government decided to relax certain exchange-control restrictions in the second half of 1984, including those on outward direct investment to other EC member states, and such restrictions were further eased at the end of 1985. In the latter year, to make for more competitive energy pricing, price controls were lifted in the domestic petroleum-product market; and the quasi-monopoly enjoyed by French refineries was broken. At the end of 1985, building on the Barre government's start to the renovation of monetary policy, Bérégovoy initiated the replacement of the long established system of quantitative credit controls – which were a bête noire of Rueff in the past – with a policy entailing a more active use of central-bank interest rates and minimum-reserve requirements for commercial banks. Furthermore, in the course of 1985, with a view to making Paris a major financial centre, Bérégovoy pushed forward various financial-market innovations, including the opening of the money market to non-financial enterprises and the creation of a financial futures market.

The Fifth Republic's first *cohabitation* government held office from March 1986 to May 1988. By then economic liberalism had become widely fashionable. Even what was subsumed under the label of Reaganism or Thatcherism had its supporters in France, as witness the neo-liberalism now espoused by the PR (the party created in 1977 to serve Giscard d'Estaing's interests). The new government, with Chirac as prime minister and Edouard Balladur as economics and finance minister, introduced an ambitious privatisation programme. Although both were neo-Gaullists from the Pompidou stable and believers in a strong state, they wished to unshackle the economy from the excesses of dirigisme. Yet, apart from privatisation, their measures of economic liberalisation were largely in line with the previous efforts of Fabius and Bérégovoy. The government *ordonnance* of 9 December 1986 swept away virtually all remaining price controls – those related to healthcare being the main exception – and the Conseil de la Concurrence was set up to regulate competition. Abrogated was the *ordonnance* of 30 June 1945 that created France's post-war system of price controls. Before the end of 1986 more exchange-control restrictions were lifted. Outward direct investment was totally freed; residents were allowed to transfer funds abroad for financial and real-estate investment purposes; and the administrative control of business firms' trade-related foreign-currency transactions was abolished. Various financial-market measures deregulated further the money and bond markets and increased banking competition. The wide-ranging economic liberalisation achieved during these two years of the first *cohabitation* government was largely the work of Balladur, who won international repute as an innovative finance minister and also emerged as a major national political figure.

After Mitterrand's reelection in May 1988 for a second seven-year term and the relatively favourable results for him of the ensuing snap legislative elections, Michel Rocard became prime minister at the head of a predominantly Socialist government, and Bérégovoy returned as economics and finance minister. Economic liberalisation remained the order of the day. The last remaining exchange-control restrictions of significance were lifted at the end of 1989. Residents were allowed to open foreign-currency bank accounts abroad. And French banks were freed of all restrictions in extending franc-denominated loans to non-residents. The liberalisation of payments for these two types of financial transaction completed France's long overdue implementation of the EEC Treaty's provisions for freedom of movement for capital. This was six months ahead of the deadline set by the EC Directive of June 1988.

The Long Wave of Privatisation

After the partial halt dictated by Mitterrand on his winning the 1988 presidential elections, large-scale privatisation proceeded anew from 1993 onwards. Tellingly, the appointment of Lionel Jospin as prime minister in 1997 at the head of a Socialist-led *cohabitation* government did not stop privatisation (now called 'capital opening'), despite earlier electoral promises to the contrary. Thus, after a short pause, the nationalisations of 1944–46 and 1981–82 continued to be rolled back. By the middle of the first decade of the twenty-first century, non-financial enterprises left wholly in the hands of the state were confined largely to the activities of nuclear energy (processing and engineering), the postal services, and railway transport. Yet many of the privatisations carried out since 1986 were not outright ones. The state kept controlling interests in leading companies across a wide swathe of sectors, including, for example, telecommunications (through a majority stake in France Télécom), electricity and gas, and the aerospace and defence industries. Indeed, because of shareholdings of this kind, the level of public ownership in France remained very high by international standards. Compared with the type of public ownership associated with the nationalisations of the GPRF and early Mitterrand periods, much had changed, however. Even if only partially privatised, companies were expected henceforth to assume full responsibility for their management and gain competitive advantage.

The receipts from privatisation in the twenty years since 1986 served partly to reduce the stock of government debt. This became an imperative in the second half of the 1990s because of the requirements of the Maastricht Treaty's public-finance convergence criteria; their fulfilment was a precondition for EMU and the launching of the euro. But the fundamental reason for privatisation lay elsewhere. In step with the economic liberalisation and deregulation initiated by the Barre government in the second half of the 1970s and continued by both left-wing and right-wing governments in the 1980s, the underlying driving force was the ever increasing integration of the national economy into the wider European economy and, indeed, into the global economy. By the 1990s public finance could no longer provide the additional capital required by the larger public-sector enterprises to drive their modernisation and expansion on keenly competitive international markets. Equity funding had become an imperative, and so dirigisme was further weakened.

Delors and the Single Market

The Renewed Search for Economic Growth

Already by the time of the Fabius government, the partial retreat from dirigisme had become enmeshed with efforts in the EC to give effect to central provisions of the Treaty of Rome that had never been properly implemented. In view of the weak economic growth in the EC area in the second half of the 1970s and early 1980s, this failed implementation had come to be viewed as a costly mistake. The blueprint for the new efforts was the Commission's White Paper entitled 'Completing the Internal Market', which was approved by the European Council at its meeting in Milan in June 1985. The institutional decision-making means for implementing the White Paper's three hundred or so proposals, namely the mandatory use of QMV by the Council of Ministers, was provided by the Single European Act. This treaty brought together in a single act – hence its name – provisions amending the EC treaties and, secondly, provisions for European cooperation in the sphere of foreign policy. It was signed in February 1986 and, after completion of the ratification process, came into force in July 1987. By virtue of the SEA (Article 13), which defines the internal market as 'an area without internal frontiers in which the free movement of goods, services, persons, and capital is ensured', the internal market had to be progressively completed by the White Paper's proposed deadline of 31 December 1992.[9]

Two of the major initiatives underpinning the ambition of the completed internal market – also called the single market – may be associated with France, or at least with French political figures. First, the White Paper of June 1985 was the flagship initiative of Delors as incoming president of the Commission. Like Roy Jenkins – his predecessor but one, who had been at the origin of the EMS initiative – Delors deemed it politic to push forward one well focused high-profile initiative at the start of his presidency. Secondly, the SEA originated in the work of the 'ad hoc' committee on institutional reform set up on a proposal from Mitterrand at the Fontainebleau meeting of the European Council in June 1984. Although it came to be called the Dooge Committee after the name of its

Irish chairman, the committee's most influential member was its rapporteur, Maurice Faure. This Radical politician was the same person who had headed France's delegation at the EEC and Euratom inter-governmental negotiations in 1956–57, and had subsequently helped persuade the National Assembly to ratify the Rome Treaties. Personally chosen by Mitterrand to be France's representative on the committee, Faure contributed much to its work and conclusions. Already at its second meeting, he proposed a draft report that had been approved by Mitterrand beforehand. It became the Dooge Committee's working document and served to shape the preliminary version of its proposals, which were presented to the European Council in December 1984.[10]

Yet the French mark on the internal-market programme should not be exaggerated. The more far-reaching suggestions made by the Dooge Committee in the matter of the internal market came above all from the British participants. Furthermore, it was an indirect tribute to the innovative nature at the time of British economic policy that the Commission's seminal White Paper was prepared in the first half of 1985 under the authority and guidance of Lord Cockfield, the British EC commissioner responsible for the internal market and taxation, who had previously served in the Thatcher government, initially as Secretary of State for Trade.

That, in this matter, a British Conservative of Thatcherite persuasions should become the right-hand man of the French Socialist heading the EC Commission might appear a little incongruous. It reflected, however, an economic-policy consensus that predated the formation of the Delors Commission. The perceived need to practise more resolutely liberal policies at European level owed much to the widespread recognition, already in the early 1980s, that the EEC was no longer providing a favourable framework for economic growth. For, after the early success in setting up the customs union, there had been a failure to proceed further in the 1970s and create a true common market – free of internal non-tariff barriers, with freedom of movement not only for goods but also for services and capital, not to speak of persons. Tellingly, in January 1983 the Council of Ministers decided on a new variant for itself in the form of a regular Internal Market Council, bringing together the appropriate member-state government ministers. Then, in June 1983, the European Council at its meeting in Stuttgart issued its 'Solemn Declaration on European Union'. Although the declaration focused mainly on the European Council's self-assumed role as the provider of the 'general political impulse to the construction of Europe', it also included a commitment to the internal market. This same concern on the part of EC member states to impart a fresh momentum to economic growth, through establishing a properly functioning internal market, had encouraged the Commission itself, presided by Gaston Thorn, to address the issue. And it had reported to the Council of Ministers before the European Council's

Stuttgart meeting. Subsequently, in June 1984, the same month as the Dooge Committee was set up, the Commission addressed a Communication to the Council of Ministers entitled 'Consolidating the Internal Market' and putting forward a series of proposals to be implemented before the end of 1985. In short, Delors's arrival in Brussels in January 1985 announced a change of regime at the Commission's headquarters, rather than a season of spring for altogether new ideas. The merit of the White Paper of June 1985 was that it was well drafted conceptually and had a determinedly practical focus, while Delors's role as an able and forceful Commission president was to ensure that it was given real political effect.[11]

It might appear that France surrendered the substance of the Luxembourg Compromise of January 1966 when it agreed at the European Council meeting in December 1985 to adopt the SEA, since it thereby committed itself to the use of QMV by the Council of Ministers for most of the measures required for completing the internal market, including decisions on the harmonisation of national legislations (SEA Article 18). Arguably, however, no such surrender occurred. What France effectively agreed was to sacrifice independence for a wide range of decisions concerning freedom of movement for goods, persons, services, and capital. Since it was generally in France's interest to have a completed internal market or single market, it was in France's interest that the EC decision-making machinery be adequate to the task. For the task was a daunting one in view of the huge quantity of legislation that had to be passed at EC and national level in advance of the deadline set for the end of 1992. A refusal of the task would have been to deny much of the purpose of the change of direction of economic policy that had started under Giscard d'Estaing and the Barre government, and that was still under way under the Fabius government when the SEA was negotiated and signed. With the exception of changes in indirect taxation (for which unanimity was still required), the measures to be taken by the Council of Ministers were scarcely of a kind to warrant, in the words of the Luxembourg Compromise itself, that 'discussion must be continued until unanimous agreement is reached'.[12]

Mitterrand's view of the SEA insofar as it bore upon the internal-market programme was pragmatic. The erosion of national independence represented by the SEA's provisions for QMV was judged to be limited and sufficiently well ring-fenced. On the other hand, the French president had no enthusiasm for strengthening institutionally the EC for its own sake. This was demonstrated by his own Eureka initiative in 1985–86, when he showed that he wanted to keep European economic cooperation in the domain of high technology free from EC control and QMV procedures, especially when such cooperation related to security or defence.

Mitterrand was persuaded of the desirability of high-technology cooperation in early 1985 by his special adviser, Jacques Attali. The international context was Ronald Reagan's 'star wars' Strategic Defence Initiative (SDI) for a space-based anti-missile defence system, to which the French president was opposed for politico-strategic reasons. However, he was convinced, like his American counterpart, that space technology opened new avenues for the enhancement of military power. In this context he considered that the American invitation to European aerospace and defence equipment manufacturers to participate in the SDI as sub-contractors would result in the surrender of the fruits of European high-technology research and development to the US. As a result of French proposals made in April 1985 and active diplomacy on Mitterrand's part, nineteen Western European countries agreed in June 1986 to set up the European Research Agency – the acronym of Eureka deriving roughly from the originally proposed English name, European Research Coordination Agency. Because of the desired military spin-offs and the involvement of EFTA countries, which were valued because of their industrial high-technology know-how, Mitterrand had insisted from the outset that Eureka be organised outside the EC framework, with the Commission having no say in it. He also sought, unsuccessfully, to have the agency's secretariat located in Strasbourg. Eureka's future was to prove disappointing when measured against Mitterrand's initial expectations. Its birth, however, testified to his conviction of the merits of an intergovernmental approach once economics became entwined with security – a conviction finding justification in the SEA, which explicitly placed the economic aspects of security in the intergovernmental domain of foreign-policy cooperation.

The Internal-market Programme and the Removal of Non-tariff Barriers

From a macroeconomic standpoint, the prime justification of France's participation in the internal-market programme was that it could allow export demand to play an even greater role in the generation of economic growth, as had been the aim of Barre and then of Delors, prior to his being appointed president of the Commission. Much of the content of 'Completing the Internal Market', the White Paper of 1985, testified to this compatibility with French policy. For instance, more than a third of its proposed measures dealt with veterinary and phytosanitary controls or food law. France, as the largest exporter of agricultural produce and processed foods in the EEC, stood to gain the most from the lowering of non-tariff barriers in respect of such goods. The bulk of these measures involved the legislative harmonisation of health and safety requirements. Also of benefit to France was the internal-market programme's alternative strategic tack to harmonisation, namely its proposals to give more widespread application to the principle of the mutual recognition of national regulations and standards, not only for trade in goods but also for trade in services. The White Paper's emphasis on this principle drew on the landmark judgment of the EC Court of Justice in February 1979 when it ruled on the 'Cassis de Dijon' case. The German authorities had banned the import of the French liqueur of this name because it did not comply with German regulations; but the ban was found to be a measure having 'equivalent effect' to the imposition of a quantitative restriction on the free movement of goods. It infringed the principle that all goods legally produced and commercialised in one member state must be admitted in all the others, and, as such, it was an abuse of the Treaty of Rome.[13]

The most visible non-tariff barrier impeding trade in goods was the presence of customs posts on the EEC's internal frontiers. Such posts should have been swept away on the completion of the customs union in 1968. They were kept in place, however, partly for purposes of VAT collection. The internal-market programme provided for their disappearance at the end of 1992, thanks to changed VAT arrangements. Again this was a measure from which France stood to gain in its pursuit of export-led growth. According to Commission estimates, the cost of customs formalities represented between 5 and 10 per cent of the value of intra-EC traded goods. The longest and most costly delays of all were those faced by road hauliers entering Italy, which was then France's second largest market.

After 1993 – a year of recession across much of continental Europe – French exports of goods generally benefited from the 'completion' of the internal market. If it is well nigh impossible to quantify the exact net effect, the average annual increase of more than 8 per cent in the franc (or euro) denominated value of such exports to other EU-15 markets in the remaining six years of the decade testified to a favourable economic environment for which the internal-market programme must take a large measure of credit.

The White Paper also proposed far-reaching steps towards the creation of a single market in services – a sphere in which there had been very little progress since 1958. Substantial progress in this sphere was seen by the Commission as a means of boosting economic growth rates across the EC area. Financial services were privileged. Thus one proposal was for a new EC Banking Coordination Directive which would provide for the mutual recognition between member states of national standards of control and supervision and for the issuing of a single EC banking licence. Other financial-service proposals covered insurance and securities. All these proposals, when put into effect through EC legislation and combined with the liberalisation of capital movements, were to make for the emergence in the 1990s of a high degree of integration of Europe's financial markets, roughly half a century after the signing of the EEC Treaty.

In the case of France, the setting in 1985 of the goal of EC-wide liberalisation of financial services tallied with the financial-market liberalisation that was taking place at national level, as witness the far-reaching reforms introduced that same year by Bérégovoy. It was already clear, before the Commission's White Paper was published, that not only was financial-market liberalisation good for French economic growth, but also that, if the opportunity were passed by, it would be to the country's long-term detriment, with Paris incapable of assuring its place as an international financial centre.

Yet the passage from the dirigisme characteristic of the post-war organisation of the financial sector to largely market-driven arrangements was not a smooth one. Even if liberalisation of this kind was perceived to be largely in France's interest, the habit of government interference in corporate decisions and a certain presumptuousness did not die easily. It was indeed with active government involvement that the state-owned commercial bank, Crédit Lyonnais, embarked in the late 1980s upon its ill-starred attempt to establish itself as Europe's biggest bank. Its domestic and international lending was expanded very rapidly, in an obsessive drive to multiply the balance-sheet total, and a plethora of subsidiaries and branches were opened in the EC area and beyond. The result in the 1990s of this politically influenced imprudence was Europe's biggest post-war bank collapse. And the mammoth scale and staggered nature of the ensuing state bail-out called into question France's respect of EC competition rules.

By 2007, a decade and a half after the formal completion of the internal market, the balance of advantage for France in respect of financial services appeared largely positive. The domestic banking sector was greatly modernised and remained largely in French hands. Major bank acquisitions abroad were limited. But they included the takeover by BNP Paribas of Italy's Banca Nazionale del Lavaro in 2006. AXA had become Europe's foremost company for non-life insurance, with major subsidiaries across the continent. Striking was the success of the Paris Bourse in progressively securing its future, notwithstanding the predatory competition from London and Frankfurt. It took the lead in the creation in 2000 of Euronext, the integrated exchange for the Paris, Amsterdam, Brussels and Lisbon bourses. Six years later Euronext embarked on a transatlantic merger with the New York Stock Exchange (NYSE), to which the European Commission gave its approval in January 2007, thereby allowing for the confluence of the forces of European integration and globalisation.

The Reorientation of Foreign Trade

Waning Colonial Trade Ties

For France, then, the watering down of its own post-war dirigisme and its acceptance of the EC's goal of completing the internal market were closely linked. Another facet of this process of change was the reorientation of

France's external trade. Reflecting the rising international ambitions of the French corporate sector and the keen demand of French consumers for foreign goods, this reorientation of trade gradually, but radically, transformed the face of the national economy by the beginning of the twenty-first century. France embraced globalisation, at least in the latter word's sense of an ever closer integration of the world's economies. To understand this change from a French standpoint, it is instructive to return anew to the time of the EEC's birth.

The EEC Treaty, besides contributing to the erosion of French dirigisme, led to a radical long-term reorientation of France's external trade, though not altogether in the way that had been hoped at the time. In the 1950s great store was still being put on the development of economic and political ties with Africa. As has been shown, the Schuman Declaration included a commitment to the African continent, and, more importantly, during the EEC negotiations in 1956–57, the Mollet government – thanks to its own considerable diplomatic efforts – secured the insertion into the EEC Treaty of its 'Association of Overseas Countries and Territories' provisions. Thus, the old idea of *Eurafrique* was revived, with a privileged role reserved for France. Then, in the first few years of the Fifth Republic, de Gaulle linked membership of the EEC to a high ambition for French Africa. He tried to create a federal Communauté Française, in which the colonies of West and Equatorial Africa would accede through 'self-determination' to a halfway-house type of statehood entailing an ongoing association with France, and so indirectly with the EEC. De Gaulle failed, however. By 1961 all these countries had opted instead for full-fledged independence. Accordingly, three years after the Treaty of Rome's entering into force, its provisions for the 'Association of the Overseas Countries and Territories' appeared redundant.

Yet, in this post-independence world, it did prove possible to maintain an 'association' of an economic kind along lines set out in the Treaty of Rome and its 'Implementing Convention on the Association of the Overseas Countries and Territories with the Community'. Under this convention, eighteen countries formed the Association des Etats Africains et Malagache (AEAM). They were all African, all francophone except for Somalia, and fourteen had formerly been under French rule. In 1963, in the Cameroon capital of Yaoundé, the AEAM signed a Convention with the EEC that provided for continuing preferential trade ties, financial and technical assistance, and the setting up of joint institutions at ministerial and parliamentary level. This was with the active encouragement of France. The first Yaoundé Convention was replaced by a second in 1969. Following the UK's EC accession, the arrangements were somewhat reshaped. Their coverage was extended to include British Commonwealth countries in Africa, the Indian Ocean, the Pacific Ocean, and the Caribbean, as well as other African countries that were neither Commonwealth members nor party to the original AEAM group. In 1975 the first convention embodying the changed arrangements was signed in the Togolese capital of Lomé. The AEAM was replaced with a new group called the ACPs (African, Caribbean, Pacific states). Three further Lomé Conventions were to follow before the end of the century, with the last of these, Lomé IV, running for a ten-year period and expiring in 2000. It was then replaced by a radically new 'ACP–EU Partnership Convention', whose principal (and highly ambitious) long-term aim was to establish FTAs between the EU and regional groups of ACPs, especially in Africa. France pushed for this new arrangement in the face of scepticism from other EU member states (Germany, Austria, the Netherlands, and the Nordic countries).[14]

The Yaoundé and later the Lomé conventions allowed France to reconcile its EC membership with the pursuit of its interests in West and Equatorial Africa. Within this wider framework, traditional bilateral relations were maintained and often had overwhelming priority. But neither the bilateral ties nor the EC's successive conventions brought prosperity to these former French parts of Africa in the last four decades of the twentieth century.

One difficulty lay in the management by the French monetary authorities of the franc zone, especially during the Mitterrand years. The CFA – Communauté Financière Africaine – franc was introduced after the Second World War as the common currency of the two French-run monetary unions in West and Equatorial Africa. From 1948 to 1994 the CFA remained at an unchanged pegged rate against the French franc. In the second half of the 1980s the CFA's international value was affected by two developments: first, the 'hard franc' policy pursued by successive French governments after the economic-policy turnaround of 1983; and, secondly, the pronounced weakening of the US dollar against the DM, the franc, and other ERM currencies from 1985 onwards. For the CFA the consequences were disastrous. The receipts from these African countries' commodity exports were largely determined by dollar-denominated international prices, and they were already low for their import needs; but they now fell still further, and dramatically so. A devaluation of the CFA franc would have helped producers of agricultural raw materials, the type of commodity most of the countries relied on, the notable exception being oil-producing Gabon. But this option was long refused in Paris. Those who stood to lose from such a devaluation were French exporters and local urban elites, whose life styles were often characterised by conspicuous consumption with a high import content of largely French provenance. It was only in 1994 that Balladur – now the prime minister of a *cohabitation* government – halved the CFA's value against the franc; this move had been urged by the IMF, while Mitterrand gave it only grudging approval.[15]

By the time of the devaluation in 1994, imports of goods into France denominated in CFA francs represented less than 1 per cent of total French imports, while the share of exports to the franc zone in total French exports was a little more than 1 per cent. Yet this group of fourteen countries had a total population that was several million in excess of Germany's. Such a low level of trade was proof that *Eurafrique* had turned out to be an empty dream, at least to the south of the Sahara.

The Maghreb and the 'Euro-Mediterranean' Area

The ambition represented by the term *Eurafrique* also covered North Africa and, in particular, the Maghreb area. Initially, on the Mediterranean's southern shores, Algeria remained the country that was economically speaking by far the most important for France. Yet this country was owed nothing under the Treaty of Rome, once it took the path to independence. After the signing of the Evian Agreements in 1962 and the last explosion of an atomic bomb in the Sahara in 1963, bilateral relations became centred on France's remaining major interest, the exploitation of Algeria's oil and natural gas resources. To assure the continued presence of French state-owned petroleum enterprises, Algeria's large financial demands tended to be met by the French government. In the later years of de Gaulle's presidency, the Algerian government's investment budget was totally covered by a mixture of French development aid and petroleum taxes – paid mainly by the French enterprises operating in the country – while hydrocarbon-product exports to France accounted for some three-quarters of total Algerian exports, paid for at prices above those ruling on the world market. In addition, Algerian workers' remittances from France contributed to about a fifth of Algeria's GNP. Some limited recognition was paid to the EEC insofar as Algeria accorded tariff preferences to the rest of the Six. Yet the degree of preference was less than that accorded to France; and Algeria's trade relations with Europe continued into the 1970s to be predominantly French-oriented, even if the Algerian government was bent on developing the oil and gas sector in cooperation with other countries besides France, notably Italy.

De Gaulle, on returning to power in 1958, had sought to establish good bilateral relations with Morocco and Tunisia, as witness their eligibility, in principle, for the never-to-be-realised Communauté Française. However, the 1960s proved to be difficult. In 1964 France abrogated a preferential trade agreement of five years' standing with Tunisia, which was in response to the unilateral expropriation of lands belonging to French nationals. The expropriation had come on top of the incident over the French naval base in Bizerte in 1961, when the Tunisian president, Habib Bourguiba, had encouraged large-scale demonstrations to block the base, essentially to protest against France's conduct of the Algerian war. By contrast, relations with Morocco in the first half of the 1960s were not quite so turbulent. Although about a third of French-owned lands in Morocco were expropriated in 1963, partial compensation was agreed in the following year, and the system of quotas allowing certain types of Moroccan export into France was not dismantled. The same trade arrangements survived the Ben Barka affair in 1965, which poisoned political relations between Paris and Rabat.

After de Gaulle's relinquishing of power, first Pompidou and then Giscard d'Estaing sought to improve and consolidate France's relations with Morocco and Tunisia. However, as from the end of the 1960s, the organisation of these two countries' trade relations across the Mediterranean began to be placed in an EEC framework rather than a French bilateral one. Thus, association agreements as provided by the Treaty of Rome's Declaration of Intent were signed in 1969 between the EEC and, on the other hand, Morocco and Tunisia. But they were modest in kind since they covered only trade – and not even all trade (Morocco's exports of fresh vegetables and wines continuing to depend on existing French preferences). Several years later, following a meeting in 1972 of EC foreign ministers in the newly created framework of European Political Cooperation (EPC), the aim of a 'global Mediterranean policy' was declared in Brussels. It was to be implemented by a series of bilateral trade and cooperation agreements that would lead in time to an FTA in industrial goods encompassing the EEC and all other countries in the Mediterranean area, and, on the agricultural side, to the extension by the EEC of a range of trade preferences.

Bilateral agreements of this kind, covering trade and promising financial assistance, were signed with the three principal Maghreb countries in 1976. For Morocco and Tunisia the agreements were potentially important, but for Algeria hardly at all, since its exports were made up almost entirely of oil and natural gas. The application of these agreements quickly proved disappointing for Morocco and Tunisia, especially when set against the rhetoric of the EC's 'global Mediterranean policy'. The deterioration of the economic climate in Western Europe encouraged protectionism in the one area of industrial activity where Morocco and Tunisia enjoyed a comparative advantage, namely textiles and clothing. If this protectionism ran counter to the agreements, it retained a veneer of legality by being effected bilaterally through (euphemistically named) voluntary export restraint arrangements (VERs). Furthermore, the widening in the scope of the CAP in the 1970s and 1980s was to the advantage of Mediterranean-type produce, notably olive oil and tomatoes, with the result that exports of this type of produce from the southern-shore Mediterranean countries faced increased EEC protectionism. By the time Spain and Portugal joined the EC in 1986, bringing the prospect to Morocco and Tunisia of still greater difficulties in exporting to European markets, any promise that formal links with the EEC would turn out to be more to their advantage than the abandoned colonial links with France seemed to have been disappointed. Deep frustration about EEC protectionism contributed to Morocco's application for EC membership in July 1987, which was a quixotic, unsuccessful gesture on the part of Hassan II.

Algeria, on the other hand, had until then little cause for complaint on the export front. Not only did the high international prices for oil and gas between 1973 and 1986 assure it of favourable terms of trade, but in the first half of the 1980s both France and Italy had chosen Algeria as their main gas supplier, which entailed, in the case of Italy, the construction of the first underwater trans-Mediterranean pipeline. On the part of France, moreover, at the outset of the Mitterrand years, there was a desire to accord Algeria a privileged place among developing countries. Many in the PS represented a younger, less jaundiced generation of French politicians than those to the fore of the SFIO at the end of the Fourth Republic, and this new generation was sympathetic to the brand of socialism associated with the Algerian one-party state. More importantly, Algeria enjoyed a prominent position not only in the Arab and African worlds but also in the wider Third World non-aligned movement. Algeria, alongside India and Mexico, merited therefore particular favour. Claude Cheysson, in charge of the Quai d'Orsay from 1981 to 1984, played a key role. That he chose to be called Minister of External Relations – the title of Talleyrand's post under the Directoire – testified to a desire to treat with the developing countries of the Third World on an avowedly fraternal basis, notably by advocating a new type of North-South relation. In late 1981, half a year after his coming to power, Mitterrand paid an official visit to Algeria. It was the first such visit by a French president since that country's independence. He agreed in Algiers to a long-term contract for the purchase of LNG by the state-owned Gaz de France (GDF). Its salient feature was a price set 25 per cent above the ruling world level. However, this sort of benevolence was limited to the early Mitterrand years, and it never led to France's taking Algeria's side in its dispute with Morocco over the future of the Western Sahara. As the 1980s progressed, the French president became more concerned with European affairs at the expense of Third World causes.[16]

Furthermore, after the sharp fall in world energy prices in 1986, the earlier generous gas contact led to a bitter price dispute between GDF and Algeria's Sonatrach. Because of this collapse in prices, Algeria found itself in straitened economic circumstances. Soon afterwards the country was rift by a long-running political crisis. By the early 1990s murderous and internecine violence bordering on open civil war engulfed Algeria. In these circumstances, it was scarcely surprising that France reduced its relative degree of dependence on Algerian gas to the advantage of Norwegian and Russian suppliers.

The Maghreb's difficulties were a major factor prompting the EC Commission in November 1989 to call for a renovated Mediterranean policy. That the loosening of economic ties with France had not given way to an effective and mutually advantageous framework for trade and investment between the EEC and the Maghreb had negative security implications for the Western Mediterranean area, while the Eastern

Mediterranean area remained bedevilled by the Arab–Israeli conflict. At the end of 1990 the EC Council of Ministers addressed this question of a renovated Mediterranean policy, but agreed on only timid measures. In April 1992 the Commission insisted on the need for more action when it proposed bilateral 'Euro–Maghreb partnership' agreements, which were to be more ambitious in scope than the trade and cooperation agreements signed in 1976. The proposal, which was targeted first at Morocco, was approved by the European Council in June 1992.[17] Not only were agreements of this kind, now called simply 'association agreements', signed with Tunisia, Morocco, and Algeria in 1995, 1996, and 2002 respectively, but they were offered to other countries to the east on the Mediterranean, with Israel being the first to sign. The economic ambition became the creation by 2010 of a Mediterranean-wide FTA for industrial goods. Tunisia's association agreement was to come into effect in 1998 and Morocco's in 2000.

A Euro-Mediterranean Conference was held at ministerial level in Barcelona in November 1995. It brought together all EU member states and a dozen other countries from the Mediterranean area, including the three Maghreb ones. Its purpose was to institutionalise ongoing coopera-tion between the participants in what was soon called the 'Barcelona process'.[18] The conference owed much to France and Spain, having been prepared and organised in the framework of their successive EU presidencies in 1995. Chirac, in particular, was very much in favour.[19] However, during the first ten years and more of the 'Barcelona process', multilateral political cooperation was to prove elusive, largely because of the refusal of Arab states to sit alongside Israel in talks with the EC.

In France a new awareness of the Maghreb's potential for economic growth took hold in the 1990s. The turn in Algeria towards more liberal economic policies was one factor at play. Yet it was Morocco's economic prospects that were seen as especially promising, at least from a French standpoint. By 2004, thanks to Moroccan privatisation, the French conglomerate, Vivendi Universal, had acquired a majority stake in the country's telecommunications operator, Maroc Telecom. And in the early years of the new century the interests of French banks – BNP Paribas, Crédit Agricole, Société Générale – were being reinforced through their Moroccan subsidiaries. Such developments reflected the hope that France – along with Spain and Italy – might benefit in the longer term from a dynamic of economic growth in the Maghreb comparable to that associated with the post-communist economic transition in Central and Eastern Europe. In 2005, however, France's exports of goods to the three Maghreb countries accounted for slightly less than 3 per cent of total French goods exports. Such a share was scarcely consonant with the dream half a century earlier of a French-led *Eurafrique*, not to speak of the professed logic of protectorates and colonisation prior to the First World War.

EC Markets and French Exports

To take the period between 1959 (the first year of intra-EEC tariff reduction) and 2005 (France's year of disenchantment with the EU), increasing exports to other member states were the main economic benefit attributable to EC membership. These exports were mainly industrial goods, notwithstanding France's longstanding interest in the CAP and its traditionally strong position as an exporter of services. In general, exports of goods and services to other EC markets played a large part in shaping the pattern of France's economic growth over the last four decades of the twentieth century and the early years of the twenty-first. Export demand tended to be the most buoyant component of aggregate demand over most of this period; and much of the export demand originated from within the EC area. Important steps for intra-EC trade creation were the progressive realisation of the customs union in 1959–68 and later the 'completion' of the internal market, with the bulk of the required legislative steps taken in 1987–92. Successive EC enlargements from the 1970s onwards played a vital role. The enlargements of 1973 and 1986 to include first the UK and then Spain were of considerable consequence, on account of the size of the countries concerned and their existing or potential trade flows with France.

In a first phase lasting up to the international oil shock of 1973–74, French trade with the rest of the EC area soared and led to a striking reorientation of the direction of foreign trade. Thus, in 1973 exports of goods to the other EC–9 and to the franc zone accounted respectively for 56 per cent and 5 per cent of France's total goods exports. But in 1959, the year of the first reduction of intra-EEC customs duties, the relative proportions had been quite different. Exports to the same eight European countries had then accounted for 33 per cent of total goods exports, only slightly more than the 32 per cent of the total taken by the franc zone, of which Morocco and Tunisia were still part.

There was then a second phase which spanned the economic adjustment in Western Europe to the first oil shock and the lesser second oil shock of 1979–80, as well as the years of so-called Eurosclerosis marking the first half of the 1980s. French exports to the rest of the EC area continued to grow, but demand no longer had the exceptional vigour that had marked the late 1960s and early 1970s – not to speak of earlier years, especially the first two years of EEC tariff dismantlement (1959–60). The share of French exports sold on EC markets slipped considerably, compared with the position in 1973. A low of 48 per cent for goods sold to the other EC–10 was recorded in 1981. The high-growth markets for France had become those of the oil-exporting countries, notably Iraq and Saudi Arabia, to the benefit of sales of French military goods.

A third phase, one of renewed buoyancy, may be dated from 1986 when the sharp fall in international oil prices brought about a substantial improvement in the terms of trade of most Western European countries. Factors that contributed to the improved demand conditions in the EC area included the entry of the Iberian Peninsula countries into the EC and the boost given to business confidence by the launching of the internal-market programme. By 1990 the share of total exports of goods sold on the markets of the other EC–12 had risen to 63 per cent in 1990, whereas five years earlier, on the eve of Spain's and Portugal's accession, the share had been only 54 per cent.

By an unexpected irony, it was in 1993, the first year of the 'completion' of the internal market, that demand conditions in Europe sharply worsened for France. The economy moved into recession, and the drop in GDP (down 0.9 per cent) was the first time GDP recorded an annual decrease since the Second World War. A major reason for the downturn lay in the earlier sharp tightening of monetary policies in Western Europe, which derived from Germany's restrictive stance in response to the inflationary pressures arising from unification.

However, French exports boomed in a long recovery running from 1994 to 2000: then the volume of exports of goods and services rose on average by an annual 8 per cent. This boom contributed greatly to the strong GDP growth from 1998 to 2000. The single market worked to the advantage of French exporters. Yet it was not the main factor at play. By the second half of the 1990s, the most dynamic elements of France's export demand tended to emanate from the wider world beyond Europe. Globalisation was paying dividends for many a large French-based enterprise, as they successfully sold goods ranging, for example, from aircraft and other aerospace equipment to perfumes and cognac.

Then, from 2001 to 2005, the French economy was marked by poor GDP growth. The role played by exports in this downturn was considerable. The dip in the US economy in 2001–2 and the dollar's pronounced weakening in 2002–4 – a weakness that persisted into 2005 and 2006 – dampened French export growth on world markets. But an even weightier factor was the depressed economic performance in the five years up to 2005 of France's foremost trading partner, Germany. French exports to Germany were adversely affected, as were French exports to the Benelux countries, whose economies were even more sensitive to German economic trends.

Germany's position as France's leading export market resulted from the size of the German economy itself, geographical proximity, and longstanding inter-industrial linkages for intermediate goods. In the early 1970s, shortly after the completion of the customs union and at the time of the first EC enlargement, exports to the FRG accounted for about a fifth of total French exports of goods. By the 1980s this share had decreased, but it still represented about a sixth of the total. By 2005 it had slipped further to less than 15 per cent, roughly a seventh.

The two major EC enlargements, bringing in the UK and Spain, were of considerable advantage to the French economy. Spain's accession in 1986 marked the start of a long period of extraordinarily fast growth in Franco-Spanish trade, which was still under way in the early 2000s. By 2003 Spain had become France's second largest export market, a position it retained in each of the following two years, taking a tenth of all French goods exports. Ironically, in the late 1970s and early 1980s it had been largely for economic reasons that, first, Giscard d'Estaing and then Mitterrand had opposed Spain's EC membership. When, at Fontainebleau in June 1984, the European Council agreed to the accession of the Iberian countries, the determining factor was Mitterrand's own change of heart. But this was essentially for political reasons, the French president having been reassured about Spain's future after nearly two years of socialist government in Madrid.

Earlier in the 1960s, when the British application for EC membership had met with such disfavour, it had been a change of president rather than a change of heart by de Gaulle that had unlocked the door for negotiations. After accession in 1973 not only did Franco-British trade grow rapidly, but later, in the 1980s and 1990s, its pace consistently outstripped that of France's overall EC trade growth. By the mid 1990s the UK had become a market for French goods comparable in size to Italy and Belgium-Luxembourg. Indeed, from 1996 to 2002, before being overtaken by Spain, the UK market was second in importance only to the German one.

Globalisation and French Hesitations

Managing Industrial Change in an Increasingly Global Economy

In the early years of the twenty-first century, the EU accounted for between three-fifths and two-thirds of French exports of goods. The figure was 65 per cent in 2005 for the EU–25. Impressive as this figure may be, it compared with a share of 56 per cent recorded in 1973 for the EC–9 alone. In 2005 the markets of what had been the EC–9 took 46 per cent of the total, down therefore by as much as ten percentage points. This decline in the older member states' relative importance as export markets may be imputed above all to the forces of globalisation. Whether for exports or direct investments, the international horizons of the French corporate sector widened very considerably in the thirty years or so following the EC's first enlargement. To take French exports of goods to North America, the Far East and Australasia, they represented a healthy enough 17 per cent of the total in 2005; and a share of more than 7 per cent went to the US, despite a very unfavourable exchange rate for French exporters.

The French economy's structural adjustment to the forces making for globalisation from the 1970s onwards was often painful. For the reshaping of the steel industry, collective EC decision making eased at an early stage the path of adjustment. Neither the problems nor the challenges were specific to France. A major crisis broke out in 1975, largely because of overcapacity and fierce international competition, which badly affected steel industries across Western Europe. A further feature of the crisis in France was the weakening of the industrial inter-linkage that had long existed between steel and coal. Coal production was in inexorable decline. Most of the French steel sector's energy requirements no longer came from coking coal, since electrical energy, increasingly generated by nuclear power, had largely displaced the product that had been at the heart of the ECSC's creation a few decades earlier. Yet the French steel industry had still potentially a viable future. It was already availing itself of high-grade iron ore shipped as hematite from overseas – for example, from Brazil – rather than relying on the uncompetitive iron ore mined in Lorraine. Because of this change in ore input, a massive modern steel complex had entered into production on the coast just outside Dunkirk. And in the mid 1970s a second coastal complex built at Fos, near to Marseilles, was starting up. However, as a result of adverse demand conditions, the enormous state investments made in the rolling mills and blast furnaces at Fos, as well as in the expansion of capacity at Dunkirk, could not guarantee an adequate economic return. From a French standpoint, what was needed to remedy the situation was a breathing space in the form of ECSC production quotas and the imposition of large-scale capacity cuts on older steelworks, not only in Lorraine but elsewhere in the EC area, most notably in the Walloon south of Belgium.

In 1975 France took the lead among the Ten in pressing the EC Commission to declare a state of 'manifest crisis' (under Article 58 of the ECSC Treaty) and impose a system of production quotas. The Commission initially demurred. It preferred instead to work with the OECD to ease competitive pressures in the EC area by arranging VERs with non-EC suppliers. Japanese exporters, in particular, showed a readiness to comply. However, the Commission gradually moved towards the French position by accepting that it was its duty to deal directly with the problem of the ECSC's own excess capacity. The first step was the Davignon Plan, named after the EC commissioner for industrial affairs, Belgium's Vicomte Davignon. Approved by the European Council in March 1977, this plan provided for minimum prices and for the coordination of national restructuring plans. It proved insufficient. At last in October 1980 the Commission declared a state of 'manifest crisis', and the EC Council of Ministers gave its approval to mandatory production quotas, drawn up by type of steel product and for each enterprise. Given the relative competitiveness of the German steel industry, the FRG acquiesced only reluctantly to this move. It was under German pressure that the EC Council of Ministers decided in June 1981 that state subsidies to the steel industry should come to an end in 1985, and that in the meantime they should be allowed only for restructuring that entailed the reduction of high-cost capacity.

Thus, over a long period between the mid 1970s and mid 1980s, the EC Commission helped to maintain orderly production levels and oversaw much needed capacity reduction. It gave the required breathing space to both the French government and the French steel industry, after the huge investment in modernisation carried out in the 1960s and early 1970s. The vulnerable Fos complex survived. Usinor and Sacilor, the two big state-owned steel groups, were merged in 1986. In 1989, in a curious twist of history, the new group acquired a large majority stake in Saarstahl, resulting, after a fashion, in a regained French control of the Saar steel industry. Usinor was privatised in July 1995. Then in 1998 it acquired a majority stake in Belgium's Cockerill–Sambre and thereby obtained control of what was left of the Walloon steel industry. The Usinor group, with plants also in Spain and Italy (as well as Brazil), was then the largest producer of crude steel in Europe. In 2001 Usinor joined forces with Luxembourg's Arbed and Spain's Aceralia to form the European giant, Arcelor. In 2006 the Indian group, Mittal, took over Arcelor to form Arcelor Mittal – incorporated in Luxembourg – by far the world's biggest steel producer. Globalisation and privatisation had transformed the face of French steel industry, now greatly slimmed down but highly performing.

Another example of a needed breathing space won by EC arrangements concerned the French automotive industry. Prior to the completion of the internal market at the end of 1992, the market for motor cars in the EC area was a highly segmented one. National restrictions were imposed by a number of member states on imports of cars from non-EC countries, above all from Japan. The severest restrictions were those imposed by Italy, and second to Italy was France. If Italy had a formal GATT-agreed quota system introduced in the 1950s, France's restrictions were applied through a VER arrangement, which aimed to hold new registrations of Japanese cars under an annual ceiling of 3 per cent of total new French registrations. The exercise of both forms of restriction depended upon the operation of administrative controls at internal-frontier customs posts (by virtue of the EEC's Article 115). It was also helped by differing national technical standards. However, internal-frontier customs posts were set to disappear at the beginning of 1993; and technical standards were to be harmonised, as part of the internal-market programme, by the introduction of a 'common type' of EC approval. Thus, a major worry in France and Italy at the beginning of the 1990s was how their automotive industries would withstand the ineluctable freeing of restrictions, especially since Japanese manufacturers were perceived to hold a competitive advantage over their volume-oriented European rivals. Heightening this worry was the pursuit of this advantage by certain Japanese manufacturers through setting up assembly plants in Europe, sometimes called 'transplants'.

The quandary was addressed through negotiations in the framework of the EEC's common commercial policy. In 1991 an EC–Japanese agreement was concluded. It governed the sale of Japanese cars and other light vehicles for a seven-year period up to the end of 1999. The agreement itself took the form of parallel official declarations by the EC commissioner responsible for external relations and the Japanese international trade and industry minister, backed by an unpublished 'elements-of-consensus' text. It was a VER arrangement; and there was claim to due form since 'an appropriate notification' was made to the GATT. The Japanese commitment was to 'monitor' the level of car exports to the EC area as a whole, and individually to the more sensitive national markets. Thus, market disruption was to be avoided over a transition period ending in 2000. Only in that year would a single EC market be truly in place for cars, with no restriction whatsoever on the import and movement of Japanese cars. The VER was duly implemented. On the French market, the ceiling on the level of sales of Japanese cars was progressively raised, before being phased out altogether at the beginning of the new century.

The EC–Japanese agreement glossed over the question of whether Japanese 'transplant' production would be included in the VER arrangements. At the time, the French prime minister, Edith Cresson, declared that Japanese 'transplant' production would be welcome on French soil. The loudest dissent came from Jacques Calvet, the head of Peugeot–Citroën, who had long advocated a strong dose of EC protectionism to assure the future of car manufacturing in Europe. But what was not widely expected in the early 1990s was that the French automotive industry would soon make great strides in enhancing its international competitiveness. In the middle of the 1990s the agreement with Japan was still of help. Before the end of the decade it was a crutch that could be dispensed with. Cresson's wish was fulfilled in 1997 when Toyota announced the setting up of a new car plant in Valenciennes. Indeed, the international tables were turned in 1999 when a reinvigorated Renault bailed out Nissan, taking a controlling stake in the financially troubled Japanese company. Under strong French leadership, an alliance between the two companies flourished to both Renault's and Nissan's advantage.

The Difficult Liberalisation of World Trade in Agriculture

The European Commission could not always be counted upon to act in France's perceived interests. High on the agenda during the Uruguay Round was the liberalisation of world trade in agricultural goods. In the last stages of these difficult GATT multilateral trade negotiations, such type of liberalisation was the main stumbling block hindering the Uruguay Round's overall conclusion. In November 1992 the Commission and the US administration had come to a bilateral compromise in

Washington. Limits were accepted on EC oilseeds production and, more importantly from a French standpoint, it was agreed to reduce CAP export subsidies, which had so benefited French wheat exporters. In particular, the agreement provided for a reduction in the volume of CAP subsidised exports of slightly more than a fifth over six years, compared with their average annual level in a 1986–90 base period. And the value of the actual subsidies paid was to be lowered by more than a third. When Balladur took office as prime minister in April 1993, he came under great pressure to refuse what had apparently been settled in Washington half a year earlier – especially from within the RPR, his own party. Chirac, the party president and the indefatigable defender of farm interests, led the objectors. Balladur gave way. The French government accordingly denounced the Commission for having overstepped its mandate; and the agreement itself was dismissed as only provisional.

Yet by the end of 1993 Balladur acknowledged that if a compromise on the lines of the Washington agreement was the price for salvaging the Uruguay Round, then so be it. On the parliamentary right, he was backed by Giscard d'Estaing and Barre, even if Chirac remained adamant in publicly opposing anything that smacked of French weakness. Thanks to the change in France's stance, the Commission was able to agree to the final Uruguay Round package in December. In the matter of CAP export subsidies, a concession was made to the EU, since it was allowed a more favourable base period (1990–92) for calculating the reductions.

During the Uruguay Round negotiations, not only the US but also the Cairns Group of 'key fair trading countries in agriculture', led by Australia, expressed fierce opposition to the CAP's effects on international trade. This opposition was to be renewed in 2001 when the Doha Round opened under WTO auspices. Both the EU and the US were again being pressed to reduce their still high levels of agricultural protection and subsidy, so as to allow exporters from developing countries to have access to their markets. When Pascal Lamy, the WTO's director general, was obliged to suspend the trouble-plagued multilateral trade negotiations in July 2006, it was partly because of the EU's obduracy over lowering its tariffs and levies on imports of agricultural goods. Lamy, after having been Delors's chief of staff at the European Commission from 1985 to 1995, had served as the EU commissioner for trade from 1999 to 2004, and had so been in charge for several years of the EU's input into the Doha Round negotiations. This Frenchman of socialist persuasion could not have been more aware of the problem posed by the strict negotiating mandate given to the Commission by the EU Council of Ministers. It largely reflected the French government's opposition to any further reforms of the CAP – an opposition dictated by Chirac from the top.

By the middle of the twenty-first century's first decade, the CAP had indeed been significantly reformed, both to reduce surpluses and rein in EU budget expenditure; its glory years belonged to the past, essentially the

1970s and 1980s. The EU's concessions in the Uruguay Round were linked to its own internal CAP reform, carried out in 1994 to implement the MacSharry proposals (named after the EU commissioner for agriculture) which had been tabled two years earlier. Under this reform, the level of price support was substantially lowered, and offsetting compensation took the form of direct income payments. The 'Agenda 2000' reform package, covering the 2000–6 budgetary period, was agreed in 1999, and its thrust was much the same. Then, under a mid-term review, the EU's agricultural ministers agreed in June 2003 to a complete decoupling of the levels of EU payments to farmers from their farm production levels, at least in principle. The new system of payment was introduced in 2005. However, as a concession to France, countries were allowed to opt temporarily for only a partial decoupling, with the effect that 25 per cent of French cereal production continued to be eligible for the traditional type of price support.

From a French standpoint, an important feature of the 2003 mid-term agreement was that it did not prejudice the overall level of funding for the CAP. For in October 2002, at the time of the worsening of the transatlantic crisis over Iraq, Chirac had won the backing of his close German ally, Schröder, for maintaining total CAP spending in 2007–13 at roughly the same level as in 2000–6. The EU Council of Ministers subsequently adopted this informal bilateral agreement. Having secured this EU commitment, the French president continued to make clear his opposition to international calls for a new, radical slimming down of the CAP – calls aimed at furthering the Doha Round.

Disenchantment with Economic Liberalism and the 2005 Referendum

Chirac's second presidential term (2002–7) – a five-year one, by virtue of a change to the constitution in 2000 – was marked by a certain turning away from the qualified economic liberalism associated with such figures as Barre and Bérégovoy. This second term got off to a worrying start, since in the presidential election's first round in April 2002 the populist and xenophobic nationalist, Jean-Marie Le Pen, had taken second place, beating Jospin by a slight margin and falling short of Chirac, in his share of the votes, by only three percentage points. Le Pen's denunciation of France's economic ills, real and imaginary, and his complaints about the EU were a major factor encouraging a new reluctance among France's political establishment to subscribe to the virtues of economic liberalism – even in the form of the EU's own 'Lisbon Agenda' (the commitment of the European Council in 2000 to make the EU 'the [world's] most competitive and dynamic knowledge-driven economy by 2010'). Hesitations about international competition and the supposed benefits of the single market became increasingly evident in the course of Chirac's second term, on the part of successive right-of-centre governments and also the Socialist opposition.

Government promotion of 'national champions' assumed a new vigour, even if it flew in the face of the spirit of EU competition law. During Jean-Pierre Raffarin's three-year period as prime minister in 2002–5, it was Nicolas Sarkozy, in his capacity as the second of as many as four holders of the economics and finance portfolio, who was particularly zealous in creating 'national champions' or caring for old ones. In April 2004, acting in accordance with Chirac's wishes, he used his ministerial powers of suasion to bring a takeover bid to fruition in the pharmaceutical sector. The bidder was the purely French firm, Sanofi–Synthélabo, and the prey its Franco-German competitor, Aventis. The fruit of the merger was the largely French-based Sanofi–Aventis, sufficient in size to rank as one of the world's top ten pharmaceutical companies. The German Chancellor branded the French minister's role in the hostile takeover as 'nationalistic'. The burden of Schröder's complaint was that the takeover put an end to the independent existence of Aventis, a company created in 1999, through a cross-border merger, with a balanced management structure reflecting equal German and French interests. Sarkozy also deployed his energy in 2004 to keep the ailing engineering group, Alstom, intact. As a quid pro quo for allowing substantial French state aid, the European Commission was insisting that Alstom should dispose of parts of its business, as well as pressing the idea that the French company should enter into a joint partnership for the manufacture of either its TGV trains or its gas turbines. Siemens was the obvious candidate. But the French economics and finance minister resisted robustly this pressure from Brussels, which caused disappointment in Germany.

Dominique de Villepin, when he became prime minister in June 2005, was not to be outdone by Sarkozy – the latter now head of the UMP (the majority political party) and also interior minister. Already in July, partly in response to the (falsely) rumoured takeover of Danone, the food and drinks group, by PepsiCo, de Villepin began in July to vaunt the merits of 'economic patriotism'; this was in keeping with his distaste for globalisation and economic liberalism of the Anglo-Saxon kind.[20] In early 2006 he announced a 'national champion' of his own creation: the government-arranged merger of the private-sector company, Suez, and the partially privatised GDF. Suez's transformation into an energy and water conglomerate (in the case of energy, both electricity and gas) had taken place mainly in the 1990s, when it emerged chrysalis-like out of the financial holding company of the same name, and its international activities included a dominant position in the production and distribution of Belgium's electricity. The prime minister's immediate aim was to head off a hostile takeover bid for Suez from the Italian utility, Enel. His grander aim was to create a second French utility giant, comparable in size for its energy business to the state-owned Electricité de France (EDF), and also to

Germany's E.ON. However, at the beginning of 2007 the planned merger was in serious difficulty, largely because of trade-union opposition and the approaching presidential election, and so perhaps set to be an example of failed dirigisme in the service of economic patriotism.[21]

De Villepin's decision to bring about a merger between Suez and GDF was taken against the background of the ongoing EU-wide liberalisation of the energy sector. The approach of successive French governments in the 2000s to this liberalisation testified to a singular degree of ambivalence towards the continuing EU's single-market project. The deregulation of the EU's hitherto protected national markets for the supply of electricity and gas had not figured in Delors's White Paper of 1985. However, EU Directives providing for the EU-wide liberalisation of the electricity and gas markets were adopted in 1996 and 1998 respectively. The subsequent transposition of these Directives into national legislation in France proved tardy and minimalist in scope. The Jospin government, moreover, sought successfully, with the backing of the Schröder government in Berlin, to frustrate the European Commission's proposed three-stage timetable for the liberalisation process. Unveiled in 2001, these proposals would have resulted in the completion of the deregulation process by the beginning of 2005. But it was only in 2003 that a somewhat more flexible position on the part of the Raffarin government allowed the EU Council of Ministers to agree to a deadline of 1 July 2007 for completing the third and last stage, which was two and a half years later than the Commission and most other member states had wished. What rendered this French foot-dragging particularly controversial was the huge international expansion of the state-owned EDF group's activities since the 1990s, through the acquisition of subsidiaries elsewhere in Europe. This expansion aimed to benefit from the national deregulation that had taken place elsewhere, in advance of the official, delayed EU deadlines for the liberalisation of the electricity market – so there was no level playing field, but rather a field tilted in France's favour.[22]

On the Left the PS's post-1983 consensus on the broad direction of economic policy broke down further after the 2002 elections. The fissures became widely evident once Chirac decided in July 2004 to have the EU's constitutional treaty approved by referendum. For Fabius in particular, the moment had come to reposition himself within his party. From 2000 to 2002 he had served as economics and finance minister in the Jospin government, the successor but one to Dominique Strauss-Kahn, and both men had indicated in office that they favoured market-oriented economic policies, rather than the old-fashioned dirigiste approach represented by the government's own 35-hour working week legislation. Now, in choosing to lead the internal opposition within the PS to the EU's constitutional treaty, Fabius argued inter alia that it consecrated economic liberalism, prejudiced France's 'social model', and did nothing to counter the malevolent forces of globalisation, as manifest, for instance, in the relocation of French firms to the poorer areas of the newly enlarged EU, or to beyond its borders altogether.[23]

The referendum was held in May 2005. In the French debate beforehand, the issue of EU enlargement became entangled with the controversy over the European Commission's efforts to extend the reach of the single market to include a wide range of service activities, many of them typically provided by small enterprises or self-employed persons. The liberalisation of these activities was covered by an EU Directive, which had first been proposed by the Commission in January 2004 and, although subsequently watered down, was still awaiting adoption by the Council of Ministers and the European Parliament. The PS dissidents headed by Fabius, together with other politicians stretching across the political spectrum from the extreme right to the extreme left, seized on the so-called 'Bolkestein directive' (named after the responsible internal-market commissioner) to denounce the constitutional treaty itself. They raised the spectre of the 'Polish plumber', the emblematic figure representing foreign low-wage workers attracted to France under the umbrella of the EU's internal-market legislation, thereby threatening French livelihoods. When Chirac realised that the 'Bolkestein directive' and the 'Polish plumber' risked to tip the referendum balance against the treaty, he called for a further watering down of the original proposal; and a much diluted Directive was eventually adopted by the EU in 2006. But Chirac's effort was of no avail, despite the treaty's being backed by the two main right-of-centre political parties and, officially, by the PS as well. In the referendum, the opponents of the treaty accounted for 55 per cent of votes cast. The splintering of the Socialist vote, partly over a question of economic philosophy, was decisive.

When the French president had decided on the referendum, his implicit assumption was that France's mainstream politicians and political parties would back the new EU treaty and deliver a comfortable majority in favour of it. He was no doubt counting on the political class to have confidence that the entering into force of the treaty would leave the political workings the EU basically unchanged, save for the new, more permanent presidency arrangements for the European Council, which were arguably in France's interest. And, secondly, he trusted that both the PS and the majority of the electorate would instinctively recognise that considerations of high politics relating to France's leadership role in European integration dictated quite simply that the new treaty be approved.

Instead, against a background of chronically high unemployment and the related unpopularity of the Raffarin government, Fabius dissented, and large numbers of the electorate signalled their view, whether passing or otherwise, that the common market was no longer working in France's interest. In particular, as was evident in Chirac's first television appearance of the referendum campaign, a gulf of incomprehension existed between a president exercised by geopolitics and a younger generation of voters worried about poor employment prospects. The profile of the 'no' vote as established by the exit polls was clear-cut in its essentials: the younger the person, the less likely he or she was to vote in favour of the EU's constitutional treaty; and, cutting across this correlation, the lower the socio-economic class to which the person belonged, also the less likely he or she was to want the treaty. The importance of the disenchanted young, the worst hit by unemployment and worried above all by their economic future, was reflected in another feature of the referendum result. Those Catholic areas of the west and the east of the country that were historically associated with the Christian Democracy movement in post-war Western Europe (represented in France under the Fourth Republic by the MRP) failed in general to deliver their customarily strong 'pro-European' vote. The explanation in large part was surely generational change; once, in these areas of France, 'Europe' had been seen as a force for economic good, as well as a moral force for peace, whereas for the young anywhere in France in 2005, especially those experiencing employment difficulties, the message coming from on high – in different ways from Chirac, Fabius, and Le Pen – was that the 'Europe' of the single market had become contaminated by Anglo-Saxon liberalism.

The down-to-earth economic dimension to French disenchantment with the EU and the demagogic rhetoric directed against 'liberalism' were certainly important factors in 2005. However, the referendum disenchantment was also related to French perceptions of France's place in Europe and the world. Here then we may return to the history of the French quest for international power and security. Thus, going back in time, our account of this quest is to be taken up anew by the reader, at the end of the 1960s – shortly before de Gaulle's abrupt relinquishing of the post of President of the Republic.

Notes

1. Patrick A. Messerlin, 'France and trade policy: is the "French exception" passée?', *International Affairs* 72(2), 1996, 293–309.
2. *Ordo* liberalism, with its rejection of both economic planning and purely laissez-faire economics, had its beginnings at the University of Freiburg in the 1930s. The leading figure was the economist, Walter Eucken. Franz Böhm, the jurist, was also of note. Both were opposed to Nazism. After the war, in 1948, they launched the yearbook: *Ordo. Jahrbuch für die Ordnung von Wirtschaft und Gesellschaft*. Although not from the University of Freiburg, Röpke became a fellow spirit and was associated with the yearbook. Until 1933 this economist and social philosopher had taught at the University of Marburg. Stripped of his professorship after denouncing the barbaric nature of the National Socialists' onslaught against reason and freedom, Röpke went into exile, first in Turkey and then, for the rest of his life, in Switzerland, where he held a chair in international economic relations at the Graduate Institute of International Studies in Geneva. Eucken died in 1950; Röpke in 1966. See A. J. Nicholls, *Freedom with Responsibility: The Social Market Economy in Germany, 1918–1963*, Oxford, 1994.
3. De Gaulle, *Mémoires d'espoir*, vol. 1, 143.

4.   The economic and financial statistical data in this and subsequent chapters are derived from various periodical sources: Bank for International Settlements (*Annual Report*); European Commission (Statistical Annex to *European Economy*); IMF (*Direction of Trade Statistics Yearbook; International Financial Statistics; International Financial Statistics Yearbook*); INSEE – Institut National de la Statistique et des Etudes Economiques (*Les Comptes de la Nation*; website); OECD (Annex Tables to *Economic Outlook; Monthly International Trade Statistics*).

5.   Raymond Barre, *Questions de confiance. Entretiens avec Jean-Marie Colombani*, Paris, 1988, 36.

6.   Peyrefitte, *C'était de Gaulle*, vol. 2, 377.

7.   Interviewed by François Furet in 1983 for the periodical *Le Débat*, Barre distinguished between 'palaeo-liberalism' and his own Tocquevillian kind. He argued for 'a market economy backed by mechanisms of social solidarity, allowing for the intervention that is incumbent on the state, but a state which serves as an enabler … [having] recourse to incentives rather than to regulation or control'. See Raymond Barre, *Réflexions pour demain*, Paris, 1984, 421–69. See also Barre, *Questions de confiance*, 43–44, 333–43.

8.   Peter Ludlow, *The Making of the European Monetary System: A Case Study of the Politics of the European Community*, London, 1982, 84–85.

9.   For the internal-market programme set against its broader economic background, see Loukas Tsoukalis, *The New European Economy Revisited*, Oxford, 1997, 33–50.

10. Pierre Favier and Michel Martin-Roland, *La Décennie Mitterrand*, 3 vols, Paris, 1990–96, vol. 2, 210–11; Moravcsik, *The Choice for Europe*, 360–61.

11. For Delors's own recollection of the launching of the internal-market programme and the SEA, see Jacques Delors, *Mémoires*, Paris, 2004, 182–92, 202–28.

12. The internal-market programme bore little on high politics. For France, as for other EC member states, economic considerations were uppermost – see Moravcsik, *The Choice for Europe*, 335–41.

13. For the 'Cassis de Dijon' judgment, see Harryvan and van der Harst (eds) *Documents on European Union*, 199–203.

14. Philippe Lemaître, 'L'Europe et les pays ACP réforment leur relation privilégiée', *Le Monde*, 4 February 2000.

15. 'IMF persuades French Africa to go for growth', *Financial Times*, 13 January 1994; 'France–Afrique : la coopération dévaluée', *Le Monde*, 20 January 1994.

16. For Mitterrand and the Maghreb, see Hubert Védrine, *Les Mondes de François Mitterrand. A l'Elysée, 1981–1995*, Paris, 1996, 326–37.

17. Michael Sutton, 'Euro-Maghreb Partnership: a new form of Association?', in The Economist Intelligence Unit, *European Trends*, 4th quarter 1994, 61–67.

18. Agence Europe, 'Rapport du Conseil sur les relations entre l'Union européenne et les pays méditerranéens, en préparation à la conférence qui se déroulera les 27 et 28 novembre à Barcelone', *Europe Documents*, no. 1930/31, 27 April 1995.

19. 'M. Chirac a lancé, au Maroc, l'idée d'une pacte de stabilité pour la Méditerranée', *Le Monde*, 22 July 1995.

20. *Le Monde*, 29 July 2005. See de Villepin's related interview in *Les Echos*, 23 September 2005. Also Dominique de Villepin, *Le Cri de la gargouille*, Paris, 2002, 9–13, 48–50, 186–87, 201–5. The slogan 'economic patriotism' (*patriotisme économique*) had already been used by the PS, just after 9/11, in connection with the presentation by Fabius, then finance minister, of an unduly optimistic budget for 2002 – see *Le Monde*, 20 September 2001.

21. For the promotion and care of 'national champions' by the Raffarin and Villepin governments, see the Economist Intelligence Unit's quarterly *Country Report: France*, January, April, October 2003; January, April, July 2004; October 2005; April, July, October 2006; January 2007.

22. The Economist Intelligence Unit, *Country Report: France*, 2nd Quarter 1999; May 2000; April 2001; April 2002; January 2003; July 2004; January, October 2006.

23. Laurent Fabius, *Une certaine idée de l'Europe*, Paris, 2004, 10–11, 23–40, 55–62, 91–94, 97–100.

Part III

PRESERVING POWER AND SECURITY
AFTER DE GAULLE

Chapter 7

EUROPEAN POLITICAL INTEGRATION UP TO THE COLD WAR'S CLOSE

While the Treaty of Rome opened up new economic perspectives, the Gaullist vision of a union of states, with France to the fore, was never put aside. After the UK's admission to the EC, Pompidou's and Giscard d'Estaing's diplomacy transformed the essence of the Fouchet proposals into the institution of the European Council. France's often strained relations with the US under the Nixon, Carter and Reagan presidencies, and the Cold War's final throes, contributed greatly to the development and strengthening of the Franco-German partnership. Mitterrand and Kohl, in particular, harnessed Elysée Treaty decision making to their European ambitions.

The Rapprochement with Albion

The 'Soames Affair'

After the half-century story of France and the common market, a return is now necessary to the 1970s and 1980s, and indeed the end of the 1960s. From the end of de Gaulle's presidency in 1969 to Europe's geopolitical upheaval at the close of the 1980s, France played an innovative role in the high politics of European integration. But it was not a straightforward one. The early 1970s, under Pompidou's presidency, were marked by a return to much of the spirit of the Fouchet proposals. The ambition was European union in the shape of a confederation, without any privileged Franco-German partnership. The situation changed gradually in the second half of the 1970s and in the 1980s under Giscard d'Estaing's and Mitterrand's

---

Notes for this chapter begin on page 207.

presidencies. The Franco-German partnership was revived, and the Elysée Treaty began to count.

Yet Franco-British relations flourished at the outset. This development had its roots in a reappraisal of European international relations under de Gaulle's own presidency at its very end. His refusal in 1967 of the UK's second application for EC membership had not been in the style of his refusal of 1963, brusque if not brutal. But it was a refusal for all of that. Towards the end of 1968, however, signs of a new mood emerged in Paris. De Gaulle's go-it-alone policy of détente, pursued since 1965, had been predicated on the restored strength of France's standing in the world and a willingness of the USSR to exercise moderation in its rule in Central and Eastern Europe. Within the space of a summer, this policy was thrown seriously into question, first by the riots and unrest of May 1968 that appeared almost to topple the Fifth Republic, and then in August by the USSR's resorting to military force to quash the bid for political freedom in Czechoslovakia. Shortly afterwards, in November 1968, West Germany gave proof of a new spirit of independence when it sought, albeit unsuccessfully, to dictate a substantial devaluation of the French franc. The state of Franco-German relations was therefore little better than at their nadir during Erhard's chancellorship between 1963 and 1966. Under these circumstances, the time was propitious for the exploration of new foreign-policy options in Paris, especially since there had been a change at the Quai d'Orsay in the government reshuffle following the May *événements*, with Debré – the former prime minister (1959–62) – becoming foreign minister instead of Couve de Murville, now prime minister. Like his predecessor, Debré was essentially the agent of a foreign policy determined by de Gaulle. Yet, also like his predecessor, he was no mere cipher. And it was Debré who counselled de Gaulle to reconsider France's ties with the UK for the shaping of Western Europe's future.

Debré was an Anglophile. 'Ever since the origin of the negotiations of the treaty that founded the European Coal and Steel Community', he later remarked in his memoirs, 'I have blamed supranationalism, among its other vices, for having distanced us from England.'[1] That he was not opposed to the UK's assuming a substantial part in the leadership of Western Europe had been manifest in 1955 when he led the Gaullist support in the Council of the Republic for ratification of the Paris Accords – the solution to the German problem engineered by Eden after the EDC failure. What attracted Debré in 1968 to the idea of a rapprochement between France and the UK was not only his judgement that the latter could not be permanently excluded from EC membership (otherwise, he believed, France's partners would never agree to a definitive financial arrangement for the CAP), but also his conviction that the two countries' common opposition to creeping supranationalism, within the framework of the Treaty of Rome, made them potentially close allies for the future. He was reinforced in his position by the knowledge that most of France's ambassadors in the major capitals of Western Europe were in favour of EC enlargement and the UK's inclusion.

To advance matters, the foreign minister succeeded in persuading de Gaulle to meet with Christopher Soames, who was Churchill's son-in-law and, since September, the new British ambassador in Paris. Like Debré, Soames was keen to contribute to ending what he felt was virtually an Anglo-French war over Europe. Originally planned for the second week of January 1969, the meeting eventually took place nearly a month later on 4 February 1969, and only less than twelve weeks, so it proved, before de Gaulle's relinquishing of the presidency.[2]

What exactly was said by de Gaulle to Soames on that day at the Elysée – word for word, with all its nuances and ambiguities – can never be known. The only first-hand account was that written afterwards by Soames, and he was helped by embassy colleagues in the teasing out of an adequately precise recall. The French president certainly expressed a willingness to envisage wide-ranging Anglo-French talks about the shaping of Europe's future. As to the proposed content of these talks, a pithy summary came much later from the pen of Bernard Ledwidge, who was then the Minister at the British Embassy in Paris and so one of the first to be informed of the General's overture:

> De Gaulle said that he believed there could be much closer cooperation. It might be possible to change the Treaty of Rome so as to make economic collaboration easier for Britain. Political and defence cooperation, which were not subjects for the EEC, would need to be concerted in regular meetings between the four great European powers, France, Britain, Germany, and Italy. When Soames asked how this arrangement would fit in with NATO, the General replied that NATO would continue in existence for a time, but that in the longer run Europe would have to organise its own defence. The Americans would remain allies of course, but not present in Europe.[3]

Two days afterwards, the British ambassador showed his completed account of de Gaulle's proposals and ruminations to Bernard Tricot, secretary general of the Presidency of the Republic, and two days later on 8 February he met the French foreign minister, Debré, to be informed that he too had read the account. Only a few changes to the text were called for. After this quasi-vetting from the French side, the record of the meeting was dispatched by Soames to his masters at the Foreign Office. There, however, a mood of suspicion and resentment towards de Gaulle prevailed. And Soames himself was out on a limb. He had been appointed ambassador to France when George Brown, a strong advocate of EC membership, was Foreign Secretary, but Brown had now been replaced, in Harold Wilson's Labour government, by Michael Stewart, who was ill disposed towards de Gaulle and held jaundiced views about the UK's links with continental Europe. As it so happened, the British prime minister was due to meet the German Chancellor, Kiesinger, for talks in

Bonn on 11 February. At the urging of Stewart and Foreign Office officials, who feared that de Gaulle might be springing a trap, Wilson decided with some misgiving to tell briefly his German host of de Gaulle's overture. No British response had yet been made to Paris. It was only on 12 February that Soames, on instructions from London and in the deepest of embarrassment, informed the secretary general of the Ministry of Foreign Affairs, Alphand, about Wilson's having informed Kiesinger; and he also admitted to the communication already made to other EC governments, through normal diplomatic channels, of the dispatch that he, the British ambassador in Paris, had prepared a week earlier.

On 21 February, following an article in *Le Figaro* on London's deliberate diplomatic waywardness, the British Foreign Office took the very unusual step of publishing, without any prior consultation with Paris, extracts of Soames's now controversial report of his meeting with the French president. Furthermore, in reading the extracts to the press, the Foreign Office's chief spokesman added the gloss that de Gaulle was bent on dissolving both the EEC and NATO, whereas British policy was to uphold and develop both institutions. Since the new US president, Richard Nixon, was due to arrive in London a few days later and then go on to Paris – his first official visits to the two capitals – this public show of virtue by the Foreign Office may have been judged especially timely by the Wilson government. In any case, Stewart and the Foreign Office mandarinate had wreaked a revenge of sorts on France. Satisfaction was exacted, first, for the two rebuffs suffered at de Gaulle's hands since 1963, first over EC membership and, secondly, for what was perceived, no doubt correctly, as Couve de Murville's talking down of the pound sterling during the EC talks on the UK's second application; these talks had preceded the crisis that rocked sterling in November 1967, thereby precipitating the currency's 14.3 per cent devaluation, an event which, like the Suez crisis a decade earlier, was a particularly sombre moment for the UK in the quarter century after the Second World War.[4]

On what was to be the last occasion when he felt himself wronged by perfidious Albion, de Gaulle was enraged at the turn of events. As to the hapless Soames, after the Foreign Office's culminating mischief, he was summoned to the Quai d'Orsay to be informed by Debré of French displeasure about the UK's blatant disregard for diplomatic niceties and conventions. The French foreign minister added that relations between the two countries lay temporarily in ruins, a bleak judgement to which the British ambassador could not but assent.

Pompidou's Leaning towards the UK

In his discussions with Soames, de Gaulle had situated the prospect of the UK's EC membership – entailing perhaps a radical revamping of the

Treaty of Rome – in his preferred conceptual framework of a European union of states. In keeping with the spirit of the earlier Fouchet proposals, there was the mooted goal of political cooperation between states in the sphere of foreign policy and defence, but now with the UK's conceivably taking part. He reiterated his view that larger states should play a privileged role in the shaping of Western Europe's future.

To a large extent, this mindset was shared by Pompidou, de Gaulle's longest serving prime minister (1962–68), who, after having separated himself from the French president in the wake of the *événements* of May 1968, became his successor in June 1969. In particular, Pompidou's view of the EC was also centred on the primacy of intergovernmental cooperation, with the Commission relegated to a clearly subordinate role. A native of the Auvergne, he was endowed with the proverbial hard-headed commonsense of that region, and he tended to be wary of any plans for Europe's future that smacked of misplaced rationalism in politics. But what he did believe in was the importance of occasional meetings of EC heads of state or government to keep the whole enterprise on a proper course, as witness his leading role in convening two summits, that in The Hague in December 1969 and that in Paris in October 1972, where the larger member states could pull more freely their weight than was possible in the institutional straitjacket of the Treaty of Rome.

Given such views, the idea of EC membership for the UK posed no insuperable problem for Pompidou. By the winter of 1968–69, when he was no longer in government, he had become convinced that the UK should not be continually barred from EC entry. And during his presidential election campaign in May 1969 he publicly declared himself in favour of its accession. However, there was one key precondition for Pompidou, as there had also been for Debré at the time of the latter's initiating what became the 'Soames affair'. The financial arrangement governing the automaticity of the CAP's financing had to be in place before any accession talks could open. After his election as president, Pompidou's choice of Chaban-Delmas as prime minister and the appointment of Maurice Schumann – a centrist from the defunct MRP – as foreign minister signalled that he would take a positive attitude towards the EC's future, with enlargement viewed as a major step forward.

There were changed perceptions in Paris of, first, West Germany's place in the EC and, secondly, the tightness of the relation between the US and the UK. A few years earlier, Kiesinger's replacing Erhard as Chancellor had allowed for some improvement in Franco-German relations, but the unwelcome German forcefulness on the monetary front in November 1968 had been a setback. Pompidou himself, on taking over from de Gaulle, was haunted by the fear that Germany's economic weight would eventually lead to Bonn's role in shaping the EC's future becoming the preponderant one, and, in this perspective, he thought that the UK's accession might well serve France's longer-term interest, especially since the two countries would be objective allies in their shared aversion to supranationalism. He was encouraged in such thinking by the altered nature of Anglo-American relations at the end of the 1960s, which, at least for the moment, consigned to the past de Gaulle's fear that the UK, in the event of EC membership, would act as a Trojan horse for the US in the latter's pursuit of hegemonic power. The swearing in of Nixon as US president in January 1969, three months before de Gaulle's departure from the Elysée, had brought a Republican to the White House who better understood and respected the old French statesman's international vision than did either of his two Democrat predecessors, Kennedy and Johnson. Pompidou, on becoming French president under a Gaullist banner, benefited from this new American sympathy for France. And a corollary of the same sympathy was a downplaying in Washington of the famed 'special relationship' between the two Anglo-Saxon powers.

Yet a favourable disposition on Pompidou's part towards the British application for EC membership was not a sufficient condition for the latter's success. Making circumstances more propitious was the surprise win of the Conservatives in the British general election of June 1970. That passionate European, Edward Heath, who had been the Macmillan government's chief negotiator in 1961–63 for the first accession attempt, took office as prime minister. All was now to depend on how Heath and Pompidou dealt with settling the French objections that had stood in the way of British membership. A good augur was that the strength and extent of the new prime minister's commitment to the EC, as well as to other European cooperation, could be directly vouched for by Pompidou's right-hand man at the Elysée, Michel Jobert, who was secretary general of the Presidency of the Republic from 1969 to 1973, before becoming foreign minister. Jobert and Heath were old friends, having first met in 1960 when holidaying at the same hotel in Spain. Serving as a gage of good will were the British prime minister's views on security and defence. In 1967, Heath had delivered the Godkin Lectures at Harvard University: speaking about defence policy in a Western European context, he had envisaged the 'possibility of an eventual European defence system', and he had expressed as his own view that such a system might include 'a nuclear force based on the existing British and French forces which could be held in trusteeship for Europe as a whole'.[5] When the lectures were published in 1970, Jobert translated some passages, including the reflections on defence, for Pompidou. 'We can work together with that man' was apparently the immediate response.[6] From 1970 the 'Soames affair' was forgotten, and, at Downing Street, there resided a prime minister for whom the 'special relationship' with the US held little attraction, at least as a foreign-policy lodestar.

Already before Heath became prime minister, the EC's leaders had cleared the ground for the opening of serious negotiations with the UK and the other three applicants, namely Denmark, Ireland, and Norway.

This advance forward occurred at the EC summit held in The Hague in December 1969, the conditions for its success having been established beforehand by Pompidou. Thus, it was the French president who had taken the initiative in July 1969 in calling for the summit itself and entering into an understanding with Brandt, the new German Chancellor. Then, during the months that followed, he was to insist on the need for the EC to pursue, as mutually complementary aims, 'completion' (primarily financial arrangements for the CAP), 'deepening' (above all, in French eyes, new arrangements to achieve currency stability), and, last in the triptych, 'enlargement'. Because of the progress made at the Hague summit on 'completion' and 'deepening', Pompidou was ready to join the heads of government of the other five member states in a commitment to enlargement.

A fresh momentum was thereby imparted to EC affairs. Only three weeks after the summit, the EC Council of Ministers agreed in principle to the creation of the EC's system of 'own resources' to replace direct financial contributions to the EC budget from member states. The EC Decision, formalising this agreement (with effect from 1 January 1971), was adopted in April 1970. The financing of the CAP was finally taken out of national hands, a step that had so long been a French objective. As to the achievement of greater currency stability – the other French priority – the package agreed at the Hague summit included an ambitious commitment to EMU, and this led in March 1970 to the setting up of the Werner Committee.

EC negotiations were reopened with the UK in July 1970. The decisive breakthrough took place the following year. In March 1971, Soames, who had been kept on in Paris at the express request of the incoming French prime minister, now gave his opinion to Heath that Pompidou would prefer to settle the outstanding crucial issues bilaterally and at the highest level – rather than leave the task to Schumann, the French foreign minister, acting through the EC Council of Ministers. The other EC member states, according to Soames, would see the practical advantage of such an approach. He was duly instructed to explore with Jobert the possibility of a summit meeting between the French president and the British prime minister. The response proved a favourable one. A two-day meeting was held in Paris in May 1971. Schumann and the Quai d'Orsay were allowed no part. And Heath's advisers, who were at least present at the Elysée, also found themselves redundant. Perhaps the most difficult issue was that of the sterling balances, and Heath convinced Pompidou that the British government would seek to reduce these balances and, more generally, reduce sterling's role as a reserve currency. This was partly an assurance that sterling would not stand in the way of EMU. At the end of the summit, the French president – sitting alongside the British prime minister in the Elysée Palace's Salle des Fêtes, where de Gaulle had announced theatrically his first veto in 1963 – told the assembled press corps that the time for French vetoes was over. A month later the EC negotiations with the UK and the other three applicants were completed, and, in January 1972, the treaties of accession bringing the four into the EC on 1 January 1973 were signed in Brussels (Norway's accession terms, however, being rejected in a national referendum shortly afterwards).

Pompidou called a referendum in France in April 1972 to ratify the EC accession treaties, rather than simply submitting them, as allowed by the constitution, to parliament. Various reasons influenced his choice, the most obvious being his desire that the French electorate give plebiscitary approval to the considerable part he had played since 1969 in improving relations with the UK and making this first EC enlargement possible. It was a miscalculation. The treaties were approved in the French referendum, but, with 68 per cent of votes cast in favour, not as overwhelmingly as he had hoped. What was galling for Pompidou was that only three-fifths of the electorate deigned to vote at all. This show of public indifference deeply disappointed him. Domestically, it contributed to his decision in preparation for the 1973 legislative elections to change prime minister, with the orthodox Gaullist, Messmer, taking over from Chaban-Delmas in July 1972. On the EC stage, where Pompidou had emerged as the leading European statesman since his initiative three years earlier in convening the Hague summit, he now found his wings clipped because of the referendum's expression of lack of strong support at home for what he had achieved. Henceforth he was to consecrate less of his energies to EC affairs. The second and last EC summit he was to convene, that held in Paris in October 1972, proved a pale affair, especially when compared with the almost phoenix-like nature of the previous EC summit in the Dutch capital in December 1969.

Outside the EC framework, the idea of substantial nuclear defence cooperation between France and the UK, as had been proposed by Heath in his Harvard lectures in 1967, turned out to be a nonstarter. The possibility of such cooperation was discussed secretly by Pompidou and Heath in March 1972 and again in May 1973. However, it would appear that the French president evinced no enthusiasm for any ambitious venture.[7] Perhaps the fact that France was benefiting now from secret nuclear cooperation with the US may have influenced his seemingly lukewarm attitude. In any case, there was to be no further return to Heath's idea of privileged cooperation between the two countries in the building of a European defence identity. By mid 1973 Pompidou was ravaged by the leukaemia that led to his death in office in April 1974. Only a month beforehand, after a snap British general election at a time of industrial discontent, Heath's premiership had come to an end and, with it, 'pro-European' Tory rule.

Echoes of the Fouchet Proposals

EPC and France's Part in the Helsinki Final Act

A leading feature of the Fouchet proposals had been the aim of establishing a common foreign policy, at least in areas where states shared a common interest. The idea was revived at the EC summit held in The Hague in December 1969. However, on this occasion, the running was made not by France but by West Germany and Belgium in the persons, respectively, of Brandt and Gaston Eyskens. Largely as a result of the impetus they provided, the summit leaders agreed to the setting up of a committee, comprising the political directors of the foreign-affairs ministries of the Six, whose brief was 'to study the best way of achieving progress in the matter of political unification', which meant, more prosaically, cooperation in the sphere of foreign policy. In October 1970 the result of this committee's work was submitted to the EC foreign ministers and adopted by them. Known either as the Davignon Report (named after the future EC commissioner, then the political director at the Belgium's Ministry of Foreign Affairs, who chaired the committee) or else as the Luxembourg Report, it opened the way to 'European political cooperation'. This was the process of foreign-policy cooperation managed outside the framework of the EC treaties until the SEA, after its ratification in 1987, formally provided for it.

Pompidou at the Hague summit had been willing to countenance twice-yearly meetings of the foreign ministers (rather than quarterly ones, as preferred by Germany and Belgium), and the twice-yearly formula was that put forward in the Davignon Report. A change to quarterly meetings came as the result of the Copenhagen Report, the Davignon Report's successor, in November 1973. This move to EPC was partly in the spirit of the Fouchet proposals. However, the French ambition expressed in the first Fouchet Plan's proposal for setting up a European Political Commission in Paris had found no support in The Hague in 1969. The French president had resurrected this particular proposal inasmuch as he suggested, unsuccessfully, that a political secretariat should be set up in Paris at the service of the foreign ministers. Such a secretariat was eventually to be created, by virtue of the SEA, but it was located in Brussels rather than Paris, before its being merged, pursuant to the Maastricht Treaty and the establishing of the CFSP, with the General Secretariat of the Council of Ministers.

Although positively disposed towards EPC, Pompidou was sceptical about how far it could be advanced towards a truly common policy under any arrangements that put all EC member states on an equal footing, especially after the increase in their number following EC enlargement, and also at a time when West Germany had become bent on its own Ostpolitik. Lacking was a sufficient common will. His pragmatism, as

Schumann related many years later, prevented him from 'entertaining the illusion that our European partners were ready, during his seven-year term or even much later, to put into practice an independent foreign policy'.[8]

Nonetheless, it was mainly during the period of Pompidou's presidency that the EC member states, acting together in the EPC framework, played a major part in the preparation of the most important pan-European treaty to be drawn up in the long aftermath of the Second World War. This was the Final Act of the Conference on Security and Cooperation in Europe (CSCE), which was signed in Helsinki in August 1975, more than a year into Giscard d'Estaing's presidency; there were thirty-five signatory states in all, including two from outside Europe, the US and Canada. Prior to the introduction of EPC, Pompidou had played some role in the tortuous diplomacy that paved the way to the CSCE negotiations. For in October 1969 the French president had been the first Western leader to respond favourably to Soviet overtures for a conference on European security, a readiness to participate having been signalled from Paris in June 1970. The prime Soviet aim was to use the force of international law to consecrate Europe's existing frontiers, not least the intra-German border and the Oder–Neisse Line. Assuring the permanence of Europe's post-Yalta order was not an aim from which Pompidou was inclined to demur. However, he urged from the outset that the question of human rights should also be addressed by the proposed conference. Nixon and other Western leaders were later to make the same precondition, which was the origin of the inclusion in the Helsinki Final Act of its 'Basket III' provisions on human rights, sitting uneasily alongside its 'Basket I' provisions relating to the permanence of existing borders and its 'Basket II' provisions relating to economic cooperation. In the following decade and half, this commitment in the Final Act to human rights was to be a considerable source of strength for the increasing number of people in Central and Eastern Europe who dared to protest against the stifling of freedom under communist rule.

In the wake of the initial French response, the EC's foreign ministers had put the proposed European security conference on the agenda of their very first EPC meeting, held in November 1970. Subsequently, in 1972 and 1973, they used the EPC framework to exercise collectively a leading role in the preparation of the organisation of the conference itself and, in particular, in arranging its negotiations around the three sets of issues that led to the Final Act's three 'baskets'.

The CSCE's formal opening in Helsinki in July 1973 provided Jobert, by then France's foreign minister, with the occasion for insisting that Europe should no longer be the playground of the two superpowers. His peppery and much remarked-upon address showed a sense of assurance that derived from the EC's role in the successful launching of the CSCE and from France's contribution to that role. As to his rhetoric of independence, it owed something to his and Pompidou's refusal two months earlier of the Nixon administration's controversial 'Year of Europe' initiative. This rhetoric reflected more a French view of the world than a universally held EC one – though Heath was sympathetic to it. In those matters that were to come under the Helsinki Final Act's 'Basket I' heading and had a bearing on Germany's future, a divergence of interests existed between France and the FRG. As the shaping of the Helsinki Final Act neared completion two years later, the US was to look to the long-term interests of the Bonn government, then headed by Schmidt, when the US Secretary of State, Kissinger, negotiated the insertion into the Final Act of a formula qualifying the principle of inviolability of Europe's post-war frontiers. By this insertion, allowance was made for the possibility of changed frontiers, including implicitly their abolition, provided any such change was 'in accordance with international law, by peaceful means, and by agreement'. This was not in the spirit of the original Soviet design for a European security conference, nor in the spirit of Pompidou's early willingness to respond positively to it.

The Concept of a European Confederation and the European Council's Creation

More than three years into his presidency, Pompidou remained as wedded as ever to the Gaullist idea of Europe as a 'Union of States'. At the EC summit held in Paris in October 1972, which brought together the leaders of both the Six and the incoming three new member states, the final communiqué was penned in large part by him. It contained not only an expression of approval of the objective of the progressive realisation of EMU (to be recalled in the SEA's preamble in 1986), but also a commitment 'to transform the whole complex of [member-state] relations into a European Union before the end of the decade', though without any real precision of what this term 'European Union' meant.

In fact, Pompidou had hoped to use the occasion of the summit to have the more precise term 'confederation', beloved of de Gaulle, introduced into the consecrated EC lexicon; it had the advantage of denoting clearly that any future European union was not to be at the expense of the nation state. But when the French ambassador in Bonn broached the matter with the German Foreign Office in July 1972, it was made clear that the term 'confederation', with its resonances from nineteenth-century German history, would not wash with the FRG's citizenry. Eleven years earlier a similar objection had been raised in Bonn to de Gaulle's preference for the same term. The word 'union' – de Gaulle's own second-best option – was proposed instead by the Foreign Office, the word's very vagueness and conceptual elasticity being put forward as a virtue. Pompidou consented.[9] Later he was to say that, in accepting the term 'European Union', he had been attracted by its very Delphic quality, which obviated any need to choose between the terms 'federation' and 'confederation' to describe whatever new political arrangements might pragmatically be decided upon, alongside or around the Treaty of Rome.[10] But that was perhaps to put a good face on the rebuff he had received on the occasion of the initial soundings in the German capital.

Between March and October 1973, Jobert sought to persuade his master of the desirability of holding more regular and structured EC summit meetings. Initially, he had mooted the idea of a formally privileged role for France, the UK, and Germany in representing 'Europe'. But Pompidou evinced no enthusiasm. The French foreign minister then enlisted the help of Monnet, who, in the summer of 1973 and at the ripe age of eighty-four, drew up a project for a 'provisional European government'. Such 'government' was to consist essentially of quarterly meetings of the EC heads of state or government to pursue the aims of 'European Union' and EMU, as established by the Paris summit of the previous year. The Luxembourg Compromise of 1966 had been approved by Monnet for essentially pragmatic reasons, and he now took care to insist on the need for an intergovernmental approach, even if his own personal vision for the long-term future went well beyond it. Both Heath and Brandt, who were consulted and kept informed by Jobert, encouraged the French president to take an initiative in institutionalising the summit meetings. Thus, in October, a month after receiving Monnet's report, Pompidou announced that the French government would be proposing to its EC partners that the heads of state or government meet regularly to debate and harmonise their positions in the matter of political cooperation. This was the origin of the Copenhagen summit in December 1973. The principle of the French proposal – now fleshed out a little more, with a preference declared for two ordinary meetings each year at summit level – was largely accepted. However, France's EC partners wanted the remit of the institutionalised summit meetings to extend beyond EPC and deal also with EC matters. And a month later the French president rallied without enthusiasm to this idea of a broader remit.

It was left to a further summit, held in Paris in December 1974 when France held the EC half-year presidency, to arrive at a final agreement. Pompidou was now dead. Giscard d'Estaing reformulated the French proposal and won approval for the institution of the European Council. It was to meet three times a year in ordinary session, though when, a decade later, the SEA formally brought the European Council under the umbrella of EC treaty law, the minimum requirement was put at twice a year. It was also at this Paris summit that Giscard won assent for the holding of direct elections for the European Parliament from 1979 onwards. However, it was to the institution of the European Council that he attached by far the greater importance; the enhancement of the European Parliament's position was the price to be paid for it.[11]

In view of Monnet's role in 1973, this establishment of the European Council, which was to prove of far-reaching consequence for the EC's future, might be seen as a return to the spirit of a bolder, pristine age. The Gaullist imprint lay heavy, however. Giscard was in no doubt that the creation of the European Council accorded well with the foreign-policy decision-making mechanisms in France as shaped by the constitution of the Fifth Republic. For even if, formally speaking, foreign policy was never part of a 'reserved domain' of the President of the Republic, the framing of foreign policy had lain squarely in presidential hands ever since 1959. The European Council appeared therefore an ideal forum for the exercise of French power or influence, especially since any French president, on account of the prestige of his office and the length of his presidential mandate, would tend to enjoy a privileged position on what was now to be the supreme EC policy-making body. What the creation of the European Council brought to mind was not so much the Schuman Declaration as the failed Fouchet proposals. 'A major initiative whose inspiration is to be seen as inherited from de Gaulle rather than Jean Monnet', was the apposite remark of Jean François-Poncet when he looked back in 1983 on his years as French foreign minister under Giscard; and he stressed that the French president's policy, like that of his two predecessors, was shaped by the vision of a 'confederal Europe'.[12]

In the remaining years of his presidency, after the setting up of the European Council, Giscard d'Estaing associated the role of the new body with the organisation of a 'European confederation'. In this French president's view, it was by virtue of the European Council's concentrating powers into its hands that it would be possible for a 'European confederation' to take shape.[13] The powers of the European Council were later to be formally set out in the SEA and built upon in the Maastricht Treaty.

America's 'Year of Europe' and the Atlantic Alliance

Rethinking the Alliance

The EC's development in the period running from the Hague summit of December 1969 to the first meeting of the European Council in March 1975 did not take place in an international vacuum. The years in question were ones of adjustment for the US. As he extricated his country with difficulty from the imbroglio of the Vietnam war and the wider conflict in Indochina, Nixon sought to redefine America's world role and, in particular, to remould relations with Europe in the widest sense, including the USSR, and also with China. In this endeavour, he was especially keen to cooperate with France, initially for three brief months with de Gaulle himself, and then with Pompidou, who, he considered, had the merit of remaining faithful to the General's realism in international politics.

Indeed, Nixon was ready to treat Pompidou as his privileged interlocutor among Western European statesmen and thereby to treat France as Western Europe's leading state – at least up to the time of the Yom Kippur War in October 1973.

Not only did the American president choose to favour France in this way in the diplomatic handling of the international monetary crisis of 1971 (see next chapter), but it was also the approach tried when Nixon and Kissinger, then the National Security Advisor, launched their ill-starred 'Year of Europe' initiative in 1973. The context was East–West détente: the first Strategic Arms Limitations Talks treaty (SALT I) had been signed by the two superpowers in May 1972, and it was followed in June 1973 by their Agreement on the Prevention of Nuclear War. Détente pointed to the need, in American eyes, for the working out of a new Atlantic Charter, including a renovated defence strategy for the US and its allies. Kissinger's brainchild, the 'Year of Europe', was intended to serve as the occasion for the negotiations to this end.

In late April 1973, Kissinger announced this 'Year of Europe' in a speech delivered in New York. He believed that he had the support of Pompidou, and, indeed, he was later to assert that the initiative had partly originated with the French president in December 1972. However, this influential member of the Nixon administration paid himself no favour in contrasting the 'global interests and responsibilities' of the US with the (mere) 'regional interests' of its European allies, and he was later to regret this lack of presentational tact. The speech appeared to call for a pliant Western Europe. Yet Pompidou reassured Kissinger in Paris in mid May that he had not taken offence since the asserted imbalance in geopolitical interests was largely true. The stumbling block for Pompidou was of a different order. He thought the American eagerness for détente to be imprudent, and he questioned the wisdom of the forthcoming Agreement on the Prevention of Nuclear War. Backing Pompidou, and perhaps even more wary of American policy in respect of Western European security, was Jobert, who had replaced Schumann as foreign minister just a few weeks before Kissinger's 'Year of Europe' speech. The large degree of mutual trust generated by Jobert's longstanding collaboration with Pompidou, combined with the debilitating effects of the president's deepening fatal illness, gave the mecurial Jobert wide latitude for manoeuvre as foreign minister. This latitude he amply used to foil Kissinger and kill off any idea of a far-reaching revision of the Atlantic Charter.

The crucial occasion was the two-day meeting between Pompidou and Nixon which opened in Reykjavik at the end of May 1973. By this time, the French president was wary, like Jobert, of the American initiative, fearing that a hidden purpose of the 'Year of Europe' was to facilitate a new sort of US–Soviet condominium. He remarked wryly to Nixon of his uncertainty whether the 'Year of Europe' was meant to be 'a year of beatification or of strangulation'.[14] The initiative, moreover, was clouded by the

Watergate affair, which had weakened the US president's position, even internationally. The final mapping out of the ground for the talks between the two presidents had been carried out by Jobert and Kissinger after their arrival in the Icelandic capital. Here Jobert succeeded in making the presidential talks little more than a general review of the international situation. His sharp style of diplomacy, first in limiting the agenda of the Reykjavik meeting and afterwards in manoeuvring the EC member states as a bloc into a confrontational stance against the US over the 'Year of Europe', disabused Kissinger of the advantages of continuing to privilege France in the conduct of American relations with Western Europe. 'France', he wrote later, 'wanted to curtail neither its independence in the Alliance nor its claim to the leadership of Europe. On this rock an aspiration to greater Atlantic coherence was bound to run aground.' Thus, when Kissinger became Secretary of State in September 1973, the idea of 'conceding Paris a leadership role' – his own words describing his earlier readiness to work with Jobert – could no longer be countenanced.[15] Indeed diplomatic relations between the two countries were to come under serious strain in the closing months of the same year when the French president effectively took Egypt's side in the Yom Kippur War, while, at the same time, the foreign minister openly attacked US policy towards the Middle East.

Yet saying no to the 'Year of Europe', and later dissenting from the US position in the Arab–Israeli conflict, was far from tantamount to a rejection of the Atlantic Alliance. Throughout his presidency, Pompidou remained convinced of the imperative of a strong American military commitment to Western Europe and worried frequently about its being eroded or abandoned, notably in the context of East–West détente. Notwithstanding France's continued absence from NATO's integrated military command and the development of the independent nuclear *force de frappe*, there were further adjustments of national defence strategy in the spirit of the Ailleret–Lemnitzer agreement. Thus, in 1972 the Defence White Book *La Politique de défense de la France* underlined France's attachment to the Atlantic Alliance and its shared security interests with its European neighbours. Negotiations started in the same year between General Valentin, Chief of Staff of France's 1st Army, and General Ferber, CINC–AFCENT, to arrange for the placing of the entire 1st Army, rather than just the army corps stationed in Germany, under NATO command in the event of a European war. The two generals were to sign their agreement in July 1974, three months after Pompidou's death.[16]

Pompidou's commitment to the status quo of the Atlantic Alliance was also manifest in his rejection of overtures from West Germany for the creation of a new European defence organisation as part of a changed security framework for the continent. As from December 1972, following Brandt's reelection and the signing of the Treaty on the Bases of Relations between the FRG and the GDR (a decisive step forward for Brandt's

Ostpolitik), differences had hardened between Paris and Bonn over the extent to which the fruits of the Ostpolitik should now be sought in the form of force reductions by both sides in Europe. The talks on Mutual Balanced Force Reductions (MBFR) were due to open in Vienna in October 1973. No sympathy existed in Paris for the ideas of Egon Bahr – Brandt's right-hand man for all pertaining to the Ostpolitik – who desired a radically new security system for Europe, entailing notably the departure of all American troops. On this score Pompidou feared collusion between the FRG and the USSR. In June 1973, at a twice-yearly Franco-German summit meeting, the Chancellor proposed 'an organisation of common defence supplementing or replacing NATO', in which West Germany would be accorded more than just 'an infantry role'; this was after Brandt had complained about the uncertainty created for Germany by France's having brought tactical nuclear weapons into service in 1972. Then in November 1973 it was the turn of the German foreign minister, Walter Scheel, to propose to his counterpart, Jobert, the establishing of a common defence policy in an EC framework, partly or completely independent of the US, with nuclear defence treated as a supranational competence. But these overtures met with no positive response from Pompidou.[17]

Under Giscard d'Estaing, security and defence policies were further shifted in the direction of greater cohesion with those of France's allies in the Atlantic Alliance. In June 1974 the new French president was party to the North Atlantic Council's Ottawa Declaration under which France's power of nuclear deterrence, as well as the UK's, was stated to represent a contribution to the 'overall strengthening of the deterrence of the Alliance'. The Declaration had been a year in the making. In keeping with both the Defence White Book of 1972 and the Ottawa Declaration, the concept of the 'national sanctuary' as the touchstone of security and defence strategy discreetly gave way to the wider concept of the 'enlarged sanctuary'. This meant that the planned use of France's military power, including nuclear weapons, should henceforth be assumed to extend to the defence of its European neighbours, with West Germany above all in mind, and that, geopolitically, France's vital interests could enter into play anywhere in Europe or the Mediterranean area. This concept of the 'enlarged sanctuary' was implicit in the preamble to the military programme law for 1977–82, which was debated and voted by parliament in the course of 1976, and it was made explicit in an article written for the *Revue de défense nationale* of June 1976 by General Méry, Chief of Staff of the Armed Forces. In practice, the concept had already begun to be implemented in 1975 when General Méry and SACEUR, General Haig, opened talks on about how best NATO's integrated military command and the French general staff could coordinate any move to nuclear war, especially their use of tactical nuclear weapons. Yet France's possession of such weapons remained a bugbear for West Germany on account of their short range, which meant that, if ever they were used, their targets would likely to be on German territory.[18]

Nuclear Collaboration and New Frictions

The reinvigoration of the French commitment to the Atlantic Alliance under Pompidou and Giscard d'Estaing, in the shape of an increasing de facto rapprochement with NATO's integrated military command, owed something to an American readiness to covertly assist France in the development of its nuclear defence programme. Such a readiness would have been unthinkable under the Kennedy or Johnson presidencies. The initiators were Nixon and Kissinger during their failed launching of the 'Year of Europe'. Their reasoning was that the independent French nuclear force made a positive contribution to Western security, and that it was accordingly in the interest of the Alliance that it be as effective as possible, provided the national security of the US was not prejudiced by the sharing of knowledge or expertise. The actual offer of American technical assistance was first made by Kissinger to Jobert in June 1973 at the western 'White House' in San Clemente, California, just after the signing there by Nixon and Brezhnev of their bilateral Agreement on the Prevention of Nuclear War. For assistance with the design of nuclear weapons, there could be only 'negative guidance' – that is, answering French queries through signalling fruitless paths of exploration – since much of the relevant information was classified. On the other hand, for assistance with the design of delivery systems or the sharing of intelligence data concerning the USSR, there could be more largesse. Having relayed the American overture back to Paris, Jobert, in his remaining eleven months as foreign minister, was apparently under the impression that it had been spurned. However, Pompidou, while being at one with Jobert in the stymieing of the 'Year of Europe', was receptive to this more practical idea of nuclear collaboration, and so it started on a secret footing.

On the French side, the key persons involved at the outset were the heads of the CEA and the Délégation Générale pour l'Armement (the government agency responsible for arms production), as well as the French ambassador in Washington. Secrecy was assured by the bypassing of normal government channels; all arrangements were made at a very high level through the offices of the Presidency of the Republic at the Elysée and the National Security Council at the White House.

The collaboration gathered pace under the presidency of Giscard d'Estaing with, on the American side, Jimmy Carter succeeding Gerald Ford at the beginning of 1977. To some extent, it developed into a two-way traffic, with the Americans benefiting from the high quality of the CEA's research work, notably in the domain of safety and technical security.[19]

More generally, the early years of Giscard's presidency were marked by improving Franco-American relations, even if there was essentially no change to the post-October 1973 stance adopted by Pompidou and Jobert towards the Arab world and its oil-exporting countries. Within the Atlantic Alliance, the shift in French defence planning in 1975–76 towards the concept of the 'enlarged sanctuary', coupled with a greater readiness on France's part to coordinate planning with NATO's integrated military command and also to increase (much needed) defence expenditure on conventional capabilities, met with Washington's satisfaction. It represented a partial move towards NATO's doctrine of 'flexible response'. Furthermore, in an unstable Africa, France's role as a regional gendarme – strongly pushed by Giscard – was often in keeping with American interests.

In January 1979 it was Giscard d'Estaing who hosted the Western Four-Power summit in Guadeloupe. Coordinating his position with that of Schmidt, who was the summit's dominant European figure, the French president gave discrete backing to what was to emerge as NATO's 'twin-track' response to the Soviet build-up of SS-20 intermediate-range nuclear ballistic missiles (approximate range: 4,500 kilometres). This 'twin-track' response, which took its inspiration from NATO's Harmel Report of 1967, consisted essentially of the carrot – the offer of disarmament negotiations – and the stick – the deployment of new US intermediate-range nuclear missiles in Western Europe in the absence of such negotiations. It was formally agreed by the North Atlantic Council in December 1979. However, determined to forestall Soviet pressure for French nuclear missiles to be counted in any future East-West disarmament negotiations, Giscard refrained from associating France formally with the December agreement, and a ready reason was at hand, namely France's thirteen years of self-exclusion from NATO's integrated command.

Before the end of 1979, because of Giscard's increasing reservations about Carter's international policies (reservations shared by Schmidt), France's relations with the US were following essentially the same trajectory as they did under Pompidou. A first phase of largely excellent relations was being followed by a second phase of strains and mutual reticence. In 1980 the strains were aggravated. At stake were relations with the USSR and the Arab world.

After the start of the Soviet invasion of Afghanistan in December 1979, Giscard refused to follow Carter in reacting vigorously to the Soviet move. Not only did the French president's stance bring a chill between Paris and Washington, but it also prevented the European Council or the EC's foreign ministers, acting in an EPC framework, from strongly backing the US. The French president's self-appointed and fruitless role as honest broker when he met Brezhnev in Warsaw in May 1980 made matters only worse. And it cost him some loss of support in France, notably after Mitterrand scathingly described him as Brezhnev's telegraph boy ('*le petit télégraphiste*').[20]

Then, in June 1980 when the European Council met in Venice, Giscard played a considerable part in influencing or persuading his fellow EC leaders to issue a joint statement on the situation in the Middle East. Thus, in what was to become known as the Venice Declaration, the leaders of the EC–9 affirmed the Palestinian people's right to self-determination. Furthermore, they asserted that the Palestinian Liberation Organisation (PLO) must be associated with negotiations for settling the Arab–Israeli conflict and that the basis of these negotiations must be UN Security Council Resolution 242 (adopted in 1967). Only four months earlier Israel and Egypt had exchanged formal diplomatic recognition in the framework of the Camp David peace settlement of September 1978. The Venice Declaration made clear that the European Council, under the French president's prompting, wanted urgently a 'comprehensive solution to the Israeli–Arab conflict', which, by implication, was to question the less ambitious and more pragmatic American approach.[21]

At the beginning of the 1980s, therefore, Giscard d'Estaing was bent on showing that the interests of Western Europe, especially across the continental divide in Soviet-bloc Europe or on the eastern shores of the Mediterranean, did not necessarily coincide with those of the US. He was convinced that, alongside the need for military firmness towards the USSR, economic détente was also required. Like Schmidt, Giscard attached great importance to the beneficial effects of trade and economic cooperation with the USSR and the rest of the Soviet bloc. And he had worried from the early years of Carter's presidency about how such economic ties would be affected by the US president's concern with human rights in the USSR, a concern the French president judged to be excessive (notwithstanding its matching the spirit of the Helsinki Final Act's 'Basket III' provisions). Now, in 1980, the 'great game' excursion of the USSR into Afghanistan was perceived by Giscard to be remote from Western European interests, and therefore not meriting the response pushed by the Americans. As to the Venice Declaration and the Arab–Israeli conflict, the French position – transmuted into an EC one – was in line with French foreign policy since the Yom Kippur War of 1973, if not since the Six Days' War of 1967. In short, Giscard was using the European Council and EPC for pushing a foreign-policy agenda that had a distinctly Gaullist echo.

Prior to the deterioration in Franco-American relations in the closing years of Giscard d'Estaing's presidency, the Barre government had started to play down the significance of the shift in French defence-planning strategy which had occurred in 1975–76 as a result of the introduction of the concept of the 'enlarged sanctuary'. The subject remained a controversial one in political and policy-making circles in France until the end of Giscard's seven-year term, and defence planning strategy took on, anew, a somewhat more Gaullist hue. Yet neither for this reason nor on account of foreign-policy disagreements was there a halt to Franco-American collaboration in the sphere of nuclear weapons.

Back to the Elysée Treaty

French and German Uncertainties about the Superpowers

The seven-year period between the Soviet invasion of Afghanistan and the meeting between Mikhail Gorbachev and Ronald Reagan in Reykjavik towards the end of 1986 was an extraordinary one, covering, as it did, the final bout of tangible Cold War friction (1979–85), Reagan's SDI initiative in 1983, and, finally, the same American president's willingness in the Icelandic capital to contemplate total nuclear disarmament with his Soviet counterpart, to the surprise and dismay of Western Europe's leaders. Reduced to its essentials, such was the international background to Mitterrand's new reshaping of French security and defence policy during his first presidential term. Growing reservations about American leadership of the Atlantic Alliance during the Reagan years, combined with persistent nagging fears that the FRG might be tempted to forsake its mooring to the West in exchange for national unification, led Mitterrand to increasingly accept that defence ties between France and West Germany should be especially privileged. There was thus a gradual return in Paris to much of the spirit of de Gaulle's handling of German relations in 1958–63.

A first step was taken in Paris in February 1982, at one of the regular twice yearly Franco-German summits, when Mitterrand and Schmidt decided to give substance to the defence provisions of the Elysée Treaty of 1963. The summits would henceforth include meetings of the two countries' foreign and defence ministers to discuss jointly questions of security and defence. They would be served by a Commission on Security and Defence comprising high-ranking representatives of the four ministries. Under its umbrella, three standing committees would concern themselves with, respectively, politico-strategic coordination, cooperation in the sphere of armaments, and military cooperation. These agreements, making for a closer tie between defence and foreign policies in the framework of the cooperation prescribed by the Elysée Treaty, were subsequently finalised and given effect at the following bilateral summit held in Bonn in October 1982, by which time Kohl had replaced Schmidt as Chancellor.

This Franco-German summit of October 1982 and its preparatory meeting earlier in the same month, when Kohl had introduced himself to Mitterrand in Paris on his first official visit abroad as Chancellor, marked indeed the beginning of their thirteen-year political friendship. An element of irony lay in the fact that this good start owed much to Schmidt, who for different reasons was no natural political friend of either of the two men. For in the reactivation of the defence provisions of the Elysée Treaty eight months earlier it was Schmidt, rather than Mitterrand, who played the leading part. The idea was one that he had entertained for a few years, that he had long discussed with Giscard d'Estaing, and that he was now promoting anew with the latter's successor.[22]

Despite his regret at the outcome of the French presidential election in May 1981, Schmidt had been the first foreign statesman to pay a visit to the Elysée's new incumbent, and in October of the same year he had two days of talks with Mitterrand at the latter's country house at Latché in the Landes. Much discussed was the US under Reagan's leadership and the state of the Atlantic Alliance. The Chancellor expressed his unease about the Cold War hawks surrounding the American president, and his worry that insufficient attention was being paid to the more measured views of the Secretary of State and former SACEUR, Alexander Haig. Schmidt's own position was that NATO's 'twin-track' decision of December 1979 had to be rigorously respected. In the absence of a Soviet climbdown over the SS-20s, there should be no tergiversation about the deployment of the state-of-the-art Pershing II ballistic missiles (approximate range: 1,800 kilometres) in West Germany and, additionally, the Tomahawk cruise missiles (approximate range: 2,500 kilometres) in the UK, Italy, the Netherlands, Belgium, and West Germany. On the other hand, what appeared to Schmidt to have been forgotten in Washington was that the 'twin-track' decision entailed also a commitment to seek the opening of talks with the USSR for an agreed reduction of intermediate-range nuclear forces (INF) in Europe. Once there were such talks, he told Mitterrand, his own preference was for the so-called zero option, meaning that the Soviet dismantlement of all such forces (SS-20s and, accessorily, the older-generation SS-4s and SS-5s) would be matched by the cancellation of the entire threatened NATO deployment. Thus, his desired end result was the elimination from the continent of intermediate-range nuclear missiles, at least those of the superpowers.

Mitterrand readily agreed with the need for a tough NATO stance, especially that represented by the planned deployment, if necessary, of Pershing II missiles in West Germany. He shared also Schmidt's hope that the Soviets would come to the negotiating table. Like his predecessor Giscard d'Estaing, but outspokenly so, the new French president had always supported the 'twin-track' decision.

No doubt to Mitterrand's and Schmidt's surprise, Reagan announced shortly after the time of the Latché talks that the US was entering into INF and other arms-control and disarmament negotiations with the USSR. These were to start in Geneva already at the end of November 1981. But the French president now became worried that the question of the size of France's nuclear force would be dragged into the INF negotiations – a similar concern having contributed to the muted nature of Giscard's support in 1979 for the 'twin-track' decision. It was therefore requested of Washington that there be no mention of France's nuclear force in any bilateral agreement between the US and the USSR. The same worry also led the French president to distance himself from the zero option favoured by Schmidt, since such an outcome, rather than the less ambitious one of mutual reductions in the numbers of deployed missiles, risked giving rise to international pressure on France to participate seriously in nuclear disarmament.

Mitterrand's Twentieth-anniversary Address to the Bundestag

A new adjustment of French defence policy occurred alongside these international developments. Marking a further step back from the 'enlarged sanctuary' thinking of 1975–76, this adjustment in 1981–83 served to emphasise that France's nuclear weapons were not automatically in the service of the Atlantic Alliance, and should not therefore be associated with it in any arms-reduction negotiations between the superpowers. Thus, as a general principle, nuclear deterrence became reserved anew for the protection of the 'national sanctuary', which, in the parlance of the time, was also termed the 'first circle' (the second of the 'circles' covered by French defence arrangements being Western Europe, essentially West Germany, and the third being the area of French interests outside Europe, mainly in Africa). To this end, it was decided by Mitterrand that the future generation of tactical nuclear weapons, the ground-launched Hadès (range: some 400 kilometres), should not be put under the command of the French 1st Army – which had been the original intention – since the latter might in time of crisis be made subordinate to NATO, by virtue of the Valentin–Ferber agreement. Instead the nature of these weapons was to be considered 'prestrategic': recourse might be had to the Hadès missiles only as an 'ultimate warning' of the possible use by France of strategic nuclear weapons; their use for purely tactical battlefield purposes was excluded. All the country's nuclear arsenal was thereby clearly ring-fenced for national purposes, and a justification was that France should not be sucked into a nuclear war if ever NATO, with perhaps the French 1st Army in tow, were to resort to tactical nuclear weapons in the face of a Soviet attack on German territory.[23]

At the Geneva negotiations, neither the US nor the USSR was pressed to reach a quick agreement. And they had soon differed over the question of whether British and French intermediate-range missiles should be considered part of the American nuclear arsenal in Europe. The talks entered into periods of temporary suspension. In June 1982, on the occasion of a visit to the FRG for a summit meeting of the North Atlantic Council, Reagan addressed the Bundestag and reaffirmed his resolve concerning the Pershing II and cruise missiles that were due to be deployed at the end of 1983. The American president's words were welcomed by the majority of Bundestag deputies, notwithstanding the growing opposition in the SPD's ranks, encouraged notably by Brandt, to Schmidt's defence stance. Outside the Bundestag the mood was very different as more than 200,000 demonstrators marched in the streets of Bonn in protest. The mammoth post-war clash between West Germany's political establishment and a domestic peace movement led by the Greens and the radical left had come to a head. In October the FDP deserted the SPD after thirteen years of coalition rule and threw in their lot anew with the CDU–CSU, allowing Kohl to take over as Chancellor. Although the reason for the FDP's transfer of allegiance pertained to economic policy, not defence policy, the SPD in opposition – unencumbered by Schmidt – quickly adopted a neutralist stance on the issue of intermediate-range nuclear missiles. Kohl called for early Bundestag elections, which were set for March 1983. It was clear that the question of the deployment of the Pershing II missiles would be a major electoral issue, and that the CDU–CSU, but not the SPD, would be in favour of what had been Schmidt's position when Chancellor.

A significant turn taken by the INF negotiations affected the political debate in West Germany and heightened French concerns. In November 1982 Reagan proposed the zero option in respect of American and Soviet weaponry. Then in December the Soviet leader, Yuri Andropov, countered by reiterating the Soviet position that there should be no Pershing II deployment and by expressing a readiness, on the other hand, to reduce the number of SS-20s to the west of the Urals to a level comparable to the total of British and French intermediate-range nuclear missiles. The SPD's candidate for the post of Chancellor, Hans-Jochen Vogel, was favourable to this Andropov proposal. Accordingly, when paying a visit to Mitterrand in Paris in mid January 1983, exactly a week before the French president was due to address the Bundestag on the occasion of the twentieth anniversary of the Elysée Treaty, Vogel expressed views that were the exact opposite of his host's. Mitterrand was hostile to the American zero option and even more to the Soviet counter-proposal.

Thus, some seven years before the fall of the Berlin Wall, the INF controversy exposed one of the constants governing French security interests since the creation of the FRG, namely that France's regional leadership role in Western Europe actually took sustenance from the continuing conflict or rivalry on the European continent between the superpowers. Furthermore, the question of the deployment of the Pershing IIs made Mitterrand an objective ally of Kohl, despite their differing socialist and Christian Democrat persuasions. The French president feared the international consequences of the SPD's returning to power in Bonn, while the new German Chancellor was keen to have French support as he stood firmly behind a NATO policy that had raised bitter feelings among so many of his fellow citizens.

For Mitterrand, the Bundestag address on 20 January 1983 marking the twentieth anniversary of the Elysée Treaty provided an exceptional opportunity for influencing the debate. Whether he had long harboured an ambition of this kind is unclear. What is known is that the text of the address was prepared in haste and at the last minute, yet with great care. Only a week beforehand the French president's concerns regarding Germany had been heightened by Vogel's visit. However, later on the day of the same visit, Mitterrand left Paris for five days of official visits in French West and Equatorial Africa. And it was in Gabon that Mitterrand dismissed a preliminary draft of the Bundestag address, prepared by the Quai d'Orsay, as quite inadequate. Consequently, only after his return to Paris on 19 January did he and his collaborators prepare the actual address during an intense twenty-four hours, with the president making the final changes on the flight to Germany and indeed in the Bundestag itself, prior to entering the chamber. 'His obsession', noted Attali, accompanying him, 'is to head off German neutralism, as much as to avoid French arms being taken into account in the American-Soviet negotiations.'[24] Both 'obsessions' were patent in the important middle part of the French president's address, devoted to the question of security in the context of Franco-German relations, which came after a flowery introduction (linking the Hague congress of 1948, the endeavours of the trio of Adenauer, Monnet, and Schuman, and the Elysée Treaty itself), and before the prosaic enough last part devoted to current EC affairs.[25]

If one key passage of the address may be privileged, it is where Mitterrand resorted to the principle of the balance of power to justify, first, the deployment of Pershing IIs (and, by implication, France's nuclear missiles as well), and, secondly, to warn of the danger represented by an American nuclear disengagement from Western Europe:

> Our analysis and conviction, expressed in the name of France, is that nuclear weapons … remain the guarantee of peace once an equilibrium of forces has been established. Only this equilibrium, after all, can lead to good relations with the countries of the East, our neighbours and historical partners. It has provided the sound basis for what has been called détente. It has allowed you to implement your 'Ostpolitik'. It has rendered possible the Helsinki agreements.
>
> But the maintenance of this equilibrium entails, to my mind, that entire regions of Europe should not be deprived of the means of defence against nuclear weapons targeted against them. Whoever opts for the 'decoupling' between the European and American continents would endanger, in our judgement, the equilibrium of forces and hence the maintenance of peace.[26]

On the question of the INF talks, Mitterrand stressed that France could not become involved in them. There was, he said, a problem of comparability of weapons, meaning that no missiles similar to SS-20s or Pershing IIs existed on the French side. Furthermore, France was not a superpower and possessed relatively few nuclear weapons. If there were to be reductions in their numbers, the national policy of nuclear deterrence risked losing credibility. In general, France had its own 'vital interests', which paralleled, and were partly separate from, both its membership of the Atlantic Alliance and its friendship with the FRG. The independence of the French nuclear force had therefore to be preserved.[27]

Despite these precisions, the main message contained in the French president's address was widely considered to be a call for a strengthening of the Atlantic Alliance, and it met with Reagan's fulsome praise. The backing for the deployment of Pershing IIs, the rejection of any 'decoupling' on the nuclear front between the US and Western Europe, and amiable words about the recent creation of the Franco-German Commission on Security and Defence and the more general need for bilateral consultation between France and the FRG on security matters, all combined to give an Atlanticist-cum-European hue to Mitterrand's intervention. Yet the views he expressed were intended above all to serve France's more particular interests. Keeping West Germany locked into the Atlantic Alliance was a means to an end, namely to ensure that France retained the largest independent voice in security matters in Western Europe, and this itself was the precondition of France's continuing to carry weight in the eyes of Moscow and so being able to act sometimes as a privileged intermediary between the two superpowers. Mitterrand indeed maintained, not disingenuously, that his Bundestag address was not directed unilaterally against the USSR.[28]

The main result of the Bundestag address was a debt of lasting political gratitude on the part of Kohl to Mitterrand. The March 1983 elections in West Germany swept the coalition between the CDU–CSU and the FDP back to power, with the Christian Democrats winning their highest share of the vote since 1957. The intervention of the socialist French president had contributed to the SPD's disarray. It was in the same month of March that, coincidentally, Mitterrand took the important decision to keep the franc in the ERM (see next chapter). Henceforth, because of security and defence considerations as well as economic and monetary policies, the pursuit of close relations with the FRG became a still greater priority for French foreign policy, as well as a distinguishing mark of Mitterrand's own presidency.

The FAR and the Reactivation of WEU

In the sphere of security and defence, further developments initiated in the two years following the Bundestag address were the creation of the FAR (Force d'Action Rapide), a conventionally-armed rapid deployment force, which was announced by the defence minister, Charles Hernu, in June 1983, and the reactivation of WEU twelve months later. Both developments had a strong Franco-German dimension. Important in Mitterrand's mind were two considerations: a perceived need to foster closer non-nuclear defence ties with West Germany as a way of lessening the temptation of neutralism (the breakthrough achieved by the Greens in the

Bundestag elections constituting a warning in this respect); and a heightened concern about the strength of Reagan's defence commitment to Western Europe after he revealed his SDI ambition to the world in March 1983, without prior consultation with his partners in the Atlantic Alliance.

In the case of the FAR, one of the multiple roles planned for it was that its airmobile division be deployed in France's 'second circle' of defence, notably in the event of war on West German territory. What this role might represent in practice was to be indicated in September 1987 when the FAR and the Bundeswehr carried out their 'Bold Sparrow' joint exercise, a feature of which was the airlifting of some 20,000 French troops into the western end of Bavaria (just across the border from Baden-Württemberg near to Ulm). The intended military message was that the FAR was capable of making a contribution to West Germany's forward defence. That the joint exercise took place outside of a NATO framework, in the presence on the ground of both Kohl and Mitterrand but not of SACEUR, whose attendance as an observer had been vetoed by France, testified to the strong Gaullist leanings of the French president.

As to the so-called reactivation of the dormant WEU, it took initially the form of an official memorandum from its Council when it met at ministerial level in June 1984; then, four months later, in October, the memorandum provided the basis of the WEU Council's Rome Declaration. Formally speaking, this declaration by the foreign and defence ministers of the seven WEU member states marked the thirtieth anniversary of the modification of the original Brussels Treaty. The reactivation consisted in little more than an enhancement of the role of the Council itself and, accessorily, of the Assembly. To this end, it was agreed that the Council should meet at ministerial level twice rather than once a year. The declaration itself was carefully crafted to take account of differing views of the limits that should restrain WEU's relative degree of independence vis-à-vis NATO, the furthest apart being France and the UK, leaving West Germany uneasily in the middle. Initiating a practice that was to be repeated in the years ahead – most importantly, in the main WEU Declaration annexed to the Maastricht Treaty – the Council balanced a leaning towards a certain degree of autonomy with a repledged fealty to the Atlantic Alliance:

> Conscious of the continuing necessity to strengthen Western security and of the specifically Western European geographical, political, psychological and military dimensions, the Ministers underlined their determination to make better use of the WEU framework in order to increase cooperation between the member states in the field of security and to encourage consensus … The Ministers are convinced that a better utilisation of WEU would not only contribute to the security of Western Europe but also to an improvement in the common defence of all the countries of the Atlantic Alliance and to greater solidarity among its members.[29]

It was on the initiative of both the French and Belgian governments that the WEU Council met in Rome. However, the idea of breathing new life into the moribund WEU had originated earlier in discussions of the Franco-German Commission on Security and Defence. Here the initiative had come from the French rather than the German side. It met with a positive reaction, one reason being the desire of the foreign minister, Hans-Dietrich Genscher, to pursue his Ostpolitik in tandem with the strengthening of German ties with other Western European states in a new, bolder framework, as witness the (failed) Genscher–Colombo initiative of 1981 to extend EPC to security matters. A precondition set by Bonn for the reactivation of WEU was a lifting of the restrictions imposed in 1954 on West German conventional rearmament, and France was duly instrumental in having the WEU Council accede to this request.

However, the Rome Declaration bore scant fruit. The second French move to resuscitate WEU began just more than two years later, shortly after the Reykjavik summit meeting between Reagan and Gorbachev in October 1986. Perhaps surprisingly, in view of the prerogatives accorded by the Fifth Republic's constitution to the head of state in the domain of security and defence, the initial steps were taken by Chirac, the *cohabitation* prime minister, who was acting largely off his own bat. Concerned at Reagan's flirtation in the Icelandic capital with the idea of total nuclear disarmament – and stretching the limits of his constitutional powers as prime minister – Chirac addressed the WEU Assembly in December 1986 and called for a new security charter for Western Europe. This charter would, on the one hand, emphasise both the continuing importance of nuclear deterrence and the continuing need for US conventional and nuclear forces in the Western half of the continent, and, on the other hand, stress the importance of an adequate defence effort on the part of Western European countries themselves. In the course of 1987, pursuing this initiative, Chirac met Kohl, who had also been alarmed by Reagan's disarmament mood in Reykjavik, to discuss what might be agreed in the framework of WEU. This bilateral consultation at the level of the French prime minister and the Chancellor served as a catalyst for the preparation by the WEU Council of a report which led to WEU's foreign and defence ministers adopting the 'Platform on European Security Interests' at their meeting in The Hague in October 1987.

Much of the Hague Platform reflected the principles enunciated by Chirac ten months earlier. It built, moreover, on the SEA, which had entered into force only that summer. Thus, the Preamble to the Hague Platform referred to the authority of the SEA and, in particular, to the latter's commitment in its own preamble to the establishment of a European Union. According to the SEA's provisions for EPC, 'closer cooperation on questions of European security would contribute in an essential way to the development of a European identity in external policy matters', even if such cooperation had to be confined initially to the 'political and economic aspects of security' (Article 30). WEU's foreign and defence ministers wished to go beyond this timid introduction of the security dimension into

EC affairs. 'We are convinced', they declared, 'that the construction of an integrated Europe will remain incomplete as long as it does not include security and defence.' Yet this was not to be in separation from the US. Rather it was incumbent on WEU member states 'to strengthen the European pillar of the Alliance'. The language of diplomacy was carefully used to affirm the inherent reasonableness of the goal of a separate European security and defence identity within a wider American-led organisation.

The adoption of the Hague Platform marked the end of WEU's reactivation phase in the 1980s. In December 1987, only six weeks later, Gorbachev and Reagan signed the INF Treaty. It ordained the 'first and double zero options': the removal from all Europe of Soviet and US nuclear missiles with ranges of, respectively, between 5,000 and 1,000 kilometres and between 1,000 and 500 kilometres. The USSR, if only because of the dominant strength of its conventional forces in Europe, would have preferred, additionally, the 'third zero option', so as to eliminate tactical nuclear weapons – those with a range of less than some 500 kilometres. This, for obvious self-interested security considerations, would also have been the preference of the FRG, a bystander to the INF treaty.

Enhanced Defence Ties with West Germany

During this phase of reactivation of WEU, Mitterrand's own priority became the further cultivation of the bilateral Franco-German partnership, for its own sake and as the basis in the longer term for wider Western European security and defence arrangements. The French president's hostility to Reagan's SDI was partly founded on the perception that any formal subordination to the US in this domain could result in France's being effectively forced back into NATO's integrated command. However, what he could have only dimly realised in April 1985, at the time of the launching of Eureka to counter (in his eyes) the SDI, was that the Cold War was soon to draw to an end. Gorbachev had come to power in the USSR in the previous month. The long drawn-out Geneva disarmament talks started in earnest towards the end of the same year. A little like Stendhal's Fabrice del Dongo caught in the cloud of the battle of Waterloo, Mitterrand was to find himself in the second half of the 1980s in a maelstrom of events whose full significance was to become clear only later.

In May 1985 a meeting took place between Mitterrand and Kohl on the shores of Lake Constance. The SDI dominated much of their talk. The French president complained that, in the event of a breakdown in continental peace because of grave turbulence in communist-controlled Central Europe, the SDI would not prevent the USSR's launching of missiles from, say, Dresden on West Berlin or from Gdańsk on Hamburg.[30] The meeting marked an early step in Mitterrand's becoming disposed to the idea of more substantive security cooperation between France and

West Germany than that represented by the activities of the Franco-German Commission on Security and Defence. Kohl, for his part, was to prove a willing and active partner, being ready, as he was to show, to take the initiative.

Mitterrand's doubts about the US were heightened by Reagan's position at the Reykjavik superpower summit of October 1986. Not that he maintained his earlier opposition, evinced at the time of the Bundestag address, to the zero option. As soon as it had become clear that Gorbachev would not insist on the inclusion of French and British nuclear forces in the agreed arms reductions, which took place well in advance of the signing of the INF Treaty in December 1987, Mitterrand had been won over to acceptance of the 'first and double zero options'. And he started indeed to be open to the idea of the 'third zero option'. Thus, in March 1988 at a meeting of the North Atlantic Council in Brussels, Mitterrand backed Kohl and Genscher in their favouring of the superpowers' proceeding to the 'third zero option', though it was not to be until January 1990 that he decided to scale down greatly France's own Hadès programme. More fundamentally, by 1987 what the French president was insisting upon was not the need for a presence on European soil of American missiles, but rather the need for an equilibrium between the two superpowers' strategic forces and, on the American side, a continued commitment in the exercise of nuclear deterrence to Western Europe's security. However, because of doubts about this commitment in the long term and also continued concerns about Germany's future, which were reinforced by his perception of the new vistas opened to Bonn's Ostpolitik by the transformed situation in the USSR, he was even more receptive after Reykjavik to the idea of binding France and West Germany closer under a reinforced security umbrella of their own making.

Fresh discussions on security and defence were held with Kohl at the chateau of Chambord in March 1987. The running was now being made by the Chancellor. Kohl too had been shocked by what he took to be Reagan's apparently blithe disregard of Western European security, and he was worried about the effects of the future INF Treaty. Furthermore – shades of Adenauer – he was fearful of growing pressures in West Germany in favour of neutralism, especially if Gorbachev remained in power in Moscow. His best way of countering such domestic pressures, Kohl told Mitterrand, was through their putting a new Franco-German security and defence agreement into place, and he proposed that their two security advisers, Horst Teltschik and Attali, should lead secret talks to this end.

Later, on the fringe of the Group of Seven summit held in Venice in June 1987, Kohl sounded out Mitterrand about the possibility of creating integrated Franco-German army units. The French president reacted favourably, but cautioned that he would need the approval of Chirac, his *cohabitation* prime minister. Shortly afterwards Kohl was told that a proposal would be welcome. In July the talks between Teltschik and Attali led to the former's raising the idea of a full-fledged Franco-German Defence Council, whose competences would extend well beyond those of the existing Commission on Security and Defence. The Council, suggested Teltschik, would establish a common understanding of how best to deploy armed forces in Western Europe's defence; it would adopt a common position on disarmament negotiations; it would direct Franco-German cooperation in all domains of defence; and it would act as a forum for joint consultation at the highest level on the use of nuclear weapons. Again there was a basically positive, if guarded, reaction on the French side.

At the fiftieth twice-yearly Franco-German summit held in Karlsruhe in November 1987, formal blessing was given to the setting up of a Franco-German army brigade. Then, on 22 January 1988, on the twenty-fifth anniversary of the Elysée Treaty, a protocol was added so as to establish the Franco-German Defence Council. Sitting twice yearly, the new body was to comprise the French president, the French prime minister, the Chancellor, the two foreign ministers, the two defence ministers, France's Chief of Staff of the Armed Forces, and Germany's Inspector General of the Bundeswehr.

This use of the Elysée Treaty was strong in political symbolism. However, the reality was that France and West Germany did not see altogether eye-to-eye on the role of the Franco-German Defence Council and, indeed, on the nature of security and defence cooperation between the two countries. For large as was the overlap of their interests, their relations continued, as in the time of de Gaulle and Adenauer, to be bedevilled by France's jealously guarded independent nuclear force and Mitterrand's inheritance of the Gaullist mantle. Neither the determination that France should remain outside NATO's integrated command, nor the ambition that France should continue be the main power in continental Western Europe in the face of the USSR, sat easily with German policies. Contrary to what Teltschik had originally proposed to Attali, the remit of the Franco-German Defence Council did not extend to consultation concerning nuclear weapons, as witness Article 4 of the January 1988 protocol.[31] Furthermore, as long as France possessed tactical or 'prestrategic' nuclear weapons, Mitterrand remained adamantly opposed in principle to any idea of sharing decisions with West Germany about their use, even on German soil.

However, in his public pronouncements for domestic political purposes, Mitterrand overlooked such difficulties and expressed unalloyed pride in both the implementation of the defence provisions of the Elysée Treaty, as agreed by Kohl and himself in October 1982, and the later creation of the Defence Council. Thus, in April 1988, in penning his long tract *Lettre à tous les Français* for the forthcoming French presidential elections, he stressed that it was he and Kohl who had at last given substance to the defence plans of de Gaulle and Adenauer. The 4,000-strong Franco-German army brigade 'foreshadowed' a common European army, while, in general, Franco-German cooperation constituted a 'good starting point' for any wider European defence design. After having alluded in this electoral tract to debates about NATO, the nature of deterrence, and 'France's role at the centre of Europe', Mitterrand concluded his disquisition by asserting rhetorically that 'the common defence of Western Europe will soon take centre stage'.[32]

In brief, between the Reykjavik superpower summit of October 1986 and the setting up of the Franco-German Defence Council in January 1988, Mitterrand and Kohl devoted much effort to finding some kind of mutual assurance through new bilateral defence arrangements, even if the significance of these arrangements was far from devoid of ambiguity. Encouraging the two men to adopt this course were their anxieties and, arguably, their confusion in the face of the disappearing certainties of the Cold War era. Each sought an added element of insurance in the support of the other, without either of them quite believing that there would be a total withdrawal of the American commitment to Western Europe. Yet their jointly agreed defence schemes contained a large element of political theatre. This was particularly true of the Franco-German army brigade, which was described in April 1989 by the French Senate's foreign-affairs standing committee as having only low military value.

Mitterrand's deeper concerns in these years were twofold: the traditional French preoccupation, so characteristic of the post-war era, of how best to bind the FRG into formalised European arrangements, thereby preventing it from being tempted by neutralism for the sake of German unification; and, secondly, a fierce determination to preserve France's role as an independent nuclear power, whatever the push for disarmament on the part of the superpowers. The siren call to Bonn was now Gorbachev's. Long gone by Mitterrand's reign was Pompidou's hope that the UK would play an important positive role in offsetting German power. In the sphere of security and defence, what Mitterrand preferred was a return to some of the spirit of de Gaulle's presidency – hence a readiness to explore the unrealised scope of the Elysée Treaty.

However, by the 1980s there was one major sphere of public policy in which France was very much West Germany's junior and subordinate partner, namely the monetary sphere. How this situation came about and how France chaffed at the bit, basically for reasons of power, is the subject of the next chapter.

Notes

1. Debré, *Trois Républiques pour une France*, vol. 4, 264–65.
2. Debré's leading role in initiating the talks between de Gaulle and Soames is underlined in Vaïsse, *La Grandeur*, 607–8, 613–14.

3. Bernard Ledwidge, *De Gaulle*, London, 1982, 363.
4. On the Foreign Office's role in the 'Soames affair', see Hugo Young, *This Blessed Plot: Britain and Europe from Churchill to Blair*, 2nd edn, London, 1999, 197–208.
5. Edward Heath, *Old World, New Horizons: Britain, the Common Market and the Atlantic Alliance*, Oxford, 1970, 70–76.
6. Edward Heath, *The Course of My Life: My Autobiography*, London, 1998, 361–62.
7. For this lack of enthusiasm as recorded in Pompidou's own papers, see Eric Roussel, *Georges Pompidou, 1911–1974*, 2nd edn, Paris, 1994, 503–8, 652–56.
8. Maurice Schumann, 'Témoignage sur l'identité européenne', in Association Georges Pompidou (ed.), *Georges Pompidou et l'Europe. Colloque – 25 et 26 novembre 1993*, Brussels, 1995, 137.
9. For the recollection of François Puaux, the French ambassador in question, see Association Georges Pompidou (ed.), *Georges Pompidou et l'Europe*, 87.
10. Roussel, *Georges Pompidou*, 523.
11. For the Paris summit communiqué, see Harryvan and van der Harst (eds), *Documents on European Union*, 181–84.
12. 'Témoignages et interventions', in Samy Cohen and Marie-Claude Smouts (eds), *La Politique extérieure de Valéry Giscard d'Estaing*, Paris, 1985, 111–13.
13. Françoise de La Serre, 'L'Europe communautaire entre le mondialisme et l'entente franco-allemande', in Cohen and Smouts (eds), *La Politique extérieure de Valéry Giscard d'Estaing*, 89–91.
14. Roussel, *Georges Pompidou*, 570.
15. Henry Kissinger, *Years of Upheaval*, Boston, 1982, 165, 178.
16. Soutou, *L'Alliance incertaine*, 324–26.
17. Ibid., 327–49.
18. Ibid., 357–65.
19. This nuclear collaboration between the US and France was a well kept secret until the end of the 1980s. It was divulged in Richard H. Ullman, 'The covert French Connection', *Foreign Policy* 75, Summer 1989, 3–33. And it was confirmed in Valéry Giscard d'Estaing, *Le Pouvoir et la vie*, 3 vols, Paris, 1988–2006, vol. 2, 183–92.
20. For Giscard's own account of his break with Carter over Afghanistan and his meeting with Brezhnev in Warsaw, and his related criticism of Mitterrand, see Giscard d'Estaing, *Le Pouvoir et la vie*, vol. 3, 205–22.
21. For the Venice Declaration, see Harryvan and van der Harst (eds), *Documents on European Union*, 207–9.
22. Helmut Schmidt, *Menschen und Mächte*, 2 vols, Berlin, 1987–90, vol. 2, 284–86; Barry Blechman and Cathleen Fisher, 'West German security policy and the Franco-German relationship', in Robbin F. Laird (ed.), *Strangers and Friends: The Franco-German Security Relationship*, London, 1989, 50–52.
23. Soutou, *L'Alliance incertaine*, 373–78.
24. Jacques Attali, *Verbatim*, 3 vols, Paris, 1993–95, vol. 1, 385.
25. For the address itself, see Mitterrand, *Réflexions sur la politique extérieure de la France*, 40–44, 183–208. For the address's preparation, see Favier and Martin-Roland, *La Décennie Mitterrand*, vol. 1, 264–71; Attali, *Verbatim*, vol. 1, 383–86; Védrine, *Les Mondes de François Mitterrand*, 234–37.
26. Mitterrand, *Réflexions sur la politique extérieure de la France*, 193.
27. Ibid., 194–97.
28. Soutou, *L'Alliance incertaine*, 378–81.
29. For the Rome Declaration, see Harryvan and van der Harst (eds), *Documents on European Union*, 224–25.
30. Attali, *Verbatim*, vol. 1, 814–17.
31. Text of the protocol in Soutou, *L'Alliance incertaine*, 452–54.
32. François Mitterrand, 'Lettre à tous les Français', *Le Monde*, 8 April 1988, and 9 April 1988.

Chapter 8

OPPOSITION TO GERMAN MONETARY HEGEMONY

Dissatisfied with the Bretton Woods system, France had nonetheless lived with it until its collapse in 1973, which torpedoed the plans then afoot for EMU. The introduction of the alternative 'snake' arrangements, partly outside the EC framework, marked the emergence of the FRG as Western Europe's leading monetary power. In 1979 the DM's position as anchor currency in the 'snake' and the matching dominant role of the German monetary authorities were effectively transferred to the EMS, dashing French hopes for equality. The redressing of this imbalance in French and German monetary power became a priority during the Mitterrand years.

The Death of the Bretton Woods System

The Gold Exchange Standard, the Franc, and de Gaulle

The post-war international monetary system was founded on a dollar-based gold exchange standard. Although its design had been agreed in July 1944 at the Bretton Woods international conference, it started to function normally in Western Europe only at the end of 1958 under the European Monetary Agreement (EMA). Then the currencies of the EC member states and the UK became externally convertible for current-account transactions. Subsequently, in 1961, the same European countries, together with Sweden and Ireland, joined the US, Canada, and a number of Latin American countries in accepting the obligations of Article VIII of the IMF Agreement signed at Bretton Woods seventeen years earlier. Under this key article, the European countries committed themselves to current-account currency convertibility with no restrictions on current-account payments.

Never was French dissatisfaction with this international monetary system more strongly expressed than on the occasion of de Gaulle's press conference of February 1965. His complaint was that the role of the American currency as the effective anchor of the system had conferred upon the US the exorbitant privilege of running a chronic balance-of-payments deficit (on current account and long-term capital transactions), on the strength of limitless credit from the rest of the world. The French president's prescribed remedy, as urged at this press conference, was a return to the fully-fledged gold standard, which had functioned relatively satisfactorily up to the time of the First World War. Accepting the diagnosis made by Rueff, de Gaulle remarked that the gold standard had been fatally compromised by the decision taken at the Genoa Conference of 1922 to economise on the use of gold through the partial use of sterling and the dollar as reserve currencies. But this gold exchange standard, both subsequently in the interwar years and in its more ambitious post-war form, had not worked. Hence, he argued, the need for a revived gold standard through a new effort of international cooperation:

> The International Monetary Fund, instituted to maximise currency stability, should provide an appropriate forum for all the states concerned; their purpose should no longer be the preservation of the 'gold exchange standard' but rather its replacement. The 'Group of Ten', which, in addition to the United States and England, includes France, Germany, Italy, the Netherlands, and Belgium on the one hand, and Japan, Sweden, and Canada on the other, should prepare the necessary proposals. Furthermore, the six states that appear to be in the process of realising a European Economic Community should establish a system of monetary solidarity between themselves, as recommended by common sense, and then show its worth to the rest of the world. Such initiative would be in keeping with the renascent power of our old continent.[1]

Yet a revived gold standard was a will-o'-the-wisp. The decisive impediment was that the US was not to be tempted into such a venture. Even in France there was no consensus on the part of the political establishment and senior monetary officials that gold was the way forward. The prime minister, Pompidou, was lukewarm. Giscard d'Estaing was definitely not in favour, though he was replaced as finance minister in January 1966 by Debré, ever faithful to de Gaulle and an admirer of Rueff to boot. As to the French president's suggestion that the EEC create a system of monetary solidarity of its own, what he would seem to have had in mind was the achievement regionally of an even greater fixity of exchange rates than that which could be realised globally in his proposed new international system – in which, whatever the margins of fluctuation, all parities would be based directly on gold. However, by the late 1960s, the pressures at work in Western Europe were making for less currency stability, not more, as de Gaulle desired.

Thus, sterling, after a long crisis marking its dying role as a reserve currency, was devalued in November 1967. It was then the turn of the French franc to move into the eye of the storm. In France, de Gaulle's faltering response to the quasi-insurrectionary mischief of May 1968 not only badly battered his own political credibility, but it also led to serious economic trouble. The balance-of-payments current account worsened in the second half of 1968 as a result of a surge of imports on the back of the large wage increases accorded under the Grenelle Agreements. Pompidou had engineered the increases to defuse the crisis by weaning the trade unions away from their (less than whole-hearted) support of the protesting students. Because of this current-account deterioration, speculative pressures mounted against the French currency. Other factors at play, making for a flight from the franc, were the fears of the French moneyed classes for the value of their financial assets and reduced international confidence in both the franc and the Fifth Republic's future.

In November 1968 de Gaulle faced what proved to be his last major crisis. Speculative pressures had reached such a peak that newspaper rhetoric spoke of a 'financial putsch' against the regime or of a '*grand Clamart*' (an allusion to the failed assassination attempt against the French president in 1962 at Petit Clamart). At an emergency meeting of the Group of Ten, the German finance minister, Strauss, and the German economics minister, Karl Schiller, refused a DM revaluation, and thereby gave proof that an unabashed West Germany was now determined to pull its economic weight in the pursuit of its own international interests, irrespective of the views of France or any other major state. The SPD's Schiller made no bones about criticising openly French (and British) economic policy. In the face of the German refusal of a revaluation, the French finance minister, Ortoli, bowed to what appeared inevitable and accepted instead a devaluation of the franc. However, in the course of the weekend immediately following the Friday meeting in Bonn, the decision was countermanded by de Gaulle. He was persuaded, partly on the advice of the EC commissioner for economic and financial affairs, Barre, that a devaluation could be avoided if the requisite monetary support was made available in the Group of Ten framework and if appropriate domestic economic measures were taken. Hence de Gaulle, in the twilight of his presidency, barred the way to the desired German option, which he considered would be an unacceptable humiliation for France.[2]

Pompidou, Money Matters, and the Hague Summit

Yet it was only a devaluation postponed. In August 1969, two months after his election as President of the Republic, the more pragmatic Pompidou decided with Giscard d'Estaing (once again finance minister) to swallow French pride and devalue the franc by a hefty 12.5 per cent. The aim was to redress the balance of payments and spur on export-led economic growth.

Further help was to materialise in October 1969 when the DM was revalued by 8.5 per cent. As a result of September's Bundestag elections, an SPD–FDP coalition had replaced the CDU/CSU–SPD 'grand coalition' in power since 1966. Schiller remained economics minister. Worries about domestic inflation had led him to change his mind about the need for a realignment against the dollar; and the redoubtable Strauss was no longer in office to champion the interests of German exporters. However, October's revaluation was not a smooth one. It was preceded by a brief period of floating for the German currency – a practice which not only raised problems for the functioning of the CAP, but was also contrary to the operating rules of the Bretton Woods system itself. If this system provided for orderly currency realignments under IMF auspices, it did not allow for the suspension, even temporarily, of declared parities. This German disregard for due procedure, less than a year after the franc crisis of November 1968, showed that international monetary cooperation, even between EC member states, had fallen on less clement times.

Against this background, the EC-6 held their summit meeting in The Hague in December 1969. Despite the Dutch venue it was a French initiative. Pompidou had proposed that there should be a meeting of the leaders of the Six on the occasion of the completion of the EEC Treaty's twelve-year transitional period. It was not his intention that this gathering in the Dutch capital be primarily a celebration of the EEC's completed transition; rather it was to be the occasion of addressing a number of urgent matters. These included the question of the UK's continued quest for EC membership and the challenge of how best to set course for calmer exchange-rate waters, in view of the monetary strains and currency adjustments of the preceding twelve months.

On the monetary front, Pompidou certainly needed to act. One of the effects of the franc's weakness in 1968 and 1969 had been a compromising of France's hitherto largely dominant political role vis-à-vis West Germany. Further weakness of this kind had therefore to be avoided. Directly practical was the French president's second concern, ensuring that the CAP's future was not jeopardised by prolonged currency disorder affecting the EC area. For the CAP's design – at the time of the laborious laying down of its foundations in 1958–64 – had been predicated on the stability issuing from a successfully functioning Bretton Woods system. Although French farmers by 1962 had already started to benefit from CAP expenditure, the changeover on the financing side from member states' direct contributions to a reliance on the EEC's 'own resources' had yet to take place. This changeover risked being endangered if monetary instability became endemic.

Conveniently at hand for Pompidou was the EC Commission's memorandum on economic-policy coordination and monetary cooperation within the EEC. This memorandum had been submitted to the Council of Ministers in February 1969. It was the work of the commissioner for economic and financial affairs, the Gaullist-leaning Barre – hence its name, the Barre Memorandum. Proposed were the coordination and convergence of national economic policies and, secondly, the setting up of EEC machinery for monetary support. The memorandum explicitly suggested that there should eventually be fixity of exchange rates within the EEC, in the sense of 'the elimination, for the currencies of the member states, of day-to-day fluctuations around the parities'.[3] This fixity would have represented a loose form of monetary union, without a single currency or even a parallel common one. Barre's aim became Pompidou's too when the latter looked to advance French interests at the December 1969 summit. The French president did not conceive such a weak form of monetary union as an alternative to the Bretton Woods system, but rather as a consolidation of it at regional level through the securing of a maximum degree of exchange-rate stability. Gaining approval for monetary union, in the sense of fixity of exchange rates, was indeed the chief priority Pompidou had set himself before travelling to The Hague.[4]

However, it was Brandt, the new German Chancellor, who stole much of the limelight in stating that negotiations for EC enlargement could start within six months. His desired aim was the inclusion not only of the UK but also of other EFTA countries, the Scandinavian ones being those he had in mind. For Brandt, such an enlargement would facilitate the pursuit of his Ostpolitik, the policy to which he had nailed his colours at home. To ease acceptance of the same policy, he also favoured formalised EC cooperation in the sphere of foreign policy. His calculation was that it was only in a clearly established Western European framework, in which West Germany would not be overly beholden to France, that he and his successors could strive for the long-term goal of German unification. 'All our interests', Brandt declared at the EC summit, 'would be served if the Community expanded at a time when we were striving for closer cooperation between West and East.' To win agreement to this marriage between Westpolitik and Ostpolitik, the Chancellor was willing to be accommodating over the CAP and monetary union, as witness his readiness, in respect of the latter, to 'fully cooperate in establishing a European Reserve Fund'.[5]

Thus, to the satisfaction of France's interests, the Hague summit resulted in a commitment to the immediate laying down of a definitive financial arrangement for the CAP. And there was also the promise to advance on the monetary front. The Barre Memorandum, stated the summit's final communiqué, was to provide the basis for 'a plan in stages [which] will be worked out during 1970 with a view to the creation of an economic and monetary union'.[6]

The Werner Report

It was left to the EC Council of Ministers to arrange the preparation of this plan for EMU. However, Pompidou was most concerned that his monetary-union initiative should not be hijacked by other member states, notably the Benelux ones, with a view to their own European ambitions. The fear was that they might seek to advance beyond the purely inter-governmental approach that he had in mind for organising the convergence of economic policies and moving progressively towards fixity of intra-EC exchange rates. Soon after the summit in The Hague, he instructed the foreign minister, Maurice Schumann, to exercise great vigilance on this score. The locus of decision making, the French president wrote in his note, should be either the Council of Ministers or else the EEC's Committee of Governors of the Central Banks. Not only should there be no insistence on the role of the Commission, but the European 'Parliament' – put disdainfully in inverted commas by Pompidou – should not be allowed to figure in the plan prepared under the auspices of the Council of Ministers. 'If there has to be question somewhere of the transfer of competence or attributions', he continued in the same note, 'one must say "from states, to institutions of the Community"', in specifying that, on our understanding, this formula designates above all the Council of Ministers or the Committee of Permanent Representatives.'[7] Although Schumann was from the defunct MRP, he was a Christian Democrat of distinctly Gaullist sympathies, having rallied to de Gaulle in London in June 1940 and having served in the following four years as the Free French spokesman (*'la voix de Londres'*) for the BBC's daily broadcasts to France. Pompidou's instructions, relating to the safeguarding of the prerogatives of the nation state, were not therefore of a kind to trouble his mind.

In fulfilment of the commitment given by the EC heads of state and government in The Hague, the EC Council of Ministers set up an 'ad hoc' committee in March 1970 to report on the realisation by stages of EMU. Heading this committee was Pierre Werner, the prime minister of Luxembourg and also the Grand Duchy's finance minister. Each member state and also the Commission provided two committee members, a full member and a deputy. The latter in Germany's case was the young Hans Tietmeyer; he was to be a powerful figure at the Bundesbank in the 1990s, playing a major role in the realisation of EMU under the Maastricht Treaty.

The senior figure representing France on the Werner Committee was Clappier – Robert Schuman's *directeur de cabinet* twenty years earlier – who by 1970 had become the First Deputy Governor of the Banque de France and also chairman of the Monetary Committee of the EEC. Since he was close on policy matters to the confident and independently minded Giscard d'Estaing, whom Pompidou had somewhat reluctantly appointed as finance minister, Clappier was amenable to a bolder approach than that allowed by the French president in his instructions to Maurice Schumann. Thus, in both the interim and final versions of the Werner Report, which were presented to the Council of Ministers in May and October 1970 respectively, Clappier gave his signature to a series of conclusions which included the recommendation that a 'Community ... centre of decision for economic policy' be set up 'on the institutional plane' in EMU's third and final stage. This would be a body exercising some right of control over national governments in the matter of public-finance deficits and enjoying exclusive authority to decide upon currency parity changes vis-à-vis third countries. It would also be 'politically responsible to a European Parliament'. Clappier and his fellow committee members agreed, moreover, that monetary union should ideally entail the adoption of a single currency. This was not strictly required under the committee's definition of monetary union: 'the total and irreversible convertibility of currencies, the elimination of margins of fluctuation in rates of exchange, the irrevocable fixing of parity ratios, and the total liberation of movements of capital'. Nonetheless, a single currency was recommended to 'guarantee the irreversibility of the undertaking'.[8]

The Werner Report spoke vaguely of a start to the final stage by the end of the 1970s, provided there were sufficient political will. But, since Pompidou's reaction to the proposed arrangements for the final stage was one of extreme displeasure on account of their supranational character, the requisite political will was not to be forthcoming from France. Yet Pompidou's total opposition to the institutional aspects of the Werner Report's design for the final stage of EMU did not prevent French approval of its immediately practical recommendations for the first stage. These were broadly in line not only with the Barre Memorandum, but also with what had been advised by the Committee of Governors of the Central Banks in September 1970, in a prudently-framed report responding to various questions that Werner had posed on behalf of the 'ad hoc' committee. The French were indeed gratified that the Werner Report recommended an experimental reduction in the permissible margins of fluctuation between EC currencies. It marked a first, albeit timid, step towards fixity of exchange rates.

The explanation of this step calls for some technicalities. Under the Bretton Woods system, with the dollar as anchor currency, the permissible margins of fluctuation of a European currency against the dollar (which the EMA in 1958 had set at 0.75 per cent either side of parity) translated into permissible margins of fluctuation between any two European currencies that were twice as large (1.5 per cent either side of cross-parities). The system allowed therefore for a lesser degree of day-to-day stability between any two European currencies than between any European currency and the dollar. To rectify partially this anomaly, the Committee of Governors of the Central Banks suggested that the permissible intra-EC margins of fluctuations be narrowed to 1.2 per cent either side of cross-parities. This move was agreed once the Council of Ministers had given its approval in March 1971 to the Werner Report's recommendations for the (uncontroversial) first stage of EMU.

The Dollar Crisis

This new narrower intra-EC fluctuation band was due to come into effect in June 1971. The change represented essentially no more than a relatively minor modification to the workings of the dollar-based gold exchange standard. As had been insisted in the Barre Memorandum, the strengthening of EC internal monetary stability was designed to contribute to the effective operation of the Bretton Woods system, not to serve as a substitute for it.[9] Yet the planned narrowing of the intra-EC fluctuation band never materialised. For, as events were to prove, the Bretton Woods system had entered into its mortally terminal phase by the summer of 1971. The fundamental reason lay less with Western Europe's increased monetary instability, than with the growing unwillingness, and indeed incapacity, of the US to underpin a system whose functioning no longer matched its interests.

Already in March 1968 it had been decided in Washington to abandon the attempt, through the operation of the Gold Pool, to keep the market price of gold in line with the official price ($35 per fine ounce). A major irritant for the Americans had been de Gaulle's policy of converting large amounts of the dollar reserves of the Banque de France into gold. However, it was not until 1971 that the dollar's gold convertibility, as a matter of right for foreign central banks, came to be judged untenable. Partly because of the build-up of structural inflationary pressures arising from the pursuit of the Vietnam War, which had been financed largely by monetary creation rather than extra taxes, the overall deficit on the US balance of payments deteriorated in a startling fashion. No direct recourse could be had to devaluation – the normal policy prescription for a chronic balance-of-payments deficit – since the US was formally the one country in the system whose currency could not be realigned in relation to all the others. Continuing weakness threatened a run on the dollar.

In May 1971, Schiller decided to float the DM – he was still the German economics minister and later the same month became the finance minister as well. The Dutch monetary authorities followed suit in floating the guilder. The Germans wanted to avoid the inflationary consequences of the large-scale foreign-exchange market intervention that would have been required to maintain the DM within its IMF-agreed margins of fluctuation against the dollar. A German proposal for a joint EC float had been rebuffed beforehand by France, and Pompidou reacted angrily to Schiller's ensuing unilateral move.

The response of the US president, Nixon, and his Secretary of Treasury, John Connally, to the increasingly difficult international monetary situation came brutally and unilaterally in August 1971. The gold convertibility of the dollar was officially suspended; and among other measures an emergency 10 per cent surcharge was slapped on about half of all goods imported into the US. Connally's wider message, in putting together the August package, was that the US should not be beholden to the countries of Western Europe in arranging an international monetary order, especially since their contribution to burden sharing within NATO, for assuring their own security, left so much to be desired.

The Deutsche Mark as Anchor Currency

France's Role in the Abortive Salvage of Bretton Woods

In 1965 de Gaulle had railed against the Bretton Woods system, seeing in it the arm of American hegemony. However, by 1971 the system itself was crumbling. The floating in May of the DM, which dashed hopes for the planned narrowing of intra-EC fluctuation margins, and then the suspension in August of the gold convertibility of the dollar, made for monetary turmoil. Pompidou's reaction was to seek to salvage what could be usefully saved from the arrangements planned at Bretton Woods a quarter of a century earlier. Unlike his predecessor, he remained unpersuaded of the feasibility of the resurrection of the gold standard; and indeed the events of the intervening six years had rendered even more quixotic the ideas put forward by Rueff, to which de Gaulle had been so attentive. Yet, in line with his European monetary union proposals at the Hague summit, which were predicated on the continued existence of the Bretton Woods system, de Gaulle's successor was still convinced that fixity of exchange rates lay very much in France's interest.

On this matter, the French president found himself in effective alliance with some of the more internationally-minded elements of the Nixon Administration, led by Kissinger, then at the head of the National Security Council, who believed that Connally's tough Texan approach to international monetary matters was prejudicial to good American relations with Western Europe and Japan. In the absence of a common front in Western Europe on the question of currency reform, it was decided in Washington – as Kissinger later put it – 'to permit Pompidou to establish a position of leadership in Europe by negotiating the terms of a settlement with us'.[10] It was thus that Nixon and Pompidou met in the Azores on 13 and 14 December 1971. The French president acted as Europe's de facto representative, with the prior acquiescence of West Germany and the other four EC member states, as well as the UK. This was the last occasion on which the US was to allow France a larger role than Germany in international monetary diplomacy. However, in the short term the meeting was successful, inasmuch as it opened the way to the Group of Ten's formal agreement to establish a modified Bretton Woods system. This agreement was signed at the Smithsonian Institute in Washington on 18 December, only several days after the Azores meeting.

Pompidou preferred to handle the Azores negotiations directly rather than rely on Giscard d'Estaing. From the outset, the French president conceded to the Americans that the gold convertibility of the dollar could not be restored. The common ground in the negotiations was the Franco-American understanding that a radical currency realignment should serve to restore a system of fixed but adjustable exchange rates under the auspices of the IMF. This would entail substantial upward adjustments of the Western European (and Japanese) currencies against the dollar. It was also accepted that the dollar be devalued in terms of the official price of gold – though, in the absence of convertibility, this promised to be no more than a notional adjustment. A series of new 'central rates' (replacing the term 'parities') was worked out against the US currency. It involved much haggling, with Connally playing the hard man on the American side and Kissinger serving as the diplomatic go-between.

Thus, as formalised in the Smithsonian Agreement, the DM was revalued by 13.6 per cent, the Dutch guilder and Belgian franc by 11.6 per cent, the French franc and the pound sterling by 8.6 per cent, and the lira by 7.5 per cent. As to the official price of gold, Nixon and Pompidou agreed in the Azores that it be raised from $35 to $38 per ounce. This change, also incorporated into the Smithsonian Agreement, was relatively advantageous to France in purely book-keeping terms, since gold – thanks partly to de Gaulle – accounted for a relatively large part of the reserves of the Banque de France.

However, on the question of the modified system's permissible margins of fluctuation, Pompidou won no satisfaction in his talks with Nixon and Kissinger. In keeping with his perception that it was in France's interest to have the greatest possible degree of monetary stability, he would have preferred the restoration of the pre-May 1971 margins of fluctuation (0.75 per cent either side of the new dollar central rates for European currencies; 1 per cent for all others, the standard established IMF norm). But Connally, refusing any such degree of fixity, proposed 2.5 per cent either side of dollar central rates. As a small sop to the disappointed French president, Nixon allowed at their Azores meeting that this margin of fluctuation could be reduced to 2.25 per cent. Embodied in the Smithsonian Agreement, this precise margin of fluctuation – proposed by an American president – was destined to a long future: it was to define the width of the fluctuation bands around the central rates of, first, the European 'snake' and then, up to 1993, around the central rates of the Exchange Rate Mechanism (ERM), the heart of the European Monetary System (EMS).[11]

The 'Snake in the Tunnel'

The Smithsonian Agreement was to prove no more than a holding operation. In March 1973, only fifteen months after its signing, it collapsed. It was the end of the dollar-based Bretton Woods system. In the meantime the European 'snake' had been formed. The enlargement in December 1971 of the permissible margins of fluctuation to 2.25 per cent either side of dollar-defined central rates had meant that the permissible margins of fluctuation between any two European currencies became as wide as 4.5 per cent either side of their implicit bilateral central rates. This was a far cry from the 1.2 per cent planned early in 1971 for the first stage of EMU. After Pompidou and Brandt agreed in February 1972 to put EMU back on the rails, the EC Council of Ministers resolved in March to reduce the permissible margins of fluctuations between EC currencies to 2.25 per cent either side of their bilateral central rates, so that they would all tend to 'snake' (*serpenter*) together against the dollar.[12] By way of exception, the still narrower Benelux margins applying between the Dutch guilder and the Belgian franc were maintained. This narrowing of intra-EC margins of fluctuation took place in late April 1972, thereby creating a 'snake in the tunnel' configuration, as the market exchange rates of the same currencies moved against the dollar well inside the band limits set by the Smithsonian Agreement.

Quickly the new 'snake' was to experience trouble. In advance of the enlargement of the ECs at the beginning of 1973, sterling and the Danish krone were put into the 'snake' in May 1972, just a week after its birth. But, in the following month, the dollar's chronic weakness – and accessorily sterling's – led to large speculative capital flows into DM-denominated assets; and the ensuing strengthening of the German currency made for severe strains on the 'snake' narrow band. In the maelstrom of a new international monetary crisis, both the British and Danish currencies had to be withdrawn from the 'snake'. In the case of sterling, the exit was to prove permanent. It was not an auspicious start for the 'snake'. Ireland was still de facto in monetary union with the UK, which meant that all three future EC member states had failed in June 1972 to bind their currencies into the German-led arrangement.

The 'snake' itself survived, as a result of Schiller's resignation from the West German government in the same month. For reasons of economic principle concerning the convertibility of the DM, Schiller had been adamantly opposed to the introduction of even temporary controls on inward capital movements. Isolated on this issue, and generally unpopular within his own party, he resigned and was replaced as economics and finance minister by his rival, Schmidt. The temporary exchange controls, acting as a brake on the DM's appreciation, helped then to keep the 'snake' arrangements in place, which was to France's evident satisfaction. It was, moreover, a step in keeping with received French ideas on exchange-rate management. Prior to the liberal inflexion of French economic policy towards the end of the decade under Giscard d'Estaing and Barre, the universal assumption in Paris was that currency stability within the EC area required the retention of national exchange controls on movements of capital, especially short-term capital; and this was despite the obligation imposed by the EEC Treaty on member states to have lifted the bulk of restrictions on capital movements by the close of the transitional period at the end of 1969, an obligation that only the FRG had respected.

Pompidou was partly reassured by the turn of events in Bonn, especially the ditching of Schiller, who had been a thorn in the French side ever since 1968. In October 1972, at the EC's Paris summit on the eve of enlargement, his main concern was still EMU. However, all that was agreed was to set up the European Monetary Cooperation Fund (EMCF) by April 1973. There was also a joint pledge – naïvely optimistic or cynically vacuous – to take the necessary decisions to allow the transition to EMU's undefined second stage at the beginning of 1974.

The Floating 'Snake' with its DM Anchor

Half a year later the EMU project, as launched at the 1969 summit in The Hague and elaborated in the Werner Report, was to be no more than a dream from the past. In February 1973, despite German exchange controls, speculative capital movements were exerting strong upward pressure on the DM and hence on an increasingly uncomfortable 'snake'. One consequence was that the Italian monetary authorities were obliged to withdraw the lira. Like sterling, it was never to return. The other consequence was American acceptance of a 10 per cent devaluation of the dollar. This was to be the last gesture of the US in favour of what remained of the system of fixed but adjustable exchange rates created at Bretton Woods. The month of March brought no respite to the currency disarray. It was then that the six EC member states participating in the 'snake' arrangements – West Germany, France, the Benelux countries, and (a returned) Denmark – decided to float the 'snake' against the dollar. The Smithsonian 'tunnel' existed no more. Germany's leading role was evident to all at this juncture, especially since the DM had to be revalued by a further 3 per cent against the French franc and the other currencies of the 'snake' to ensure a successful start to the float.

On the other side of the Atlantic, Connally's successor as Secretary of Treasury in the penultimate year of the Nixon administration was George Shultz, an economist intellectually committed to floating exchange rates. The German-led 'snake' move met with his approval. In March Shultz announced that the Federal Reserve Bank of New York would no longer intervene to support the dollar and that all capital controls would be abolished by the end of 1974. The American policy of 'benign neglect' of the dollar's fortunes on the foreign-exchange markets had thus begun. It made indirectly for a qualitative change in the nature of Franco-German relations. France's quest for a high degree of currency stability became a strictly regional quest. Since both the UK and Italy had been forced to abandon the 'snake', it was a quest that had to be pursued with West Germany alone among the larger Western European states. In a way that had never been envisaged at the time of the preparation of the Elysée Treaty, France had effectively been thrust into the arms of its economically powerful neighbour on a terrain that was decidedly not to French advantage.

What the floating 'snake' assured on a regional basis was currency stability of the Bretton Woods kind, but with the DM instead of the dollar fulfilling the anchor role. The monetary hegemon was now West Germany: the last word on currency realignments within the 'snake' tended henceforth to be that pronounced in Bonn, while the levels of short-term interest rates in all 'snake' countries were dependent on decisions taken by the Bundesbank in Frankfurt for purely German domestic monetary-policy reasons. In short, the 'snake' area had patently become a DM zone, even if some of the arrangements still fell under the formal authority of the EC Council of Ministers.

Already in 1973 the German-biased dimension was underlined by the admission to the 'snake' of the Swedish krona and the Norwegian krone on an associate-member basis. They were to remain in the 'snake' until 1977 and 1978 respectively. Although these two Scandinavian currencies were less in the DM's orbit than, say, the Dutch guilder or the Belgian franc, both Sweden and Norway were countries with very strong trade ties with West Germany, finding it therefore in their interest to be linked to the DM in this way. Furthermore, it was largely because of its own high trade dependency on West Germany that Switzerland sought in 1975 to have its currency join the 'snake' on a similar associate basis. However, during the course of several months' negotiations, the Swiss franc's inclusion was blocked by the French finance minister, Jean-Pierre Fourcade. One of the reasons he put forward was that the Swiss franc would drag the 'snake' upwards on the foreign-exchange markets and so be prejudicial to the eventual reentry of sterling and the lira. More generally, the French concern in 1975 was that the German-centred character of the European 'snake' or joint float would be further accentuated by the Swiss currency's inclusion.

The putative EC identity of the 'snake' had already been badly compromised in January 1974 when the French franc itself had been temporarily withdrawn. For Pompidou had deemed it prudent to allow the French currency to depreciate against the DM because of the deteriorating economic conditions in Western Europe in the wake of the international oil shock, and, to this end, an independent downward float had been preferred to a 'snake' devaluation. It was on the occasion of the

French franc's rejoining the 'snake' in July 1975 that Fourcade bargained successfully to disallow the French currency's being accompanied back into the 'snake' by Switzerland's much harder franc (an enlargement of the 'snake' that West Germany then favoured). However, a new bout of weakness was soon to affect the French currency. As from the beginning of 1976, the French currency became the victim of large-scale speculative pressure on the foreign-exchange markets; and the rate of loss of official reserves, as the Banque de France intervened to keep the franc from falling through the floor of the 'snake', accelerated to the point of being unsustainable. In March 1976, at a crisis meeting of the finance ministers whose currencies were in the 'snake', Fourcade proposed a general realignment, with a 3 per cent devaluation of the franc matched equally by a 3 per cent DM revaluation. But the German view was that a unilateral franc devaluation was called for. In the absence of compromise, the French franc was withdrawn anew from the 'snake' for a second time. This goodbye to the German-led joint float proved to be final.

Pompidou's concern with international monetary stability at the time of the Hague summit in 1969 had been largely dictated by economic considerations and, in particular, by the need for near fixed exchange rates in the EEC, if the CAP were to thrive. Yet his fears about the viability of the CAP – once exchange rates became subject to frequent change or were even floated – turned out to be excessive. For many years the arcane system of Monetary Compensatory Amounts (MCAs), first introduced in 1969, was to insulate both producers and consumers of CAP agricultural produce against the effects of intra-EC exchange-rate changes. Even so, reassurance on this score did not mitigate subsequent French anxieties about the future of international monetary arrangements. Especially after the death of the Bretton Woods system in March 1973, the future of such arrangements was seen in Paris as having a direct bearing on France's place generally in the world, regionally in Europe, and bilaterally in relation to West Germany. Thus, by the late 1970s, the shaping of European monetary relations – and, by implication, wider international monetary relations as well – had become a major concern of Giscard d'Estaing, with what were essentially political considerations taking precedence over purely economic ones.

The EMS and its Ambivalent Design

Overlapping German and French Interests

The EMS ball was set rolling by Jenkins in 1977 in the course of his first year as president of the EC Commission. In October of that year he used the occasion of his being invited to give the first 'Jean Monnet' lecture at the European University Institute in Florence to advocate a European monetary union within the political framework of a 'slimline federation'. However, it was not until April 1978 that the political will emerged to return to the drawing board after the failed Werner Plan of eight years earlier. This happened when Giscard d'Estaing and Schmidt met at Rambouillet and discussed their positions prior to a European Council meeting in Copenhagen, They agreed to present a plan for a new monetary system, entailing fixed but adjustable exchange rates, but with a long-term view to replacing the DM-anchored 'snake' with monetary union.

The double act was duly performed in the Danish capital. The German Chancellor, while acknowledging that their plan fell short of Jenkins's proposal, indicated that the new system would have an EC dimension that the 'snake' so patently lacked. There would thus be the creation of a European Monetary Fund (EMF), a partial pooling of official reserves, and an increased use of EC currencies rather than the dollar for central-bank intervention purposes. The existing European Unit of Account (EUA) – based on a currency basket – would become the new parity-grid numeraire, as well as a means of settlement between central banks and, eventually, a new form of reserve asset. For his part, the French president, who was the inspirer of the EMF idea, hailed the proposed system as a 'new Bretton Woods for Europe'.[13]

Schmidt and Giscard d'Estaing – both of them longstanding members of Monnet's Action Committee for a United States of Europe – appeared as equals in presenting their plan at the Copenhagen meeting of the European Council. In feigning an answer to a query posed by a participant about the origin of the plan, Giscard peddled Napoleon's dictum that no more than hypotheses could ever be entertained about any question of paternity. Yet, in the year of negotiations that followed before the setting up of the EMS in March 1979, the Chancellor tended to take the leading part. According to the French president's memoirs, this had been agreed at Rambouillet:

> Helmut Schmidt and I decided upon a division of roles. Although I was [even] more convinced than him about the project's usefulness, I asked him to act as its advocate before the rest of the world and, in particular, at the forthcoming meetings of the European Council in Copenhagen and Bremen. Since the key to success was the winning over of the German financial community, you are better placed than me for the task, I told him.[14]

However, united as they were in purpose, their interests were not identical. Schmidt was concerned above all by the implications for West Germany of what he took to be inadequate American leadership. In measuring the qualities of American leadership, Schmidt could benefit from his long experience in dealing with security and defence issues. It was largely on such issues that he had nationally made a political name for himself, after being elected to the Bundestag in 1953. After the sea change represented by the SPD's approval in 1959 of its Godesberg programme, his and Erler's views had become the party's new and Westward-leaning defence policy; both men were pro-NATO and in favour of a strong conventionally armed Bundeswehr (ideally backed, so Schmidt had argued in 1961, by sea-based intermediate-range nuclear missiles). He had subsequently served as defence minister from 1969 to 1972, before being appointed economics and finance minister and finally displacing Brandt as Chancellor in 1974. He had been positively disposed towards the Kennedy administration's military strategy of 'flexible response' and, more generally, towards the design of an Atlantic 'partnership of equals' proposed by Kennedy in his Independence Day speech in Philadelphia in 1962. All the more bitter therefore had been his disappointment at the end of 1964 when Johnson killed off the MLF project. On this occasion Schmidt's confidence in American handling of the Atlantic Alliance, and of Germany's place within it, took a severe knock; and it was only under Ford's brief presidency that he was to feel again that a partnership was being proffered on equal terms to the Europeans.[15]

But when Ford was succeeded by Carter, the Chancellor questioned anew the reliability of the US as an ally. In early 1977, at the beginning of his presidency, Carter sought to block a major agreement between Germany and Brazil in the domain of civil nuclear energy. Then there was the new American president's perceived reluctance in 1977 and 1978 to respond adequately to the USSR's build-up of SS-20 intermediate-range nuclear missiles. Prior to Carter's agreement at the Western Four-Power summit in January 1979 to NATO's 'twin-track' response and then his resolute reaction in December of the same year to the Soviet invasion of Afghanistan, Schmidt had been prey, like Adenauer before him, to doubts about the strength of the American commitment to defend Western Europe in times of crisis.

Schmidt's discontent about the approach of the Carter Administration to international economic and monetary policies in 1977–78 was the proximate cause of his espousal of the EMS idea. Against this wider international background his discontent took on a more political and indeed geopolitical significance. For in agreeing with Giscard d'Estaing to seek to organise the EC area into a formalised regional monetary bloc, the Chancellor was above all concerned with Western Europe's taking its own destiny in hand, with West Germany to the fore, and winning some sort of equal partnership with the US.[16] Not that the complaints on the economic and monetary front were minor ones. A massive deterioration in the US balance of payments in 1977, partly due to rapidly increasing oil imports, led to a very pronounced weakening of the dollar exchange rate from mid 1977 onwards. This weakening continued throughout 1978, when there was no recovery in the current-account position, and into 1979. The dollar's slide adversely affected the price competitiveness of the Western European economies; and Schmidt blamed it on American irresponsibility, inasmuch as the official policy of 'benign neglect' towards the dollar's exchange rate had allowed Washington to dispense with an adequate energy-saving programme for containing oil imports.

Schmidt had also been displeased at the Group of Seven's London summit meeting in May 1977. Carter had urged that both West Germany and Japan should help to redress the US balance of payments by stimulating domestic demand in their own economies, thereby acting as 'locomotives' for the world economy. Although Schmidt reluctantly pledged that Germany's real GDP growth for the year would be raised to 5 per cent (an outturn never attained), he feared the inflationary consequences, and also regretted that the EC countries could not pull more weight collectively so as to resist such American pressure.

If Schmidt's forcefully taking up the cause of European monetary integration was largely a response to American policies in the early years of the Carter administration, Giscard d'Estaing's approach reflected convictions and ambitions for France of long standing. As befitted the person who had served as finance minister for four years under de Gaulle and throughout Pompidou's presidency, Giscard continued to hanker for stable or fixed exchange rates. On his initiative an international economic summit of leading industrialised countries had taken place at Rambouillet in November 1975 – effectively the launching of the Group of Seven (once the original group had been enlarged in 1976 to include Canada). The problem he had put at the top of the agenda was what he described as the 'international monetary crisis', meaning essentially floating exchange rates and the turmoil that he associated with the dollar and the 'snake'. At Rambouillet, with token German backing, the French president had Fourcade sign with the US Secretary of Treasury, William Simon, a memorandum under which they agreed to increased central-bank cooperation and intervention to counter erratic exchange-rate fluctuations between the dollar and the 'snake' currencies. However, this agreement represented a merely pious declaration of intention, at least on the American side.

Half a year later, at the European Council meeting held in Luxembourg in April 1976, Giscard focused on regional monetary stability and argued in favour of another attempt at EMU. But he elicited no favourable response from Schmidt, who emphasised the prior need of economic-policy convergence and expressed a certain satisfaction with the existing 'snake' arrangements. At that time the Carter presidency was in its infancy, and the dollar had yet to begin its precipitous fall.

Two years were to elapse before Giscard and Schmidt teamed up to make their joint EMS proposals in Copenhagen. Even then, the political horizon of the French president's ambition was far from identical to that of his German ally. Giscard was adamantly opposed to the US policy of 'benign neglect'. However, his primary concern lay less with Western Europe's relation to the US than with France's relation to West Germany. In particular, he wished to replace the German-dominated 'snake' – whose modus operandi gave exceptional influence to the Bundesbank – with a more balanced system of currency management and policy-making, allowing for equality between the two countries and the assurance of France's due rank. A monetary system that was asymmetrical in its obligations needed therefore to give way to a symmetrical one, even if it was still very much in France's interest to benefit from the monetary stability resulting from the effective pegging of the franc to the DM. Only through an improved monetary system could there be a reinvigoration of France's economic power that would prevent its being overshadowed in Europe by West Germany. In October 1978, as the planned EMS neared final shape, Giscard d'Estaing felt confident to declare that his aim was to consolidate France's position as the fourth of the world's leading economic powers (ahead, that is, of the UK), and then to have France catch up in economic strength with West Germany within the space of some fifteen years.[17]

The EMS Negotiations, the Symmetry Issue, and the ECU

In April 1978, at the European Council meeting in Copenhagen, the German Chancellor was keen that the UK should participate in the future EMS, despite the misgivings of the British prime minister, James Callaghan. The matter was discussed together by Callaghan, Schmidt, and Giscard. Without great enthusiasm, Callaghan accepted that the EMS project in its early stage should be pushed forward through confidential discussions and negotiations by individual representatives of their three governments, all chosen personally by themselves. This arrangement was to prove important on the French and German sides. Both Giscard d'Estaing and Schmidt put forward immediately the names of their intended delegates. The perennial Clappier, now Governor of the Banque de France, was to represent France. Schmidt's choice was Horst Schulmann, the chief economic adviser in the Chancellor's Office. Hence the Bundesbank was to be sidelined in the decisive first few months of negotiation. Its president, Otto Emminger, and his fellow directors had not cared even for the snake. Also sidelined were the other six EC member states. Italy's exclusion had been foreshadowed three years earlier when Giscard had initially sought to confine the Rambouillet summit of leading industrial countries to a group of only five (the US, Japan, West Germany, France, and the UK).

Because of the lukewarm British attitude, much of the shaping of the EMS between April and December 1978 was to consist essentially in the securing of an agreement between France and West Germany. The Clappier–Schulmann duet lasted until the European Council meeting in Bremen in July 1978, at the start of Germany's six-month EC presidency. There the heads of state or government agreed in principle to the establishing of a 'scheme for the creation of closer monetary cooperation leading to a zone of monetary stability in Europe'. Important for the orchestration of the Bremen meeting was Giscard d'Estaing's visit beforehand to Schmidt at his home in Hamburg. After Bremen the negotiations passed to various EEC bodies, notably the Council of Ministers (in its 'Ecofin' variant, comprising economics and finance ministers), the Committee of the Central Bank Governors, and the Monetary Committee. Symbolically, Aachen marked the apogee of the negotiations. In September the German Chancellor and the French president held a two-day meeting in Charlemagne's city for joint consultation about the EMS; on the first evening, they visited Aachen's cathedral, still the repository of the Holy Roman Emperor's throne, to attend a concert to mark the occasion and celebrate the closeness of Franco-German relations. Albeit in a more religiously neutral mode, it was reminiscent of de Gaulle and Adenauer coming together in the cathedral in Rheims sixteen years earlier. The EMS's final shape was then agreed at the December meeting of the European Council, held in Brussels.[18]

However, the inauguration of the EMS (with all nine EC member states formally participating) and the start of operation of the ERM (with sterling as the absentee) did not take place until March 1979. The delay was due to last-minute French reservations about whether the modifications to the MCA system served adequately the interests of French farmers. These reservations had arisen in connection with the internal politics of the ruling RPR–UDF parliamentary coalition. For the day after the December agreement to the EMS in Brussels, Chirac had issued a pronunciamento, in the name of the RPR, from the Cochin hospital in Paris where he had been confined after surgery resulting from a motor car accident. He denounced nameless politicians for having sacrificed France to Europe; and his purpose was to profit from any unease about Giscard d'Estaing's advertised enthusiasm for European causes by championing a hardline nation state stance in advance of the first direct elections for the European Parliament to be held in June 1979. The French president's prudent response was to make a show of concern for the country's farmers – hence the EMS delay. In the event, Chirac's position proved disastrous for his party in the elections to the Strasbourg parliament. Taking his lesson, he liberated himself from the political embrace of Pierre Juillet and Marie-France Garaud – two formidable éminences grises whose advice had earlier been prized by Pompidou – and henceforth he evinced more enthusiasm for the European cause.[19]

In the negotiations preceding the December 1978 agreement in Brussels, the crucial question had been whether the ERM would operate symmetrically or asymmetrically. In principle, all participating currencies were to be on an equal footing, bound to one another in a parity grid, with permissible margins of fluctuation set normally at 2.25 per cent either side of central rates – identical to the 'snake' fluctuation margins. Importantly, symmetrical operation in French eyes excluded a privileged role for the DM; in other words, no national currency should be allowed to serve as the anchor for all the other currencies within the ERM. Furthermore, symmetry also required that the burden of policy adjustment should be shared and equitable. It should therefore be incumbent upon those governments and monetary authorities of member states with stronger currencies – normally Germany with the Netherlands in tow – to take anticipatory remedial action to forestall excessive appreciation. No longer should it be simply left to those with weaker currencies – notably France – to gear their policies to the avoidance of excessive depreciation. This was a key issue for France. At the heart of it lay obviously the question of the degree of subordination of France to Germany in the monetary sphere.

The desired French solution was twofold. First, the European Unit of Account (EUA) – until then no more than a currency basket – should be transformed into an embryonic parallel currency and serve as the ERM's numéraire. To give the metamorphosed EUA a proper garb, Giscard d'Estaing had successfully proposed at the European Council meeting in Bremen that the EUA be renamed the European Currency Unit (ECU). This acronym, when put into French lower case as 'écu', made it synonymous with a type of gold coin minted in France in the thirteenth century in the reign of Saint Louis, and also with a type of silver coin minted later during the French Revolution. Secondly, on the substantive issue rather than the window dressing, Clappier argued throughout the negotiations that the ECU should be used as the yardstick for a divergence indicator, which – for each currency, strong or weak – would signal the need for a corrective policy response by the currency's national authorities, and indeed make it obligatory. Equal burden sharing was imperative.

Schmidt was ready to indulge Giscard in the matter of a new name for the EC currency basket. But there was strong German opposition, first expressed by Schulmann, to the introduction of a divergence indicator that could well lead to the FRG's being regularly identified – because of the DM's very strength – as an EC member state formally required to undertake major policy adjustment. This prospect of being obliged to pursue reflationary monetary or fiscal policies for the sake of its EC partners, regardless of the consequences for domestic monetary stability, was anathema in Bonn and, even more so, in Frankfurt, the home of the Bundesbank. The implicit logic of the French-proposed intervention system smacked of the 'locomotive' principle recommended in the previous year by Carter. It raised the spectre of EC-legitimised pressures for lower German interest rates, on the premise that the demand management of the German economy should be subordinated to EC-wide imperatives. The German Chancellor and the French president had seen eye to eye on those aspects of the EMS that were in line with the thrust of the ten-year-old Barre Memorandum – whose author was now the French prime minister. These included the arrangements for short-term monetary support and the credit mechanisms. But there was never any real agreement between the two men over a new intervention system and over the role of the ECU.[20]

The European Council chose to fudge the issue, helped by the opacity arising from the issue's technical complexity. According to its Resolution of December 1978, the ECU lay at 'the centre of the EMS'. Each currency was to have 'an ECU-related central rate', and the ECU was to be used as an official reserve asset and as a means of settlement between EC central banks. The ECU also lay at the heart of the intervention system. For 'an ECU basket formula' would serve as 'an indicator to detect divergences between Community currencies'. The 'threshold of divergence' for each currency was set at 75 per cent of the maximum spread of divergence allowed by the ERM's permissible margins of fluctuation; and when any particular currency crossed it, there was to be 'a presumption that the authorities concerned will correct this situation by adequate measures'. These were classified under the four headings of 'diversified intervention' on the foreign-exchange markets, 'measures of domestic monetary policy', 'changes in central rates', and 'other measures of economic policy'. The equivocal word was 'presumption', since it fell short of a binding obligation.

If a central bank failed to take required measures, whether in the form of either interest-rate changes or intra-marginal intervention on the foreign-exchange markets, it would be expected under the terms of the Resolution to explain the 'special circumstances' justifying its inaction to the other central banks operating the ERM. However, the Resolution left essentially unaltered the feeble character of the appropriate response; the crossing of the 'threshold of divergence' created just 'a presumption' to act and no more. The Bundesbank was thereby let off the hook. Almost any refusal to cut interest rates, or to intervene intra-marginally by selling DM in support of a weaker currency (thereby expanding the domestic money supply), could be justified by the Bundesbank's prior and binding obligation to hold down inflation at home. In the matter of ERM foreign-exchange market intervention, all that was indisputable was that action had to be taken once the bilateral limits between any two currencies' exchange rates had been reached. Intervention then became obligatory by central banks to avoid overshooting the permissible margins of fluctuation, unless the central rates themselves were changed. But this was already the modus operandi of the 'snake'. *Plus ça change, plus c'est la même chose.*

The Dictates of the ERM and French Dissatisfaction

Temporary Acquiescence to German Monetary Hegemony

After the first few years of the ERM's existence, it was clear that the fudge over the ECU and the intervention system had resulted in the ERM itself emerging as no more than a rebaptised 'snake'. Although the daily computations of the ECU divergence indicator were regularly published by the international financial press, there was no evidence in the case of the DM that the Bundesbank paid much heed to them. Eventually, with the passage of time, even the pretence that the divergence indicator mattered was to be quietly dropped. As to the ECU's appointed role as numeraire for the ERM parity grid, it was essentially a facade. On the occasion of currency realignments, the negotiations revolved around bilateral central rates vis-à-vis the DM; only when the new rates were decided in these practical terms was the agreement then dressed up in ECUs.

To give the new monetary system its own institutional authority, there had been the French-inspired promise to set up the EMF as a sort of regional IMF, largely independent of the Washington-based institution and largely independent too of EC national central banks. This promise had figured in the brief EMS Annex released as part of the European Council's formal conclusions after its July 1978 meeting; and it was reiterated, but only vaguely, in the European Council's Resolution of December 1978. It proved an unfulfilled promise. The German Chancellor, in tactical collusion with the French president, had called for the EMF's creation. But this cut little ice with the Bundesbank. From the German central bank's standpoint, the EMCF – established in 1973 as a result of the Werner Report – was quite adequate for the EMS's purposes. Under the 'snake' arrangements, the BIS had acted from Basle as the agent for what was a disembodied EMCF. It had administered the multilateral settlement of central banks' very short-term debts and claims vis-à-vis one another, and also the credit mechanisms for short-term monetary support and medium-term financial assistance. This international cooperation under BIS auspices suited the Bundesbank, and under the EMS arrangements, so it turned out, the role of the EMCF was not essentially changed. In 1981, at a meeting of the EEC Monetary Committee, the Bundesbank had the satisfaction of finally killing off the planned supranational EMF.[21]

Hence, contrary to Giscard d'Estaing's intentions in 1978, France became subject in the 1980s to the constraints of a German-led EMS whose mechanisms were not significantly different from the old 'snake'. Once Mitterrand embarked upon the risky and ultimately unsuccessful economic-policy course dictated by his presidential electoral platform of 1981, these constraints were to be keenly felt. In particular, neither the Bundesbank in Frankfurt nor the federal government in Bonn felt under any obligation to ease their monetary or fiscal stance to accommodate French needs. The franc's central rate against the German currency had already been adjusted downwards by 2 per cent in September 1979, though this had been in the shape of a general ERM realignment formally effected through a DM revaluation (and a devaluation of the Danish krone) against all the other participating currencies. Now, in October 1981 and June 1982, in the course of the Mauroy government's pursuit of socialist goals through a policy of economic expansion, the French currency had again to be adjusted downwards, but by 8.5 per cent and 10 per cent respectively, through formal devaluations of the franc. Although these realignments were again of a general kind, involving all participating currencies, the biggest devaluations against the DM and the guilder in October 1981 were those of the French franc and the lira (the latter ranked as a second-class member of the ERM on account of its 6 per cent permissible margins of fluctuation.) In the general realignment of June 1982, the franc's change against the DM and the guilder – the two hard currencies – was the biggest of all the bilateral devaluations.

These downward adjustments of the franc's value took place at a time when the franc-denominated import prices of commodities were already being ratcheted upwards by the dollar's sustained recovery from its position in 1977–79, dog years for the American currency. The conjunction of the franc's ERM devaluations and the dollar's appreciation heightened domestic inflationary pressures. Hence much of the increased international price competitiveness accruing from the franc's depreciation was eroded by fast price rises at home – the inflation differential vis-à-vis West Germany stood at more than 7 percentage points in both 1981 and 1982. France was in the throes of an inflation and currency-depreciation spiral. To make matters worse, speculative pressures against the franc on the international financial markets, engendered by lack of confidence in the Socialist-dominated government, only complicated further the task of the prime minister, Mauroy, and the economics and finance minister, Delors.

Such was the background to the crucial moment of choice for Mitterrand in March 1983. The franc was yet again under considerable strain. Keenly debated at the Elysée and in the upper reaches of government since 1982 was how best to change course in the face of growing evidence of policy failure. The key issue was the French currency's continued participation in the ERM. Either the franc would be withdrawn from the ERM – as the franc had been withdrawn from the 'snake' in 1976 – in the hope that a floating exchange rate and a more flexible interest-rate policy would be more conducive to industrial expansion; or, alternatively, the franc would remain in the ERM, but would be backed in the future by a more credible economic policy, involving a significant tightening of fiscal policy. The latter course of action was urged by Delors with the backing of Mauroy. On the other hand, an influential voice calling for the franc's withdrawal from the ERM was that of Jean Riboud, a longstanding friend of Mitterrand and head of the large Schlumberger industrial group, who had been pressing his case since August 1982. In the same camp as Riboud were Bérégovoy (secretary general of the Presidency of the Republic), Fabius (budget minister), and Michel Rocard (economic planning minister).

The president himself hesitated. Tipping eventually the balance of economic argument was the advice proffered by the Director of the Treasury, Michel Camdessus, the most powerful civil servant in the economics and finance ministry, and a future head of, first, the Banque de France and then the IMF. He convinced Fabius that an exit from the ERM was likely to precipitate an excessive depreciation of the franc. The fall, moreover, would be a difficult to arrest because of France's limited foreign-exchange reserves (following their haemorrhage in 1982). For Camdessus, the only action left open to the monetary authorities at that stage would be to raise short-term interest rates to 20 per cent or more, disastrously slamming the brakes on economic growth. Fabius, belonging at the time to Mitterrand's charmed circle, announced his conversion to the pro-ERM camp – with, apparently, immediate and decisive effect.[22]

Not that the French president would have been altogether swayed by any purely economic argument. What was to prove his decisive political overture to West Germany had taken place only two months earlier, in the shape of his Bundestag address, providing succour to a beleaguered Kohl. A concern to maintain the momentum of this new phase of Franco-German rapprochement now discouraged Mitterrand from taking precipitate action on the monetary front, since an ERM exit would have been to the detriment of cooperation between the two countries.

In any event, for a mixture of economic and political reasons, Mitterrand finally declared his preference in March 1983 for the prudent yet uncomfortable ERM option. The decision to maintain the franc in the ERM required draconian accompanying measures. It led immediately to a downward adjustment of the franc against the DM of 8.8 per cent. However, appearances were preserved inasmuch as the ERM realignment, agreed only after considerable difficulty in Brussels, was of a general kind entailing across-the-board changes to bilateral central rates in the parity grid. The DM was revalued a little against the guilder, while all the other currencies were devalued in varying degrees against the Dutch one. The French currency was placed yet again in the company of the lira, but their devaluation against the guilder was somewhat less than that of the even weaker Irish pound. Yet there was no hiding the fact that at the heart of the ERM realignment lay France's economic troubles. For Delors in particular, the downward adjustment of the franc had now to be made to work. Swingeing budgetary austerity measures were introduced to restrain domestic demand, hold down inflationary pressures, and allow scope for export growth. These were on top of a variety of prices and incomes restrictions that had already been introduced in June and September of the previous year – including the abolition of wage indexation in the public sector. In 1984, when Fabius replaced Mauroy as prime minister and Delors was dispatched to Brussels to head the EC Commission, exports did surge, contributing to a modest acceleration in GDP growth, while inflation, although still at a high level, eased further.

The rigour associated with the serious post-1983 commitment to the ERM option took its toll on economic growth. In 1976–81 when Barre was prime minister, the rise in France's real GDP had been similar to that of West Germany and somewhat better than that of the EC area taken as a whole. Then, in the first years of Socialist rule, France fared considerably better than West Germany and continued to outperform the whole EC area. Strong public-sector demand sustained economic growth. However, after the policy turnaround of 1983, France's comparative position changed. Thus, in 1984–88, real GDP growth was slower in France than in either West Germany or the whole EC area. During these years the unemployment rate climbed into the 10–11 per cent bracket, double-digit figures for the first time in the post-war period.

The pain had its compensation. By 1988–89 there was a considerable degree of nominal convergence between the French and West German economies. Price inflation in France was down to roughly German levels, and general-government deficits were similar when expressed as a percentage of GDP. The last ever downward adjustments in the ERM of the franc's central rate against the DM had taken place in April 1986 and January 1987, when Balladur was economics and finance minister in the Chirac *cohabitation* government, and they contributed to the favourable conditions for the export boom of 1988–89. The realignments on both occasions were general ones; all other currencies were devalued in varying degrees against the DM and the guilder. In the case of the French currency, the devaluations were 6 per cent and 3 per cent respectively. The final 1987 devaluation brought the franc's cumulative downward adjustment against the German currency since the EMS's inauguration in 1979 to as much as 33 per cent.

EMU, the SEA, and the Internal-market Programme

Towards the end of the decade, the question of the future of European monetary integration came back to the top of the EC agenda. The ground had been prepared by the ERM's painful but successful fostering of nominal convergence – meaning broadly the pursuit of lower inflation and fiscal-policy discipline on the West German model. This at least was the case for the inner core of Germany, France, and the Benelux countries. The long-standing German and Dutch demand that the harmonisation of economic policies should precede monetary union was now partly satisfied.

The ground had also been prepared politically by the SEA, which gave expression, for the first time in EC treaty law, to the goal of EMU. This was arguably by a sleight of hand, since EMU figured in the SEA only in passing. First, there was the mention in the SEA's preamble of the approval that had been given to EMU as a long-term goal by the EC heads of state or government when they decided to set up the EMCF at the Paris summit convened by Pompidou in 1972. The second mention took the form of a convoluted chapter heading, in the body of the treaty itself, entitled 'Cooperation in Economic and Monetary Policy (Economic and Monetary Union)'. However, nothing was explicitly said about EMU in the actual chapter – itself a very brief one, virtually an empty box. Thus, almost surreptitiously, the goal of EMU was formally established under treaty law when the SEA entered into force in 1987.

At the European Council meeting in December 1985, which agreed the SEA, the pressure for including some commitment to EMU in it had come primarily from France in the face of German reticence and outright British hostility. Mitterrand was convinced that the completion of the internal market called for monetary union, not for reasons of economic theory but of national interest. He reportedly told the Irish prime minister, Garret FitzGerald, a few days before the Luxembourg meeting: 'We will not allow the *grand marché* to be put in place if there is not the promise of an agreement on monetary union. Otherwise it is suspect: the *grand marché* would serve only the interests of a nationalist Great Britain or an imperialist Germany.'[23]

No mention had been made of monetary union in the Commission's White Paper of June 1985, even if Delors had called five months earlier for the creation of 'a true European currency' in his declaration to the European Parliament as the Commission's incoming president. Mentioned instead in 'Completing the Internal Market' was the need to strengthen the EMS. It became increasingly clear in the next few years that this was no idle platitude. The full liberalisation of capital movements across the EC area, which was of fundamental importance for the internal-market programme, risked seriously disturbing the functioning of the ERM and hence the internal market too. This was pointed out in the influential Padoa-Schioppa Report of April 1987 (*Efficiency, Stability and Equity: A Strategy for the Evolution of the Economic System of the European Community*), prepared by the Study Group on the Integration Strategy of the Community, set up by the EC Commission in 1986 and headed by the Deputy General Manager of the Banca d'Italia, Tomasso Padoa-Schioppa, who had previously been head of the Commission's Directorate-General for Economic and Financial Affairs. The crux of the problem, as emphasised in the report, was that exchange-rate fixity, capital mobility, and national autonomy in the conduct of monetary policy were essentially incompatible. The Padoa-Schioppa Report proposed a revamped EMS, largely in keeping with the original French vision. Through the strict coordination of monetary policies in the interest of all, both capital mobility and a high degree of exchange-rate fixity could be possible. The personal preference of Padoa-Schioppa, however, was to go a stage further and opt for a single currency, and his view influenced Delors.

In fact, with the exception of West Germany, the provider of the anchor currency, all countries with currencies in the ERM had already lost much of their autonomy in the setting of interest rates. But the Bundesbank continued perforce to set its interest rates as a function of domestic monetary conditions. And the weaker-currency ERM participants still relied on exchange controls on capital movements to protect their currencies against adverse speculative pressures.

Once this instrument was removed, there was the likelihood of greater exchange-rate instability within the ERM. If the concern about the consequences of the liberalisation of capital movements was particularly keenly felt in Italy on account of the lira's past chronic weakness, it was also a source of anxiety in France. The ERM participants that allowed full freedom of capital movements were Germany and the Netherlands, the possessors of the two hardest currencies. Although Belgium and Luxembourg allowed full freedom in principle, the freedom was not total in practice because of the operation by the Belgium-Luxembourg Economic Union of a two-tier foreign-exchange market. Among other ERM participants, France had made considerable progress since the late 1970s towards allowing full freedom of capital movements. But – as already indicated – two major controls were still in place when the EC Directive providing for the full liberalisation of capital movements was adopted in June 1988. These were the prohibition, applying to most French residents, against opening foreign-currency bank accounts abroad and, secondly, the limitations on the amounts of franc-denominated loans that French banks were permitted to extend to non-residents. Such controls represented an important safety net – as would be demonstrated, four years after their removal, by the franc's vulnerability in the ERM crisis of 1993.

The concern in the late 1980s about the consequences of full freedom of capital movements contributed to a heightened and widespread perception that the EMS had failed to be qualitatively different from the old 'snake' arrangements. France was at the forefront in indicating dissatisfaction on this score. In September 1987 the Basle–Nyborg Agreement was concluded with a view to reducing asymmetry in the ERM's functioning; this was largely the result of an initiative taken by Balladur on the occasion of the ERM realignment of January 1987. Yet the Basle–Nyborg Agreement amounted to little more than a tinkering with the system. It merely made more flexible the EMCF's operating rules, under which a weaker-currency central bank could borrow limited amounts of a stronger ERM currency from another central bank on a very short-term basis for intervention purposes (in practice, borrowing mainly the DM).

In 1988, twelve months after the Basle–Nyborg Agreement, the question of European monetary union came back to the fore. French patience with the operational asymmetry of the ERM and German monetary hegemony had worn thin. However, the positive German response to French proposals was to cause some surprise. That was not all. A year later, Europe's geopolitical upheaval was to transform the EMU endeavour, imparting to it a huge new political significance compared with the first abortive attempt to achieve monetary union two decades earlier.

Notes

1. De Gaulle, *Discours et messages*, vol. 4, 330–34.
2. For de Gaulle's handling of the devaluation question, see Lacouture, *De Gaulle*, vol. 3, 734–38.
3. 'Commission Memorandum to the Council on the coordination of economic policies and monetary cooperation within the Community', *Bulletin of the European Communities* 3, 1969, Supplement, 3–5.
4. Roussel, *Georges Pompidou*, 337.
5. Brandt, *People and Politics*, 244–47.
6. For the summit communiqué, see Harryvan and van der Harst (eds), *Documents on European Union*, 168–69.
7. Roussel, *Georges Pompidou*, 340–42.
8. For the Werner Report's conclusions, see Harryvan and van der Harst (eds), *Documents on European Union*, 169–72.
9. 'Commission Memorandum to the Council on the coordination of economic policies and monetary cooperation within the Community', 4, 12.
10. Henry Kissinger, *The White House Years*, New York, 1979, 958.
11. For a detailed account of the Azores meeting, see Roussel, *Georges Pompidou*, 461–89.
12. For the Council's Resolution, see Harryvan and van der Harst (eds), *Documents on European Union*, 177–78.
13. For the respective roles of Jenkins in Florence and Giscard and Schmidt in Copenhagen, see Ludlow, *The Making of the European Monetary System*, 37–62, 88–94.
14. Giscard d'Estaing, *Le Pouvoir et la vie*, vol. 1, 143.
15. Dennis L. Bark and David R. Gress, *A History of West Germany*, 2nd edn, 2 vols, Oxford, 1993, vol. 1, 524–25, vol. 2, 24.
16. For Schmidt's wider vision, see David Marsh, *The Bundesbank: The Bank that Rules Europe*, London, 1992, 232–33; Kenneth Dyson, *Elusive Union: The Process of Economic and Monetary Union in Europe*, London, 1994, 98.
17. *Le Monde*, 18 October 1978.
18. For the text of the European Council's Resolution establishing the EMS, see Ludlow, *The Making of the European Monetary System*, 303–8; for key extracts, Harryvan and van der Harst (eds), *Documents on European Union*, 196–98.
19. Ludlow, *The Making of the European Monetary System*, 201–5, 263–64, 279–83; Franz-Olivier Giesbert, *Jacques Chirac*, Paris, 1987, 310–25.
20. For the question in 1978 of the ERM and symmetrical or asymmetrical burden sharing, see especially Ludlow, *The Making of the European Monetary System*, 102, 106–8, 140–42, 159–65, 230–39.
21. Connolly, *The Rotten Heart of Europe*, 19–23.
22. On the policy transformation between June 1982 and March 1983, see Philippe Bauchard, *La Guerre des deux roses. Du rêve à la réalité, 1981–1985*, Paris, 1986, 101–76.
23. Attali, *Verbatim*, vol. 1, 886–88.

Chapter 9

GEOPOLITICAL UPHEAVAL AND THE MAASTRICHT TREATY

The EMU project was relaunched by France and West Germany less than two years before the opening of the Berlin Wall. The goal on the French side was the curtailing of German monetary hegemony. The dramatic events of 1989 led Mitterrand to attach even more importance to EMU and, for a few months, to seek to forestall the emergence of a greater Germany. Then, bowing to the ineluctable in the matter of unification, he cooperated with Kohl in creating an EC-wide political union. The outcome was the Maastricht Treaty, whose design for political union was remindful of the Fouchet proposals.

Monetary Union Proposed from Paris and Bonn

The Balladur and Genscher Memorandums

At the time of the setting up of the Franco-German Defence Council in 1987–88, French concerns about the future of the two countries and their privileged partnership were far from exclusively concerned with security and defence. As had been the case five years earlier, at the time of the Euromissile crisis and Mitterrand's Bundestag address, much anxiety existed about France's weakness in the face of German monetary power as exercised in the ERM framework. Tellingly, when the idea of the Defence Council was proposed by Bonn in July 1987, the French reaction had been to make acceptance of it conditional on German acceptance of a parallel French proposal: the setting up of a Franco-German Economic and Financial Council for the coordination of monetary policies. This second proposal, which emanated from the Elysée rather than from the Chirac *cohabitation* government, won German agreement. Hence the Economic and Financial Council was set up in January 1988 at the same time as the Defence Council. Yet on the French side the economics and finance minister, Balladur, evinced no enthusiasm. More importantly, on the German side the Bundesbank and its president, Karl-Otto Pöhl, were adamantly opposed to the Economic and Financial Council from the outset, objecting on legal or quasi-constitutional grounds to its very existence. Because of the Bundesbank's refusal to play ball, it was never to prove a meaningful or influential decision-making body.

The French escape from German monetary hegemony was to take a different route. On 8 January 1988, two weeks before the formal creation of the Franco-German Economic and Financial Council and four months before the end of the Chirac government's term of office, Balladur addressed a memorandum entitled 'Europe's Monetary Construction' to his fellow EC finance ministers for discussion when they met in early February. Its origin was the French government's dissatisfaction with the functioning of the ERM, and it was to be the first in a series of initiatives that resulted, within the space of a year and a half, in EMU's becoming the new high ambition for the EC, after that of completing the internal market. For the period prior to 1993, which was that of the execution of the internal-market programme, the French economics and finance minister suggested that the EMS be strengthened, so as to create an institutional structure that would give all EC member states participating in the ERM a real say in the framing of coordinated economic and monetary policies. This would, he indicated, put an end to a situation in which German monetary policy tended, by the logic of the system, to be imposed on the rest of the ERM area – the concern on the French side back in 1978, when the design of the future ERM had been such a difficult issue with Germany.

Specifically, Balladur called for a greater symmetry in exchange-market intervention, with the Bundesbank purchasing other ERM currencies rather than the dollar. He also urged sterling's participation in the ERM and the lira's inclusion in the narrow band, since he wished to put an end to the ERM's excessive tendency to function around a DM/French franc axis. The boldness of Balladur's initiative concerned the period from 1993 onwards. Towards the end of the memorandum, he suggested the introduction of a 'single currency' (*monnaie unique*) after the completion of the internal market. This currency would be supported by a federal central-banking system, with a European Central Bank (ECB) sooner or later placed at its apex. What this meant – though, of course, he did not say it – was that the Bundesbank's rule in Europe would be brought to an end. Crucially, despite his use of the term 'single currency', Balladur explicitly left open the question of whether the new currency should be a true single currency, displacing national currencies, or else a (parallel) common currency – though his own personal preference was for the latter.[1]

Shortly afterwards, in February 1988, Giscard d'Estaing and Schmidt, out of office and so acting as elder statesmen, used the platform of their Committee for the Monetary Union of Europe to present proposals for the statutes of a future European Central Bank. They also suggested that EMU be put on the agenda of the European Council at its meeting in Hanover in June – the six-month EC presidency then being in West Germany's hands.

That this actually happened was due above all to Genscher, the German foreign minister. On 26 February he presented his fellow EC foreign ministers with a memorandum in favour of EMU entitled 'A European Currency Area and a European Central Bank'. In charge of the Foreign Office since 1974, he had long given proof of commitment to the cause of European union – as witness his role in the preparation of the 'Solemn Declaration on European Union', issued by the European Council after its Stuttgart meeting in June 1983 at the end of the FRG's previous EC presidency. Because of his vast experience, his position as the leading FDP figure in the Kohl government, and the relative independence enjoyed by the Foreign Office, Genscher had the clout to take this initiative and so place Germany's weight behind the EMU endeavour. And he was strikingly insouciant about German hostility to any European move threatening the country's monetary independence, an independence represented by the DM itself and the autonomy of the Bundesbank.[2]

What prompted the German foreign minister to back the French finance minister – and so start a process that would lead eventually to the Maastricht Treaty – has been variously interpreted, particularly in the absence of a sufficiently clear indication on his own part.[3] Mitterrand, acting through his then former (and future) foreign minister, Roland Dumas, may have given some indirect encouragement to Genscher for reasons of internal French politics (to take the initiative and any credit away from the right-of-centre Balladur, as the French presidential election approached). Be that as it may, German interests and geopolitical considerations were what really underpinned the German foreign minister's stance. At the beginning of 1988 a decisive EC advance in the spirit of the Stuttgart Declaration could usefully parallel the inauguration of a new era in the FRG's relations with the USSR. Among leading Western statesmen, Genscher was no doubt the most aware of the tectonic-like political shifts then taking place to the east of the Elbe.

Coincidentally or not, Genscher's monetary-union initiative in February 1988 – effectively adding considerable weight to Balladur's own proposal – followed two exceptionally intense months of high-level contacts between the FRG and the USSR. First, in December 1987, Gorbachev had received Strauss, who had flown himself to Moscow as a private visitor and who spoke afterwards about Europe's being on 'the eve of a new age'. Secondly, in January 1988, Eduard Shevardnadze came to Bonn to meet his counterpart, Genscher, on what was the first visit to the West German capital by a Soviet foreign minister for five years –

Shevardnadze was to claim in 1991 that he had already been convinced in 1986 that German unification was inevitable and that the issue of unification would soon take centre stage. Earlier, in July 1987, Genscher had accompanied Richard von Weizsäcker, the President of the Federal Republic, on a state visit to Moscow, and this was the occasion of Gorbachev's admitting that Germany's division might not last for ever. Genscher's role at that time contrasted with Kohl's much lower profile. Indeed, the first summit meeting between Kohl and Gorbachev was not to take place until October 1988; relations between the two men had been decidedly chill during much of the previous two years because of an extraordinary act of political clumsiness on the Chancellor's part in October 1986, when in an interview for the American weekly *Newsweek* he had compared Gorbachev's skills in public relations to those of Goebbels.[4]

To the extent, therefore, that the German proposal for monetary union reflected wider European political considerations, it was fitting that it came from the FRG's foreign minister. Mitterrand, for his part, proved keen to exploit the opportunity raised by the Genscher Memorandum. This document was seen at the Elysée in February 1988 as a most welcome step in France's direction. However, for Mitterrand, there was the hurdle of the presidential elections to cross. In early April he embarked upon his last-minute election campaign, at the centre of which he put the long *Lettre à tous les Français*, his political epistle to the French nation. Prominent in it was a statement of high ambition for Europe. Although he chose to make only the briefest mention of monetary union, he did signal that he was well disposed to it. What was desirable, he said, was the development of the ECU as a 'genuine reserve currency'; and this, in turn, would call for the establishment of a European central bank, so as to manage the new reserve currency.[5]

The Delors Report

Early in June 1988, fresh from his success in the presidential elections, Mitterrand met Kohl in Evian. It was the occasion to prepare jointly their positions for the European Council meeting in Hanover at the end of the month. Free now to engage anew in high politics, the French president wished to achieve progress on EMU and the ECB. The Chancellor's less lofty concern, which he felt to be more pressing than the ambition represented by the Balladur and Genscher memorandums, was that France should not block the planned adoption of the draft EC Directive providing for the full liberalisation of capital movements – a key measure in the programme for completing the internal market. To advance his own priority, Mitterrand provided the requisite assurance that France would back the Directive, to which, however, he added the request that Kohl support French efforts aimed at the EC-wide harmonisation of taxation of savings or investment income. The Directive providing for the full liberalisation of capital movements was indeed to be adopted by the EC Council of Ministers less than two weeks later. But German support for the harmonisation of withholding tax proved no more than lukewarm; and it was effectively to collapse altogether in 1989, creating much bitterness in Paris.

Partly because of the understanding struck in Evian over the full liberalisation of capital movements and its translation into action by the EC Council of Ministers, Kohl was ready to allow the EMU project to be pushed forward when the European Council met in Hanover. Yet, in deciding to give satisfaction to both the French president and his own foreign minister in putting EMU on the European Council's agenda, Kohl had needed extra persuasion from the president of the EC Commission. The Chancellor had not instantly taken to Genscher's advocacy of monetary union as expressed in the February memorandum. However, in the run-up to the European Council's meeting in Hanover in June 1988, Delors encouraged Kohl to adopt a more positive view of the merits of EMU.

At the Hanover meeting, Kohl responded to the discussions and politicking generated by the Balladur and Genscher memorandums by agreeing to put EMU on the agenda. The result was the European Council's decision to set up a committee and charge it with 'the task of studying and proposing concrete stages leading towards [EMU]'. The committee's remit was not to pronounce on the desirability or otherwise of the goal of EMU, especially since that goal had already been posited in EC treaty law by the SEA; rather the remit was practical in kind, inasmuch as it was essentially technical expertise that was being called upon. The European Council accordingly decided that the bulk of the committee's members were to be the governors of the EC's national central banks acting in their personal capacity. In need of a prominent figure to look to the EC's wider interests, the European Council, on Kohl's prompting, chose the Commission's president as the committee's chairman. Three independent experts were thrown in for good measure. Delors, in turn, chose Padoa-Schioppa as the committee's rapporteur. The latter had been responsible a year earlier for the Commission-sponsored report on the consequences for the EMS of the EC-wide liberalisation of capital movements (see previous chapter). Pöhl was a reluctant member of the committee since he took a dim view of the prospect of EMU, but the Bundesbank president's voice proved paradoxically the most constructive one. Despite his disagreement with the goal he worked in the spirit of the remit, in that he considered how best to achieve EMU, instead of questioning it as an end. He argued successfully for an independent ECB, on the lines of the Bundesbank, and he likewise pressed for the eventual introduction of a single currency, rather than a common one existing alongside national currencies.[6] Swimming with the tide, Delors chaired adroitly the committee, encouraging Pöhl and the other central bankers to arrive at a consensus.

However, the independence that would be characteristic of a Bundes-bank writ large at European level was not a prospect meeting with wide-spread favour in Paris, inasmuch as a large degree of central-bank autonomy sat uneasily with the centralising tradition of the French state. As the Delors Committee began its deliberations, a major concern in French government circles was that of the answerability of the future ECB to national governments. In particular, the economics and finance minister, Bérégovoy, felt strongly about the need for political control, and his views were shared by the prime minister, Rocard. Furthermore, within the French finance ministry, the Director of the Treasury, Jean-Claude Trichet, and other elite Treasury civil servants feared the loss of power over monetary policy to which they were accustomed, even if that same power had been much eroded in practice by the constraints imposed by the ERM. Unlike the Bundesbank, the Banque de France – a Napoleonic creation – had been very tightly controlled by the state ever since its full nationalisation in 1945.

Yet neither Bérégovoy nor Rocard had any real say in the matter. Not only had the Governor of the Banque de France, Jacques de Larosière, been appointed to sit on the Delors Committee in, formally speaking, a personal capacity – like all the other central bank governors – but his say was enhanced by his past as the IMF's Managing Director. In November 1988 he chose to rally to the German and Dutch position in favour of independence for the ECB, an independence also to be extended to the other national central banks operating, satellite fashion, in the proposed federal European System of Central Banks (ESCB). Apart from de Larosière, the one other person who really counted on the French side was the French president himself, since the Delors Committee was to report directly back to the European Council. No longer shackled by a *cohabitation* government, Mitterrand was beholden only to himself when pronouncing for France in the European Council. Crucially, in December 1988 he gave the go-ahead to de Larosière, when the latter, bypassing Bérégovoy and Trichet, sought approval for moving to the German and Dutch position on central-bank independence. Having welcomed the Genscher Memorandum and having then contributed to winning Kohl over to the cause of EMU, Mitterrand was politically well disposed to the work of the Delors Committee, even if it came down on the side of central-bank independence on the German or Bundesbank model. De Larosière, as a central banker, was glad enough to rally France to the camp of German monetary orthodoxy. What mattered for Mitterrand was that EMU, even on German terms, was politically far preferable to a German-led EMS.[7]

The fruit of the Delors Committee's work, the *Report on Economic and Monetary Union in the European Community*, was published in April 1989. Agreed and proposed by the committee was the eventual replacement of EC national currencies by a single EC one; and the ECB, at the apex of the

ESCB, would be fully independent. The move to EMU was to be a three-stage process, whose start would be linked to the completion of the internal market, especially the full liberalisation of capital movements so as to make for a 'single financial area', while the third and final stage would start with the 'irrevocable locking' of the exchange rates of national currencies. The design of the process was essentially that of EMU's evolving out of the EMS. The latter was to be consolidated through the inclusion in the ERM of all EC currencies, and the application to all of them of the standard permissible margins of fluctuation, rather than the wider margins that had until then been allowed exceptionally to the lira. Within the consolidated EMS, it was implied in the report, the DM would continue to serve as the 'anchor' currency: the EMS, it was pointed out, had benefited from the role played by the German currency as the 'anchor' for 'participants' monetary and intervention policies'. Pöhl remarked, perhaps only half in jest, that these words about the DM's solidity formed the best sentence in the entire report.[8] The eventual emergence of the single currency, under the arrangements agreed by the Delors Committee, would virtually mean the reemergence of the DM under another name, at least initially.

In Paris, two weeks after the publication of the Delors Report, the Governor of the Banque de France was summoned to the finance ministry for a dressing down over his signature to a document that was 'too Germanic' in design. But de Larosière silenced Bérégovoy and Trichet in telling them that his support of the Bundesbank model for central-bank independence had been authorised by the French president himself four months earlier.[9]

The Delors Report was duly approved at the Madrid meeting of the European Council in June 1989. Mitterrand pressed keenly for the launching without delay of an IGC to amend the EEC Treaty on the basis of the Delors Report. Thatcher blocked that move, however. Instead, the European Council agreed that the first stage leading to the realisation of EMU would start on 1 July 1990, the date already serving as the deadline for the completion of the liberalisation of capital movements by EC member states. Only afterwards would an IGC be held 'to lay down the subsequent changes' required for detailing out the second and third stages.

Few imagined that before that date the geopolitical map of Europe would be radically changed, lending a new political urgency, at least from a French standpoint, to the EMU project. For the months following the Madrid summit were those of the last convulsions of communism in much of Central and Eastern Europe, including the GDR. By the end of 1989 Mitterrand would become even more convinced of the need to pursue EMU for political reasons – that is, to contain German power and channel it in the right direction.

France and the Fall of the Berlin Wall

Mitterrand at the Bar of History

The Berlin Wall was abruptly opened by the GDR authorities on 9 November 1989, twenty-eight years after its construction had sealed the main escape route to the West from East Berlin and the East German state. This opening of the Wall, followed by its dismantling, was the climax of several months of intensifying unrest in East Germany. One aspect of the unrest had been a growing mass exodus to the FRG. Many had profited from Hungary's opening of its border with Austria. After the Nemeth government had dismantled physically its part of the Iron Curtain in May by cutting down the barbed-wire fencing, the route was opened wide in September when it was decided to abrogate a consular agreement with the GDR and allow East Germans 'on vacation' in Hungary to leave freely, once they had acquired an FRG passport from the West German embassy in Budapest. Other West German embassies, notably that in Prague, served as places of refuge for thousands more who had resolved to turn their back on the East German regime. Furthermore, the regime itself was falling apart fast. Increasing numbers of East Germans peacefully demonstrated in the streets of their cities in the summer and autumn of 1989. The demonstrations, especially in Leipzig, were of epic quality. But demanded by them was what was to prove to be impossible, the radical reform of the regime itself through a change of leadership. Gorbachev, visiting East Berlin in early October for the GDR's fortieth anniversary, intimated that such reform was feasible and necessary. Yet when East Berliners found to their amazement a month later that the days of the city's physical division were now over, a subterraneous revolution rather than just a reform of the existing regime was far advanced; on the heels of the momentous events that had occurred earlier in 1989 in Poland and Hungary, it would reach its term within the period of less than a year, the existing East German structures of government and power being entirely swept away.

In Paris, as in other Western capitals, there was no doubt after 9 November 1989 that Europe's post-war order was in the process of being utterly transformed. Yet difficult to appraise was the momentum of the far-reaching developments under way, the extent to which they were controllable, and their likely consequences for the FRG and the USSR, the two major powers the most directly affected. The French president's immediate concern was that any destabilisation of an East German state in dire need of reform should be no more than temporary, and certainly not serve as a catalyst for a precipitate movement in Bonn in favour of German unification.

But German reunification did take place on 3 October 1990. And Mitterrand for the remainder of his life was to be sensitive to the charge that he had initially sought to block this outcome. In December 1995, half a year after stepping down from the presidency and only weeks before his life finally slipped away, he completed *De l'Allemagne, de la France*, an apologia for the honourable and constructive nature of his intentions in relation to Kohl's designs for a greater Germany. In this book he chose to emphasise that he held a different view of Germany from that taken by de Gaulle and Churchill towards the end of the Second World War. Both, he said, had laid much of the blame at a militaristic Prussia's door for the decades of European strife that came to a climax with the emergence of the Third Reich. De Gaulle and Churchill had therefore favoured Germany's permanent division, whereas Mitterrand insisted in this posthumously published book that he had never considered Prussia to be such a bogeyman. The implication was that he had never entertained any stereotyped historical objection to German unification. To substantiate the point, Mitterrand praised Prussia, first, as epitomised in the eighteenth century by Frederick the Great and the spirit of the French Enlightenment he had cultivated so assiduously at his Potsdam court and, secondly, as epitomised in the twentieth century by the moral uprightness of many of Prussia's aristocratic army officer caste, in particular those who had turned to resistance against Hitler. Here the outstanding noble figure was Henning von Tresckow, one of the leading plotters in the failed assassination attempts of both March 1943 and July 1944.[10]

More generally, what *De l'Allemagne, de la France* conveyed was a sense of deep personal interest in the two countries' intertwined past and a keen sentimental attachment to the furtherance of good Franco-German relations. This had been given expression at the very end of his presidency in the moving address he pronounced in Berlin on 8 May 1995 on the occasion of the ceremonies marking the fiftieth anniversary of the end of the war in Europe, the text of which was republished as the final pages in this personal testament.[11]

Looking back on the more concrete issue of whether he had actually sought as French president to prevent German unification in 1989–90, Mitterrand used *De l'Allemagne, de la France* to stress two points. First, he said, it was the UK in the person of its prime minister, the redoubtable Thatcher, who had tried to arrest the process of unification; no similar spoiling role had been played by France. Secondly, it was thanks primarily to his own efforts that the question of the new Germany's frontier with Poland was settled, with Bonn at last fully accepting the permanence of the Oder–Neisse Line. Without France's contribution to the resolution of this matter, he strongly implied, the path to unification would have been blocked.[12]

However, his stance in 1989–90 was far from clear-cut. During the decisive period between the opening of the Berlin Wall and the spring and summer of 1990, when the key decisions were taken concerning the political process of unification and the future of the transformed FRG within the Atlantic Alliance, Mitterrand gave definite signs of foot dragging – at least initially – in the face of Kohl's designs for a new Germany and the rapidly changing geopolitical situation. The French position was accordingly less straightforward than that of the US, the sole of the four major powers with a say in Germany's future to be fundamentally and consistently well disposed to the Bonn government's ambitions. Especially in the very uncertain days of December 1989, certain of Mitterrand's actions appeared ambivalent indeed.

The French Proposal for a European Bank

Fortuitously, the EC presidency happened to be in French hands in the second half of 1989. Partly because of the momentous events in Berlin, Mitterrand was persuaded to convoke an extraordinary meeting of the European Council in Paris on 18 November, though without any expectation that it would serve much immediate purpose. Indeed, the French president focused much of the initial discussion on the more widespread political instability across Central and Eastern Europe and, regrettable from a French standpoint, the dangers that the same instability posed to Gorbachev personally and to Soviet interests in general. There was ready agreement in the European Council to the principle of the intangibility of Europe's existing frontiers; it could scarcely have been otherwise. Kohl himself chose to speak at length about both Europe's and Germany's future, but in a quite non-committal way about the latter, eschewing any mention of the question of unification.

The signs of a breakdown in the European continental order provided the cue for Mitterrand's proposal at this meeting to set up a pan-continental 'Banque de l'Europe', this being an idea that had emanated at the end of August from the ever fertile mind of the French president's special adviser, Attali. The bank's specialisation would be large-scale project finance and its shareholders would be limited exclusively to European states, including the USSR. Before putting this proposal to the European Council, the French president had already briefly aired it in an address to the European Parliament on 25 October. The French aim, put crudely, was to minimise the role of the US and the Bretton Woods institutions, notably the World Bank, to the advantage of France and the EC, in the economic reshaping of what was hoped would be a reformist and yet still largely communist Central and Eastern Europe.

The cue for this French initiative had come several months earlier on the occasion of the annual Group of Seven summit meeting, which was held that year in Paris around the date of 14 July 1989 to coincide with the bicentenary celebrations of the French Revolution. The less sentimental and more immediate context was George H. W. Bush's state visit immediately beforehand to, first, Poland and then Hungary. On the eve of his departure for Poland, the US president had sounded out his fellow summiteers with a proposal for a substantial Group of Seven package of economic assistance to that country; this was after the semi-free parliamentary elections that had taken place there in June, resulting in the Solidarity-led opposition's triumph. At the Elysée the initiative was dismissed as tantamount to an unwarranted exercise of American leadership in European affairs. Yet it was not the general view and, at the summit itself, the initial Bush proposal was modified rather than rebuffed. This took the form of an agreement on the part of the Seven to launch the PHARE (Pologne–Hongrie: Assistance pour la Restructuration Economique) programme of technical assistance under the wider auspices of the OECD, to the benefit of both Poland and Hungary. It constituted a first major international step in assuring the two countries' economic transition.

However, Attali, who was the leading organiser of the Group of Seven meeting, felt piqued that the responsibility for the administration of the PHARE programme – later to be extended to other countries of Central and Eastern Europe – was put in the hands of the EC Commission, rather than in France's hands by virtue of its having been the summit's host.[13] Subsequently, when he made his 'Banque de l'Europe' proposal less than two months later, he deemed that a precondition for its successful creation would be its physical location in Paris. Yet, at the November meeting of the European Council, there was no ready agreement from the EC heads of government for setting up such a bank. Indeed, the reception given to the proposal as voiced by Mitterrand was largely negative, even if, crucially, there was not total rejection. The door thus slightly ajar, some astute French diplomatic footwork followed, notably in the framework of preparations for the European Council meeting in Strasbourg in December 1989. The eventual outcome in May 1990 was the treaty setting up the European Bank for Reconstruction and Development (EBRD), with a remit to promote private enterprise and, accessorily, improved public infrastructure across Central and Eastern Europe on the widest possible geographical definition of the continent's eastward extension – that is, including all of the USSR. Although Attali himself was appointed the first president of the EBRD in 1990, London was chosen rather than Paris as the location for the bank's headquarters; and even more to his dismay was the (limited) say won by the US in the bank's running (its 10 per cent shareholding comparing with a total stake of 51 per cent for the EC member states together plus the Commission). Furthermore, the emphasis on the promotion of private enterprise had not been in Attali's mind when he had first proposed the idea of a development bank for Central and Eastern Europe. His move to London, for a presidency of the EBRD that was to be dogged by controversy and acrimony and was to last only a little more than two years, took place in April 1991.[14]

A measure of circumspection had marked Mitterrand's stance in the saga of the EBRD's creation. Although from October 1989 the French president had judged it in France's interest to push forward the proposal for a European Bank, he was less committed to the idea than Attali. And in January 1990, to the disappointment of his special adviser, Mitterrand turned against the idea of locating the EBRD in Paris. One concern was not to provide ammunition to those who objected to the longstanding French insistence that the European Parliament continue to be formally based in Strasbourg, despite the fact that Brussels was a much more convenient location and that many of its activities were already being carried out there. An even more important consideration was that other priorities had come to the fore, especially once it became apparent that the opening of the Berlin Wall was not, as initially thought, the harbinger of a radically reformed GDR, but instead the signal that German unification was no longer to be relegated to a distant future.

Kohl's Ten-Point Programme

The crucial day, as regards the French president's perception that events were galloping even faster than he and most of the rest of the world had anticipated, was 28 November 1989. It was then that Kohl announced to the Bundestag his Ten-Point Programme for achieving German unity in the framework of a new 'peace order in Europe'. After free elections in the GDR, said the Chancellor, 'confederative structures' were to be developed between the two German states with a view to putting into place, eventually, a federal system for all Germany. The unwelcome subtext was clear to Mitterrand: his German partner was not really willing to envisage the halfway house of a German 'confederation' (the word figuring nowhere in the Ten-Point Programme); rather his aim from the start was to achieve unification through the enlargement of the Federal Republic. The Chancellor had opted for the diplomatic fait accompli, a practice at which the French president himself was a past master. But, if one is to rely on Attali's memory and testimony, this sort of mimetism was not of the kind to lessen Mitterrand's ire, and the immediate reaction of the president was to think of what help might be forthcoming from Moscow:

> But [Kohl] told me nothing. Nothing at all! I shall never forget this! Gorbachev will be furious; he will not allow it to happen, it is impossible! I have no need to oppose it; the Soviets will do it for me. Just think: they will never accept to have this greater Germany [*cette grande Allemagne*] facing them! ... Nothing will be agreed by me on this score until considerable progress has been achieved in the furthering of the unity of Europe. The GDR, moreover, will not want any change [to its independence of statehood]. They are Prussians; they do not want to be under Bavarian control.[15]

Mitterrand's metaphorical use of 'Prussian' and 'Bavarian' to denote the East German and the West German, as Attali relates it, was no more than a foible to which he occasionally resorted, though, as befitted a longstanding admirer and friend of the controversial Nestor of German literature, Ernst Jünger, there was perhaps a whiff of condescension in this sort of dichotomy drawn at the expense of the 'Bavarian'. However, as regards his loosely labelled Prussians, it was not primarily to the likes of an Egon Krenz (the GDR's short-lived Communist party leader and head of state following Erich Honecker's downfall) or a Hans Modrow (prime minister since mid November) that the French president now looked to calm overly eager aspirations for German unification. Towards the close of 1989 he did not believe that rapid unification was desirable; nor did he believe that it was possible. In particular, he counted on a firm reaction from Moscow to the developments in Germany, since an unwelcome prospect for the Soviets would be German unification under the roof of the FRG. In promoting the 'Banque de l'Europe' idea at the European Council meeting ten days earlier, Mitterrand had been concerned for the future of Gorbachev and perestroika in the USSR; such concern gave way now to the expectation that one of the traditional priorities of Soviet foreign policy since 1945 would be given due effect, namely that of Moscow's preventing the reemergence of a greater Germany, outside the Soviet zone of influence.[16]

Looking to the USSR, the GDR, and the UK

On 6 December 1989 the French president flew to Kiev, having taken the initiative of seeking talks with the Soviet president several days after the latter's summit meeting with the US president in Malta, and just prior to the regular meeting of the European Council to be held under France's presidency in Strasbourg on 8–9 December. The subject at the heart of their discussions in the Ukrainian capital was perforce Germany. In their different ways both Mitterrand and Gorbachev expressed their discontent with Kohl's Ten-Point Programme. The French president's line of argument was that any German unification, necessarily within existing frontiers, had to await a strengthening of both the EC and the CSCE, and that in the meantime the integrity of the East German state must be fully respected.[17]

Two weeks before going to Kiev, Mitterrand had decided upon the dates for a state visit to the GDR, which was to be the first (and last) such visit by a head of state from any of the three Western powers having a say in Germany's future. The visit's formal justification, at this extraordinary juncture, was the French president's acceptance of a standing invitation from his East German counterpart in return for the state visit Honecker had made to France in January 1988. The question of the return visit's timing had been raised in early October 1989 on the occasion of the GDR's fortieth-anniversary celebrations when Honecker was still in power, but without any sense of great urgency. A month and a half later, however, the changed circumstances persuaded Mitterrand that the standing invitation provided an opportunity that should be quickly seized. Thus, on 22 November – before Kohl's surprise unveiling of his Ten-Point Programme – it was announced from Paris that the French president would visit the GDR on 20–22 December. In Kiev the matter of this visit was touched upon. According to a Soviet memorandum, Mitterrand even suggested that Gorbachev might like to join him in the GDR in a gesture of public support for the regime and for Modrow, its embattled leader; it was a suggestion, however, that the Soviet president ignored.[18]

On 8 December, only two days after his journey to Kiev, Mitterrand discussed the German problem with Thatcher. These bilateral private talks took place, at the French president's behest, on the fringe of the European Council meeting in Strasbourg. The two apparently expressed agreement on the need to stop or slow down the drive towards German unification. The time, said Mitterrand, had come for the reestablishment of the 'special relations' that had existed between France and the UK on the eves of the First and Second World Wars. Thatcher concurred in judging that a 'solid Anglo-French political axis' was called for. Later, in *De l'Allemagne, de la France*, Mitterrand denied any collusion between the 'Iron Lady' and himself.[19]

Strasbourg and the Starting Date

If Gorbachev had no real means at his disposal for countering Kohl's high ambition, even less so did Mitterrand or Thatcher, especially since Bush viewed positively and straightforwardly any prospect of a greater Germany firmly anchored to the West. However, in Strasbourg the question of unification was not on the European Council's official agenda, and although the prospect of unification was discussed around the dinner table by the assembled heads of state or government – giving rise famously to a heated altercation between Thatcher and Kohl – no adoption of a formal position on the part of the EC-12 was called for. On the other hand, at the top of the official agenda as set by the French presidency, was a matter that greatly concerned the future of both the FRG and France, namely the setting of a starting date for the IGC that would draw up the EC treaty provisions for the second and third stages of EMU. For Mitterrand, a commitment to a firm date had become even more of a priority in the wake of November's dramatic events.

Not only did the French president want a firm starting date but he also preferred the date to be set as soon as practically possible. His desire was that the IGC's work, consisting essentially in the drawing up of EC treaty changes on the basis of the Delors Report, should take place in the second half of 1990, with the further aim that the new treaty arrangements should be ratified by all EC national parliaments before the end of 1992, the official deadline for the completion of the internal-market programme. But as late as 27 November 1989 the German Chancellor had been saying that all that was required before the end of 1990 was a report, addressed to the European Council, spelling out the guidelines for the future IGC. Solicitous for the electoral fortunes of the CDU–CSU, Kohl had come to the view that it would be inopportune for the IGC on monetary union to commence any time before the Bundestag elections of December 1990, since domestic opposition in West Germany to the combination of the DM's planned demise and the downgrading of the Bundesbank risked to cost votes at the expense of the ruling majority (especially in Bavaria, through a swing away from the CSU). Mitterrand, in the run-up to the Strasbourg meeting, had accordingly become concerned by the possibility of the emergence of an unholy alliance between West Germany and the UK over monetary union. Even if only an alliance of a short-term tactical kind, it would have married the interests of Kohl, leaning towards prevarication over EMU, with those of Thatcher, bluntly hostile to monetary union on principle.

However, intense French diplomacy working on the government in Bonn was successful in putting paid to any prospect of a tactical Anglo-German alliance. Allaying Mitterrand's worst fears, Kohl wrote to the French president on 5 December to say that he would agree to a definite starting date for the IGC, though not a date before December 1990 – once the Bundestag elections were over – when the European Council was set to meet in Rome. The British prime minister, promptly informed of this new lease of life in the Franco-German partnership and so warned of the prospect of finding herself in a minority of one in Strasbourg, decided already before she arrived in the Alsatian capital that discretion was the better part of valour. On the issue of the IGC's starting date, the 'Iron Lady' had effectively surrendered.

Hence, at the European Council meeting of 8–9 December, Mitterrand's main objective was achieved once Kohl signalled his approval of the December 1990 date for launching the IGC, as he did at lunch on the first day. Thatcher reserved her vigorous opposition for France's second objective, the introduction of an EC Social Charter, whose aims as drafted by the EC Commission were in line with the longstanding French ambition that the EC should move towards the harmonisation of social legislation on the basis of French-type norms. For the French president, the UK's dissociation from the Social Charter was no doubt the lesser of two evils, being far preferable to its blocking the launching of the IGC on monetary union. After the Strasbourg meeting, Mitterrand was able to express his quiet satisfaction that 'whereas today we run up against the hegemony of the DM, tomorrow we shall exert our full weight in the taking of monetary decisions'.[20] By setting the IGC's starting date, EMU had at last been put securely on the rails; it was no longer purely in the realm of declaratory intention, a realm to which it had hitherto been largely confined ever since the Hague summit exactly twenty years earlier.

Yet there proved to be a quid pro quo when Kohl succeeded later at the same Strasbourg meeting in winning agreement to a short declaration by the European Council on Germany's future, a declaration whose message at this particular juncture was not what either Mitterrand or, a fortiori, Thatcher would have spontaneously applauded. 'We seek the strengthening of the state of peace in Europe', ran the opening of the relevant single paragraph in the Conclusions of the Presidency, 'in which the German people will regain its unity through free self-determination.' This pledge was scarcely innovative, inasmuch as the wording was virtually the same (indeed, from the words 'state of peace' onwards, exactly the same) as that of the pledge contained in the FRG's 'Letter on German Unity' which had been annexed to the bilateral Moscow Treaty signed in August 1970 by the FRG and the USSR – the first fruit in treaty form of Brandt's Ostpolitik. The European Council was simply taking over a longstanding West German pledge. It was qualified in the remainder of the declaration. The 'process' had to 'take place peacefully and democratically' in respect of the Helsinki Final Act and 'in a context of dialogue and East–West cooperation', and, not least, it had to be 'placed in the perspective of European integration'. But on Kohl's insistence there was no explicit mention of the intangibility of existing borders.[21]

The State Visit to the GDR

After the French president's success in winning a firm EC commitment to the launching of the IGC on monetary union, he turned his mind to the encouragement of reform in the GDR, where unrest was increasing despite Modrow's having taken over from Krenz. On 13 December Mitterrand confirmed to his entourage that he was going ahead with his state visit for the threefold reason that unification was not yet on the agenda, that Kohl had not requested the visit be cancelled, and that he himself was personally committed to honouring the invitation. If he was not hostile to unification in principle, yet he partly agreed with Gorbachev in considering that no precipitation was called for, which is what he said to Bush three days later when they met for bilateral talks in Guadeloupe.

The state visit to the GDR took place between 20 and 22 December. 'Fate not yet having set its seal on German unity', Mitterrand wrote in *De l'Allemagne, de la France*, 'I wished France to be present there and to exercise its rights in a manner that it deemed appropriate.'[22] In 2005, ten years after these words were written, Kohl's own, bitter judgement was blunt: his longstanding European political partner had wished his visit to be 'destructive of the process of radical change in the GDR'.[23]

Mitterrand's basic message to the East Germans in December 1989 was straightforward enough: the GDR still existed as a state in its own right and should have its proper part to play in determining Germany's long-term future; unification could only come about with the assent of the two Germanys; and, if there was a move towards unification, it had to be bound into the wider process of European integration.

In East Berlin, at the state banquet in his honour on the eve of his arrival, the French president reassured the dignitaries of the increasingly rickety regime that they could 'count on France's solidarity with the GDR', and that the two states had 'still a great deal to do together'.[24] In the polite formalities of the same banquet speech, Mitterrand gave expression to his theme of predilection regarding Berlin's and Brandenburg's past. This was when he praised the contribution of the Prussia of Frederick the Great to the philosophy of the Enlightenment, a theme to which he was to return briefly on the last day of his visit when in Berlin he met a small group representing East Germany's political opposition. They included the idealistic and passionate Bärbel Bohley of the New Forum opposition movement; Manfred Stolpe, the president of the Consistory of East Germany's League of Evangelical Churches; and Ibrahim Böhme, the president of the East German SPD, which had been founded in October of that year. Diverse as were their backgrounds, they were at one in expressing their hopes for a reformed socialism in a reinvigorated GDR, rather than in a unified Germany, and Mitterrand's sympathies lay with them.[25]

What counted most in this state visit, at least in the public eye, was the symbolism associated with the French president's visit to Leipzig on 21 December. There he addressed students and others from the worlds of arts and letters at the Karl-Marx University. More importantly still, he lunched with Kurt Masur, the chief conductor of the Gewandhausorchester; it was this standard-bearer of reform, who, on the occasion of the potentially most explosive mass demonstration of all in Leipzig, that of 9 October, had taken the leading role in heading off brutal paramilitary repression on the part of the regime and so avoiding what could have been a bloodbath for the city. In the same spirit, Mitterrand also visited Leipzig's two great Gothic churches, that of Saint Nicolas, whose weekly pacifist-inspired prayer meetings had been at the centre of the mass demonstrations between September and October, and that of Saint Thomas – famous for its link with Johann Sebastian Bach, who had been the cantor of its choir school.

There had perhaps been the opportunity for another highly symbolic act involving France on 22 December. On that day the West German Chancellor and the East German prime minister formally reopened the Brandenburg Gate lying at the centre of the divide between the two Berlins. It is unclear whether the French president was ever actually invited to make the gesture of accompanying Kohl and Modrow in passing from one side to the other, thereby testifying to Berlin's new found (if yet uncertain) unity. Mitterrand certainly considered that he had had the opportunity to do so; and it would have entailed a delay to his departure of only some hours. However, as he later explained in *De l'Allemagne, de la France*, he had needed to take account of the susceptibilities of France's other EC partners, and, in any case, the celebration at the Brandenburg Gate was essentially an affair for the Germans themselves.

Mittterrand's Call for a European Confederation

On 31 December 1989 – some ten days after the state visit to the GDR, during which time the Ceausescu regime had been brought to a bloody end in Romania and Václav Havel had been elected president of the Czechoslovak Republic – the French president addressed his customary New Year message to the nation. He availed of it to propose, albeit vaguely, the creation of a 'European Confederation'. It was, so it appeared, to be no more than a loose association of states, essentially a spin-off, in terms of its membership, from the CSCE (excluding necessarily the latter's two non-European members, the US and Canada). Its raison d'être was to be the fostering of cooperation in the framework of Europe's existing state structure. It would serve to consolidate Europe's existing borders in keeping with the Helsinki Final Act's (qualified) provisions concerning the same. What was clear was that the European Confederation would be a second-tier organisation, unconnected to a first-tier organisation such as the EC, and, indeed, said Mitterrand in his New Year message, the latter's structures needed to be independently strengthened.[26]

This essentially conservative European Confederation proposal, to which the coup de grâce would eventually be delivered by Havel, was linked to another of Mitterrand's proposals, made shortly beforehand in East Berlin, that Paris should host a CSCE summit towards the end of 1990 as a sort of 'Helsinki II'. He was effectively taking up a proposal made by Gorbachev during their meeting in Kiev. The summit was to materialise and bear fruit in the shape of the Charter of Paris for a New Europe, which was signed in the French capital in November 1990. It formalised the continent's adherence in principle to 'human rights, democracy, and the rule of law', and it opened a process that resulted in 1994 in the CSCE's transformation into the Organisation for Security and Cooperation in Europe (OSCE). However, in Mitterrand's eyes at the end of 1989, the future CSCE summit was intended to be an even more important event than it turned out to be, making agreements that would buttress both the proposed European Confederation and the continued existence of the GDR.

But he knew even when he delivered his New Year message that he had been unable to put a brake on Kohl's accelerating drive towards German unification. His one substantive achievement at the end of 1989, after several intense weeks of personal diplomacy, remained the European Council's commitment in Strasbourg to a definite date for the opening of the IGC on monetary union.

The Drive for German Unification

The FRG's Absorption of the GDR and the 'Two Plus Four' Process

By early February 1990, only a month later, it had become clear that German unification was probably approaching at a much faster speed than scarcely anyone could have imagined when Kohl had announced his Ten-Point Programme towards the end of November. Large numbers of East Germans were evincing little or no enthusiasm for any promise of reformist socialism in a renovated GDR. Neither Gorbachev nor Modrow was signalling an unshakeable commitment to the permanence of the East German regime. There was a growing awareness in Washington of the opportunity that had now presented itself to push for unification on terms that would be very largely favourable to the FRG and to the Atlantic Alliance. Mainly on American initiative, talks were afoot to organise all negotiations concerning the external aspects of eventual German unification through a 'Two Plus Four' process – that is, a diplomatic process restricted to the FRG, the GDR, and the Four Powers with a right of say over Germany's future. In the case of France, Mitterrand's initial preference for settling German issues in the forum of the CSCE gave way to an acceptance of the proposed approach. Crucial meetings were held in Moscow, first, between Gorbachev, Shevardnadze, and the US Secretary of State, James Baker, and then between Gorbachev and Kohl. They led to the announcement on 13 February, at a meeting in Ottawa of NATO and Warsaw Pact foreign ministers, of the imminent launching of the 'Two Plus Four' process by the six states concerned. By the beginning of March, Kohl was stating publicly that unification under Article 23 of the FRG's Basic Law, incorporating the territories of the GDR directly into the FRG, was the only feasible way forward. On 18 March 1990, when parliamentary elections were held in the GDR after having been brought forward from their earlier planned date in May, the Chancellor's boldness was shown to have paid off. The clear victory of the East German CDU and the other two right-wing parties in the Alliance for Germany, which was at the expense of both the East German SPD and the East German communist party, the renamed PDS, testified to the will of the majority to join the FRG.

The stage was set for six highly charged months of international and intra-German negotiations. The culminating point was unification itself, which took place on 3 October 1990, named the Day of German Unity. Constitutionally, unification was under Article 23 of the FRG's Basic Law, as allowed by the Unification Treaty signed by the two German states on 31 August. Political unification had been preceded on 1 July by monetary union between the FRG and the GDR, with the DM replacing the Ostmark on a one-to-one basis, which was a ratio that made political but not economic sense. On the international front, the most important step was taken at the fourth and final 'Two Plus Four' ministerial meeting held in Moscow. There on 12 September 1990, nearly half a century after the Potsdam Conference, the Final Settlement on Germany was signed, for want of the once promised peace treaty closing the Second World War. The rights of the Four Powers in Germany were terminated on 3 October. On 9 November, on the first anniversary of the opening of the Berlin Wall, a Friendship Treaty and a further treaty providing for economic cooperation were signed between the enlarged FRG and the USSR. Finally, on 14 November the FRG and Poland signed a frontier treaty committing them anew to the intangibility of the Oder–Neisse Line.

In 1990 France's direct role in all these events tended to be a secondary one compared with that played by either the US or the USSR, not to speak of the FRG's own role. In the 'Two Plus Four' process there were clearly three big players and, therefore, in different ways, three lesser ones – France, the UK, and the fast disappearing GDR.

Mitterrand and the Oder–Neisse Line

However, on one particular issue, that of the international status of the Oder–Neisse Line, France, in the person of its president and, accessorily, its foreign minister, spoke with a strong voice. This was notably the case in February and March 1990. The French demand was that, prior to any unification treaty, an international treaty providing for the permanence of the post-1945 frontier, namely the Oder–Neisse Line between Germany and Poland, had to be drafted; and then, immediately after unification, duly signed. In his personal dealings with Kohl, Mitterrand was at his most insistent at a private meeting held at the Elysée on 15 February 1990. The Chancellor's legalistic response was essentially the same as it had been when the French president had raised the issue with him at an earlier private meeting, six weeks beforehand – only a unified Germany could give its name to such a treaty. On 1 March, on Mitterrand's instructions, Dumas spoke publicly on the issue in West Berlin, urging that Poland be promptly and formally reassured of the intangibility of the Oder–Neisse Line. Genscher, who was in the audience, appeared to approve of his French colleague. On the other hand, the reaction of the Chancellery in Bonn and especially of Kohl himself was one of anger. However, on 8 March the Bundestag passed almost unanimously a motion declaring the inviolability of Poland's western border.

On the following day, the Polish president and prime minister, General Jaruzelski and Tadeusz Mazowiecki, were in Paris in response to an invitation from the French president. Mitterrand agreed that the Bundestag declaration was by itself insufficient. And he promised that France would support Poland's request to be included in the 'Two Plus Four' process when it touched upon the border question. But the promise did not go so far as to commit France to pressing for the process's transformation into a full-fledged 'Two Plus Five' arrangement, this being the bold Polish request.

In the second half of March the intertwined incipient crises in Franco-German and German–Polish relations were defused. Kohl's vicarious personal success in the East German elections put him in a more assured position when speaking with Mitterrand. Less than a week after these elections Mazowiecki visited Washington, where he was given firm reassurances by Bush concerning the intangibility of the Oder–Neisse Line. The American president suggested to Kohl at the time of Mazowiecki's visit that the key wording of the future post-unification treaty between Poland and the enlarged FRG could be informally agreed, in advance of unification, by Warsaw and Bonn. This was in line with Mitterrand's urging. Kohl accepted, and progress was subsequently smooth in settling this sore issue. Important in this respect was the third of the 'Two Plus Four' ministerial meetings, which took place in Paris in mid July. Prior to that meeting, both the Bundestag and the GDR's Volkskammer had formally committed themselves to the bilateral treaty that was to be signed with Poland after unification. At the 'Two Plus Four' ministerial meeting in Paris, the Polish foreign minister, Krzysztof Skubiszweski, participated in the negotiations, in keeping with French policy on the border issue.[27]

Kohl's cussedness over the Oder–Neisse Line prior to the East German elections, contrasting with Genscher's more emollient stance, was dictated to a large extent by his ambition for the electoral success of the East German CDU and the wider-based Alliance for Germany. He had no wish to prematurely deprive the GDR's pro-unification coalition of the irredentist Silesian vote. But his refusal to give any reassurances until the month of March worried and peeved Mitterrand. The relative quiescence of the US, the UK, and the USSR, on the other hand, derived from a widely shared and largely unspoken understanding that there was no real threat to the Oder–Neisse Line. That a unified Germany would be amenable to sign a frontier treaty with Poland was also widely expected. Whether such a treaty was even necessary from the standpoint of international law was debatable once the chosen path to unification was through recourse to Article 23 of the Basic Law. After all the FRG had already recognised the permanence of the existing German–Polish border in December 1970 when the Warsaw Treaty was signed by Brandt and Poland's communist leader, Władysłav Gomułka. To understand Mitterrand's concerns in early 1990, some of the explanation must be sought on the side of worldly wise prudence, but some also in the initially traumatic effect on him of the events of November 1989, especially Kohl's unilateral announcement of his Ten-Point Programme. First to Gorbachev, then to Thatcher, and then to Bush, within the space of ten days in the following month of December, the French president spoke ominously of the parallel of 'Europe in 1913'.[28] The perceived imperative of guaranteeing the intangibility of the Oder–

Neisse Line beyond any shred of doubt, as championed by Mitterrand in early 1990, had its logic in the furtherance of future European security; it also must have drawn at least a little on deep-seated and atavistic fears about the ambitions of France's newly transformed neighbour.

The Enlarged Germany and NATO

Perhaps the most difficult question to be resolved in the framework of the 'Two Plus Four' process was that of Germany's future relation to Europe's two main security and defence alliances, NATO and the Warsaw Pact. In Germany itself political views were divided. In West Germany, on the side of the opposition, the SPD opted for neutralism, a position it shared with the East German SPD. The latter not only became a party of government in the GDR in April 1990 – when Lothar de Maizière, the East German CDU's leader, formed a grand coalition government – but it also obtained the foreign-ministry portfolio and thus, in the person of Markus Meckel, representation in the 'Two Plus Four' process. As to the West German government coalition, both the CDU–CSU and the FDP wanted the future Germany to be a member of NATO, a view that was effectively reinforced from March 1990 onwards when there was no longer any doubt that the Basic Law's Article 23 would be the path of unification. However, there were important nuances. Genscher tended to show more willingness than Kohl to soften the USSR's opposition by allowing for the possibility of some sort of exclusion of the territories of the GDR from NATO's reach. Crucially the Bush administration was on Kohl's side. In Moscow neutralism was the preferred solution and, when that was no longer on the cards, a permanent bar on NATO's being allowed to move eastwards into the territories of the GDR.

Yet, starting with the visit of Gorbachev and Shevardnadze to Washington at the end of May 1990, the position of the Soviet leadership changed. By mid July the Soviet president was proffering his assent to Kohl for the inclusion of all of the future FRG in NATO, with relatively few restrictions on the eastward reach of NATO's integrated military command. A number of developments contributed to this remarkable turnaround: Gorbachev's need of Western economic assistance for the continued pursuit of perestroika; the strengthening of his own domestic political position at the twenty-eighth congress of the Communist Party of the Soviet Union (CPSU) in early July; and, as that congress drew to an end, the American-inspired Declaration emanating from the North Atlantic Council summit in London, which provided inter alia for regular diplomatic liaison between the states of the Warsaw Pact and NATO – a provision leading in 1991 to the creation of the North Atlantic Cooperation Council (NACC). The arrangements for the enlarged FRG's place in NATO, largely in line with Gorbachev's conciliatory position, formed an important part of the Final Settlement on Germany, as agreed in mid September.

This course of events posed a particular challenge to Mitterrand. His often jaundiced view of American foreign policy and also of the role of NATO as a defence organisation ill disposed him to any idea that NATO would be strengthened politically and militarily by Germany unification. The French president was certainly no closet supporter of German neutralism, but he was opposed to any arrangements that led to the US having an even greater say over Western European defence. His frame of mind was perceptively noted by Brent Scowcroft, Bush's National Security Advisor, on the occasion of Mitterrand's meeting with the American president at Key Largo in April 1990. Although Bush himself was upbeat about the direction of their talks, Scowcroft noted from the sidelines that Mitterrand was unfavourable to any change in NATO's role enabling it to adjust positively to Europe's transformed geopolitical configuration; its role in the French president's eyes was to remain 'confined to [that of] defence against a massive attack on Western Europe', which, according to Scowcroft, promised the 'atrophy of the alliance', and he at least was to return to Washington 'even more convinced that the US and France had significantly differing views of the future of Europe and [the American] role in it'.[29] Scowcroft was not alone, since parallel talks at Key Largo between Baker and Dumas pointed to the same conclusion on the American side.[30]

Yet Mitterrand did not seek actively to frustrate Bush's and Kohl's shared design to maintain post-unification Germany in NATO's integrated military command. In late May the French president went to Moscow for one-to-one talks with his Soviet counterpart, their first since the hastily arranged meeting in Kiev half a year earlier, and the question of the FRG's future military status figured prominently on their agenda. Reporting to Bush several days afterwards to recount what had passed between himself and Gorbachev, Mitterrand said that Gorbachev's hostility to the participation of a unified Germany in NATO appeared neither fake nor tactical. He suggested, however, to the US president that there might be some room for a breakthrough, since, in response to his arguing for full German membership of NATO, there had been a hint on the Soviet side of the acceptability of a French-type membership for the enlarged FRG – that is, leaving Germany outside the military command.[31] Attali, who was present at the Moscow meeting, was to assert five years later that the idea of French-type membership had been mooted not by Gorbachev but by Mitterrand. But this tale of French duplicity was purely imagined – and indeed, effectively, eventually retracted by Attali.[32]

Mitterrand's chief concern was not so much the issue of unified Germany's membership of NATO as American plans for reshaping NATO itself. The North Atlantic Council's Declaration of 6 July 1990, which was to persuade Gorbachev and Shevardnadze to bow to the prospect of the new Germany's having full NATO membership, including insertion in the integrated command, was not at all to the French president's liking. The Declaration was essentially a text prepared by the Bush administration and amended at the summit when other NATO member states had been allowed their say. Two French objections to the American text were acted upon. The first related to the American proposal for an enhancement of NATO's political role, under which the USSR and other Warsaw Pact countries would become involved in matters of common concern by establishing diplomatic liaison missions at NATO headquarters in Brussels and having ambassadors accredited to the alliance. The idea that NATO as an American-led organisation should have added clout in the sphere of European security as a result of the encouragement of such diplomatic ties was anathema to the French. However, when the NATO foreign ministers thrashed out a mutually acceptable version of the Declaration, Dumas accepted a compromise under which the states of the Warsaw Pact were invited individually 'to come to NATO, not just to visit, but to establish regular diplomatic liaison with NATO', but without there being any mention of the accreditation of diplomats of ambassadorial rank.

In their second objection to the American proposals, Mitterrand and Dumas, at the summit's respective meetings of heads of government and foreign ministers, had a greater degree of success. The draft version of the Declaration, as sent by Bush to the other NATO heads of government, had called for the creation already in peacetime of multinational corps, including American forces, notably in the area under NATO's CINC–AFCENT, by tradition a German general. This would replace the long-standing 'layer cake' system of national corps sectors in West Germany. The proposal cut right across Mitterrand's longstanding efforts to wean West Germany away from what he considered to be too great a dependence on NATO military structures. Nor was the proposal popular with all other NATO member states. Prompted by Dumas, the foreign ministers excised from the Declaration the commitment to the peacetime creation of such corps in the integrated military command under CINC–AFCENT, though the ministers retained a vaguer pledge to 'rely increasingly on multinational corps made up of national units'.

On another important question for the French, that of a proposed change in NATO's own nuclear strategy, Mitterrand failed to win any concessions at the London summit. In the early 1960s de Gaulle and Adenauer had been greatly perturbed by the Kennedy administration's shifting NATO's strategic doctrine from 'massive retaliation', in the event of a hypothetical Soviet-led attack, to one of 'flexible response'. Now Bush was proposing a further shift in doctrine: according to the wording that was to be retained in the summit Declaration, there was to be 'a new NATO strategy making nuclear forces truly weapons of last resort'; it was to entail 'moving away from "forward defence" towards a reduced forward presence and modifying "flexible response" to reflect a reduced reliance on nuclear weapons'. There would therefore no longer be any provision for the early first use of nuclear weapons in NATO employment guidelines. Part of the context for this proposal was the massive reductions in Soviet force levels promised by the Conventional Armed Forces in Europe (CFE) treaty negotiations, which were near to conclusion in Vienna. Kohl willingly took America's side in this new change in security policy. But neither of Western Europe's nuclear powers, France or the UK, was happy. Immediately prior to the London summit, Bush prevailed upon Thatcher to hold her dissatisfaction in check. Mitterrand, on the other hand, was unwilling to give even muted assent to a proposal that made France's own defence policy still more out of kilter with Europe's changing security environment, devaluing, as it did, France's independent nuclear *force de frappe*.

The French president's annoyance at the way in which the US had organised if not stage-managed the North Atlantic Council summit was considerable. Before the end of July he announced that France would withdraw all of its 46,000 troops out of Germany by 1994, and also that France would refuse to contribute to any NATO multinational corps. The Franco-German Defence Council appeared to count for nothing in Mitterrand's announcement of the French troop withdrawal from Germany; the decision was a unilateral one, not the result of any prior bilateral discussion.[33]

Providing a Treaty for European Union

Moving towards 'Political Union'

In May 1990 Mitterrand had remarked to Gorbachev that, in view of Kohl's haste, it was essential that German unification be synchronised with a further advance in European integration. In fact, a major step to this end had been taken on 19 April, more than a month earlier, by the French president and the German Chancellor when they addressed conjointly a letter to the other EC heads of government. In advance of the extra-ordinary meeting of the European Council convened by the Irish prime minister for 28 April, they proposed that 'the European Council should initiate preparations for an intergovernmental conference on political union', which would 'be held in parallel to the conference on economic and monetary union'. The term 'political union' was left undefined. No matter; the objective of the second IGC, according to the Franco-German letter, would be fourfold: strengthening the democratic legitimacy of the union; rendering its institutions more efficient; ensuring the unity and coherence of the union's activity in the economic, monetary and political spheres; and, not least, defining and implementing a common foreign and security policy.[34] The other heads of government responded positively in Dublin by agreeing to examine the joint proposal, as well as a Belgian memorandum on EC institutional reform, though not without Thatcher's suggesting that there was a large measure of confusion over the purpose of the exercise.[35] When the European Council met again in Dublin at the end of June, a month after Mitterrand's Moscow visit and a week before the key NATO Council Declaration opening the way for the completion of the 'Two Plus Four' process, the EC heads of government formally agreed to the launching of the second IGC at the end of the year in Rome, at the same time as the IGC on EMU was launched.

That political union should be a goal pursued in conjunction with EMU was not a new idea. In keeping with the long-established French understanding of European 'political union' as meaning primarily a shared unity of purpose in the sphere of foreign policy and security (the understanding at the heart of the Fouchet proposals), the SEA had already been marked by a twofold aim of this kind, even if only in embryonic form. To be found in the SEA, in addition to its vague invocation of EMU, were its provisions on 'European Cooperation in the sphere of foreign policy'. By the autumn of 1989 the unfolding events in Central and Eastern Europe had led to louder calls for a political strengthening of the EC. Delors was to the fore, as witness a speech he made in mid October at the College of Europe in Bruges. Then, just two weeks before the fall of the Berlin Wall, Kohl privately told Mitterrand that a 'European political project' was needed to match the EC's advance on the economic front – that is, the programmed completion of the internal market and the plan for EMU. However, Mitterrand's second priority at the time – the first being EMU – was winning the European Council's agreement to the French-proposed Social Charter. It was not until February and March 1990 that there was the gradual distillation of a shared Franco-German view about the desirability of coupling EMU to some sort of political union.

An important informal meeting in this respect was that held between the French president and the German Chancellor at the Elysée on 15 February 1990, two days after the launching in Ottawa of the 'Two Plus Four' process. Although the two men were still at loggerheads over the Oder–Neisse Line issue, Mitterrand acknowledged that 'political union' had now to be on the EC's agenda. Then, in the aftermath of the East German elections on 18 March, which brought the prospect of German unification even nearer, a joint readiness emerged to move beyond agreement in principle, to purposeful action. Not that Mitterrand was suddenly converted. In the first few days after these vital elections he remained primarily concerned with the urgency of EMU. And the German proposals for beefing up the powers of the European Parliament and the Commission were not to his liking. Yet what happened in the second half of March 1990 was that he decided finally to swim with the German tide, though not on German terms. Mitterrand's intention was to press for the French concept of political union – that is, essentially an intergovernmental one, with the leading institutional role played by the European Council.

Here then was the origin of the Kohl–Mitterrand proposal addressed to the Irish presidency in April 1990 and of the European Council's agreement to it in the following June. It laid the ground for the future European Union (EU). Playing the key role on the French side in preparing this initiative had been Elisabeth Guigou. Appointed to the General Secretariat of the Presidency of the Republic after a year of serving on the political staff of Delors when he was economics and finance minister, Guigou combined two important posts between November 1985 and October 1990 (when she replaced Cresson as minister for European affairs). The first was that of adviser on European affairs to the president; and the second that of head of the Secrétariat Général du Comité Interministériel pour les Questions de Coopération Economique Européenne (SGCI), a responsibility making her the senior official for the coordination of government policies on EC matters. Furthermore, in the second half of 1989, by virtue of France's holding the EC presidency, she was chosen by Mitterrand to chair a high-level group of representatives of foreign and finance ministers preparing the IGC on EMU. Subsequently, it was Guigou who pressed Mitterrand to be open to Kohl's idea of linking EMU to 'political union', provided the end result was an EU transcending the EC and driven by the European Council. Her advice to this effect, in the first half of February 1990, was a catalyst for the French president's gradual change of mind; her further advice in the second half of March contributed significantly to his final decision.[36]

Later in 1990 the Franco-German initiative took on an added momentum. Thus, a week prior to the European Council meeting of December 1990 and the formal opening of the IGCs, Mitterrand and Kohl penned a further joint letter to the other EC heads of government. They proposed what was in fact to be approved as the agenda for the negotiations on political union. Kohl had taken a step in Mitterrand's direction, since the two leaders called for a substantial enlargement of the role and duties of the European Council. It should, they said, lay down the guidelines for a common foreign and security policy. Reflecting a major French concern in the face of the Bush administration's ambitions for NATO, the letter proposed that defence should eventually become a responsibility of the Union through bringing WEU into its orbit.[37]

For Mitterrand, however, EMU remained the top priority. Nothing was to be allowed to prejudice its realisation. If the German desire for political union could only be accommodated by Bonn's largely accepting the French vision of such union, his own desire for EMU entailed continued acceptance of the German view of monetary integration.

As the IGCs got under way, Bérégovoy, the economics and finance minister, was given a dressing down for failing to appreciate the nature of this trade-off. In November 1990, marking his dislike of the Delors Report's option in favour of an independent ECB, Bérégovoy had evinced interest in the British proposal for a 'hard ECU' – a common currency

existing in parallel to national currencies, the latter remaining the responsibility of national monetary authorities. He was not so presumptuous as
to argue that a parallel currency approach could be retained indefinitely for
the final stage of EMU, thereby dispatching the Delors Report to the
dustbin of history, but he did feel that a strong case could be made for its
provisional use. Furthermore, shortly before the opening of the IGCs in
December, Bérégovoy advocated the idea of a 'fully democratic economic
government', suggesting that in the framing of monetary policy the future
ECB should be partly subservient to the European Council and the Council
of Ministers. In January 1991 he signalled anew his interest in the British
'hard ECU' proposals. Normally one of the most loyal of Mitterrand's
political servants, Bérégovoy was called to heel towards the end of that
month. To discuss European questions, Mitterrand assembled the prime
minister, the economics and finance minister, the foreign minister, and the
minister for European affairs. It fell to the last and youngest of the four, the
recently promoted Guigou, to set matters straight. The idea of a common
currency was highly questionable, she said, and there would be no EMU
without France's working immediately for a single currency. Mitterrand –
no natural enthusiast for the niceties of economic debate – then intervened
to insist that a common currency and a single currency were incompatible
concepts, and that Bérégovoy had therefore to choose. As the economics
and finance minister floundered, the president fired a political warning
shot. 'No reversal of alliance!', he reportedly exclaimed. 'The ally is
Germany! As to the British, they are aligned with the United States!'
Bérégovoy, a man of more Anglophile leanings than the president, found
himself with little choice but to back down ruefully.[38]

The Proposed EU 'Pillar' Structure and the CFSP

The twin IGCs having been formally launched in December 1990 at the
Rome meeting of the European Council, it became the lot of the Luxembourg presidency in the first half of 1991 to organise the preparatory
drafting of the future Maastricht Treaty. Thus, in April 1991 the presidency
submitted a 'non-paper', or embryonic version of the future treaty, for
discussion. It provided for a clear separation between the EC and, on the
other hand, the two new spheres that in the Maastricht Treaty were to be
called 'a common foreign and security policy' (CFSP) and 'cooperation in
the fields of justice and home affairs'. This proposed structure was soon to
be known as the 'pillar' system, and, in respect of the two new 'pillars', the
'non-paper' accorded preeminence to the European Council and intergovernmental decision making. In particular, it provided for the European
Council's full control of the CFSP, as earlier proposed by Mitterrand and
Kohl. This was a success for French diplomacy. The idea of a 'pillar' structure had been successfully advocated in the early months of 1991 by Pierre

de Boissieu, the career diplomat who was the representative of the French foreign minister and the French minister for European affairs at the weekly negotiations of the IGC on political union (acting in tandem with Trichet as the representative of the French finance minister for the IGC on EMU).[39]

However, partly because of Dutch and Belgian opposition to the inter-governmental approach privileged in the 'non-paper', the Luxembourg presidency presented modified proposals in June 1991, now in the form of a draft treaty. The first article, in which it was stated that the EC must serve as the main foundation of the future EU (thereby acknowledging the preeminence of the *communautaire* principle over the largely intergovernmental one adopted for the second and third pillars), concluded with the further statement that 'this treaty marks a new stage in a process leading gradually to a Union with a federal goal'. Yet, as regards the essentials, the draft treaty retained the 'pillar' structure favoured by France. At the end of June the European Council endorsed this Luxembourg text as 'a basis for further negotiations', though not before the UK and Denmark had rejected outright any idea of a federal goal.

Events at this stage took a sharp turn. The Netherlands held the presidency in the second half of the year, and in August 1991 the Dutch foreign ministry drafted a radically new version of the proposed treaty. The 'pillar' structure was entirely abandoned. In its stead was a more homogeneous structure, with the CFSP just one element of the 'External Relations of the Community', on the same footing, in terms of the draft treaty's architecture, as 'commercial policy' or 'development cooperation'. Although the European Council was to remain at the apex of decision-making in matters of foreign and security policy, for which it would act unanimously in setting both general and special objectives, the Commission's formal role in the elaboration of such policy was to be enhanced compared with the Luxembourg draft treaty's provisions.

Part of the reason for this change of course was a conviction that the Dutch foreign minister, Hans van den Broek, had acquired in June at an informal meeting in Dresden of EC foreign ministers, hosted by Genscher in connection with German unification. A large majority of member states, he thought, could be persuaded to favour an institutional arrangement under which the Union and the Community would be coterminous or identical, rather than one in which the latter would be relegated to being no more than a component – albeit the major one – of the EU as a whole. From a French standpoint, however, the change was totally unacceptable. There was a strong suspicion at the Elysée that the Dutch were acting in collusion with the Commission in the person of Delors.[40] The drawing up of the Dutch draft treaty proved yet another mishap in the long history of frequently strained EC relations between Paris and The Hague.

In September a round of bilateral diplomacy on the part of the Netherlands established not only what was obvious, namely that both France and the UK were adamantly opposed to the Dutch initiative, but also that Germany as well as Italy had serious doubts too. Yet at the end of the month van den Broek persisted and tabled the draft treaty at a meeting of EC foreign ministers. He found it rejected by as many as ten of the other eleven member states. Almost by default, therefore, the Luxembourg draft treaty of June 1991, as revised by a chastened Dutch presidency, was now put back on the table and served as the basis for the final negotiation.

At the European Council meeting held in Maastricht on 9 and 10 December, which brought the twin IGCs to a conclusion, it was agreed that QMV under the CFSP would be limited to the implementing measures of a 'joint action' (Article J.3.2). Otherwise the rule of unanimity would apply. This limitation was in keeping with the positions taken by France, Germany, the UK, and most other member states; it meant, however, that the CFSP in practice could not advance far beyond existing EPC arrangements in the sphere of foreign policy as defined by the SEA.

But where there was some advance, at least on paper, was in the area of security and defence. In keeping with what had been proposed by Mitterrand and Kohl in their joint letter of December 1990 and also, in more detail, in yet another joint letter of October 1991, the new treaty – formally the Treaty on European Union – provided for the extension of the CFSP to 'the eventual framing of a common defence policy, which might in time lead to a common defence' (Articles B and J.4.1). Furthermore, WEU was stated to be 'an integral part of the development of the Union' (Article J.4.2).

Security and Defence

The introduction of the wording 'common defence' into the Maastricht Treaty and its association with WEU represented a triumph for Franco-German diplomacy, notably in the light of the agenda set by the Mitterrand–Kohl joint letter of December 1990 – not to speak of Mitterrand's own *Lettre à tous les Français* in 1988. The ball was set rolling in February 1991 when a Franco-German document on security-policy cooperation was put before the IGC. It proposed the setting up 'in due course' of a 'common European defence system' founded on WEU and operating under 'guidelines' established by the European Council. Implicit in the proposal was the EU's swallowing up of WEU. The proposal won particularly strong support from Belgium. But it was robustly resisted by the two stalwart Atlanticists among the EC's member states, the UK and the Netherlands (the latter as ever combining a strong degree of commitment to NATO's integrated command with a highly *communautaire* approach to the EC), and it caused, moreover, serious anxiety in Washington.

Little Luxembourg, in charge of the presidency, took note of these differences, and the draft treaty as tabled in June spoke solely of the 'eventual framing' of a common 'defence policy', this being a policy that could be implemented, facultatively, in the framework of WEU. A few weeks later the European Council decided to postpone the resolution of the question of 'strengthening the Union's [non-existent] defence identity' until the closing stages of the IGC negotiations, and the matter did not figure in the Dutch draft treaty as tabled in September. In the first half of October two rival sets of proposals were presented to the IGC, one by the UK and Italy allowing in the long term for a European defence identity in the form of a common defence policy, and the other by Spain, France, and Germany holding out the prospect of an actual common defence.

At this juncture Mitterrand and Kohl decided to intervene at the highest level. The Franco-German partnership had moved anew into high gear, partly because of shared doubts about the future of the American commitment to Europe in the wake of the Gulf War and the start of the break-up of Yugoslavia. Also goading Mitterrand since May had been the moves afoot in NATO to set up an Allied Rapid Reaction Corps (ARRC) under British command. In mid October, against this international background and only three days after the presentation of the Franco-German–Spanish document to the IGC, the French president and the Chancellor returned to their joint epistolary endeavour. By way of the Dutch presidency, they addressed yet another letter to the other EC heads of government to emphasise the need for progress on security and defence. Attached to the letter were proposed draft treaty provisions. Although these new treaty proposals made no immediate headway, they greatly shaped the final stage of the negotiations on the matter in December.

According to the Franco-German draft treaty provisions, one of the 'objectives of the Union' should be 'to affirm its identity on the international scene, in particular through the implementation of a common foreign and security policy *which will eventually include a common defence* [our italics]'. In the Maastricht Treaty itself (Articles B and J.4.1), this wording, as already indicated, was to be partly retained and partly watered down (the words in italics becoming '*including the eventual framing of a common defence policy, which might in time lead to a common defence*'). Thus, some account was taken in Maastricht of the objections or reservations of the UK and the Netherlands, and also of Ireland's neutrality; yet, in respect of Franco-German demands, the essential was conceded.

Mitterrand's and Kohl's proposed draft treaty provisions also covered the whole of what was to become the long article (J.4), dealing with security and defence, in the Maastricht Treaty's Title V providing for the CFSP. Compared with the corresponding provisions of the Luxembourg draft treaty, where WEU's availability for future EU's purposes was qualified (any decisions by the EU involving WEU being restricted to the latter's 'sphere of competence'), the Mitterrand–Kohl proposals insisted that WEU was 'an integral part of the *process of European union* [our italics]'. This new emphasis was accepted at the Maastricht summit. In the agreed Treaty (Article J.4.2), the changes compared with the Mitterrand–Kohl wording were of mere form (*'development'* replacing *'process'*, and *'the Union'* replacing *'European union'*).

The Franco-German proposals included a draft Declaration to be made, as a treaty appendix, by the EC member states that were also WEU members (Belgium, France, Germany, Italy, Luxembourg, the Netherlands, Portugal, Spain, and the UK). This proposal inspired much of the content and some of the wording of the Treaty's Declaration on Western European Union. For instance, as regards WEU's operational role, the Declaration agreed in Maastricht followed the proposed Franco-German draft in allowing: a WEU planning cell; closer military cooperation, complementary to the Atlantic Alliance, especially in the fields of logistics, transport, training, and strategic surveillance; meetings of WEU chiefs of defence staff; and, notably, the creation of 'military units answerable to WEU'. Furthermore, common to both the proposed draft Declaration and the wording eventually agreed was the implicit promise of a further strengthening of WEU after a review in 1996. However, the agreed Declaration also stressed that any extension of the organisation's activities should be compatible with NATO interests, as witness the assertion that 'WEU will be developed as the defence component of the European Union and as the means to strengthen the European pillar of the Atlantic Alliance'.

What could not be explicitly written into the Maastricht Declaration was the postscript memorandum to the Mitterrand–Kohl draft. According to this postscript, Franco-German military cooperation would be reinforced beyond the existing stage of the two countries' joint army brigade, so that the 'reinforced Franco-German units' could serve as the nucleus of a 'European corps' open to the forces of other WEU member states. This was the origin of the Franco-German agreement, announced by the German Chancellor and the French president in La Rochelle in May 1992, to set up a joint army corps with 'a European vocation'. The plan was that it should be operational, with or without contributions from other WEU forces, by the end of 1995. It gave birth to the Eurocorps, in which France and Germany were to be joined successively by Belgium in 1993, Spain in 1994, and Luxembourg in 1996.

On the French side, the idea of a European multinational army corps – independent of NATO's integrated command – had been in gestation since the fractious North Atlantic Council summit of July 1990. From a political standpoint, though not in terms of military content, it rivalled the NATO concept of a multinational corps that had figured so importantly at the summit and had led to the ARRC's conception less than a year later. More concretely, the setting up of Eurocorps in 1992 would effectively allow Mitterrand to go back on his July 1990 announcement to withdraw all French troops from Germany by 1994, and this served both French and German interests.[41]

EMU's Irreversibility

On the eve of the Maastricht summit, EMU remained the question that preoccupied Mitterrand above all others. In the course of the previous ten months – ever since France's submission of a draft treaty on EMU in late January, only a few days after Bérégovoy had been called to order over the 'hard ECU' – Bérégovoy himself and the Director of the Treasury, Trichet, sought to advance French interests in the framework of the IGC on EMU. However, there was a radical difference between this IGC and that dealing with political union. Whereas the parameters of the latter IGC and indeed the goal of political union itself were ill defined, the route to EMU had been well charted beforehand. For the Delors Report had laid it down: the three-stage process leading to a single rather than a common currency, with the ECB enjoying independence in the conduct of monetary policy. Furthermore, in November 1990, the Committee of Governors of the EC's national central banks had filled in important details by agreeing to a draft statute for the future ECB. Here the Bundesbank's influence was strong, and in April 1991 it fell to Pöhl to present the same draft statute to the Luxembourg presidency, with the polite warning that there should be no unpicking of it by the IGC. What was left to be resolved in the course of 1991 was the following: whether satisfaction should be given to proposals from France and other quarters regarding 'economic government' (a legitimate issue for the Elysée, at least in respect of the apportioning of powers between the Council of Ministers and the Commission for what lay outside the ECB's independent preserve); the criteria governing eligibility for EMU's third and final stage; how best to deal with the UK's reluctance to embark upon the third stage and adopt the single currency; and, crucially, the manner and setting of the timetable for the start of both the second and third stages, especially the latter.

On the issue of 'economic government', Bérégovoy and Trichet met with only limited success. It was agreed at the IGC that the Council of Ministers should be allowed certain circumscribed powers in the area of exchange-rate policy, either to conclude target-zone agreements with third countries (akin to the Louvre Accord concluded in 1987 in a Group of Seven framework), or else to formulate general orientations for exchange-rate policy in respect of the single currency. This was the small extent of 'economic government' agreed under the Maastricht Treaty, apart from its provisions for the policing of 'excessive government deficits'. Here the Commission was accorded some real powers, which were to become a matter of major dispute in 2003–5. But otherwise it failed to win an important role in EMU decision-making processes.

As to what were to be called the 'convergence criteria' governing eligibility for the third stage, France's position during the IGC was to ensure that the criteria were not so restrictive as to prevent the Mediterranean countries, especially Italy and Spain, from having any real chance of adopting the single currency. Crucial was to be the permissible size of the general-government deficit ('general government' being the EC's broad definition of 'government', comprising central government, regional or local government, and social-security funds). The choice of 3 per cent as the normal ceiling for the ratio between the general-government deficit and GDP was actually a French suggestion. It was a ratio to which Mitterrand had given approval, in a purely domestic context, in the early 1980s. It was also a ratio with which the French negotiators felt comfortable in 1991, the outturn in France in the previous year having been no more than 1.6 per cent.

The British question was both delicate and highly political. The approach chosen by the Dutch presidency was to favour the principle of 'opt-ins', allowing each member state to declare its choice on the eve of the third stage. Such an approach was totally unacceptable to Mitterrand, since it opened the possibility of a German change of mind, particularly if Kohl were no longer Chancellor. A treaty 'opt-out' for the UK was far preferable from a French standpoint. Linked to the French aversion to the principle of 'opt-ins' was the imperative need, as perceived by the French president, to make the three-stage process leading to the single currency an irreversible one. The fulfilment of the 'convergence criteria' should not provide member states with an option, but rather with a binding obligation, to proceed to EMU's third and final stage. These were the two related areas in which Mitterrand was to concentrate his efforts at the Maastricht summit. Agreement to the principle of a British 'opt-out' was the more readily forthcoming. With the help of the Italian prime minister, Guilio Andreotti, and some prior softening up of the German Chancellor, the French president finally had his way on the question of irreversibility. Agreement was had to a possible start of the third stage at the beginning of 1997 if a majority of member states met the 'convergence criteria', or otherwise to a mandatory start at the beginning of 1999 by all states meeting the 'convergence criteria' in 1998. It was very far removed from being just a technical issue. According to Hubert Védrine, secretary general of the Presidency of the Republic since May 1991, this agreement to a binding timetable represented one of the most important moments, if not the most important moment of all, at the European Council meetings held during Mitterrand's fourteen years in office.[42]

The Treaty's Troubled French Infancy

The Treaty of European Union was formally signed in Maastricht on 7 February 1992. Viewed from the standpoint of French interests, the treaty may be seen, at the risk of oversimplification, as having served four major aims: the recovery of France's power, albeit on a shared basis, in the sphere of monetary policy; the acceptance by other member states (apart from the

UK) of pursuing high standards of social protection in line with France; the enhancement of France's role as a foreign-policy actor through the vehicle of the reinforced European Council; and the start of a solution to France's European defence-role quandary. Of these four aims, it had been amply clear in the long run-up to the treaty's signature that Mitterrand viewed the first as also the foremost.

To come into effect, the Maastricht Treaty had now to be ratified, and in the case of France it was not plain sailing. On 9 April 1992 the French Constitutional Court ruled that, before the introduction of any bill providing for the treaty's ratification, the Fifth Republic's own constitution must first be revised because of the treaty's innovations, including its provisions for the introduction of a single currency. Several day later, in a broadcast television and radio interview, the French president set out his programme for the (limited) revision of the constitution and also for the ratification of the treaty, with a plea to parliament to act expeditiously and in the national interest. For the revision of the constitution, a brief bill was to be put before parliament forthwith. Once the bill was approved in identical terms by the National Assembly and the Senate, the proposed change would be submitted to the two chambers of parliament assembled together – constitutionally speaking, 'convened in Congress' – and expressing their approval through a three-fifths majority of votes cast. This was one of the either of the two routes that had to be taken to seal the constitutional revision and make it definitive. The alternative route would have been by way of referendum. The latter route, Mitterrand strongly hinted, would be the one chosen for the subsequent bill providing for the treaty's ratification. There was no lack of confidence on the president's part that the treaty, if put to a referendum rather than laid before Congress, would be readily ratified. 'I am confident', he declared, 'that I shall have the historical privilege to receive the assent of the French people to this great act.' To stress its legitimacy and importance, he declared that 'the Maastricht Treaty' was 'a design conceived by France (*un projet de la France*)' and, as such, squarely in the tradition of Monnet and Schuman. He asserted, moreover, that his support for EMU was based on a refusal of the prospect of France's continuing to be bound into a DM currency zone.[43]

For the revision of the constitution, the arithmetic of the composition of the two chambers of parliament was such that a three-fifths majority in the assembled Congress could be counted upon. Conditions were favourable for the passage of the bill through the National Assembly, where the Socialist-led government enjoyed a working majority. In addition, two of the chamber's three opposition parliamentary groups, namely the UDF and the UDC, representing respectively the liberal and centrist camps, were in favour of the Maastricht Treaty. The neo-Gaullist RPR's parliamentary group, the biggest of the three, was divided. Yet its leadership was grudgingly in favour or passively acquiescent, reflecting the position taken nationally by Chirac, the party's president. This left the Communists as the only parliamentary group adamantly opposed to the treaty. In mid May the National Assembly adopted the constitutional bill, with minor amendments, on its first reading. A month later, after the defusing of a minor constitutional crisis over the Senate's power of amendment, a bill adopted by both chambers was ready for voting by the Congress.

The Congress approved the constitutional bill on 23 June, with the requisite majority of three-fifths of votes cast easily attained. However, the RPR's internal divisions were scarcely masked. Almost all the RPR's deputies and senators had walked out before the vote was taken. A similar walkout had taken place in the Palais Bourbon on the bill's second reading. Chirac had opted for what he termed 'hostile non-participation': his argument was that, since the Danish electorate had just rejected the Maastricht Treaty by referendum, the treaty was effectively already dead and constitutional revision pointless.

Séguin's Stand

These divisions had already surfaced in May when the constitutional bill was given its first reading in the National Assembly. A quarter of the RPR's deputies – more than 120 in all – had been unwilling to toe the party's pro-abstention line and voted against the bill. The leader of this sizeable rump was a former minister, Philippe Séguin. Prior to the vote, this socially progressive Gaullist, known for his strong Jacobin streak and Anglophile leanings, moved a motion to the effect that the constitutional bill was incompatible with the principle of national sovereignty enshrined in the constitution. It provided him with the occasion for an eloquent speech against the Maastricht Treaty. When the motion was voted, the RPR was split roughly in two (between supporters and those abstaining). Even if the motion garnered more than a hundred votes, with support from the PCF, it was still massively defeated. However, Séguin had established his credentials as the leader of France's anti-Maastricht politicians.

In making his May speech, Séguin tested the endurance of his listeners. Lasting for two-and-a-half hours, it was more suited for reading than being listened to. Indeed the speech was published immediately afterwards as a short book entitled *Discours pour la France*. Invoked were Republican patriots: Gambetta, Mendès France, and de Gaulle. The real debate, Séguin argued, was between those who considered the nation to be an outmoded form of social organisation in the rush towards globalisation, and those, like himself, who considered the nation to have a continuing spiritual dimension providing for a sense of political community.[44]

In addressing the question of whether the treaty would contribute to peace and prosperity, the RPR deputy's answer was a resounding no. The introduction of the future single currency would bring economic harm rather than benefit; and he raised the spectre of the Depression. Nor would peace be favoured. In the treaty's effective disregard of the challenges facing the formerly communist countries of Central and Eastern Europe, there was 'an extraordinary posthumous victory for the Europe of Yalta'. France was forgetful of the moral debt it owed to these countries, first because France's liberation towards the end of the Second World War had effectively been in exchange for their subjugation, and, secondly, because France's post-war security had been based on their abandon. It was surely in France's interest, urged Séguin, that these countries' nascent democracies and fragile economies be given the greatest of support. Otherwise Europe would be a more dangerous and explosive place than during the Cold War.[45]

Hence Séguin's 'Europe' extended eastwards. At its heart would be the continent's more powerful nation states, since they were the only competent actors on the world stage, as witness, he said, the decisive roles played by the UK in the momentous year of 1940 and, in a different key, by France in 1983 in stiffening West Germany's resolve over the Euromissiles crisis. He called for the creation of a European Confederation, but one distinct from Mitterrand's, which had been 'conceived as consisting in a hard core (*noyau dur*), made up of a community of the well-off, around which gravitate subordinate states'. Yet his proposal for a regional Security Council (modelled on that of the UN, with permanent members and implicitly no role for NATO) shared something in common with the French president's desires for a more independent Europe. Like Mitterrand too, he envisaged the EC would be an inner circle of the wider confederation. Despite his refusal of EMU as defined by the Maastricht Treaty, Séguin did allow for EC monetary union by way of a common currency – alongside the franc and other national currencies – and he praised the different proposals to this effect of Balladur and John Major. Politically, the scandal of the EC's 'democratic deficit' would be resolved by rolling back the European Parliament's prerogatives and establishing the precedence of national law over EC law. A revamped EC would be based on 'delegations of competence', rather than on 'any irrevocable transfer' of sovereignty. That the latter path had been favoured, under the EMU provisions of the Maastricht Treaty, to 'truss up' (*ficeler*) Germany was futile and misconceived. A Franco-German axis was needed, the RPR deputy averred. But it would only work if France were a credible partner, and so the priority was its reinvigoration as a nation state. This depended on social justice at home and a refusal of large-scale unemployment. Imperative were 'the restoration of the state and the rehabilitation of the Republic', which was the end and the beginning of the argument from this independently minded Gaullist.[46]

Dénouement

Séguin's call for the rejection of the Maastricht Treaty resonated within the RPR, but Chirac quickly dampened the party's unrest by imposing his own policy of 'hostile non-participation' in the parliamentary process for changing the constitution. At the beginning of June, in the immediate aftermath of the Danish referendum's negative verdict on the treaty, Mitterrand decided that he would nonetheless brave fortune and, following his earlier inclination, seek authorisation for France's ratification of the treaty also by way of referendum, rather than by going back again to parliament and Congress.

Thus, at the beginning of July the date of 20 September was set for the referendum. And so the campaign took place mainly during the summer-holiday months. Two politicians distinguished themselves by their energy on the stump: Guigou for the government, and Séguin, effectively leading the campaign for all those on both the right and the left who were opposed to the treaty. By late August opinion polls were indicating that the likely 'no' vote had increased considerably, and that the result of the referendum would be very tight.

The three weeks in September therefore counted. TF1, the privatised television channel, presented a special Maastricht Treaty programme in the distinguished surroundings of the Sorbonne on 3 September. The French president played the principal role throughout the long pro-gramme. Lending personal support through a special television link was the German Chancellor. Kohl was thus able to repay the favour of Mitter-rand's Bundestag address of nearly ten years earlier. The climax of the evening was a one-to-one exchange of views between Mitterrand and Séguin. The latter was satisfied with what he took to be a real debate, though he was to be widely criticised afterwards for having been too deferential in manner.[47] The carefully stage-managed programme served the Maastricht cause. In the following week Mitterrand was hospitalised for urgent surgery in connection with a prostate cancer that had hitherto been hidden from the public. The official announcement of the cancer four days before the referendum, as well as Mitterrand's own public show of courage and humour, raised sympathy for him and may have swayed slightly the referendum result.

Some 70 per cent of the electorate voted in the referendum, which was a relatively high turnout by French standards. Of valid votes, 51.05 per cent were cast in favour of treaty ratification; 48.95 per cent were against. A close-run thing, but just enough in favour for the treaty to count as an emanation of the general will.

But in the longer term the Maastricht Treaty was to prove no panacea for France, at least as viewed by the electorate. By 2005, as has already been shown, disenchantment with the economic promise of the EU's first pillar, the EC, had set in. By that year, also, the EU's continued enlarge-ment and its internal foreign-policy dissensions had soured French perceptions of the high politics of *la construction européenne*, and these perceptions too were to weigh on the French electorate's negative judgement on the EU's new constitutional treaty. It is to the shape of this post-Maastricht Europe – and indeed post-Yalta Europe – that the reader's attention is now finally directed.

Notes

1. Edouard Balladur, 'Mémorandum sur la construction monétaire européenne' – addressed to the EC's 'Ecofin' Council. Published in *ECU* 3, 1988, 17–20. See also *Le Monde*, 15 January 1988; Edouard Balladur, *Passion et longueur de temps. Dialogues avec Jean-Pierre Elkabbach*, Paris, 1989, 347–52; Kenneth Dyson and Kevin Featherstone, *The Road to Maastricht: Negotiating Economic and Monetary Union*, Oxford, 1999, 163–66; David Howarth, *The French Road to European Monetary Union*, Basingstoke, 2001, 88–98.
2. Hans-Dietrich Genscher, 'Memorandum für die Schaffung eines europäischen Währungsraumes und einer Europäischen Zentralbank' – addressed to the EC's General Affairs Council. Published in Deutsche Bundesbank, *Auszüge aus presseartikeln* (1 March 1988). Published in French translation in *ECU* 3, 1988, 21–23. See also Dyson and Featherstone, *The Road to Maastricht*, 170–72, 327–32.
3. Hans-Dietrich Genscher, *Erinnerungen*, Munich, 1995, 387–89.
4. Timothy Garton Ash, *In Europe's Name: Germany and the Divided Continent*, London, 1993, 99–100, 106–11. Shevardnadze's claim that already in 1986 he considered German unification to be around the corner was made in his autobiographical work (Eduard Shevardnadze, *The Future Belongs to Freedom*, New York, 1991), and he confirmed it personally to Garton Ash in 1992.
5. *Le Monde*, 8 April 1988.
6. Karl Otto Pöhl, 'The further development of the European Monetary System', in Commission of the European Communities – Committee for the Study of Economic and Monetary Union, *Collection of Papers submitted to the Committee for the Study of Economic and Monetary Union*, Luxembourg, 1989, 129–84.
7. On the role played by de Larosière, in opposition to the French finance ministry but backed by the French president, see Dyson and Featherstone, *The Road to Maastricht*, 180–87.
8. 'Un entretien avec le président de la Bundesbank', *Le Monde*, 23 May 1989.
9. Ibid., 186.
10. François Mitterrand, *De l'Allemagne, de la France*, Paris, 1996, 19–26, 125.
11. Ibid., 241–47. Cf. Jean Lacouture, *Mitterrand. Une histoire de Français*, 2 vols, Paris, 1998, vol. 2, 89–91.
12. Mitterrand, *De l'Allemagne, de la France*, 39–44, 135, 148–54.
13. Delors was not only pleased with this new responsibility for the Commission, but also considered Bush's initiative to have been of decisive importance. 'Credit where credit is due, George Bush was the first to argue for a political and economic opening-up to Poland and Hungary, the two countries leading the movement for emancipation' – Delors, *Mémoires*, 273–74.
14. For Attali's own account of the EBRD's tortuous conception and birth, and his strong desire from the outset to keep the Americans out, see Jacques Attali, *Europe(s)*, Paris, 1994, 17–94, and *Verbatim*, vol. 3, passim.
15. Attali, *Verbatim*, vol. 3, 350. Especially in respect of *Verbatim*, Attali's reliability as a witness has often been questioned. Caution is certainly required, as is shown later in this chapter in connection with what Attali initially said about Mitterrand's visit to Gorbachev in Moscow in May 1990. But it does not at all mean that Attali's voluminous testimony should be systematically discounted or disbelieved. For the present subject

matter – France and German unification – see the criticism of Attali in Frédéric Bozo, *Mitterrand, la fin de la guerre froide et l'unification allemande. De Yalta à Maastricht*, Paris, 2005, 380–81.

16. The view that Mitterrand sought actively to block German unification has owed much to the publication in May 1992 of two books: Jacques Jessel, *La Double Défaite de Mitterrand. De Berlin à Moscou, les faillites d'une diplomatie*, Paris, 1992; and, of less substance, Alain Genestar, *Les Péchés du prince*, Paris, 1992. It was given added credence by the publication in 1995 of the third volume of Attali's *Verbatim*, covering the 1988–91 period. A radically opposing view was put forward in 2002 by Tilo Schabert, a German political scientist who was given privileged access between 1992 and 1995 to staff and documents at the Elysée. His book *Wie Weltgeschicte gemacht wird. Frankreich und die deutsche Einheit*, Stuttgart, 2002, was revised, expanded, and translated into French as *Mitterrand et la réunification allemande. Une histoire secrète (1981–1995)*, Paris, 2005. For a critique of Schabert's selectiveness, argument, and benign conclusion, see the book review by Jacques Bariéty in *Politique étrangère* 2, 2004, 441–45. See also the nuanced article: Daniel Vernet, 'Mitterrand, l'Europe et la réunification allemande', *Politique étrangère* 1, 2003, 165–79.

17. Mitterrand, *De l'Allemagne, de la France*, 87–96. Cf. Attali, *Verbatim*, vol. 3, 359–67; Vernet, 'Mitterrand, l'Europe et la réunification allemande', 175–78; Bozo, *Mitterrand, la fin de la guerre froide et l'unification allemande*, 156–60.

18. Philip Zelikow and Condoleezza Rice, *Germany Unified and Europe Transformed: A Study in Statecraft*, 2nd edn, Cambridge, Massachusetts, 1997, 137, 412.

19. Mitterrand, *De l'Allemagne, de la France*, 39–44. Cf. Attali, *Verbatim*, vol. 3, 368–70; Margaret Thatcher, *The Downing Street Years*, London, 1993, 796–97. Attali's and Thatcher's accounts broadly tally.

20. Attali, *Verbatim*, vol. 3, 375.

21. Conclusions of the Presidency, European Council, Strasbourg, 8 and 9 December 1989. For the West German pledge in 1970, see Garton Ash, *In Europe's Name*, 71, 472.

22. Mitterrand, *De l'Allemagne, de la France*, 107.

23. Helmut Kohl, *Erinnerungen, 1982–1990*, Munich, 2005, 1033.

24. Jessel, *La Double Défaite de Mitterrand*, 75–77.

25. Mitterrand, *De l'Allemagne, de la France*, 122–25.

26. *Le Monde*, 2 January 1990.

27. Claire Tréan, 'La question de la frontière germano-polonaise a été « définitivement réglée »', *Le Monde*, 19 July 1990. More generally, see Zelikow and Rice, *Germany Unified and Europe Transformed*, 217–22, 433–35; Bozo, *Mitterrand, la fin de la guerre froide et l'unification allemande*, 228–41, 442–45.

28. Attali, *Verbatim*, vol. 3, 363–64; Zelikow and Rice, *Germany Unified and Europe Transformed*, 141–42.

29. George Bush and Brent Scowcroft, *A World Transformed*, New York, 1998, 265–68.

30. Zelikow and Rice, *Germany Unified and Europe Transformed*, 442.

31. Ibid., 270, 453.

32. Attali, *Verbatim*, vol. 3, 495–501; Jacques Attali, *C'était François Mitterrand*, Paris, 2005, 339–40. See also Bozo, *Mitterrand, la fin de la guerre froide et l'unification allemande*, 264–66, 450–51. Attali's initial and totally misleading account of this meeting would have been noted in Washington by no less a person than the future US Secretary of State, Condoleezza Rice – see the 'new preface' in 1997 to Zelikow and Rice, *Germany Unified and Europe Transformed*, xiii–xv, where the authors, speaking of the third volume of *Verbatim*, state that 'the one story that we wish we had known better before our book was [first] published [in 1995] was that of François Mitterrand and French diplomacy', and that, in contrast to the apologia in *De l'Allemagne, de la France*, '[Attali's] important new evidence supports the much more ambivalent portrait offered in our book'.

33. Zelikow and Rice, *Germany Unified and Europe Transformed*, 303–24; Bozo, *Mitterrand, la fin de la guerre froide et l'unification allemande*, 274–78. See also Bush and Scowcroft, *A World Transformed*, 291–95; Thatcher, *The Downing Street Years*, 810–12.
34. For the text of the letter, see Harryvan and van der Harst (eds), *Documents on European Union*, 252–53; Finn Laursen and Sophie Vanhoonacker (eds), *The Intergovernmental Conference on Political Union: Institutional Reforms, New Policies and the International Identity of the European Community*, Dordrecht, 1992, 276.
35. Thatcher, *The Downing Street Years*, 761–62.
36. Bozo, *Mitterrand, la fin de la guerre froide et l'unification allemande*, 196–99, 244–46. See also Attali, *Verbatim*, vol. 3, 412, 448; Védrine, *Les Mondes de François Mitterrand*, 420–21; Cohen, *Mitterrand et la sortie de la guerre froide*, 149.
37. Laursen and Vanhoonacker (eds), *The Intergovernmental Conference on Political Union*, 313–14.
38. Eric Aeschimann and Pascal Riché, *La Guerre de sept ans. Histoire secrète du franc fort*, Paris, 1996, 90–92.
39. Cohen, *Mitterrand et la sortie de la guerre froide*, 143–45.
40. Védrine, *Les Mondes de François Mitterrand*, 463.
41. For the text of the October 1991 joint letter, see Laursen and Vanhoonacker (eds), *The Intergovernmental Conference on Political Union*, 415–18. On the genesis of the Eurocorps idea, see Bozo, *Mitterrand, la fin de la guerre froide et l'unification allemande*, 307–17, 337–38, 464–65, 471.
42. Védrine, *Les Mondes de François Mitterrand*, 472.
43. *Le Monde*, 14 April 1992.
44. Philippe Séguin, *Discours pour la France*, Paris, 1992, 17, 35–36, 109, 113–14, 115.
45. Ibid., 58–71, 79–81.
46. Ibid., 75–77, 93–102.
47. Philippe Séguin, *Itinéraire dans la France d'en bas, d'en haut et d'ailleurs*, Paris, 2003, 388–400.

Chapter 10

Post-Yalta and Post-Maastricht Europe

In the 1990s French monetary policy was subordinated to the goal of EMU, sometimes painfully so. The Maastricht Treaty's CFSP provisions proved problematic, and the US and NATO returned centre stage in Europe. Chirac created a fully professional French army, attempted but failed to persuade the US to reshape NATO's integrated command, and took steps, initially bilaterally with the UK, to launch new European security and defence arrangements. During both the Mitterrand and Chirac years, French handling of the EU's eastward enlargement was unsure in touch, and the new-look EU was a factor contributing to the 2005 referendum result.

Implementing EMU and 'La Pensée Unique'

The Maastricht Convergence Criteria and Germany's 'Asymmetric Shock'

In keeping with Mitterrand's successful resolve in 1989–91 to win German agreement to a binding timetable for implementing EMU by the end of the century, successive French governments holding office after the signing in Maastricht of the Treaty on European Union gave ample proof of their firmness of purpose – first under Mitterrand himself and then under Chirac, elected president in 1995 – and the goal of monetary union was eventually achieved in 1999–2002. The move to EMU's third and final stage in the framework of the Maastricht Treaty benefited from an ongoing powerful political impetus. To speak of France alone, the efficiency of the machinery of government in Paris for handling economic matters, the closeness of the Franco-German partnership in the first half of the 1990s,

---

and the power exercised by the European Council in the management of the EMU timetable, were all factors that enabled the French political establishment to play a large part in bringing to fruition the ambitious project of building on the existing EMS to establish monetary union.

In France's favour at the time the Maastricht Treaty was agreed was that it met all of the ordained economic convergence criteria for the adoption of the future single currency (Article 109j). Thus, France had already achieved a 'high degree of price stability' as measured by its relative rate of consumer price increase (the norm being no more than 1.5 percentage points above the average of the three best performing member states); it had given proof until then of the 'sustainability of the government financial position' as shown by the absence of a 'deficit that is excessive', whether the criterion be the size of the annual general-government deficit (the norm being a deficit no more than the equivalent of 3 per cent of GDP) or the level of general-government debt (no more than 60 per cent of GDP); it had its currency slotted into the normal narrow band of the ERM 'for at least two years, without devaluing against the currency of any other member state'; and, lastly, it provided a token of the 'durability of convergence' through the level of its long-term interest rates (the norm being a level no more than 2 percentage points above the average of the three best performing states in respect of price stability).

This position at the time of the Maastricht Treaty's signature was largely the result of the tight monetary policy that had been pursued by Bérégovoy as economics and finance minister from 1988 to 1992. During these years he wielded exceptional power in running the domestic economy, even if he was held on a tight leash by Mitterrand for the IGC negotiations on EMU. On his appointment as prime minister in April 1992, Bérégovoy ensured that he retained this power, dividing up his erstwhile empire at the Quai de Bercy – the home of the economics and finance ministry – between three full-ranking ministers, so as to exercise overarching control from Matignon. Nothing was to be allowed to endanger a stewardship during which his overriding concern, both before and after his becoming prime minister, was the continued pursuit of policies aimed at establishing the franc as a hard currency (*'le franc fort'*) and improving the competitiveness of the economy by squeezing out inflation (*'désinflation compétitive'*).

Monetary policy was conducted with a constant eye on a single privileged exchange-rate target, the ERM's bilateral central rate of 3.35 francs against the DM – set in 1987 – which, it was ordained in Paris, had to be preserved at all cost. Shadowing the DM tended to lower franc-denominated unit import prices, while the relatively high level of French short-term interest rates, needed to maintain the exchange-rate target, served to dampen domestic demand and so also to lower inflation. From 1990 onwards the underlying trend in the rate of increase of domestic prices did indeed fall, and economic growth was export oriented throughout the period (partly because of the adverse effect of monetary policy on domestic demand), and both developments were favourable for the franc. There was a narrowing of the short-term interest-rate differential between France and Germany, and the policy aim was that the differential would eventually be eliminated, with French short-term rates down to German levels. Long-term interest rates, notably on French government bonds, would also eventually fall to German levels once the financial markets perceived that the degree of monetary stability was effectively the same in the two countries. Such was the goal of Bérégovoy's endeavour; conditions would then be favourable for sustained and faster economic growth and a correspondingly brighter future. This *franc fort* policy was to remain France's quasi-official orthodoxy for the management of the economy in the run-up to EMU's third and final stage, and by 1994, when it was in the hands of the *cohabitation* government headed by Balladur, dissenters were sarcastically labelling it '*la pensée unique*', that is, the received, though not necessarily correct, wisdom of most of the country's political establishment.

During his time as economics and finance minister, Bérégovoy was encouraged in the belief that his policy stance was right by the top functionaries or advisers closest to him, especially Trichet at the head of the Treasury and Hervé Hannoun, the finance minister's own *directeur de cabinet* – both were to be promoted to the Banque de France in September 1993, Trichet as Governor and Hannoun as one of the two Deputy Governors.[1] Yet even the best laid plans may be hostage to the vagaries of fate, and by the end of 1991, when the Maastricht Treaty was agreed, it was becoming progressively clear that the currency area represented by the ERM had suffered, in economists' jargon, an 'asymmetric shock' of considerable proportion. The asymmetry resided in just one of the ERM's national economies having been destabilised. But the economy happened to be the biggest, Germany's, and the shock consisted in the more unpalatable economic consequences of unification, notably a strong rise in inflation.

In particular, the income windfall resulting from the very generous one-to-one exchange-rate applied in July 1990 for converting most of the East German household sector's Ostmarks into DM had made for an inflationary surge in consumer spending. The raising of East German wages to West German levels contributed, moreover, to cost inflationary pressures. Most important of all, the parlous structural state of the erstwhile GDR's industrial sector – far worse than had been anticipated in Bonn – meant that public-finance transfers through the federal budget from west to east, notably to cope with unemployment, were even more massive than planned in early contingency plans. Kohl chose political expediency in refraining from raising taxes to finance these transfers, and so the already record federal-government budget deficit in 1990 widened greatly in 1991, and then still further in both 1992 and 1993. These deficits were in turn the source of inflationary pressures. The Federal Republic's famed monetary stability had become seriously impaired by unification.

To respond to the 'asymmetric shock' and curb rising inflation, the Bundesbank was obliged to push up its key official interest rates – the Lombard rate (for central-bank credits to commercial banks to bridge their temporary financing gaps) and the discount rate (for credits to banks through the rediscounting of trade or treasury bills). These increases served, as intended, to push up money market rates and so the levels of interest rates fixed by the commercial banks themselves. A first turn of the screw occurred in September 1991 and another followed in December of the same year, nine days after the Maastricht Treaty had been agreed, bringing the Lombard rate to a record post-war high of 9.75 per cent. There was a further hike in July 1992 though, on this occasion, only of the discount rate. The worry about inflation was only too well founded. The year-on-year increase in German consumer prices was to be 5.1 per cent in 1992, as compared with 4.1 per cent in 1991 and 2.7 per cent in 1990.

This tightening of German monetary policy had disastrous consequences for the rest of the ERM area. In the case of France, inflation was not worsening as in Germany. On the contrary, the year-on-year increase in consumer prices in 1992 was 2.5 per cent – half the German rate – and was on a decelerating trend, down from 3.4 per cent in 1991. However, the modus operandi of the ERM dictated not only that the key official interest rates of the Banque de France had to be pushed up pari passu with German ones, but also that a positive interest-rate differential had to be maintained by way of a risk premium for international investors holding franc-denominated assets rather than DM-denominated ones. Thus, in 1991 and 1992, representative money-market rates in France were respectively 0.7 and 0.9 percentage points higher than corresponding money-market rates in Germany. The cost of credit, notably to the business sector, became extremely high. For instance, in 1992 the overnight money-market rate averaged 10.35 per cent; this rate set effectively the floor for the cost of short-term finance to large enterprises. Since inflation in France was on the low side in 1992, the money market's 'nominal' rate translated into a 'real' rate of some 8 per cent (year average), which was unsustainably high for the economy over the long term. For small and medium-sized enterprises, not to speak of the household sector, the situation was even worse, since the cost of short-term finance available to them stood near to a 'nominal' 12 per cent in 1992 and not far short of a 'real' 10 per cent. Not surprisingly, the French economy moved into recession in 1993. Unemployment mounted as economic growth stalled. In 1992 the unemployment rate crossed the 10 per cent threshold for the first time in the post-war period; in 1993 it rose to 11.6 per cent.

The economic effects of the *franc fort* policy contributed to the landslide victory of the parliamentary right in the legislative elections of March 1993. When Bérégovoy tragically took his own life several weeks later on the national May Day holiday, the symbolism was not lost on the public. The suicide of this fundamentally decent man appeared to have been precipitated by a variety of factors (including a controversy over an interest-free loan for the purchase of an apartment). What is sure is that he was disheartened by his failure to have stemmed rising unemployment and by the related criticisms of his economic management voiced in the wake of the electoral debacle, including allegations from within his own party that he had betrayed the Left.

The Message from the Sorbonne, Sterling's Battering, and the 'Sweetheart Deal'

Well before the end of Bérégovoy's year as prime minister, Germany's 'asymmetrical shock' was playing havoc with the functioning of the ERM, which had become a more ambitious arrangement since its enlargement in October 1990 at the beginning of EMU's first stage to include the pound sterling. The interest-rate differentials required for maintaining the exchange-rate stability between the DM, the 'anchor' currency, and the other participating currencies were market-driven. The size of any particular differential hinged on market credibility. By 1992 market operators – banks, hedge funds, corporate treasurers, and institutional investors – were questioning the sustainability of the ERM's existing exchange-rate configuration, if not the very viability of the system, and the nub of their concern related to the extraordinary heights to which various national monetary authorities appeared ready to let their short-term interest rates rise, rather than to accept an ERM devaluation or an ERM exit, temporary or otherwise. Their concern made for a hard calculation of when and how governments would be forced to change course, simply because of the huge cost in foregone economic growth and mounting unemployment.

The first great storm hit the ERM at the time of France's ratification of the Maastricht Treaty. Mitterrand's carefully staged Sorbonne performance on 3 September, prior to the referendum on 20 September, indirectly contributed to an unsettling of the financial climate. When Séguin in the course of his debate with the president had broached the question of the single currency and had opined that it would be managed by technocrats, the latter's reply was brazenly disingenuous. Monetary policy, Mitterrand reassured the television viewers, was a mere instrument of economic policy, which itself was safely in the hands of politicians elected by universal suffrage, notably those forming the European Council.[2] This blatant misreading of the Maastricht Treaty caused instant worry outside France. In particular, the Bundesbank's president, Helmut Schlesinger, was appalled by Mitterrand's saying effectively that the letter of treaty could be ignored and the principle of independent monetary policy cast to the wind. The foreign-exchange markets were already at the beginning of the month in a state of turbulence as operators sized up critically the credibility of the central rates of the ERM's weaker currencies, with the lira appearing the most vulnerable. On the weekend of 5–6 September an 'Ecofin' informal meeting, bringing together the EC's finance ministers and its central-bank governors proved a very testy affair. There were repeated attempts by British, Italian, French and other ministers to persuade Schlesinger of the imperative need for a cut in German interest rates. But he saw no reason to oblige. The meeting's patent failure to win any meaningful agreement was the harbinger of havoc on the foreign-exchange markets.

It came immediately. On 16 September – the British 'Black Wednesday' or 'White Wednesday', depending on the predilections of the observer – the pound sterling and the lira were forced out of the ERM, forever in the case of the British currency and temporarily in the case of the Italian one. And the peseta was devalued in the wake of the day's events. In the following week of September 1992 it was the turn of the French franc to be in the eye of the storm. The *petit oui* to the Maastricht Treaty in the French referendum held on 20 September failed to convince the markets that the Bérégovoy government's *franc fort* policy made economic sense. In the course of the week ending 24 September, to defend the severely buffeted franc, the Banque de France was obliged to intervene on a massive scale, with official figures showing that it sold foreign currency equivalent to about Fr 80 billion, which was four-fifths of the French central bank's published currency reserves at the end of the previous month. But, in contrast to the outcome of the desperate efforts ordered in London a week earlier by Major, the French monetary authorities finally succeeded in bucking the markets and maintaining their currency's ERM parity.

The explanation of the different outcomes owed much to the decade-long partnership between Kohl and Mitterrand. Despite Schlesinger's jaundiced view of the EMS as an albatross round the Bundesbank's neck, the German central bank was ordered by the Chancellor to give exceptional support to the French currency. Political reasons dictated that there should be no change in its parity against the DM. This was the 'sweetheart deal', in the apposite words of the Irish finance minister, Bertie Ahern. On 23 September 1992, after two days of battering for the franc, the German and French finance ministers, together with the Bundesbank president and Governor of the Banque de France, took the unusual step of issuing a joint communiqué stating that the current central rate between the DM and the French franc was fully justified by economic fundamentals. Then, in what was a crucial step, the Bundesbank announced that it was intervening intra-marginally to support the franc. Under the ERM's operating rules, a central bank was obliged to intervene on the markets only when its currency hit its upper or lower limit, as set by the ERM's permissible fluctuation margins around bilateral central rates, and this was the first ever occasion on which the German central bank had intervened to support a weak currency before it was strictly necessary. Total Bundesbank support amounted to the equivalent of roughly Fr 160 billion. Combined with the intervention of the Banque de France and the psychological effect of the steely show of Franco-German resolve, the franc was saved and, with it, Bérégovoy's *franc fort* policy.[3]

The Implosion of the EMS and its Metamorphosis

When the Socialists were defeated in the March 1993 legislative elections, Mitterrand signalled to Chirac – the Right's leader by virtue of his presidency of the RPR – that the next prime minister must follow Bérégovoy in also upholding the *franc fort* policy. Balladur was accordingly chosen. Neither he nor the new economics and finance minister, Edmond Alphandéry, was to be found wanting. The latter's enthusiasm for the *franc fort* precipitated the second great storm to hit the ERM in the early 1990s. In a chain of events, one of them a clumsy act of lese-majesty on Alphandéry's part that offended simultaneously his opposite number in Bonn and the Bundesbank, the ERM was nearly killed off altogether. No 'sweetheart deal' saved the day. Instead, in an unplanned fashion, the ERM rose from the ashes in a metamorphosed state.

The background was a strengthening of the franc on the exchange markets, helped by a recession-induced improvement in the balance-of-payments position, with a trade surplus of unprecedented proportion, and further evidence of weakening inflationary pressures. It induced an element of overconfidence on the part of the French monetary authorities, and encouraged the idea, first mooted by Trichet in April 1992, that the franc could become actually stronger than the DM. There was renewed talk in Paris of the effective transformation of the ERM, its being henceforth 'co-anchored' by both the French and German currencies. On 21 June 1993 the Banque de France lowered its key intervention rate to 6.75 per cent, so that for the first time since 1967 the official floor rate to the French money market was below the Bundesbank's discount rate. Then on 24 June Alphandéry committed his gaffe. He announced to the listeners of France's Europe 1 radio station that he had invited the German finance minister, Theo Waigel, and the Bundesbank president, Schlesinger, to Paris 'in order [to] discuss together the conditions of a concerted lowering of interest rates in France and Germany'. This brief was news to the two Germans, even if they were scheduled to talk with the French finance minister and the Governor of the Banque de France on the following day in the framework of a routine meeting of the Franco-German Economic and Financial Council. Alphandéry's radio remarks on the lowering of interest rates were interpreted as a diktat to Germany. Waigel's peeved reaction was to brusquely cancel the meeting, and this sudden strain in Franco-German relations unnerved the financial markets.

In this new, less assured context what transformed market perceptions of the French franc's position was the much heightened awareness in the first half of July 1993 of the acute weakness of demand in the French economy and hence, in the absence of a sharp reduction in short-term interest rates in Germany, of the unsustainable nature of the current stance of French monetary policy. As the franc came under increasing pressure, the Bundesbank did seek to provide some exceptional help through intra-marginal intervention. However, when the German central bank decided on 29 July to leave its discount rate unchanged until at least the end of August, the movement across the exchange markets of funds out of the French franc was on such a scale that the existing ERM parity-grid constellation of central rates became untenable. The French currency was not alone. The Belgian and Luxembourg francs, the Danish krone, the peseta, and the escudo were also under considerable pressure. Confusion reigned across the ERM area on 30 July. The stage was set for the weekend's meeting in Brussels of the EC's Monetary Committee, perhaps the strangest and certainly the most far-reaching meeting held by that body in its thirty-five years of existence.

For much of the Monetary Committee's two-day meeting on 31 July and 1 August, stalemate prevailed. The first move had been the total refusal of France to budge from the *franc fort* policy and accept a devaluation of its currency against the DM, whether presented as a downward realignment of the franc or as an upward realignment of the German currency. The French proposal was instead that the DM should be temporarily withdrawn from the ERM. However, neither the Netherlands nor Belgium and Luxembourg – the last two partnered in their own bilateral monetary union – wished to break their respective special currency links with Germany. Since 1983 the guilder had been pegged to the DM (with narrower margins of fluctuation than under ERM rules), and in 1990 a similar link was put in place in Brussels for the (interchangeable) Belgian and Luxembourg francs. For the Nederlandsche Bank – the Dutch central bank – its DM peg was non-negotiable, while, in the case of the twin Belgian and Luxembourg francs, the Belgian monetary authorities were aware that even a temporary termination of the two currencies' DM peg could prompt the Luxembourg monetary authorities to tie the Luxembourg franc to the guilder rather than to the Belgian franc, thereby breaking up the Belgium–Luxembourg Economic Union. The French proposal was therefore a non-starter: 'too many planets would follow the sun', remarked dryly one of the participants.[4] One way to have broken the stalemate would have been to accept that the ERM was finally dead and, with it, no doubt, EMU. Apart from the bilateral DM pegs, there would be a generalised float. The Bundesbank had no objection to this idea. For Schlesinger, who was about to retire as president and be replaced by Tietmeyer, it was a solution serving the cause of German monetary stability. But Kohl would have none of it. He telephoned repeatedly to

Waigel, who as finance minister attended the Brussels meeting, to insist that a generalised float had to be avoided at all costs. This left only one way forward: the introduction of a significant element of floating into the ERM, by widening substantially the permissible margins of fluctuation. Various figures for the wider upper and lower limits were mooted. At the last minute, late on Sunday evening in Brussels but already Monday morning in Tokyo, it was agreed that the new margins of fluctuation should be as much as 15 per cent either side of bilateral central rates, nearly a sevenfold widening compared with the existing margins of 2.25 per cent that had been in place since the 1970s. The ERM had been formally saved but, operationally, entirely transformed.[5]

It proved, moreover, a transformation for the better. As the Padoa-Schioppa Report had warned in 1987, the full liberalisation of capital movements promised difficulties for the functioning of the ERM. In particular, it increased the opportunities for essentially speculative transactions and, when these were to be conducted by the huge hedge funds, they proved very destabilising. But the radical widening of the ERM's fluctuation bands now limited such opportunities. Furthermore, if the economic situation was dire in 1993, monetary conditions were improving. German short-term interest rates fell each year from 1993 to 1998 – that is, until the eve of the start to EMU's third and final stage on 1 January 1999. French short-term interests fell too, with the exception of a spike in the first half of 1995, and so the impact of the 'asymmetric shock' arising from German unification gradually lessened. Importantly, low inflation was becoming the rule. Already in 1994 the national rates of increase in consumer prices in the core ERM area – Germany, France, Netherlands, Belgium, and Luxembourg – were all low and within one percentage point of one another, ranging from 1.7 per cent for France to 2.7 per cent for Germany. Under these conditions, the underlying trend for the differential between French and German short-term interest rates after the 1993 exchange-market crisis was one of reduction, and the differential was to be virtually eliminated in 1997.

By and large, a remarkable degree of stability prevailed between the franc and the DM after the widening of the ERM's bands. In 1997 the franc's market rate against the DM was very near to the central rate, and in 1998 – in anticipation of the following year's 'irrevocable locking' of exchange rates for the introduction of the single currency – the market and central rates were identical. The *franc fort* policy had therefore succeeded towards the century's end in making the French currency as 'hard' as the German one; and the DM's 'anchor' role was imperceptibly phased out in 1997 and 1998.

By then monetary policy was determined by the Banque de France, no longer by the French Treasury. As the exchange-market storm raged in July 1993, the French parliament adopted a law that accorded a measure of independence to the national central bank in the sphere of monetary policy

– especially for the setting of interest rates – by establishing a nine-member Monetary Policy Council. This body was set up in January 1994 at the beginning of EMU's second (intermediate) stage, even though national central-bank autonomy was not required by the Maastricht Treaty until the setting up of the ESCB at the beginning of the third stage. It was proof of Mitterrand's determination to drive the EMU project forward. Six of the Council's members were drawn from outside the central bank on the basis of political nominations. However, its three ex officio members were the Governor of the Banque de France and his two deputies. Since during the entire five-year period of the Monetary Policy Council's existence, the Governor was Trichet and one of the two deputies was Hannoun, the flame of the *franc fort* was effectively in safe keeping.

Locating the ECB, Naming its Currency, and Choosing its President

The Maastricht Treaty had left in abeyance a number of decisions of an institutional character, particularly the choice of location for the future ECB and the choice of name for the future single currency. And there was also the sensitive question of the choice of the ECB's first president. At the end of October 1993, shortly after the near fatal exchange-market crisis, the first of the two decisions was settled at an extraordinary meeting of the European Council. The meeting was held to herald the formal birth of the EU on 1 November, the day of ratification of the Maastricht Treaty by Germany, the last member state to give its approval. Frankfurt – home to the Bundesbank – was chosen by the European Council as the location of both the future ECB and its precursor, the European Monetary Institute, with the latter being set up on 1 January 1994 at the start of EMU's second stage. Although the French government had staked out Lyon as its preferred location, it was without conviction; in the eyes of all member states, the choice of Frankfurt was virtually a foregone conclusion from the time of the Maastricht Treaty's signing.

In the matter of the future single currency's name, serious hopes had been entertained in Paris that France's preference would prevail. But there was to be disappointment on this score. Giscard d'Estaing, in his negotiations with Schmidt in 1978 over the design of the EMS, had entertained as a long-term goal that the ERM's official numeraire, the ECU currency basket, would evolve into a parallel currency called the écu in French (or 'ecu', without the accent, in other languages including German and English). With its historical resonance, the name of écu would have symbolised a continuity with France's past and, arguably, French leadership too. But the EMS did not to give birth to any such parallel currency, save in the limited embryonic form represented by the use of ECUs for central-bank swap operations within the EC area. On the other hand, outside the EMS framework, the use of the ECU as a financial numeraire was developed in the 1980s in a number of EC countries – mainly Italy, France, and Belgium – for a variety of non-official banking purposes. Partly because of this proof of the ECU's practical worth as a measure of value, the feeling in French government circles after the publication of the Delors Report in 1988 was that the ECU's name could now be given to the future single currency, thereby more than meeting Giscard's earlier ambition.

However, German enthusiasm for the enhancing of the ECU's role was singularly lacking, both before and after the Delors Report. Not only had the Bundesbank been sceptical of the loftier ambitions held for the ECU ever since the time of the EMS's inception, but it actually forbade German financial institutions to incur ECU liabilities. The reason for this interdiction harked back to the nightmare memory of the inflation of the early Weimar Republic days. Under the FRG's Basic Law any resort to price indexation – traditionally a means of accommodating inflation – was unconstitutional, and the Bundesbank deemed the use of the ECU denominator or currency basket to be indeed a form of indexation.

A crunch of sorts had come in 1992 with the publication of the first copies of the Maastricht Treaty. The word 'écu' or 'ecu', depending on the language, figures some twenty times in the treaty and, spelt in lower case, appeared to be the name of the future single currency. However, because of strong German objections, the Office for Official Publications of the European Communities was obliged to insert a corrigendum page in these copies of the treaty, listing all the instances where the lower-case 'écu' or 'ecu' should be changed into the upper-case ECU. Since ECU was still strictly speaking the acronym for European Currency Unit, the message behind this corrigendum was that the use of the ECU's name in the treaty was no more than a pis aller, in no way prejudicing the final outcome for the choice of the single currency's name. By 1995, to French dissatisfaction, the widely mooted alternative 'euro' was proving a more acceptable name to the majority of member states. The enlargement of the EU at the beginning of that year to include Austria, Finland, and Sweden had tilted the balance a little further in its favour. And so the matter was finally settled by the European Council's adopting the euro as the single currency's name in December 1995.

There still remained the question of the choice of the ECB's first president. In principle, the nationality of the person charged to head the bank for a first eight-year term should not have been a consideration; being totally independent of national governments was a strict requirement of the Maastricht Treaty's Protocol on the Statute of the European System of Central Banks and of the European Central Bank. However, already by October 1993 the choice of president had become a sensitive issue, making for further division between France and Germany. The French claim, after that month's European Council meeting, was that the quid pro quo of the French government's acceptance of the ECB's Frankfurt location was a tacit understanding between the two countries that its first president would be a Frenchman. But the persistent French desire for some form of European 'economic government', potentially limiting the ECB's freedom of action, raised worries, at least in the Bundesbank, about the degree of independence that would be shown by any French nominee.

When the moment arrived in May 1998 for the European Council, sitting formally as the Council of Ministers, to appoint the ECB's president (as part of the launching process of EMU's final stage), the German-backed candidate was Wim Duisenberg, the head of the Dutch central bank. Kohl would have had an even stronger preference for Tietmeyer, the Bundesbank president, if such a choice had been on the cards. From a German standpoint, Duisenberg had given ample proof of his monetary rectitude – for instance, in 1988–89 as Pöhl's chief ally on the Delors Committee. Trichet's name was put forward by France, even if Chirac considered that the *franc fort* zeal of the Governor of the Banque de France had sometimes overly swayed the decisions of its Monetary Policy Committee. Duisenberg was chosen, however, though not before a squabble between Chirac and Kohl. At the time of this appointment, the French government announced that a tacit agreement had been concluded under which Duisenberg would stand down at the end of 2002, halfway through his term, with his place being taken by Trichet. But the Dutchman declared that the timing of his retirement would be decided by himself. To complicate matters, in 2002 Trichet was to find himself mired in criminal proceedings because of alleged negligence in the early 1990s, as Director of the Treasury, in supervising the accounts of the state-owned Crédit Lyonnais. Only in November 2003, after being completely cleared of any wrongdoing, did Trichet move to Frankfurt as president of the ECB. Fundamentally, the choice between Duisenberg and Trichet made for little practical difference; it mattered in Paris essentially for reasons of national prestige.

Euro Qualification and the Stability and Growth Pact

If France was never found wanting in respect of monetary policy, fiscal policy – once the Maastricht Treaty was signed – was to prove another matter. Its public-finance convergence criteria became a source of considerable trouble for successive French governments. In 1991, when France was clear of the 'excessive government deficit' danger zone, the general-government deficit ratio came to 2.4 per cent and the debt ratio to 35.8 per cent (this relatively healthy debt figure indicating that the country's public-finance situation was incomparably better than that of Italy or Belgium, to restrict the comparison to founding EC member states). However, from 1992 onwards the situation markedly deteriorated.

One force at play was the need to counterbalance the tight *franc fort* monetary policy with a looser fiscal policy. This translated into larger deficits, which in turn generated a larger stock of debt. The looser fiscal policy is shown by OECD figures for the 'cyclically-adjusted' or 'structural' general-government deficit (that is, the nominal deficit corrected to exclude the varying effects of the business cycle on fiscal flows). The 'structural' deficit rose sharply by one-and-a-half percentage points in 1992, and in each of the four years through to 1995 it was the equivalent of between 4 and 5 per cent of GDP.

By the time Alain Juppé took over in May 1995 as prime minister, it was abundantly clear that a major effort was required to reduce the size of the general-government deficit if there was to be any hope of France's qualifying in 1998 for EMU's third and final stage. Measures taken to forestall this failure and indeed to prevent the derailing of the entire EMU project included the immediate raising of the standard rate of VAT by two percentage points, the slapping of a temporary surcharge on corporation tax, and the drawing up of social-security reforms aimed at reducing the social-security debt and the sizeable deficit on healthcare spending. But even these different measures came to be seen as insufficient in view of the need to reduce the (nominal) general-government deficit to 3 per cent of GDP by 1997, the year whose outturn would be crucial for the European Council, since in the spring of 1998 it would rule on which states qualified for EMU. An accounting sleight-of-hand helped, however. Under the plans drawn up in 1996 for France Télécom's partial privatisation, the telecom operator was to a pay a huge lump sum to the French Treasury in return for the state's assumption of its long-term pension obligations, prior to its being transformed into a limited company. Despite the ongoing nature of both the pension liabilities in question and the corresponding state disbursements, this lump sum was imputed in its entirety to the receipts side of the 1997 state budget, thereby shaving 0.5 percentage points off that year's deficit. Thus, in nominal terms, the outturn for the ratio between the general-government deficit and GDP in 1997 came to 3.0 per cent exactly, as compared with 4.1 per cent in 1996, 5.5 per cent in both 1994 and 1995, and a peak of 6.0 per cent in the recession year of 1993.

When Jospin became prime minister in June 1997 – following Chirac's failure to win a snap legislative election – the new left-of-centre government soon demonstrated its own determination to take up the EMU baton. To show appropriate seriousness on the fiscal side, a second temporary surcharge was slapped on corporation tax. By then, however, France's qualification was already virtually assured. The *cohabitation* Socialist-led government could look forward to being in power when Mitterrand's all-important goal was at last achieved.

The key moment was in May 1998 when the European Council (qua Council of Ministers) decided which member states had qualified for EMU's third and final stage. Contrary to expectations at the time of the

Maastricht Treaty's preparation, the agreed euro area proved a very large one. Not confined to the economic core of Germany, France, and the Benelux countries, it included Italy, Spain, and Portugal, as well as Ireland and two of the EU's newcomers, Austria and Finland. Considerable progress had been made across the EU area in 1996–97 in reducing government deficits, spectacularly in the case of Italy, on whose credentials Germany and the Netherlands had long looked askance. From a French standpoint, the presence of Italy and Spain was politically welcome, particularly in view of the north-eastward shift in the EU's centre of gravity after German unification and the 1995 enlargement.

The euro area in its first years of existence was to prove a quite different construction than had been imagined at the time of the Delors Report, as witness the convoluted tale of the EU's Stability and Growth Pact. Its starting point, in November 1995, was a proposal for a Stability Pact – meaning a commitment to monetary stability – from Waigel, the German finance minister. At the time the German government's concern was that, once member states had qualified for admission to the monetary union, some would be tempted to relax their efforts in respect of convergence and, in particular, indulge anew in public-finance excesses, making for inflation. Such a temptation would be of a free-rider nature inasmuch as governments issuing bonds to finance excessive deficits would benefit at least initially from the (relatively low) level of long-term euro interest rates, a fruit of monetary stability; but this favourable level of interest rates would itself be eventually compromised by the profligacy in question. Hence Waigel proposed that all member states adopting the euro should be party to a pact under which the Maastricht Treaty's 'excessive deficit' procedure (Article 104c) – enabling the Commission and Council of Ministers to sanction delinquents – would be given extra teeth, notably through spelling out the system of penalties (including fines) and the circumstances under which they would be imposed.

Chirac balked at this German proposal. Although he had made clear his commitment to EMU – after some mixed signals during his presidential election campaign – he was wary of any dogmatic attachment to fiscal or monetary rectitude. The proposal was discussed at a number of European Council meetings. Finally, in December 1996 there was an agreement in Dublin on the part of the European Council to the pact's main elements, but not before a fractious exchange of views between Chirac and Kohl and a watering down of what had been proposed on the German side. The pact was renamed the Stability and Growth Pact, since the French president had insisted that the pact should not be perceived as a fiscal straightjacket, seriously prejudicial to job creation. In terms of substance, however, there was little change, apart from some dilution of the original German proposal in the matter of penalties, both as regards their automaticity and the fiscal thresholds at which they would apply.

In December 1997 Chirac took some comfort when the European Council approved another proposal, which was for setting up an informal 'euro' council, alongside the long-established 'Ecofin' Council of Ministers, with a view to promoting economic-policy cooperation between the member states adopting the single currency. The move for the creation of this very loose form of 'economic government' came from the French economics and finance minister, Strauss-Kahn, though only after Jospin had failed to win agreement for more ambitious arrangements; it was Strauss-Kahn's German counterpart, Waigel, who gave the green light.

By 2003, in the euro's fifth year of life, France and ironically Germany were both to fall foul of the Stability and Growth Pact. Both countries had breached the general-government deficit ceiling of 3 per cent of GDP in 2002. In both countries the deficit was set to breach the ceiling anew in 2003, and there was the recognition that even in 2004 matters could not be set right. In France's case, it was in early 2003 that the situation became clear as regards not only the previous year's actual outturn but also the likely outturn for the current year. The European Commission launched the first step of the 'excessive deficit' procedure against France in April, which in June led to the formal confirmation by the 'Ecofin' Council of Ministers of the existence of an 'excessive deficit' under EU law. This development did not prevent the right-of-centre government headed by Raffarin from presenting in September a budget for 2004 that would result, according to official projections, in a general-government deficit equal to 3.6 per cent of GDP, as compared with the outturns in 2002 and 2003 of respectively 3.3 per cent and 4.1 per cent of GDP. In Germany the 2002 and 2003 outturns were much the same, at 3.5 per cent and 3.9 per cent respectively. The stock of general-government debt was accordingly affected; there were to be record levels in both countries at the end of 2003, making for a debt to GDP ratio of 63.7 per cent in France and 64.2 per cent in Germany. Yet, in November 2003 when the 'Ecofin' Council of Ministers faced the prospect of threatening both Germany and France with fines in accordance with the deficit procedure, they backed away by 'temporarily suspending' the pact's sanctions mechanism. An irate Commission appealed to the European Court of Justice, which in July 2004 ruled largely in its favour. Nonetheless, the longer-term future of the tattered Stability and Growth Pact had become far from assured.

On the German side the public-finance woes testified to the greatly changed position of Europe's largest national economy. Instead of the economic Leviathan feared by Mitterrand at the time of the fall of the Berlin Wall, Germany had been weakened by poor economic growth since the early 1990s and chronically high unemployment. The incorporation into the FRG of the five eastern Länder, with far greater than anticipated economic and social costs, had weighed heavily on this change of fortune.

No such excuse existed on the French side. Just as Waigel had feared, the efforts aimed at correcting public-finance disequilibria were relaxed once EMU had been secured. The economic upturn that started in 1997 and continued into 2000 provided the Socialist-led *cohabitation* government with an opportunity for improving the public-finance situation. But scant use was made of it. In 2002 the Raffarin government inherited a poor public-finance situation. No far-reaching effort was made to improve it. In the face of flagging economic demand and high levels of unemployment, the Stability and Growth Pact tended to be disregarded.

The most notable feature of this long story is France's dogged commitment to the birth of the ECB and the single currency in the period from the Maastricht Treaty's signing to the commitment's fruition in 1999. The commitment took much of its strength from French perceptions of how best to shape the balance of power in Europe – not just monetary power but also political power. The long-term practical economic consequences have yet to be adequately weighed. Certainly, at the end of the Chirac presidency in 2007, there were few in France, as measured by opinion polls, who thought that the euro had had a positive effect on the French economy.[6]

The Yugoslav Imbroglio

Shades of the Paris Peace Conference

The main substance of the Maastricht Treaty lay in its carefully crafted provisions for EMU, and the introduction of the single currency at the end of the 1990s was accomplished largely in accordance with Mitterrand's ambitions for France and Europe at the decade's beginning. Yet the political development in Europe that came dramatically to the fore in the closing years of the Mitterrand presidency belonged to a quite different world, strife torn and violent. For the intense last phase of the IGC negotiations on the design and launching of the EU, which ran from the presentation of the Luxembourg presidency's draft treaty in June 1991 to the European Council's agreement to the final version in Maastricht in December, coincided with the opening of Europe's worst conflagration since the Second World War. Slovenia and Croatia declared their independence from the Federal Republic of Yugoslavia (FRY) in June, and before the end of that summer fierce fighting had broken out in Croatia's Slavonia and Krajina as predominantly Serb-composed military forces, under the flag of the Yugoslav army or in the form of local militias, sought to detach Croatian lands that Slobodan Milošević, the Serbian president, and others in Belgrade considered should belong to a Greater Serbia on account of their 'ethnic' composition. The siege and sacking of Vukovar and the artillery bombardment of Dubrovnik were emblematic of a Europe in which 'union' had little or no place. When Bosnia–Herzegovina declared its independence in April 1992, two months after the Maastricht

Treaty's signing, the break-up of Yugoslavia took a further giant step forward, with all its attendant mass 'ethnic cleansing'. The nascent EU, so it proved, could not cope with this challenge on its doorstep; the main thrust of European integration since 1950 had left Western European countries singularly ill prepared to deal with such a crisis.

In France the unfolding events that led to the collapse of Yugoslavia were a cause of dismay. In 1919, at the Paris Peace Conference, France as well as the UK had followed the US in backing a generous territorial settlement for the fledgling Kingdom of Serbs, Croats, and Slovenes – the name of the Kingdom of Yugoslavia being proclaimed only later in 1929. From a French standpoint, this Serbian-dominated polity of the southern Slavs would serve as a bulwark to the south-east against any revived German expansionism. There was, moreover, a certain romantic French attachment to the Serbian cause that went back to the first uprising against Ottoman rule already in the early nineteenth century; the Serbian bid for freedom and independence was celebrated, for instance, by the distinguished poet, writer, and politician, Lamartine, and the links between the two countries were reinforced later by Serbia's being effectively an ally of France in the Great War. In 1934, fifteen years after the Paris Peace Conference, the ties between France and Serbia or the wider Yugoslavia were strengthened in the public mind when Alexander I – the Serbian monarch at the head of Yugoslavia – and the French foreign minister, Louis Barthou, were assassinated in Marseille by a Macedonian in the pay of the Ustashi, the terrorist movement committed to Croatian independence. Following the Second World War, when Yugoslav partisan resistance had put some brake on the Wehrmacht's advance into Greece, there was widespread admiration in Paris of the role played by the Yugoslav communist party and, in particular, by its charismatic and ruthless leader, Tito. The action during the war of Croatia's Ustashi, who established a murderous, fascist state, appeared in stark contrast. After the setting up of the FRY, the Yugoslav model of communism, with its declared but partly feigned reliance in the economic sphere on industrial self-management, exerted a strong attraction in the early post-war period on the progressive Left in France (bringing the word *autogestion* into the French language in 1960), and, through this channel, it influenced also the economic philosophy in the 1960s of the masters of the new Algeria. Furthermore, Tito succeeded in holding the potentially fissiparous Yugoslavia together until the time of his death in 1980, a year before Mitterrand became president.

Not surprisingly then for a man of his generation and political leaning, Mitterrand sought initially to reverse what he saw as an overly hasty and rash decision on the part of Croatia's and Slovenia's leaders. Until the creation of UNPROFOR (UN Protection Force, the peacekeeping mission) in February 1992, the international efforts in favour of peace in the crumbling Yugoslavia were left largely in the hands of the EC and, in particular, the EPC troika of foreign ministers. The troika in the second half of 1991 was provided by the Netherlands (holding the presidency) and Luxembourg and Portugal (the preceding and following holders), and it was the Luxembourg foreign minister, Jacques Poos, who famously announced that the saving 'hour of Europe' had arrived. The troika's efforts did bear some fruit, but it was of a limited kind. As to Mitterrand, before the die of the FRY's break-up was considered to be really cast, he evinced a willingness to engage in meaningful action to forestall the evil day. In particular, there was a French proposal in September 1991 for a WEU peacemaking force to separate the warring sides in Croatia, but the UK, the only other WEU member capable of joining France for serious military action, demurred, effectively on Bismarck's principle that events in the Balkans merited not the bones of a single grenadier.[7]

Mitterrand's Geopolitical Conservatism

The nub of the problem on the EC's side was the sharp difference between the positions of France and the UK on the one hand and, on the other, Germany (backed, it might be added, by the Holy See – a bogeyman combination for Dumas, as he complained once he was no longer foreign minister).[8] Both Kohl and Genscher were strongly pressing in the second half of 1991 for the international recognition of Croatia as well as Slovenia. Their stance arose more out of a realistic appraisal of the FRY's condition and the state of relations between Serbia and Croatia – Slovenia's independence having already been tacitly accepted in Belgrade as a fait accompli – than out of any revanchist *Mitteleuropa* ambition. The opposition of Mitterrand and Major was initially firm. However, by the time of the Maastricht summit in December, the differing interests of the three countries in respect of EMU gave Kohl an advantage when discussing the Balkans: the French president's keenness for agreement on a binding EMU timetable, and the British prime minister's keenness for agreement on an EMU opt-out for the UK, conditioned their shared (very reluctant) assent at the summit to the principle of Croatian and Slovenian independence.[9]

Thus, five days after the Treaty on European Union was agreed by the European Council, the EC's foreign ministers accepted on Genscher's prompting to extend recognition of independence as from 15 January 1992 to any of the FRY's constituent republics that were so desirous, provided certain conditions were fulfilled in respect of notably the UN Charter and the Helsinki Final Act. The independence of Croatia and Slovenia as well as Macedonia was accordingly recognised by the EC and all its member states. It opened the path to the international recognition of Bosnia several months later, which was followed immediately by the three years of fighting between that country's 'ethnic' groups – Muslims (or 'Bosniaks'), Serbs, and Croats – and mass civilian murder, pillage, and rape.

UNPROFOR, to which France and the UK contributed the main elements, was inadequate for the task, being hampered by its Security Council mandate and, in particular, by the 'dual-key' control over the deployment of weaponry that gave a final say to a very circumspect UN Special Envoy, Yasushi Akashi.

Mitterrand's innate conservatism in the matter of Europe's borders stood in the way of a France's playing any leading role in resolving the Yugoslav crisis – rather than just seeking to keep a lid on it – during the remaining years of his presidency. Little more than a year before the Slovenian and Croatian declarations of independence, the French president had been scathing in private about Lithuania's bid for independence from the USSR because of fears about its destabilising effects.[10] Similar considerations about the need to assure stability across the continent affected his appraisal of the Yugoslav break-up. An avowed personal sympathy for the Serbs, partly on account of courage shown in the Second World War, was coupled to a tendency to equate Croatia with the Ustashi cause and to be sceptical about the political viability of an independent Bosnia. For a variety of reasons, Mitterrand found himself inclined towards a resigned acceptance of the idea of a Greater Serbia.[11]

Yet the French president was not insensitive to the scale of human suffering in the former Yugoslav lands. Sarajevo, besieged by the Bosnian Serbs, had become the symbol of this suffering by the summer of 1992. In France attention to the Bosnian capital's plight had been heightened by calls for intervention from the intelligentsia. Prominent was Bernard-Henri Lévy; on 23 June 1992 he delivered personally to the Elysée an appeal for help from the Bosnian president, Alija Izetbegović. Chirac had made an impassioned plea for action earlier in the same month.[12] Within the government, Bernard Kouchner, the minister responsible for 'health and humanitarian policy', was pressing for action. As a founder in 1971 of Médecins sans frontières, the international medical-relief organisation, Kouchner had credibility and raised widespread support. Another quite different factor was the first signs in Washington of impatience with the EC's failure over a twelve-month period to bring order to its backyard. Against this background, Mitterrand made a surprise move on 27 June by leaving the European Council's meeting in Lisbon and flying secretly with Kouchner to Sarejevo, where they landed on 28 June – seventy-eight years to the day after the assassination there of the Archduke Franz Ferdinand, the spark that set off the Great War. Since Sarajevo airport was virtually closed and exposed to frequent artillery or sniper fire from the surrounding Serb-held hills, this symbolic visit of six hours' duration by the ailing 75-year-old president was an act of courage and considerable panache. Practically speaking, after a telephone call from Mitterrand to Milošević, the Sarajevo excursion led to the reopening of the airport for the purpose of humanitarian aid, which indeed had been the French president's purpose. Yet from the standpoint of wider conflict resolution the visit served little purpose.[13]

It also seems that Mitterrand, immediately afterwards, was not greatly engaged with the complexities and the deeply dark side of the ongoing developments in Bosnia.[14] The attempted international resolution of the Yugoslav crisis had moved largely into UN hands well before his visit to Sarajevo – notwithstanding the continued presence of an official EC mediator or negotiator – and hopes existed in the second half of 1992 that a UN-brokered peace could be achieved through what eventually emerged at the beginning of 1993 as the Vance–Owen Plan. But the plan's subsequent collapse eroded gradually the UN's own credibility as an agent for peace. A stalemate situation took hold in Bosnia. The reluctance of France and the UK to envisage more draconian action in 1993 and 1994 was matched by the hesitations of the new Clinton administration in Washington. Yet the mood there did start to change in 1994. The adoption of more assertive political role was marked early in the year by the American brokering of a federation between Croatia and Bosnia (the non-Serb held parts), and later in the year by the appointment of Richard Holbrooke as Assistant Secretary of State for European Affairs and chief negotiator for the Balkans conflict. To bypass UN decision-making constraints, the Contact Group structure was set up through an American initiative to bring together, in an ongoing diplomatic process, France, Germany, Russia, the UK, and the US.

By May 1995, when the UN – in the person of Akashi – reluctantly agreed to the use of NATO air power against ammunition dumps near to the Bosnian Serb capital of Pale, the main say over former Yugoslavia's future had passed to the US and accessorily to the Contact Group. Although these limited bombing sorties were to be met with an unexpected counter-response, when the Serbs took hostage nearly two hundred UNPROFOR soldiers (about a hundred of them French), they clearly demonstrated that the preferred American policy of air strikes had gained the upper hand. And there was to be a decisive hardening of the American position in the course of the summer, as Bill Clinton was progressively obliged to take a clear stand.

It was also in May 1995 that Mitterrand's fourteen-year presidency came to an end. From his standpoint, this revitalisation of NATO and of the US's role in Europe was a severe disappointment. For the foreseeable future, it was a development that put paid to his hopes and plans in the 1980s and early 1990s for a common European defence system largely independent of NATO's integrated command – the last step having been the launching of the Eurocorps in May 1992. The initiative for reshaping the Balkans was passing into American hands with NATO in tow, and decisively so.

Chirac's Change of Course

Once Chirac – the 'Bulldozer' – was installed at the Elysée, French policy changed. The man who had protested so strongly over Sarajevo in 1992 did not trim his views in office. To some extent his way forward had been prepared by the Balladur government and, in particular, by Juppé, foreign minister from March 1993 to May 1995, who was a close political associate of Chirac. During this period of *cohabitation*, Mitterrand had allowed the prime minister and the foreign minister a certain freedom of initiative and manoeuvre in the conduct of foreign policy. Juppé availed of it in February 1994 when, after another bombardment of Sarajevo, he proposed the recourse to air strikes by NATO if the Bosnian Serb forces did not withdraw their heavy artillery from positions within a radius of twenty kilometres from the Bosnian capital's centre. The threat was duly made and the withdrawal apparently took place. Hitherto Paris and London had refused all proposals from Washington for the use of air strikes, and at this point the French stance began to diverge from the still highly cautious British one.[15]

In the three months from June to August 1995 the situation in Bosnia touched new depths, and it led eventually to real engagement by NATO. Chirac as the new French president was active throughout this period in calling for greater military resolve. In what was his first international visit, four weeks after taking over from Mitterrand, he travelled to the US. On 14 June, formally in his capacity as president of the European Council, he met Clinton. Annual EU–US summits were now a diplomatic fixture. But Bosnia, not strictly defined EU matters, dominated their talks, and Chirac impressed upon Clinton the need for more forceful action.

By coincidence, it was late on the same day after a dinner held at the White House for the French president, that Clinton was advised by Holbrooke of unwelcome news from the Pentagon. Because of UNPROFOR's failure to shape events in Bosnia, the possibility of its unilateral withdrawal was being considered by military planners; it was not Chirac's option, but the idea had earlier found favour in Paris when Balladur had been prime minister, and it also had backing in London. For his part, Clinton had secretly promised that US military ground support would be provided for any withdrawal, by virtue of NATO solidarity. But he had not allowed for the Pentagon's subsequent calculations, now divulged to him by Holbrooke, indicating that as many as 20,000 American troops would be required because of potential enemy fire power and the difficult terrain for the retreat to the Adriatic. Along with these troop numbers and the terrain came the prospect of body bags. The US president could therefore honour a NATO commitment that was now coming to be seen as rash, or else renege on it, with a loss to his international credibility and reputation. Yet a way out of this dilemma was to transcend it by shifting policy towards a decidedly more aggressive involvement. To judge by Holbrooke's own account, Chirac exerted considerable influence in persuading Clinton of the merits of resolute action, and thus the coincidence of the French visit and the Pentagon's warning marked a crucial moment in the train of events that led within a few months to the exercise of untrammelled American military and diplomatic power.[16]

But the effect was not immediate, and worse was very soon to come. Srebrenica, until then a Muslim haven, was overrun in mid July by forces under the command of Ratko Mladic, with no real resistance from the Dutch UNPROFOR contingent responsible for the town's security. Intelligence was sufficient to indicate instantly in Paris, Washington, and elsewhere that a disaster was in the making. Chirac insisted on the need for prompt action, calling for American logistic support for the transport to the town of French troops with real fighting capability. Clinton hesitated until it was too late. Yet the growing discovery before the end of the month of the enormity of the genocidal-type massacre that had taken place in Srebrenica, with a tally that was later to be established at some 8,000 men and boys, prompted a further hardening of resolve on the part of the Clinton administration, and the French president had served as an agent of this change.[17]

If Clinton needed further prodding, it came in late July. As the horror of the Srebrenica massacre sank in, the US Senate voted on a bipartisan basis to lift the embargo on the supply of arms to Bosnia (by way of exception to the UN-imposed embargo applying to all of former Yugoslavia); earlier this unilateral move had been opposed by Clinton. What the UN Security Council had refused to do, the US would now do independently. Shortly afterwards, in early August, the design of a Greater Serbia suffered a massive setback when Croatia launched a successful military campaign, involving also 'ethnic cleansing', to recover swathes of territory from Serb hands.

In the case of Bosnia, the catalyst for end-game action was a further bombardment of Sarajevo in late August. By virtue of an agreement struck between NATO and the UN after the Srebrenica massacre, aircraft, including French ones, flying from bases in Italy and from an American aircraft carrier in the Adriatic, pounded Bosnian Serb positions around Sarajevo. At the time it was NATO's biggest ever military operation. With the Serbian economy partly in ruins as the result of the UN trade embargo introduced three years earlier, Milošević finally realised that the time had come for the putative Bosnian–Serb government in Pale to be reined in. In early September the foreign ministers of Bosnia, Croatia, and the rump FRY (Serbia and Montenegro) agreed in principle to the continued existence of the Bosnian state, though on a federal basis with a 51–49 per cent split between the Bosniak–Croat and Serb parts. Then, in November, the final settlement was negotiated under American auspices in Dayton, Ohio. Partly in recognition of France's role, the Dayton Accords were formally signed in Paris in December 1995.

But there had been no readiness on the American side to share the diplomatic decision making at Dayton with France, not to speak of the UK, whose political role in the summer of 1995 had been marginal. Holbrooke's assertive management of the Dayton negotiations had been strikingly cavalier from the standpoint of French or even British susceptibilities, and it was the pointer to future transatlantic difficulties.

French Perceptions of the 'Hyperpower' and Kosovo

Such difficulties arose in 1999 during the Kosovo crisis and, in particular, during the war conducted by NATO to reverse the 'ethnic cleansing' carried out by Serbs against the Kosovar Albanians. They arose from a French dislike and distrust of American peremptoriness in matters both diplomatic and military.

The Kosovo crisis had been long in reaching its climax. Back in 1989 Milošević, as Serbia's president, had revoked Kosovo's constitutional status as an autonomous Serbian province endowed with a high degree of autonomy. And in the early 1990s the Kosovar Albanian majority was subjected to the 'Serbianisation' of public life. In 1998 the Kosovo Liberation Army – founded as a terrorist organisation – gained control through guerrilla warfare of nearly a quarter of the province's territory, albeit briefly. The Serbs retaliated with a first wave of 'ethnic cleansing' and mass murder. In the absence of an agreement on UN intervention by the Security Council's permanent members, NATO air strikes were threatened. Milošević backed off in October 1998, but the pause was short-lived. Further repression by Serbian forces entailed more 'ethnic cleansing', and this activity was stepped up after the failure in February 1999 of the Rambouillet Conference – organised under the auspices of the Contact Group (enlarged to include Italy) – to win Serbian agreement to a political settlement. NATO's Operation Allied Force was launched in March. After three months of NATO air strikes and the planning of a ground invasion, the Serbian president came to heel. Kosovo's uncertain future was then entrusted to the UN's care, with peacekeeping in the hands of the NATO-led KFOR (Kosovo Force).

The international parameters conditioning France's role in the Kosovo crisis were different from those beforehand conditioning its varied role in dealing with Yugoslavia's implosion, even during the period of rapprochement with the US in the early months of the Chirac presidency. Since the signing of the Dayton Accords, a further shift had taken place in France's relations with the US, with the effect that Chirac's honeymoon period with Clinton came to an end. In late 1995 the former had hoped that the latter could be persuaded to accept a radical reshaping of NATO's command structure as the price of France's rejoining it, but such hopes were dashed well before the situation in Kosovo reached its crisis point. Furthermore, as the harbinger of the dramatic deterioration in Franco-American relations in 2003 under another US president, frictions had accumulated between 1996 and 1998 over the question of what to do with Iraq. In November 1998 – when it appeared that the North Atlantic Council's Activation Warning to the rump FRY over Kosovo might well be working – the US and the UK embarked upon Operation Desert Fox in response to Saddam Hussein's suspension of cooperation with UNSCOM (United Nations Special Commission on Iraq). France refused its support, however. Already by the end of 1998 regime change in Baghdad was Clinton's preferred Iraqi option, to Chirac's dissatisfaction.[18]

International differences over Iraq contributed, moreover, to a change in the balance of relations within the Washington-Paris-London triangle. Here the crucial year was 1997, partly because of the transformation of the tenor of British foreign policy after Tony Blair became prime minister in May. Madeleine Albright had taken over as Secretary of State in January, while a new French foreign minister emerged in June in the person of Védrine, a man with distinguished credentials from the long Mitterrand era. The 1997–2002 *cohabitation* worked generally well in the sphere of foreign policy. It was Védrine who in February 1998 first coined the term 'hyperpower' (*hyperpuissance*) to describe the transformed position of the US after the demise of the USSR; and he liked to dwell on the theme of a 'multipolar world' in which the hegemonic pretensions of the 'hyperpower' might be checked.[19] Not that the term 'multipolar world' was new. With Gaullist overtones, it had been used frequently by Chirac since 1995.[20] Thus, when the French president steered French policy over NATO's role in the fast developing Kosovo crisis, he found himself well attuned to his new foreign minister's geopolitical vision. And partly because of the parallel Iraqi crisis he was increasingly insistent on the prerogatives of the UN Security Council and France's say as a permanent member.

Hence the French president was concerned that the US should be more respectful of its allies than it had been at the time of the Dayton Accords negotiations. Since Russian and Chinese objections in September 1998 excluded the authorisation of an international military intervention in Kosovo in the name of the UN Security Council, Chirac agreed that month to the intervention's being carried out in a NATO framework, but only on strictly humanitarian grounds. Not satisfied, however, he was still seeking in October for a Security Council resolution justifying the use of force. Such a resolution never came. To counter NATO's playing too dominant a role, there was a French insistence on the centrality for diplomacy of the Contact Group, even to the point of NATO officers being debarred from the chateau of Rambouillet during the February 1999 talks. France's military contribution to the short Kosovo War was considerable, its part in the bombing campaign being the second biggest after that of the US. Yet a salient feature of the campaign was repeated differences of view between the US and France over appropriate bombing targets, with Chirac himself to the fore in complaining of American trigger-happiness.[21]

The Franco-American frictions over these NATO air strikes in 1999 generated a practical scepticism that led George W. Bush, in the intermediate aftermath of 9/11, to dispense with immediate NATO support in Afghanistan (notwithstanding the triggering by the Alliance's member states of Article V). On the French side it encouraged a stronger determination to strive for a meaningful EU defence capability, in line with the Franco-British Saint-Malo Declaration of December 1998.

Rethinking Security and Defence

Time of Rapprochement

The French security and defence conundrum that had so preoccupied Mitterrand in the late 1980s and early 1990s did not go away. Yet the policies framed in Paris to resolve the conundrum underwent change already in the last years of his presidency. As in the handling of the question of the EU's eastward enlargement, an innovative role was played by the Balladur *cohabitation* government, notably through the publication in March 1994 of the *Livre blanc sur la défense* (Defence White Book) when the PR's François Léotard was defence minister; it superseded the first ever such White Book, published in 1972 when the ultra-Gaullist Debré had headed the defence ministry. This new White Book's main purpose was to redefine French defence strategy for the coming decades, not only in the context of the end of the Cold War but also in the framework of the EU's objectives for a common defence policy. The ambitions set out loosely in the Maastricht Treaty set many of the document's parameters. However, an important aspect of the new thinking, which marked a break with the spirit of Mitterrand's and Kohl's launching of the Eurocorps less than two years earlier, was the positive approach taken to the prospect of enhanced defence cooperation with the UK (as well as with Germany). If the planned Eurocorps had been intended by the French president to rival NATO's ARRC, the tone of the White Book indicated that fresh or less confrontational attitudes had come progressively to prevail in Paris since the Franco-German initiative of 1991–92.[22]

American and British fears were assuaged already in January 1993 by an agreement signed by France's Chief of Staff of the Armed Forces and the Inspector General of the Bundeswehr and, on NATO's side, by SACEUR. Under this agreement, the Eurocorps would be available for deployment not only by WEU but also by the wider Atlantic Alliance. In the case of its operating as a NATO force, the Eurocorps would come under the 'operating control' of NATO's command structure. This arrangement represented a halfway position between being 'integrated' in the command structure and merely working alongside other NATO forces through cooperation at general-staff level (the arrangement for France under the secret Ailleret–Lemnitzer and Valentin–Ferber agreements of 1967 and 1974). The agreement was eventually to bear fruit, with the Eurocorps being used for a number of NATO-led peacekeeping operations, notably in Bosnia from 1998 to 1999 when it took part in SFOR (Stabilisation Force), in Kosovo in 2000 when it took core command for a six-month period of KFOR, and in Afghanistan from 2004 to 2005 when it took core command also for a six-month period of ISAF (International Security Assistance Force).

A major step forward was France's partial rejoining of NATO's integrated command structure, even if only on a de facto basis. It was initiated in September 1992 when Pierre Joxe was defence minister in the Bérégovoy government, and it was advanced further when the Balladur government came to power. Joxe's contribution was to moot publicly the idea of France's becoming actively involved in the work of NATO's Military Committee when matters of direct concern were on the table – rather than continuing to rely on liaison between Brussels and Paris through the French mission to the Military Committee – and then to seek to persuade a doubting Mitterrand of the wisdom of such informal involvement in the command structure. Practical considerations relating to France's role in the conflicts in former Yugoslavia were the main catalyst for Joxe's conversion. Importantly, from start to finish, UNPROFOR's operations were dependent on logistics, communications, and intelligence support provided through NATO structures. Accessorily, a negative lesson had been learnt in 1992 from the near farcical nature of the dual command structure used by WEU and NATO, at French insistence, for monitoring the UN arms embargo in the Adriatic. However, it was after Balladur became prime minister that Mitterrand finally agreed that French representation on NATO's military decision-making bodies should be upgraded whenever peacekeeping operations, to which France was party, were on the agenda. The president and the prime minister were to decide henceforth case by case when France's Chief of Staff of the Armed Forces should sit on the Military Committee and also when the defence minister should sit on the North Atlantic Council for its regular (non-summit) meetings – that is, beside the foreign minister, whose place on the North Atlantic Council had been unaffected by France's quitting the integrated command in 1966.

Shortly before the publication of the Defence White Book, it appeared that a major advance had been made under NATO auspices to provide for the development of WEU's role as both 'the defence component of the European Union' and 'a means to strengthen the European pillar of the Atlantic Alliance', in accordance with the Maastricht Treaty's Declaration on Western European Union. The occasion was the summit meeting of the North Atlantic Council held in Brussels in January 1994, when the assembled heads of state or government – including the French and American presidents – approved the principle of a proposal allowing so-called Combined Joint Task Forces (CJTFs) to be set up on an ad hoc basis; the go-ahead for them would be a matter for the North Atlantic Council itself. In the framework of a CJTF, NATO would put infrastructure, communications, and command capabilities at the disposal of WEU for purely European operations decided upon by the latter. This CJTF formula thus allowed for the temporary dovetailing of the two organisations as defence entities. Further shape was to be given to the CJTF formula as a result of the 'Berlin-Plus' arrangements for the lending of NATO assets for WEU-led crisis operations. These arrangements were agreed by NATO's foreign ministers at a meeting of the North Atlantic Council in the German capital in June 1996. According to WEU's own Petersberg Declaration of June 1992, such operations could range from humanitarian and rescue tasks, through peacekeeping, to the deployment of combat forces for peacemaking purposes.

However, the promise of CJTFs, bringing together WEU forces and NATO assets, was not to be realised in the second half of the 1990s – that is, before WEU itself was wound down as a defence organisation. On the French side, under Chirac's presidency, there was no enthusiasm for WEU. This was despite his own role a decade earlier in the elaboration of WEU's Hague Platform. Chirac's view had changed. And towards the end of the 1990s it was symptomatic of WEU's failure to gain real credibility as a defence organisation at the behest of the EU that no call was made on it to play any part in the Kosovo War.

Chirac's High Ambition

Matters of security and defence had come immediately to the fore on Chirac's assumption of power. In June 1995, to an international outcry, the new president announced the temporary resumption of France's nuclear testing programme in the South Pacific. The testing, to be completed by January 1996, was designed to ensure that the *force de frappe* was fully modernised before the signing of the Comprehensive Test Ban Treaty (CTBT). The intention was not to accord an even greater importance to the nuclear components of France's defence; it would indeed have been hard to outperform Mitterrand on this score, at least in the area of strategic nuclear weapons. For a break with the past, Chirac's focus was elsewhere. It soon became clear that his aim for a far-reaching modernisation of France's defence was directed primarily at the army's conventional forces. In a compliment to the views of the younger de Gaulle – the unruly lieutenant-colonel who had called in the 1930s for an *armée de métier* – the president decided that, if France was to pull its weight at the beginning of the twenty-first century, it needed a truly professional army.

Thus, in February 1996 Chirac announced radical changes in defence policy in the course of a long television and radio interview. He told his listeners that the government would plan for the phasing out by 2001 of military conscription – that hallowed practice inherited from the Revolution and the First Republic. The total number of persons in the armed forces would therefore be reduced from some 500,000 to 350,000, with only the already fully professionalised (paramilitary) gendarmerie exempt from the restructuring and shrinkage. The new professional army, said Chirac, was to be modelled to a large extent on the British army, particularly in terms of its range of capabilities. After the end of the Cold War the need was above all for well-trained soldiers, handling sophisticated military equipment, who could be deployed almost anywhere at short notice. The need for this change had become urgent after the experience several years earlier of preparing for the Gulf War. The very difficult putting together of the 10,500-strong Daguet division had provided a negative lesson. Now the French president's aim was that 'France should be capable of sending abroad, rapidly and in an organised fashion, a substantial number of men, say 50,000 to 60,000, rather than just 10,000 as is the case today'.[23]

Chirac's less far-reaching plans for the modernisation of France's nuclear forces, which were outlined in the same interview, were far from unimportant. In the future the strategic nuclear force was to be exclusively seaborne or airborne, with the ground-to-ground missiles on the Plateau d'Albion scrapped by the end of 1996. And the tactical nuclear force, consisting of the army's Hadès missiles, was to fall under the same axe. On the other hand, four new nuclear submarines (Triomphant class) were to be commissioned, replacing the existing generation, and equipped with the advanced M–45 SLBMs as their principal weaponry. For the airborne component of the strategic nuclear force, a version of the Rafale would eventually be developed by Dassault to replace the existing Mirage 2000–N and the naval air force's Super-Etendard.

In this February 1996 announcement Chirac seemed to show scant respect for the ties with Germany that existed by virtue of the Franco-German Defence Council and earlier ambitions for the Eurocorps. In the FRG there was no question at the time of converting the Bundeswehr into a fully professional army, and so the French plan for ending conscription seemed to ride roughshod over any idea of enhancing the interoperability of French and German forces. Later in the year in December, Chirac and Kohl, acting in the framework of the Franco-German Defence Council, put their name to document calling for a 'common strategic concept' that would underpin a 'concerted defence' between the two countries.[24] But it was hard to discern here anything more than a platitudinous generality.

The phasing out of conscription was duly implemented, and the actual shrinkage of the size of the armed forces proved even greater than initially planned. However, on the financial side, developments did not proceed in line with the optimism shown in 1996, and this was to hamper modernisation, especially in the form of expensive new equipment. Underestimated from the start was the additional cost of signing up more professional soldiers, and also that of paying off older professional personnel whose skills were surplus to the new requirements. Furthermore, the unexpected coming to power of the Jospin government in 1997 compromised the plans for defence expenditure under the 1997–2002 military programme act (*loi de programmation militaire*) as drafted in 1996. Chirac's plans were to take a hard financial knock during the five years of Socialist-led rule.

In deciding expenditure on military equipment, the left-of-centre government made indeed swingeing cuts, particularly in 1998, 2000, and 2002. The budgetary outturn for 2001, the government's last full year in office, shows that such expenditure amounted to no more than 4.0 per cent of central-government expenditure, whereas the share had been 7.4 per cent in 1990, at a time when Mitterrand viewed with disquiet the end of the Cold War. Contrary to Chirac's intentions, the first term of his presidency was marked by a disjuncture between his ambition for France's military capabilities and the financial means at his disposal. Only after the return to power of a right-of-centre government in 2002 was a sharp change of course possible. Very large spending increases were made in the 2003 and 2004 budgets. For these two years, according to the government's plans, total military expenditure was set to rise by 6.1 per cent and 4.0 per cent respectively, and expenditure on military equipment by 11.2 per cent and 9.2 per cent respectively. This effort of making good the shortfalls of the preceding years was reflected in the 2003–8 military programme law.

If Chirac's ambition for the modernisation of France's armed forces was only temporarily thwarted – albeit for several years – his other great ambition in the matter of security and defence was to end within the space of a few years in unredeemable failure. Hand in hand with the planned transformation of the French army had gone the bid on his part to have France rejoin NATO's integrated command on largely French terms. As has already been indicated, the context for the bid was the rapprochement that had taken place between the French and American presidents at the height of the Bosnian crisis in the summer of 1995. When the bid eventually failed in 1997, Chirac was to switch from a fairly Atlanticist stance to an approach towards the US that had much in common with that of his predecessor, the more wary and more calculating Mitterrand.

The French president's bid was launched in Washington at a meeting in December 1995 between the France's ambassador to the US, François Bujon de l'Etang, and the US Deputy Secretary of State, Strobe Talbott. Thereafter in 1996 and 1997 talks and negotiations took place in different forums on both sides of the Atlantic. In July 1996, raising the bar high, Chirac authorised a French proposal that SACEUR should henceforth be a European and that the European SACEUR and the Supreme Allied Commander Atlantic (SACLANT) – the latter always an American – should be jointly subordinate to a sort of super supreme commander, a new post that would certainly be held by an American. But in September 1996 this idea was turned down by Clinton, who also poured cold water on a French idea that had already been put forward, that of restructuring AFSOUTH – NATO's Mediterranean command – so that it could be headed by a European, while, at the same time, the US Sixth Fleet would be left entirely under American control. The French president refused to be shrugged off and proposed in October that the negotiations over the future of AFSOUTH be continued. In the course of the next half year negotiations focused on working out a possible dual command structure for AFSOUTH, and there was a glimmer of possible compromise. However, domestic politics intervened in April 1997 when Chirac dissolved the National Assembly in the mistaken hope of winning the ensuing snap election and so putting into place, for a further five years, a government of his choice. The coming to power instead of a Socialist-led government, less enamoured by the prospect of France's forsaking its special semi-detached NATO status, combined with persistent reticence in Washington (especially in the Pentagon) to sink definitively the project. The twists and turns had made for 'the striking episode of the near-miss of French re-entry into the NATO military structure', as a well-informed insider in defence-policy circles on both sides of the Atlantic was later to put it.[25]

Chirac's attempt to put France back into NATO's integrated command, on condition that there was prior American agreement to the command's restructuring, had marked his desire for a major reorientation of French security and defence policy. As General Quesnot – Chief of Staff to the President of the Republic from 1991 to 1995 – disapprovingly expressed it in 1997, there was 'a real rupture with the legacy left by de Gaulle and Mitterrand concerning NATO'.[26] Yet there were also echoes of de Gaulle's own efforts in the late 1950s and early 1960s to reshape the Atlantic Alliance.

The Saint-Malo Declaration and ESDP

It was the British prime minister who threw a lifeline to the French president in the wake of the disappearing goal of NATO's radical restructuring. Since the route had been blocked to combining the promotion of what WEU termed a European Security and Defence Identity (ESDI) – with France itself to the fore – and the exercise of an influential French role within a reformed NATO, two options were at hand. One was to seek to reinvest WEU with credibility as an organisation with a worthwhile future, but this option had come to look increasingly quixotic because of the experience of the wars in former Yugoslavia in the first half of the decade and the peacekeeping arrangements put into place in their aftermath. The other option was to go back to Mitterrand's ambition at the time of the preparation in 1991 of the Maastricht Treaty, namely the ambition of bringing into existence a 'common European defence system' under the ultimate control of the European Council. The idea of a strictly EU defence system had been strongly opposed at the time by both the UK and the Netherlands. Blair's gift to Chirac in 1998 was to concede much of what had been refused in 1991.

The agreement between the British prime minister and the French president incorporating this concession was the Saint-Malo Declaration of December 1998. Issued at the end of a regular bilateral summit meeting between the two countries' leaders, it took its name from the Breton port town where this particular summit was held. The Declaration stated that the EU should have the 'capacity for autonomous action', by having 'credible military forces' at its disposal, so as to be able to respond to international crises. It was therefore no longer WEU but the EU itself that should be endowed with the appropriate infrastructure for undertaking military action – that is, action in the absence of the involvement of NATO as such. While the Declaration underlined the signatories' fealty to the Atlantic Alliance, which went without saying for the UK, a large emphasis was put on the need for the EU to engage fully in security and defence matters outside the NATO framework. Decision making was to be exercised by the European Council at the top and, below it, by the Council of Ministers in its 'General Affairs' variant (bringing together the EU's foreign ministers) and also through meetings of the EU's defence ministers. In short, it was a joint call for the EU to adopt what came thereafter to be called its European Security and Defence Policy (ESDP).

The formal justification for the Saint-Malo Declaration was the EU's Treaty of Amsterdam, which had been signed in October 1997 and which entered into force, after its ratification, in May 1999. In general, as regards matters relating to strengthening the CFSP, the substantive advance represented by the Treaty of Amsterdam, by way of amendments to the original Maastricht text, was slight. On the question of a common defence policy, however, there was some new wording. More than a year before Saint-Malo, France and the UK had sharply disagreed during the IGC about whether WEU should be incorporated into the EU. Despite the ensuing stalemate, the Maastricht Treaty's Article J.4, which became Article J.7 in the Treaty of Amsterdam, was rewritten and lengthened. If one reason was to signal the EU's adoption for its own purposes of WEU's Petersberg Declaration, much of the additional text was a diplomatic fudge on the crucial question of whether the EU should have its own defence system. To respect the right of the UK and others to privilege the Atlantic Alliance, certain member states were entitled to 'see their common defence realised in NATO'. On the other hand, under the same article's new wording, the European Council was explicitly authorised, in the event of a consensus emerging in the future, to establish a 'common defence' and to consider 'the integration of the WEU into the Union'. The operative term was 'should the European Council so decide'. At the Saint-Malo summit, fourteen months after the treaty's signature, the British prime minister converted to the cause of the European Council's so deciding.

Although Blair was already prime minister at the time of the initialling of the Treaty of Amsterdam in June 1997, he had been only a month in office and the UK's participation in the IGC had therefore been largely on the Major government's watch. In Saint-Malo, by contrast, Blair was freer to pursue his own agenda. The Kosovo crisis no doubt concentrated his mind, confronting him with the obvious truth that the EU was playing yet again second fiddle to the US on the European continent. Furthermore, there were influential voices in Whitehall, not just in the Foreign Office but pertinently in the Ministry of Defence, expressing the view that the WEU route to a European military capability had become a dead-end. Thus, at a time when there was a growing divergence between the UK and France over policy towards Iraq, a high-water mark was coincidentally reached in a Franco-British rapprochement over the EU's future security and defence.

Following the Saint-Malo Declaration, the European Council set to work in laying the foundations of the ESDP. Meeting in Cologne in June 1999 it formally approved the Saint-Malo approach and set in motion plans for the phasing out of WEU as a defence organisation towards the end of the following year. At its next meeting in Helsinki in December 1999 the European Council buckled down to the preliminary details. As the result of a proposal tabled jointly by France and the UK and backed by Italy, 'Headline Goals' were established under which the EU's member states 'must be able, by 2003, to deploy within sixty days and sustain for at least one year military forces of up to 50–60,000 persons capable of the full range of Petersberg tasks' – that is, ranging from humanitarian and rescue tasks, through peacekeeping, to combat tasks, including peacemaking. There was no understanding in Helsinki that these forces, put together on a cooperative ad hoc basis, would have any pretension to constitute a rapid reaction force in the full sense of the term (such as NATO's ARRC). Nor was there any aim to establish either permanent ESDP headquarters (as had been done for the Eurocorps) or to have separate operational planning staff (that is, separate from the operational planning staff available either in SHAPE – NATO's Supreme Headquarters Allied Powers Europe – or nationally). At WEU ministerial meetings held in Porto and Marseilles in May and November 2000 respectively, arrangements were agreed for the transfer to the EU of WEU's military-crisis management functions. Established on the EU side in the course of 2000 were its Military Committee and its Political and Security Committee. The Commission acquired permanent military staff. However, in line with the European Council's position in Helsinki, it was accepted that contingency planning for military operations, and operational command when deployment occurred, would be carried out either from within SHAPE or else by mixes of national headquarters, typically in the latter case for lower-level Petersberg tasks involving no significant loan of NATO assets.

This consensus was to be fractured in April 2003, at the height of the tensions between France and the US over policy towards Iraq, when France, Germany, Belgium, and Luxembourg called for a number of ESDP initiatives including the setting up of a separate EU operational planning unit. A year later a compromise was struck when the UK accepted a limited role for such a unit.

From the standpoint of France's and the UK's respective relations with the US, the transfer from WEU to the EU of the former's military-crisis-management functions was a sensitive affair. In Washington both the Clinton administration and Congress had been surprised by the Saint-Malo Declaration. Albright was the strongest in expressing reservations and warnings, which were embodied in the injunction of the 'three Ds' – no discrimination against NATO's non-EU European members, no duplication of effort or capabilities, and no decoupling of European security from that of North America. However, in the course of 1999 the Clinton administration came to terms with the new development, especially when some semantics were cleared up. Under the Saint-Malo Declaration, if EU military action was to be undertaken, it was 'where NATO as a whole is not engaged'. But six months later in Cologne this wording was changed by the European Council to 'without prejudice to NATO'. This could be read to imply that there was no need on the EU's side to make a first call on the Atlantic Alliance, a position associated in many minds with France. It was a sign of the awareness of American susceptibilities that, at the Helsinki meeting of the European Council at the end of 1999, the wording of the phrase reverted to that of the Saint-Malo Declaration.[27]

In the first years of the twenty-first century, the EU's progress in putting into place 'credible military forces' with a 'capacity for autonomous action' did not meet the promise entertained at the end of 1999 by the European Council. In particular, the 'Headline Goals' proved far too ambitious, notably in respect of capabilities for the top peacemaking end of the Petersberg range of tasks. A lack of economic commitment was one factor acting as a brake on progress. Critically, the successful implementation of the ESDP from 2000 onwards depended on Germany's stepping up its defence spending, but the increased allocation of resources in such a direction was not a priority for the Schröder government.

The credibility of the newly launched ESDP suffered from another shortcoming. Potentially severe limitations governed the adoption of CFSP 'joint actions' or 'common positions' by the EU Council of Ministers, in particular because of the right of individual member states to refer any 'joint action' or 'common position' matter to the European Council for decision by unanimity (Treaty of Amsterdam's Article J.13). The EU's own decision-making process could therefore stymie 'joint actions' to implement the putative ESDP. When the IGC preparing the Treaty of Nice carried out its work in the second half of 2000 under France's presidency, so as to further amend the EU's founding Maastricht Treaty, it was proposed that 'enhanced cooperation' – that is, closer cooperation between a limited number of member states – be allowed for CFSP matters. However, in December when the European Council met in Nice and wound up the IGC, British insistence led to the specific exclusion of 'matters having military or defence implications' from the agreed CFSP 'enhanced cooperation' provisions (Treaty of Nice's Article 1.6). Several years later this British objection was partially waived. For in the EU's constitutional treaty, signed in October 2004, a Declaration allowed for 'structured cooperation' in the defence field between member states with stronger military capabilities. But such cooperation would still fall short of the French ambition for a common European defence.

The European Union and the Other Europe

In the Wake of the Call for a European Confederation

How to extend the Schuman process of European integration to the rest of the continent was the greatest long-term political challenge facing the prosperous countries of Western Europe in the immediate aftermath of the collapse of the Yalta order and the related decision to transform the EC into the EU. Initially there was reluctance in many EU capitals, including Paris, to face fully this challenge. Nonetheless, a first practical step, which was to prove far-reaching, was taken at the European Council's meeting in Dublin in April 1990. It was agreed that bilateral association agreements should be offered to Czechoslovakia, Hungary, and Poland. They were soon to be labelled 'Europe Agreements', to stress their importance and to distinguish them from all of the EC's other association agreements. At the heart of the design of the Europe Agreements were their provisions for establishing FTAs (for industrial goods) on a hub-and-spoke basis between the EC and each of the associated countries, with the tariff dismantlement during the transition period taking place faster on the EC side (normally over five years) than on the side of the associated country (ten years). In addition, the agreements contained provisions for economic and political cooperation, including EC financial assistance and, on the part of the associated country, for the reshaping of national legislation to match the EC's own legislation governing the functioning of the internal market.

The first Europe Agreements were signed in December 1991 with each of the said three countries (constituted as the Visegrád group following a tripartite meeting in the Hungarian town of the same name earlier in the same year). The Europe Agreements with Hungary and Poland came into effect in 1994 after completion of the ratification process. In Czechoslovakia's case, the break-up of the country at the beginning of 1993 into the Czech Republic and Slovakia necessitated the signing of new agreements, thereby delaying their formal EC association. However, for all the countries concerned, the inception of the planned association had started already in March 1992 by virtue of interim trade agreements. Between 1993 and 1995 further Europe Agreements were signed with Bulgaria and Romania, with Estonia, Latvia, and Lithuania, and with Slovenia. And thus, in the rarefied world of Brussels acronyms, the PECOs (Pays d'Europe Centrale et Orientale) came into being.

The Europe Agreements owed much to the EC Commission, and from the start strong backing came from Germany and the UK. If French enthusiasm for these new-style association agreements was not greatly evident in the first half of the 1990s, one reason was a concern that this effort in favour of the formerly communist countries of Central and Eastern Europe could be prejudicial to the EC's preferential ties with countries on the southern shores of the Mediterranean, especially those of the Maghreb. Linked to this concern was a deep-seated feeling in Paris that this extension of EC or EU interests into East–Central Europe served above all German interests. Neither the memory of the *Petite Entente* of the interwar years – a fading memory and an unsuccessful entente – nor the attachment to the special ties between France and Romania – the PECO in the worst shape politically and economically – was sufficient to dispel the feeling that a new sort of *Mitteleuropa* might be created under the umbrella of the EC and, after Maastricht, the EU.

What could not be gainsaid was Germany's position as the dominant trade partner for the PECOs, particularly the important Visegrád group. A radical reorientation from East to West of the direction of the Visegrád countries's foreign trade was taking place, and it was largely (though far from exclusively) to the advantage of Germany. This change had started for Poland and Hungary in the late 1980s; for Czechoslovakia it was at the beginning of the 1990s. Thus, in 1991, when their Europe Agreements were signed, Germany accounted for 57 per cent of the EC-12's total exports to the Visegrád countries and also for 57 per cent of the EC-12's total imports from the three countries. These shares owed only a little to the incorporation of the five eastern Länder into the FRG. If such a pattern of trade flows cannot be linked simplistically to any putative German economic hegemony in Central Europe, they do illustrate why policy makers in Paris saw the Europe Agreements as favouring, through the liberalisation of trade, German interests in the new Europe freed from Soviet control.

Such perceptions were to be echoed in Mitterrand's ruminations in January 1994 as he discussed the fate of his European Confederation idea with the two journalists to whom he had long given privileged access for the chronicling of his presidency:

> As to the Germans, basically, they want a confederation, but for their own purposes. Their only thought is to reconstitute a sort of Austro-Hungarian Empire by reinforcing their domain in *Mitteleuropa* with Poland, Hungary, Bohemia and Slovakia, and Ukraine, as well as with Slovenia and Croatia. For this reason my

confederation was a substitute for their imperialist ambition. Kohl was saying: 'Why share the decisions about the future of these countries when they fall into our sphere, that belonging to the Germans?'[28]

A contentious issue already in 1990 was whether the Europe Agreements should be considered passports to eventual membership of the European organisation that aimed, in its own official rhetoric, to realise 'an ever closer union among the peoples of Europe'. To dampen hopes in Czechoslovakia, Hungary, and Poland, the EC Commission stated in August 1990 that such membership was not among the objectives of the newly proposed agreements. The issue did not go away, however. And less than two years later both Germany and the UK came out in favour of the eastward enlargement of the future EU. In February 1992 – the month when the Maastricht Treaty was signed – the German foreign minister, Genscher, stated in Warsaw that the three Visegrád countries should become members as soon as possible, and he buttressed his argument by pointing out that the Europe Agreements, containing provisions for the removal of all barriers on trade in non-agricultural goods over a ten-year period, meant the path to membership need not be excessively long.[29] Several days later this German position was publicly backed by the British Foreign Secretary, Douglas Hurd, who expressed the hope that such accession would take place by 2000 at the latest.[30]

These German and British views were provocative and, in particular, deliberately at odds with the hardline position that had been adopted by the French president. Until then it had been widely assumed that the Europe Agreements with the Visegrád group of countries would have obviated any real need on their part for membership of the EU before, at the very earliest, sometime in the first decade of the twenty-first century. But even this timing had been strongly opposed by Mitterrand in June 1991 on the occasion of the Assises de la Confédération Européenne, a congress held in Prague to discuss his own fairly nebulous idea of a European Confederation. On the day the congress opened, a French radio station broadcast an interview with him, in which, to justify his idea of a loose confederation, he stressed that it would be 'decades and decades' before countries such as Czechoslovakia, Hungary, and Poland would be ready for accession.[31] This view scarcely endeared him to his host, Havel, the Czech president. Miterrand had no more appetite for eastward enlargement than he did earlier, immediately after the fall of the Berlin Wall, for German unification.

Balladur and the Pact on Stability in Europe

A change in French policy on the question of the EU's eastward enlargement had to await the legislative elections of March 1993, with its landslide victory for the parliamentary right, and the subsequent formation under Balladur of a *cohabitation* government, exercising within limits a considerable measure of freedom in the sphere of foreign policy. This freedom was used largely and imaginatively in the matter of Central and Eastern Europe.

Prior to the legislative elections, both Balladur and the future foreign minister, Juppé, had signalled the need for a change. In a book published in December 1992 Balladur argued that 'the countries of Western Europe … should welcome [these fragile young democracies] into the Community – immediately on the political plane, at the appropriate moment on the economic one', a position which represented some advance on the almost begrudging view that had come to be associated with the French president.[32] In March 1993, speaking in his capacity as the RPR's secretary general, Juppé was more forthright when he explicitly distanced himself from Mitterrand's controversial 'decades and decades' remark made nine months earlier.[33] However, the real move forward occurred a month later when the prime minister outlined his government programme in his inaugural policy address to the National Assembly. On the subject of Central and Eastern Europe, he reiterated his view that countries from this part of Europe should be welcomed into the EU, first politically and at a later date economically. The element of surprise came in Balladur's proposal for an international conference on stability in Europe, to be held under EU auspices – a proposal that met initially with bemusement on account of its very vagueness.[34]

Matters were clarified in a French government memorandum – informally labelled the Balladur Plan – which was put before the European Council at its meeting in Copenhagen in June 1993. Proposed was an internationally agreed Pact on Stability in Europe, essentially as an exercise in preventive diplomacy. It concerned those 'Central and Eastern European countries whose vocation was to belong sooner or later to the EU'. The intended fruit of the diplomacy was to go beyond the provisions of both the Helsinki Final Act and the Charter of Paris, and so secure even tighter commitments to the safeguarding of minority rights and the preservation of existing frontiers. The prime example of what the French prime minister had in mind was the safeguarding of the rights of the large Hungarian national minority in Romania, and, on the other side of the coin, the preservation of the existing frontier between Hungary and Romania, with Transylvania put definitively beyond the reach of any Hungarian revanchism. Similar concerns related to relations between Hungary and Slovakia. Furthermore, it was suggested in the memorandum that WEU might admit as 'associate members' those countries with Europe Agreements, in order to bolster security in East–Central Europe.[35]

The great advance made at the Copenhagen meeting of the European Council in June 1993 was its recognition that the proper end of the Europe Agreements was indeed EU membership. What came to be called the Copenhagen criteria for accession were drawn up at this meeting. As to the Balladur Plan, it was decided that full consideration should be given to it when the European Council convened anew in Brussels six months later. For France – Mitterrand, Balladur, and Juppé – the significance of the Copenhagen meeting was that there were no longer any French objections of principle to the EU's preparing plans for eastward enlargement, provided it took place in a stable geopolitical framework.

The European Council's meeting in Brussels in December 1993 took place only six weeks after the Maastricht Treaty entered into force. It was decided that the Balladur Plan should be adopted as one of the EU's first 'joint actions' (Treaty Articles J.1 and J.3). The inaugural meeting of the EU-sponsored Conference on Stability in Europe accordingly took place in Paris in May 1994. The participants, effectively headed by the EU-12 and the Europe Agreement countries, comprised thirty-nine of the CSCE's fifty-two member states. Two regional 'round tables' were at the heart of the negotiations. One brought together the three Baltic states and Poland (because of its sometimes troubled relation with Lithuania). At the other 'round table' were Bulgaria, the Czech Republic, Hungary, Romania, Slovakia, and again Poland. The two groups accounted therefore for seven of the eight PECOs that were to join the EU in 2004. The purpose of the 'round tables' was to win agreements to a series of bilateral treaties on the respect of minority rights and the intangibility of frontiers, which were then to be brought together under the overarching Pact on Stability in Europe. In March 1995, when the conference's closing meeting was held in Paris, a treaty was signed between Hungary and Slovakia. Hungary and Romania made a joint declaration expressing their intention to come to an agreement, and their bilateral treaty was to be signed in September 1996. The Pact on Stability was signed by all participants; and nearly a hundred bilateral good-neighbourliness and cooperation accords, predating the conference, were included in a list annexed to the pact.

The Pact on Stability in Europe had its detractors. At the outset the Balladur Plan was viewed with suspicion in both Warsaw and Prague. For the Poles the view was that the French initiative was a needless distraction that risked delaying the EU's eastward enlargement – Poland's accession application was lodged in April 1994 only a month before the conference opened. The one big fear over the country's post-1945 borders had related to the Oder–Neisse Line, but this fear had finally been put to rest by the signing of the German–Polish frontier treaty in November 1990. There was no desire whatsoever in Warsaw to question the country's post-1945 border with Lithuania, while any concerns for 'ethnic' Poles in Lithuania or the Czech Republic were not judged to warrant bilateral treaties. In Prague there was also the worry that EU enlargement could be delayed. In addition, the sensitive issue of the Sudetenland Germans in the context of Czech–German relations had long made for an aversion to any idea of legally enshrined minority rights. For the small fraction of the Sudetenland Germans who had not taken the route of forced exile in 1945–46 and their descendants, the strongly expressed view held in Prague was that appropriate safeguards for their protection lay in the equal rights enjoyed by all Czech citizens. Russia was the other country to seriously question the French initiative as adopted by the EU at the end of 1993. The ground for Moscow's objection at the time was that the EU's 'joint action' usurped the CSCE's prerogatives. However, the Pact on Stability in Europe, after its signature in 1995, was formally entrusted to the OSCE for its safeguarding and implementation.

Even if there was a gap between the rhetoric of the Balladur Plan and the reality of the more limited outcome in 1995–96, the pact did contribute to the creation of a more stable international climate in Central and Eastern Europe. For Hungary and Slovakia, it facilitated the long diplomatic process that led to their EU accession in 2004, and it eased the path too for Romania's accession in 2007. A side effect, moreover, of the Balladur Plan was WEU's decision in May 1994 to admit Bulgaria, the Czech Republic, Estonia, Hungary, Latvia, Lithuania, Poland, Romania, and Slovakia not as 'associate members' – the French prime minister's recommendation – but at least as 'associate partners'. Although the significance of this move was overshadowed by the launching of NATO's 'Partnership for Peace' programme at the beginning of the same year and, more importantly, by Clinton's diplomatic drive that led to Poland, Hungary, and the Czech Republic actually becoming members of NATO in March 1999, the modest WEU step was another element in the making of a more secure Central and Eastern Europe.

In France itself the initiative launched by Balladur in April 1993, combined with Juppé's efforts in the following two years to adapt French foreign policy to the changed circumstances in Central and Eastern Europe, encouraged a more positive attitude towards the EU's eastward enlargement. Furthermore, fears about the consequences of such enlargement, especially those pertaining to its effects on the EU budget and the CAP, began to be put in a more measured perspective. An example was the careful and detailed study undertaken by the Observatoire Français des Conjonctures Economiques (OFCE) – arguably the country's leading economic think tank – at the behest of the Senate committee dealing with EU affairs.[36] A sign of the times, moreover, appeared to be Chirac's stance. He had already come out in favour of eastward enlargement in 1992. Then, in the summer of 1994, when he opened his presidential-election campaign with the first of two short books outlining his proposed policies, he beat the same drum, declaring grandiloquently that 'the East was our new frontier'.[37]

Forgetting Mickiewicz

Poland is the country to the east of the Elbe with which France has had the longest and deepest historical links. Nancy's jewel, the Place Stanislas, recalls the association in the person of Stanislas Leszczyński, the eighteenth-century king of Poland, whose daughter, Marie, married Louis XV, and who became Duke of Lorraine after being deprived for a second time of the Polish crown. Earlier, in relatively happier times for Poland, the future Henri III, king of France, had briefly served as the Polish monarch as the result of a royal election swayed by his mother, Catherine de' Medici. If Catholicism made for political affinities between the two countries in the early modern period, these affinities survived the French Revolution at a time when Poland as a state no longer existed. Thus, Napoleon created the short-lived Duchy of Warsaw, while Prince Józef Poniatowski commanded a resurrected Polish army as part of the French emperor's military coalition in the campaigns against both Austria and Russia, before being made a Marshal of France at the Battle of Leipzig where he died covering Napoleon's retreat. Later in the nineteenth century Paris was home to many of the exiled Polish elite, including – apart from Frédéric Chopin, whose father was French – the Polish poet and patriot, Adam Mickiewicz, who held a chair at the Collège de France alongside Jules Michelet and Edgar Quinet. If at the Paris Peace Conference in 1919 France was particularly supportive of the newly created states of Czechoslovakia and Yugoslavia as well as a greedily expansionist Romania, this went hand in hand with the strongest of French support for the political rebirth of Poland. And, following Hitler's seizure of Danzig and invasion of Poland, the immediate trigger of the wider conflict was the longstanding Franco–Polish alliance, sealed against Germany in 1921, together with the British guarantee given to Poland as late as March 1939.

De Gaulle had a strong feeling for Poland's past and present. As a young army captain, he had been a member of General Weygand's military mission to Warsaw from 1919 to 1921. He witnessed the fierce and ultimately successful five-month war against the Bolsheviks; conducted by Józef Piłsudski at the head of the new Polish army in the spring and summer of 1920, the war culminated in the 'miracle on the Vistula'. If in 1944 de Gaulle's visit to Moscow resulted in the signing of a Franco-Soviet Treaty of Alliance of no great value, it was partly due to his refusal to acquiesce to Stalin's demand that France accord full diplomatic recognition to the Lublin Committee, the Soviet-controlled puppet government claiming to be Poland's lawful authority. Later, on the occasion of his state visit to communist Poland in 1967, de Gaulle angered his host, Władysław Gomułka, by declaring in public in Gdańsk (the former Danzig) that Poles should raise up their heads and look to a longer-term future when they would find that the obstacles that presently appeared insurmountable could be pushed away.[38] The day beforehand, when staying at the Wawel Castle in Cracow, the French president had expressed with greater clarity to Peyrefitte – his Boswell-like confidant – the nature of these hopes:

All my life I have acted as if (*comme si*) the imagined might be realised. Still, this sort of wilfulness has not always failed me ... Today I am acting as if my message to the people of Eastern Europe is destined to be heard in these countries as well as in France. I am fully aware that these regimes are totalitarian. But here I am sowing seeds that, along with others, could perhaps germinate in twenty or thirty years' time ... The young Poles of today will shake off the Soviet yoke. It is inevitable. The role of France is to help by giving them courage.[39]

For all his belief in the virtue of quixotic endeavour, de Gaulle could scarcely have imagined that the young Cardinal Archbishop of Cracow – the incumbent of the cathedral on the other side of the Wawel courtyard, the 47-year-old Karol Wojtyła – would later play such an extraordinary role as Pope John Paul II in putting an end to the Yalta divide. On that day in September 1967 the French president had hoped to be welcomed into the cathedral by the archbishop. But the latter was purposefully absent, for the instructions from the Polish Primate, Cardinal Stefan Wyszyński, was that the Church should lend no support to Gomułka's regime by blessing the French visit. In Cracow the regime itself gave proof of its customary prudence by ensuring that de Gaulle's address at the Jagiellonian University, with its praise of the great university's symbolic role during all the periods of foreign occupation of Poland, was restricted to no more than a handful of listeners.[40]

Mitterrand also paid much attention to Polish affairs; this was at a time when de Gaulle's earlier hopes for Poland's future were beginning to be realised, sooner than predicted, in the shape of the Solidarity trade-union movement, backed by many of the Polish intelligentsia. He was worried that the instability affecting Poland could be the cause of wider disorder in Europe. In December 1985 he received General Jaruzelski – the Polish prime minister and enforcer of martial law from December 1981 to July 1983 – at the Elysée Palace on the occasion of the latter's stopover in Paris when returning from Algiers to Warsaw. This private visit, requested by Jaruzelski, led to no special help for the embattled Polish regime, and during their meeting Mitterrand insisted on the importance of trade-union rights for Solidarity. Yet the French president's readiness to talk with Jaruzelski was widely criticised; even the prime minister, Fabius, signalled his displeasure.[41] Four years later Mitterrand was concerned by the geopolitical implications of the fast changing situation in Poland. In July 1989, only ten days after Gorbachev had signalled that the country was free to choose its new government following the previous month's dramatic semi-free elections, Mitterrand – on Attali's testimony – warned Bush (then in Paris for the celebrations of the bicentenary of the French Revolution and the Group of Seven meeting) that an independent Poland, dividing the USSR from the GDR, spelt trouble.[42] In 1990, as has been shown, his worry about continental instability and Poland's future was again in evidence when he insisted successfully on the need for a reinforced German commitment to the intangibility of the Oder–Neisse Line. Long-term security concerns also underscored France's decision to join with Germany and Poland in holding from August 1991 onwards regular annual meetings of their foreign and defence ministers, thereby forming what came to be called the Weimar Group or Triangle, since the first meeting was held on the anniversary day of Goethe's birth in the renowned Thuringian town.

Geopolitical concerns made Mitterrand a prudent man. On a quite different plane, Mitterrand in particular and French Socialists in general had a lack of instinctive sympathy for prominent features of the Polish patriotism that fired the Solidarity movement and, more generally, the long internal opposition since 1944 to the imposition of Soviet communism. A cocktail containing strong, conservative Catholicism, anti-Marxism, and pro-Americanism was not one to naturally endear itself to the hearts and minds of many on the French Left. Of importance here was the PS's own ideological hardening in the 1970s. Its doctrinal refusal of 'social democracy' – favoured by West Germany's SPD since the Bad Godesberg turning point in 1959 – went hand in hand with a neo-Marxism that distanced it from the defunct SFIO. The divide in 1989 between France's political establishment and the new Poland assumed a curious symbolic representation when a large group of newly elected Solidarity-backed members of the Polish Senate and Sejm travelled to France at the time of the celebrations of the French Revolution's bicentenary; however, they came not to celebrate the fall of the Bastille, but instead to pay their respect to the thousands of Catholics massacred in the Vendée in 1793 after rising against the Revolution.[43]

Mitterrand himself was dismayed in 1989 by the turn of events in Poland and elsewhere insofar as the newly liberated peoples appeared to be turning their backs on socialism and not just on a corrupted communism. To his mind, and typically of the spirit of a Jaurès, both socialism and communism were of the same commendable trunk, having sprung essentially from the French Revolution. Sharing a press conference in October 1989 with the Spanish prime minister and fellow socialist, Felipe González, on the day following the proclamation of the new Hungarian Republic and mass demonstrations against the East German regime in Leipzig, he pondered though refused the idea that 'these peoples would become lost to the point of rejecting the best of what they had received'.[44] In Warsaw, at the same moment, the non-communist government headed by Mazowiecki had been in office for two months, with a finance minister, Leszek Balcerowicz, bent on a radical policy of liberal economic reform. Mitterrand had long supported the cause of intellectual freedom in communist Europe. But this liberalism was not to his taste. Mitterrand's own leanings were largely in keeping with the mind frame of many of France's post-war intelligentsia, with their predilection – so fashionable up to the 1970s – for either Marxism or a 'third way' political philosophy that brooked no contamination of socialism by liberal capitalism. Between 1947 and 1989 Poland's most influential émigré periodical publication was Jerzy Giedroyć's *Kultura*, and it was based in Paris. However, Czesław Miłosz, after defecting to the West and choosing Paris as his home, quit the French capital in 1960 for California, since he had been ostracised by the largely Marxist-inclined Parisian intelligentsia.

Chirac's world of ideas differed from that of his predecessor. And his enthusiasm for the EU's enlargement as manifest in 1994 did not appear disingenuous. It was manifest anew in September 1996 when he paid a state visit to Poland and, in an address to the two chambers of the Polish parliament, affirmed his wish that Poland should join the EU as early as 2000. But, with the advent of the Socialist-led *cohabitation* Government in June 1997, the French attitude towards the EU's future eastward enlargement began to appear less positive. In the person of Védrine, the new foreign minister, there was more than an echo of Mitterrand's circumspection: less than a month before his appointment to the Quai d'Orsay, he had remarked at a colloquium in Paris that 'the countries of Central Europe, liberated from communism, represented the complete opposite of our Europe'.[45]

However, the first sign of a waning in Chirac's good will was not in connection with the enlargement of the EU but rather with that of NATO. As from July 1997, when the North Atlantic Council at its Madrid summit meeting agreed to NATO's enlargement to include Poland, the Czech Republic, and Hungary, the French president dragged his feet in approving Clinton's transformation of the Atlantic Alliance. If Chirac's openly stated objection in 1997 was the exclusion from this first round of enlargement of Romania, he and Védrine looked askance, more generally, at a policy that aimed to secure the stability of much of formerly communist East-Central Europe in a firmly transatlantic framework, a year before the EU accession negotiations had even started; and also, as a longer-term aim, to extend NATO's borders eastwards to encompass the Baltic states.

A few years later Poland received a jolt when the European Council met in Nice in December 2000 under France's presidency. Treaty changes to the EU's institutional arrangements had to be agreed in advance of the eastward enlargement. The size and composition of the Commission and the European Parliament as well as the QMV weightings in the Council of Ministers were on the agenda. Shaping the negotiations at the start of this bad tempered summit were German requests for an increased representation in the Parliament and an increased QMV weighting. The justification was the country's post-unification population size. Chirac was accommodating over the European Parliament, but refused to budge from the principle of equal QMV weightings for France, Germany, the UK, and Italy. There could be no question of France becoming less important than Germany on the intergovernmental Council of Ministers. Spain and

Poland were also concerned. Since Germany's population was roughly speaking 20 million greater than the populations of France, the UK, or Italy, and Spain's population 20 million less than theirs, the French view was that it would be invidious to give Spain a QMV weighting that was substantially less than that accorded to the 'Big Four'. However, despite the fact that Poland's population was nearly the same as Spain's, Chirac proposed that Poland's QMV weighting should be less than the relatively generous one offered to Spain. His reason was that Poland would be a new member state, without the experience that comes with time and hence seniority. The immediate Polish reaction was to seek help from the German Chancellor, and Schröder prevailed upon the French president to change his mind. But damage had been done in distinguishing between two categories of EU member. The second-class member on this occasion would have been Poland, a country bound by strong ties to the US and to NATO, to which it now belonged.

'Old Europe'

In the negotiations in 2002–4 over the EU's constitutional treaty, Spain and Poland were to strive hard to retain their favourable QMV weightings. Eventually, however, a new system based on simple majorities and population sizes was agreed. During the same years Chirac returned to his seniority principle, pressing Poland and other accession countries from Central and Eastern European to respect the due rank of the EU's older established member states. The issue was the question of the EU's policy in the international crisis over Iraq, once Bush had set his sights on regime change in Baghdad, while Chirac, forcefully and flamboyantly supported by de Villepin as foreign minister, came to adopt an opposing stance.

Differences over Iraq came to a head in January and February 2003. On 22 January – the day of the Franco-German celebrations in Paris and Versailles of the fortieth anniversary of the Elysée Treaty – the US Secretary of Defence, Donald Rumsfeld, used a press conference in Washington to make his barbed remark about 'old Europe', identified dismissively with France and Germany, which he contrasted with the new 'NATO Europe' whose 'centre of gravity' was 'shifting to the east'.[46] In France earlier on the same day the message had been different: the French president told the German and French parliaments assembled in Versailles that France and Germany in unison should remain the 'centre of gravity' of the EU after its enlargement in May 2004 (the enlargement decision having been taken by the European Council in December 2002). 'This reestablished Europe, richer in its diversity but also more heterogeneous, will have need more than ever of the Franco-German motor', averred Chirac. Elsewhere in his address, referring to the situation in Iraq, he insisted that 'the United Nations is the sole framework for a legitimate solution'.[47]

One European politician peeved by this reassertion of the primacy of the privileged Franco-German partnership was the Spanish prime minister, José Maria Aznar. In response to an initiative taken by the Brussels-based editorial office of the European edition of *The Wall Street Journal*, he persuaded first Blair and then other European leaders who were also favourable to the American position on Iraq to make a joint declaration, emphasising the importance they attached to relations with the US. Besides the Spanish and British prime ministers, the signatories of this 'Letter of Eight', published a little over a week after the Elysée Treaty celebrations, included, from EU member states, the prime ministers of Italy, Portugal, and Denmark and, from the states to join the EU in 2004, the prime ministers of Poland and Hungary and the president of the Czech Republic.[48] Less than week later a similar declaration from ten other Central and Eastern European countries, the 'Vilnius Ten', was published at American instigation. Of the three Central European countries signing the more influential 'Letter of Eight', Poland counted for the most; Hungary was quick afterwards to qualify the extent of its support, while, in the case of the Czech Republic, the willing signatory was Havel and it represented his last important act as head of state (standing down from office at the end of the very day the declaration was published) – earlier the Czech prime minister had balked at the idea of signature.[49]

For two weeks bad relations simmered between what were now being called the 'old' Europe and the 'new' Europe, making a mockery of any pretence that the EU might aspire to a meaningful CFSP in respect of the Middle East. Public opinion in Europe took largely the French and German side. A day of mass protest against the looming war in Iraq was held across Europe on 15 February. In a striking and extravagant remark, Strauss-Kahn was to declare that the 'European nation' had been born on that day; the immense crowds on the streets of London, Rome, Paris, and Berlin revealed at last, he said, a public consciousness of belonging to the 'European nation', thereby signalling the need for an internationally more powerful EU.[50] Chirac's anger with Poland and other Central and Eastern European countries brimmed over on 18 February when a special meeting of the European Council was held in Brussels to discuss the Iraqi crisis. The divide between France and the UK could not have been clearer. Blair signalled his displeasure that that the Greek presidency had not seen fit to invite the ten countries joining the EU in 2004, as well as the three remaining candidates, Bulgaria, Romania, and Turkey. At his press conference the French president berated Poland and the other states from Central and Eastern Europe that had lent their name to either the 'Letter of Eight' or the 'Vilnius Ten' declaration: 'an opportunity had been missed to keep quiet', he said contemptuously, for 'these countries were, to be frank, not very well mannered (*pas très bien élevés*) and also somewhat unconscious of the dangers entailed in a too rapid alignment on the American position'.[51]

Warsaw's reaction was to signal diplomatically that Poland shared neither Chirac's nor Rumsfeld's conception of 'old Europe', to refuse both the American's black-and-white dichotomy and the Frenchman's implicit presumption that the position taken in the 'Letter of Eight', even by the EU member-state signatories, was somehow non-European because it diverged from the joint French and German position. When the EU was enlarged in May 2004, the invasion of Iraq had already gone seriously awry, and these heated difficulties between France and, on the other hand, Poland and other accession states belonged largely to the past. Yet if it had been a passing storm, it was one with a lesson of wide import. In the sphere of foreign policy and thus also of security and defence, an EU with fifteen member states at the very start of the twenty-first century was no longer an entity readily led by France and Germany. Now any such shared hegemony became even more difficult to exercise in a union with nearly double that membership – as many as twenty-seven after the mini-enlargement of 2007 to include Bulgaria and Romania – especially because of the strong Atlanticist leanings of some of the newcomers in 2004.

Disenchantment with High Politics and the 2005 Referendum

It has been shown that disenchantment with economic liberalism swayed the result of the May 2005 referendum on the EU's constitutional treaty. Disenchantment with the high politics of European integration, as long practised by France, also played its part. For instance, not only were many of the electorate already disappointed with the European single currency, but the ECB was viewed as the culprit, at least insofar as a connection was drawn between unemployment and the ECB's monetary policy. Mitterrand had intended that the creation of the ECB would lead above all to a clipping of the unified Germany's wings and to an end of France's subordination in the monetary sphere. But if its creation did lead necessarily to the demise of the once proud Bundesbank, that amounted to no magic solution for France's own economic problems. A striking feature of the presidential election campaign in late 2006 and early 2007, a year and a half after the referendum, was that Sarkozy and the PS's Ségolène Royal, the two candidates who won through to the second round, were heaping opprobrium on the policies of an EU-wide central bank whose creation had been first proposed by Balladur in 1988 and so much desired by Mitterrand, especially after 1989. It was almost as if they regretted the Franco-German deal struck in 1991. Another issue in the referendum was clearly enlargement. While the 'Polish plumber' had come to represent all that was quintessentially wrong in the enlarged single market, the fracas in 2003 over the EU and Iraq had reinforced the view that eastward enlargement was serving more to boost the international influence and interests of Germany or the Anglo-Saxon world, or of both, rather than those of France. And there was also the red herring of Turkish accession. In general, the EU's constitutional treaty neither favoured nor prejudiced Turkey's chances in the long term of membership, but the correct perception that accession talks were in the offing reminded voters that in important respects Schuman's Europe was long dead and gone.

A diffuse sense of loss of French ownership of the 'European construction' had taken hold. The gradual, growing accumulation of various powers in the hands of the EU's central institutions – be it the European Commission, the European Court of Justice, the ECB, or even the European Parliament – now sat uneasily with the French idea of the integrity of the nation state, as shaped by the Bourbon monarchy, the Revolution, and Napoleon. Crucially, perhaps, confidence in the longevity and power of the Franco-German partnership had waned. Seen from this perspective, the Maastricht Treaty, signed more than a decade earlier, had marked the end of a long era, inaugurated by de Gaulle and Adenauer, when France in alliance with Germany could assume to provide political leadership to Europe almost by right.

Notes

1. An internal memorandum written by Hannoun in 1991 provides a pithy résumé of the franc fort doctrine – see Aeschimann and Riché, *La Guerre de sept ans*, 82–83.
2. For the exchange between Mitterrand and Séguin over the Maastricht Treaty's design for monetary union, see Séguin, *Intinéraire dans la France d'en bas, d'en haut et d'ailleurs*, 391–94.
3. For the franc's difficulties in September 1992 and the 'sweetheart deal', see Connolly, *The Rotten Heart of Europe*, 141–47, 149–52, 176–83; Aeschimann and Riché, *La Guerre de sept ans*, 142–60.
4. André Szász, *The Road to European Monetary Union*, Basingstoke, 1999, 191.
5. For the ERM's nearly terminal crisis, see Connolly, *The Rotten Heart of Europe*, 291–338; Aeschimann and Riché, *La Guerre de sept ans*, 205–35; Szász, *The Road to Monetary Union*, 185–95.
6. *Financial Times*, 29 January 2007.
7. Cohen (ed), *Mitterrand et la sortie de la guerre froide*, 91, 94, 97, 98, 102, 103–5; Brendan Simms, *Unfinest Hour: Britain and the Destruction of Bosnia*, London, 2001, 4.
8. For the blame cast by Dumas on Germany and the Vatican, see Paul-Marie de La Gorce, 'Les divergences franco-allemandes mises à nu', *Le Monde diplomatique*, September 1993; Roland Dumas, *Le Fil et la pelote. Mémoires*, Paris, 1996, 352–95.
9. Cohen (ed.), *Mitterrand et la sortie de la guerre froide*, 96; Dyson and Featherstone, *The Road to Maastricht*, 249–50, 443. See also Anthony Seldon, *Major: A Political Life*, London, 1997, 304–5.
10. Attali, *Verbatim*, vol. 3, 450.
11. Patrice Canivez, 'François Mitterrand et la guerre en ex-Yugoslavie', in Cohen (ed.), *Mitterrand et la sortie de la guerre froide*, 61–89.
12. Jacques Chirac, 'Devant le massacre. La démission de l'Europe', *Le Figaro*, 1 June 1992.

13. Favier and Martin-Roland, *La Décennie Mitterrand*, vol. 4, 344–48; Lacouture, *Mitterrand*, vol. 2, 419–22.

14. France's ambassador to Croatia from 1992 to 1994, Georges-Marie Chenu, was to recount how the Zagreb embassy investigated claims of the existence of Serb 'extermination camps' – such a claim having been made by Izetbegović to Mitterrand during their brief meeting in Sarajevo – and how this led to the ambassador's informing Paris in early July about the Omarska and Manjaca concentration camps; the reporting of this intelligence was followed in early August by the dispatch to Paris of a list, by name and locality, of fifty-seven concentration camps, holding an estimated 95,000 prisoners. Chenu's bald assertion in 1997 was that he, as France's ambassador, had received no response at all from Paris, whether from the Elysée, Matignon, or the Quai d'Orsay. See Cohen (ed.), *Mitterrand et la sortie de la guerre froide*, 89–92.

15. Ibid., 83–84. See also Simms, *Unfinest Hour*, 110–16.

16. Richard Holbrooke, *To End a War*, New York, 1998, 65, 67–70; Gilles Delafon and Thomas Sancton, *Dear Jacques, Cher Bill. Au Cœur de l'Elysée et de la Maison Blanche, 1995–1999*, Paris, 1999, 63–90.

17. Delafon and Sancton, *Dear Jacques, Cher Bill*, 91–104; Madeleine Albright, *Madam Secretary: A Memoir*, New York, 2003, 186–90.

18. Delafon and Sancton, *Dear Jacques, Cher Bill*, 208–13, 311–54; Albright, *Madam Secretary*, 284–87.

19. Hubert Védrine, *France in an Age of Globalization*, Washington D.C., 2001, 2–4; Hubert Védrine, *Face à l'hyperpuissance. Textes et discours, 1995–2003*, Paris, 2003, 113.

20. Yves Michaud, *Chirac dans le texte : la parole et l'impuissance*, Paris, 2004, 112–21.

21. Tim Judah, *Kosovo : War and Revenge*, New Haven, 2000, 182, 267–69; Wesley K. Clark, *Waging Modern War: Bosnia, Kosovo and the Future of Combat*, New York, 2001, 238–39, 272–73, 356; Alex J. Bellamy, *Kosovo and International Society*, Basingstoke, 2002, 92, 161–62; Albright, *Madam Secretary*, 402; Robert Kagan, *Paradise and Power: America and Europe in the New World Order*, London, 2003, 46–49.

22. 'Vers une nouvelle architecture de sécurité en Europe', in *Livre blanc sur la défense 1994*, Paris, 1994, 59–71.

23. *Le Monde*, 24 February 1996.

24. *Le Monde*, 25 January 1997.

25. Michael Quinlan, *European Defense Cooperation: Asset or Threat to NATO?*, Washington D.C., 2001, 19. For details, see Delafon and Sancton, *Dear Jacques, Cher Bill*, 137–62, 181–218, 237–310.

26. Cohen (ed.), *Mitterrand et la sortie de la guerre froide*, 186.

27. For a succinct account of the Saint-Malo Declaration and the ESDP as framed by the European Council in Cologne and Helsinki, see Quinlan, *European Defense Cooperation*, 28–51.

28. Favier and Martin-Roland, *La Décennie Mitterrand*, vol. 4, 200.

29. *Financial Times*, 5 February 1992.

30. *Financial Times*, 9 February 1992.

31. *Le Monde*, 14 June 1991.

32. Edouard Balladur, *Dictionnaire de la réforme*, Paris 1992, 116.

33. *Le Monde*, 6 March 1993.

34. *Le Monde*, 10 April 1993.

35. Agence Europe, 'Conseil européen de Copenhague, 21–22 juin 1993', *Europe Documents*, no. 1844/45, 24 June 1993; 'Mémorandum sur le Pacte de stabilté en Europe', *Europe Documents*, no. 1846, 26 June 1993. See also Edouard Balladur, *Deux Ans à Matignon*, Paris, 1995, 119–22.

36. Later published as a book: Jacques Le Cacheux (ed.), *Europe, la nouvelle vague. Perspectives économiques de l'élargissement*, Paris, 1996.

37. Jacques Chirac, *Une nouvelle France. Réflexions I*, Paris, 1994, 97–103.

38. Lacouture, *De Gaulle*, vol. 3, 538–42.

39. Peyrefitte, *C'était de Gaulle*, vol. 1, 47.
40. Ibid., vol. 1, 46–47; vol. 3, 288–98.
41. Mitterrand judged Jaruzelski to be a true Polish patriot, as did, it may be remarked, Pope John Paul II – see Tad Szulc, *Pope John Paul II: The Biography*, New York, 1995, 389–90.
42. Attali, *Verbatim*, vol. 3, 283.
43. Jacques Rupnik, 'La France de Mitterrand et les pays de l'Europe du Centre-Est', in Cohen (ed.), *Mitterrand et la sortie de la guerre froide*, 210.
44. Franz-Olivier Giesbert, *François Mitterrand. Une vie*, Paris, 1996, 614–15. See also Rupnik, 'La France de Mitterand et les pays de l'Europe du Centre-Est', 209.
45. Cohen (ed.), *Mitterrand et la sortie de la guerre froide*, 222.
46. *Financial Times*, 24 January 2003.
47. *Le Figaro*, 23 January 2003.
48. 'Europe and America must stand united', *The Wall Street Journal Europe*, 30 January 2003.
49. For the preparation of the 'Letter of Eight' and the opposing French position, see five successive 'Comment & analysis' pages in the *Financial Times* from 26 May to 30 May 2003, including an interview with Chirac.
50. Dominique Strauss-Kahn, 'Une nation est née', *Le Monde*, 26 February 2003.
51. *Le Figaro*, 19 February 2003.

EPILOGUE

A historical narrative extending forward virtually to the present at the time of its writing might be cheekily compared to Musil's epic novel *The Man without Qualities*, inasmuch as both come to an abrupt and unfinished end. Very recent events may well be too fluid or open-ended to assume any secure or assured meaning. This fluidity may be greatly to the advantage of the novel, but for the quite different, prosaic work of contemporary history it cannot but be a source of imperfection.

Still, in this historical narrative, substance has been lent to the continuities announced at the outset: the continuities between the Fourth and the Fifth Republics in respect of policies for the shaping of Europe, or at least the continent's western part; and, in the course of the Fifth Republic, the continuities from one French president to another. There have been the discontinuities too, as witness the differing views of international relations espoused by a de Gaulle or a Chirac, once their focus was the world beyond Europe's borders. In particular, the place of the United Nations in the French scheme of things was to change radically over time.[1]

Yet it was the founder of the Fifth Republic who bequeathed an approach to the 'construction of Europe' that was to prove constant on the French side. Ironically, in view of the patent lack of sympathy between the two men, de Gaulle and Mitterrand proved to be fellow spirits during their respective presidencies. By the 1980s, in the service of France's national interest, the younger of the two statesmen had pushed to a fine art both a concern with Germany and a fruitful use of the European Council – that quintessentially intergovernmental institution already conceived by de Gaulle in the Fouchet proposals of the early 1960s. In the year of Mitterrand's death, Védrine, the future foreign minister who long served as his foreign-policy advisor, could pithily write that the 'Europe of the 1980s was the pure product of a modern form of enlightened despotism'.[2]

Notes for this epilogue begin on page 329.

There was also more than a whiff of enlightened despotism at the beginning of the twenty-first century, first, when Chirac availed of the choice given to him by the European Council in 2001 to designate the President of the Convention for the Future of Europe by entrusting the task to a safe pair of hands in the person of Giscard d'Estaing, and, secondly, in the latter's conduct of the proceedings that eventually led in 2004 to the signing of the EU's constitutional treaty. At heart, in Chirac's and even Giscard's eyes, this was a constitution for an organised 'society of states', rather than for a full-blown federal union of the American kind.

But at the time of the 2005 referendum on the constitutional treaty, some in France were beginning to wonder whether this view of what was happening was really true. For the anxieties about both the economic and geopolitical implications of the new treaty, to which attention has been given in this book, were sometimes allied to the question of whether the principle *'faire l'Europe sans défaire la France'* was still operative. The process of European integration in the second half of the twentieth century period was not driven mainly by 'spillover' – pace the theories of some political scientists, first expressed in the late 1950s. There was no process of one step in integration leading almost ineluctably to another, down a path whose terminus ad quem was the emergence of a Westphalian-type federal state under the banner of 'Europe', replacing a collection of motley outdated nation states. Nonetheless, if this has not happened, the feeling did exist in France at the time of the referendum that the EU had somehow imperceptibly metamorphosed into a different type of political animal than that denoted by the term 'federation of nation states'. Perhaps, as has recently been suggested, the nature of the present EU may be best understood as some sort of neo-medieval empire in a post-Westphalian setting, an empire in which there is still room for powerful states but not autonomous ones.[3]

To return to de Gaulle, he saw the functioning of the EC and his desired European 'Union of States' as a sort of 'Archimedes lever' raising France's influence, power, and rank on the European and world stages. Monnet and Schuman had already prepared the way for this leverage at mid-century. For much of the second half of the twentieth century, the 'Archimedes lever' worked successfully, albeit in the shelter of a wider security framework provided largely by NATO and the US. De Gaulle's own vision, it should be added, was predicated on the continued existence of the Atlantic Alliance, notably at the time of his related proposals for a NATO tripartite directorate and a European 'Union of States'.[4]

However, what was originally planned in the aftermath of the Second World War as a leadership or quasi-hegemonic role falling squarely on France's shoulders was gradually transformed into what was often the exercise of a two-power cooperative hegemony with West Germany for the shaping of Western Europe. This hegemony, tending to be French-led outside the monetary sphere, lasted up to the time of the preparation of the Maastricht Treaty. But the end of the Yalta divide and German unification, coupled with a greater assertiveness in Europe on the part of other national powers – not least the UK – and the further enlargement of the EU itself, changed the international political parameters. Especially with the eastward enlargement of 2004, there was the feeling of the passing of an era. Yet the era's great achievement remained intact: the securing of a real peace between France and Germany after the strains, darkness, and turmoil of the last three decades of the nineteenth century and the first five decades of the twentieth.

This transformation of Franco-German relations in the framework of post-war European integration recalls the deep truth expressed by Hobbes in *Leviathan*, namely that the final cause or end of a 'commonwealth' lies in the achievement of security or the escape from the 'miserable condition of war'. It explains that the abiding and dominant impulse behind France's concern with European union has derived from geopolitical considerations, rather than from any notions of utility maximisation associated with narrowly defined economic advantage. Yet this is not to say that France's interest in the European enterprise has lain essentially in the politics of integration as opposed to the economics of integration. Such a division would be both false and artificial. It is rather to say that the dance has been led by politics, the leading aim being that of tying Germany firmly down under Europe's roof. And thus the achievement of European monetary union, especially after the fall of the Berlin Wall, was always seen in Paris as fulfilling primarily a political end.

For France's future place in the EU, in the wider Europe, and beyond, the present writer can have little of worth to say here, other than point to the likelihood of important developments as a result of the French presidential election in 2007, which brought Sarkozy to power, and Germany's and France's holding the rotating presidency of the EU in, respectively, the first half of 2007 and the second half of 2008. But if history has no lessons, it does pretend to a knowledge that brings meaning to the past, and here it has essentially been the past of France's interest in a half-century effort towards greater European union, set against the background of an earlier past – that of the long bitter times whose successive phases had opened in the summers of 1870, 1914, and 1939.

Notes

1. For judicious remarks on this change of view, see Jean-Claude Casanova, 'France – Etats-Unis. De Charles de Gaulle à Jacques Chirac', *Commentaire* 26(103), 2003, 705–10.
2. Védrine, *Les Mondes de François Mitterrand*, 298.
3. See Jan Zielonka, *Europe as Empire: The Nature of the Enlarged European Union*, Oxford, 2006.
4. For the 'Archimedes lever' imagery, see Peyrefitte, *C'était de Gaulle*, vol. 1, 158–59.

BIBLIOGRAPHY

Works that have been translated into English, in whole or part, are designated by an asterisk.

Acheson, D. *Present at the Creation: My Years in the State Department*, New York, 1969.

Adamthwaite, A. *Grandeur and Misery: France's Bid for Power in Europe, 1914–1940*, London, 1995.

Adenauer, K. *Errinerungen*, 4 vols, Stuttgart, 1965–68.*

Aeschimann, E. and P. Riché. *La Guerre de sept ans. Histoire secrète du franc fort*, Paris, 1996.

Agence Europe. 'Conseil européen de Copenhague, 21–22 juin 1993', *Europe Documents*, no. 1844/45, 24 June 1993.

_____ 'Mémorandum sur le Pacte de stabilité en Europe', *Europe Documents*, no. 1846, 26 June 1993.

_____ 'Rapport du Conseil sur les relations entre l'Union européenne et les pays méditerranéens, en préparation à la conférence qui se déroulera les 27 et 28 novembre à Barcelone', no. 1930/31, *Europe Documents*, 27 April 1995.

Albright, M. *Madam Secretary: A Memoir*, New York, 2003.

Alphand, H. *L'Etonnement d'être. Journal (1939–1973)*, Paris, 1977.

Amouroux, H. *Monsieur Barre*, Paris, 1986.

Aron, R. *Mémoires*, Paris, 1983.*

Association Georges Pompidou (ed.). *Georges Pompidou et l'Europe. Colloque — 25 et 26 novembre 1993*, Brussels, 1995.

Attali, J. *Verbatim*, 3 vols, Paris, 1993–95.

_____ *Europe(s)*, Paris, 1994.

_____ *C'était François Mitterrand*, Paris, 2005.

Auriol, V. *Journal du septennat*, 7 vols, (eds) P. Nora et al., Paris, 1970–80.

Balladur, E. 'Mémorandum sur la construction monétaire européenne', *ECU* 3, 1988, 17–20.

_____ *Passion et longueur de temps. Dialogues avec Jean-Pierre Elkabbach*, Paris, 1989.

_____ *Dictionnaire de la réforme*, Paris, 1992.

_____ *Deux Ans à Matignon*, Paris, 1995.
Baker, J.A. *The Politics of Diplomacy: Revolution, War and Peace, 1989–1992*, New York, 1995.
Bariéty, J. 'Les entretiens de Gaulle-Adenauer de juillet 1960 à Rambouillet. Prélude au plan Fouchet et au traité de l'Elysée', *Revue d'Allemagne et des pays de langue allemande* 29(2), 1997, 167–76.
_____ 'Lectures : Tilo Schabert, *Wie Weltgeschichte gemacht wird. Frankreich und die deutsche Einheit*', *Politique étrangère* 2, 2004, 441–45.
Bariéty, J. and J.-P. Bled (eds). 'Du plan Fouchet au traité franco-allemand de janvier 1963', special number of *Revue d'Allemagne et des pays de langue allemande* 29(2), 1997, 159–362.
Bark, D.L. and D.R. Gress. *A History of West Germany*, 2nd edn, 2 vols, Oxford, 1993.
Barre, R. *Réflexions pour demain*, Paris, 1984.
_____ *Questions de confiance. Entretiens avec Jean-Marie Colombani*, Paris, 1988.
Bauchard, P. *La Guerre des deux roses. Du rêve à la réalité, 1981–1985*, Paris, 1986.
Bavarez, N. *La France qui tombe*, Paris, 2003.
Bell, P.M.H. *France and Britain 1940–1994: The Long Separation*, Harlow, 1997.
Bellamy, A.J. *Kosovo and International Society*, Basingstoke, 2002.
Berstein, S. *La France de l'expansion. La République gaullienne, 1959–1969*, Paris, 1989.*
Berstein, S. and J.-P. Rioux. *La France de l'expansion. L'apogée Pompidou*, Paris, 1995.*
Berstein, S., J.-M. Mayeur, and P. Milza (eds). *Le MRP et la construction européenne*, Brussels, 1993.
Bézias, J.-R. *Georges Bidault et la politique étrangère de la France (Europe, Etats-Unis, Proche-Orient), 1944–1948*, Paris, 2006.
Bidault, G. *D'une résistance à l'autre*, Paris, 1965.*
Blechman, B. and C. Fisher, 'West German security policy and the Franco-German relationship', in R.F. Laird (ed.), *Strangers and Friends: The Franco-German Security Relationship*, London, 1989, 48–71.
Bossuat, G. *L'Europe occidentale à l'heure américaine. Le plan Marshall et l'unité européenne (1945–1952)*, Brussels, 1992.
_____ 'Le président Georges Pompidou et les tentatives de l'Union économique et monétaire', in Association Georges Pompidou (ed.), *Georges Pompidou et l'Europe. Colloque — 25 et 26 novembre 1993*, Brussels, 1995, 405–47.
_____ *Les Aides américaines économiques et militaires à la France, 1938–1960. Une nouvelle image des rapports de la puissance*, Paris, 2001.
_____ *Faire l'Europe sans défaire la France. 60 ans de politique d'unité européenne des gouvernements et des présidents de la République française (1943–2003)*, Brussels, 2005.
Bozo, F. *La Politique étrangère de la France depuis 1945*, Paris, 1997.
_____ *Two Strategies for Europe: De Gaulle, the United States and the Atlantic Alliance*, Lanham, 2001.
_____ *Mitterrand, la fin de la guerre froide et l'unification allemande. De Yalta à Maastricht*, Paris, 2005.
Brandt, W. *Begegnungen und Einsichten. Die Jahre 1960–1975*, Hamburg, 1976.* [Endnote references to the translation: *People and Politics: The Years 1960–1975*, London, 1978].

Bruneteau, B. «*L'Europe nouvelle de Hitler*». *Une illusion des intellectuels de la France de Vichy*, Paris, 2003.

Bull, H. *The Anarchical Society: A Study of Order in World Politics*, 2nd edn, London, 1995.

Bullock, A. *Ernest Bevin: Foreign Secretary, 1945–1951*, London, 1983.

Bush, G. and B. Scowcroft. *A World Transformed*, New York, 1998.

Canivez, P. 'François Mitterrand et la guerre en ex-Yougoslavie', in S. Cohen (ed.), *Mitterrand et la sortie de la guerre froide*, Paris, 1998, 61–105.

Carmoy, G. de. *Les Politiques étrangères de la France, 1944–1966*, Paris, 1967.

Casanova, J.-C. 'France – Etats Unis. De Charles de Gaulle à Jacques Chirac', *Commentaire* 26(103), 2003, 705–10.

Chenaux, P. *Une Europe vaticane? Entre le plan Marshall et les traités de Rome*, Brussels, 1990.

Chirac, J. 'Devant le massacre. La démission de l'Europe', *Le Figaro*, 1 June 1992.

_____ *Une nouvelle France. Réflexions I*, Paris, 1994.

_____ *Mon combat pour la paix. Textes et interventions, 1995–2007*, Paris, 2007.

Clark, W.K. *Waging Modern War: Bosnia, Kosovo and the Future of Combat*, New York, 2001.

Cogan, C.G. *Oldest Allies, Guarded Friends: The United States and France since 1940*, Westport, 1994.

Cohen, A. 'Le plan Schuman de Paul Reuter. Entre communauté nationale et fédération européenne', *Revue française de science politique* 48(5), 1998, 645–63.

Cohen, S. (ed.). *Mitterrand et la sortie de la guerre froide*, Paris, 1998.

Cohen, S. and M.-C. Smouts (eds). *La Politique extérieure de Valéry Giscard d'Estaing*, Paris, 1985.

Cole, A. *Franco-German Relations*, Harlow, 2001.

Commission of the European Communities. *Completing the Internal Market: White Paper from the Commission to the European Council, June 1985*, Luxembourg, 1985.

Commission of the European Communities – Committee for the Study of Economic and Monetary Union. *Report on Economic and Monetary Union in the European Community*, Luxembourg, 1989.

Commission of the European Communities – Committee for the Study of Economic and Monetary Union. *Collection of Papers submitted to the Committee for the Study of Economic and Monetary Union*, Luxembourg, 1989.

'Commission Memorandum to the Council on the coordination of economic policies and monetary cooperation within the Community', Supplement to *Bulletin of the European Communities* 3, 1969, 3–13.

'Les congrès de l'Europe, 1948–1998', *Commentaire* 21(82), 1998, 531–38.

Connolly, B. *The Rotten Heart of Europe: The Dirty War for Europe's Money*, 2nd edn, London, 1996.

Conseil – Commission des Communautés européennes. *Rapport au Conseil et à la Commission concernant la réalisation par étapes de l'union économique et monétaire dans la Communauté*, Luxembourg, 8 October 1970.

Cotta, A. *Pour l'Europe, contre Maastricht*, Paris, 1992.

Coudenhove-Kalergi, R.N. *Pan-Europa*, Vienna, 1923.*

Cousté, P.-B. and F. Visine. *Pompidou et l'Europe*, Paris, 1974.

Couve de Murville, M. *Une politique étrangère, 1958–1969*, Paris, 1971.

_____ *Le Monde en face. Entretiens avec Maurice Delarue*, Paris, 1989.

Creswell, M. and M. Trachtenberg. 'France and the German question, 1945–1955', plus responses (C. Cogan, W.I. Hitchcock, M.S. Sheetz) and a rejoinder, *Journal of Cold War Studies* 5(3), 2003, 5–53.

Dalloz, J. *Georges Bidault. Biographie politique*, Paris, 1992.

Debré, M. *Trois Républiques pour une France. Mémoires*, 5 vols, Paris, 1984–94.

Delafon, G. and T. Sancton. *Dear Jacques, Cher Bill. Au cœur de l'Elysée et la Maison Blanche, 1995–1999*, Paris, 1999.

Delors, J. *Mémoires*, Paris, 2004.

DePorte, A.W. *Europe between the Superpowers: The Enduring Balance*, 2nd edn, New Haven, 1986.

Diebold, W. *The Schuman Plan: A Study in Economic Cooperation, 1950–1959*, New York, 1959.

Dinan, D. *Europe Recast: A History of European Union*, Basingstoke, 2004.

_____ 'The historiography of the European Union', in D. Dinan (ed.), *Origins and Evolution of the European Union*, Oxford, 2006, 297–324.

Dinan, D. (ed.). *Origins and Evolution of the European Union*, Oxford, 2006.

Drouin, P. *L'Europe du Marché commun*, Paris, 1963.

Duchêne, F. *Jean Monnet: The First Statesman of Interdependence*, New York, 1994.

Duhamel, A. *Une ambition française*, Paris, 1999.

Dumas, R. *Le Fil et la pelote. Mémoires*, Paris, 1996.

Duroselle, J.-B. *L'Europe. Histoire de ses peuples*, Paris, 1990.* [Endnote reference to the translation: *Europe: A History of its Peoples*, London, 1990].

Dyson, K. *Elusive Union: The Process of Economic and Monetary Union in Europe*, London, 1994.

Dyson, K. and K. Featherstone. *The Road to Maastricht: Negotiating Economic and Monetary Union*, Oxford, 1999.

Eck, J.-F. *La France dans la nouvelle économie mondiale*, 5th edn, Paris, 2006.

Economist Intelligence Unit (The). *Country Report: France*, London, quarterly.

Eden, A. *Full Circle*, London, 1960.

Elgey, G. *Histoire de la IVe République*, 2 vols, Paris, 1965–68.

Fabius, L. *Une certaine idée de l'Europe*, Paris, 2004.

Faure, E. *Mémoires*, 2 vols, Paris, 1982–84.

Favier, P. and M. Martin-Roland. *La Décennie Mitterrand*, 3 vols, Paris, 1990–96.

Fitoussi, J.-P. *Le Débat interdit. Monnaie, Europe, pauvreté*, Paris, 1995.

Fontaine, A. *Histoire de la guerre froide*. 2 vols, Paris, 1965–67.

Friend, J.W. *The Linchpin: Franco-German Relations, 1950–1990*, New York, 1991.

Fursdon, E. *The European Defence Community: A History*, London, 1980.

Garton Ash, T. *In Europe's Name: Germany and the Divided Continent*, London, 1993.

Gaulle, C. de. *Mémoires de guerre*, 3 vols, Paris, 1954–59.*

_____ *Discours et messages*, 5 vols, Paris, 1970.

_____ *Mémoires d'espoir*, 2 vols, Paris, 1970–71.*

_____ *Lettres, notes et carnets*, 12 vols, Paris, 1980–86.

Genestar, A. *Les Péchés du prince*, Paris, 1992.

Genscher, H.-D. 'Memorandum für die Schaffung eines europäischen Währungsraumes und einer Europäischen Zentralbank', in Deutsche Bundesbank, *Auszüge aus Presseartikeln*, 1 March 1988.

_____ *Erinnerungen*, Munich, 1995.*

Gerbet, P. *La Construction de l'Europe*, 2nd edn, Paris, 1994.

Gerbet, P. (ed.). *Le Relèvement, 1944–1949*, Paris, 1991.

Giesbert, F.-O. *Jacques Chirac*, Paris, 1987.
_____ *François Mitterrand. Une vie*, Paris, 1996.
Gillingham, J. *Coal, Steel, and the Rebirth of Europe, 1945–1955: The Germans and French from Ruhr Conflict to European Community*, Cambridge, 1991.
_____ *European Integration, 1950–2003: Superstate or New Market Economy?* Cambridge, 2003.
Giscard d'Estaing, V. *Le Pouvoir et la vie*, 3 vols, Paris, 1988–2006.
Gnesetto, N. *La Puissance et l'Europe*, Paris, 1998.
Gordon, P.H. *France, Germany and the Western Alliance*, Boulder, 1995.
Gordon, P.H. and S. Meunier. *The French Challenge: Adapting to Globalization*, Washington, D.C., 2001.
Gordon, P.H. and J. Shapiro. *Allies at War: America, Europe, and the Crisis over Iraq*, New York, 2004.
Goriely, G. 'Il y a trente ans : La Sarre dit non au «statut européen»', *Le Monde*, 3–4 November 1985.
Grant, C. *Delors: Inside the House that Jack Built*, London, 1994.
Gros, D. and N. Thygesen. *European Monetary Integration*, 2nd edn, Harlow, 1998.
Grosser, A. *La IVe République et sa politique extérieure*, 3rd edn, Paris, 1972.
_____ *Affaires extérieures. La politique de la France, 1944–1989*, Paris, 1989.
Harryvan, A.G. and J. van der Harst (eds). *Documents on European Union*, London, 1997.
Hartley, A. *Gaullism: The Rise and Fall of a Political Movement*, London, 1972.
_____ 'The once and future Europe', *National Interest* Winter 1991/92, 44–53.
Heath, E. *Old World, New Horizons: Britain, the Common Market, and the Atlantic Alliance*, Oxford, 1970.
_____ *The Course of My Life: My Autobiography*, London, 1998.
Hellman, J. *The Knight-Monks of Vichy France: Uriage, 1940–1945*, 2nd edn, Montreal, 1997.
Hirsch, E. *Ainsi va la vie*, Lausanne, 1988.
Hitchcock, W.I. *France Restored: Cold War Diplomacy and the Quest for Leadership in Europe, 1944–1954*, Chapel Hill, 1998.
Hoffmann, S. *Decline or Renewal? France since the 1930s*, New York, 1974.
_____ *The European Sisyphus: Essays on Europe, 1964–1994*, Boulder, 1995.
Hogan, M.J. *The Marshall Plan: America, Britain, and the Reconstruction of Western Europe, 1947–1952*, Cambridge, 1987.
Holbrooke, R. *To End a War*, New York, 1998.
Horne, A. *Macmillan*, 2 vols, London, 1989.
Howarth, D.J. *The French Road to European Monetary Union*, Basingstoke, 2001.
Howarth, D. and P. Loedel. *The European Central Bank: The New European Leviathan?*, Basingstoke, 2003.
Howorth, J. 'La France, l'OTAN et la sécurité européenne : statu quo ingérable, renouveau introuvable', *Politique étrangère* 4, 2002, 1001–16.
Howorth, J. and J. Keeler (eds). *Defending Europe: The EU, NATO and the Quest for European Autonomy*, New York, 2003.
Institut Charles de Gaulle (ed.). *De Gaulle en son siècle*, vol. 5: *L'Europe*, Paris, 1992.
Jenkins, R. *European Diary, 1977–1981*, London, 1989.
Jessel, J. *La Double Défaite de Mitterrand. De Berlin à Moscou, les faillites d'une diplomatie*, Paris, 1992.
Jobert, M. *Mémoires d'avenir*, Paris, 1974.

_____ *L'Autre Regard*, Paris, 1976.
Jouve, E. *Le Général de Gaulle et la construction de l'Europe (1940–1966)*, 2 vols, Paris, 1967.
Judah, T. *Kosovo: War and Revenge*, New Haven, 2000.
Judt, T. *Postwar: A History of Europe since 1945*, New York, 2005.
Kagan, R. *Paradise and Power: America and Europe in the New World Order*, London, 2003.
Kissinger, H. *The White House Years*, New York, 1979.
_____ *Years of Upheaval*, Boston, 1982.
_____ *Diplomacy*, New York, 1994.
Kohl, H. *Erinnerungen, 1982–1990*, Munich, 2005.
Kolodziej, E.A. *French International Policy under de Gaulle and Pompidou: The Politics of Grandeur*, Ithaca, 1974.
Kyle, K. *Suez: Britain's End of Empire in the Middle East*, 2nd edn, London, 2003.
Lacouture, J. *De Gaulle*, 3 vols, Paris, 1984–86.*
_____ *Mitterrand. Une histoire de Français*, 2 vols, Paris, 1998.
La Gorce, P.-M. de. 'Les divergences franco-allemandes mises à nu', *Le Monde diplomatique*, September 1993.
Laird, R.F. (ed.). *Strangers and Friends: The Franco-German Security Relationship*, London, 1989.
Larkin, M. *France since the Popular Front: Government and People, 1936–1996*, 2nd edn, Oxford, 1997.
La Serre, F. de. 'L'Europe communautaire entre le mondialisme et l'entente franco-allemande', in S. Cohen and M.-C. Smouts (eds), *La politique extérieure de Valéry Giscard d'Estaing*, Paris, 1985, 86–109.
_____ 'France: the impact of François Mitterrand', in C. Hill (ed.), *The Actors in Europe's Foreign Policy*, London, 1996, 19–39.
Laughland, J. *The Tainted Source: The Undemocratic Origins of the European Idea*, London 1997.
Laursen, F. and S. Vanhoonacker (eds). *The Intergovernmental Conference on Political Union: Institutional Reforms, New Policies and the International Identity of the European Community*, Dordrecht, 1992.
Le Cacheux, J. (ed.). *Europe, la nouvelle vague. Perspectives économiques de l'élargissement*, Paris, 1996.
Ledwidge, B. *De Gaulle*, London, 1982.
Lemaître, P. 'L'Europe et les pays ACP réforment leur relation privilégiée', *Le Monde*, 4 February 2000.
['Letter of Eight']. 'Europe and America must stand united', *The Wall Street Journal Europe*, 30 January 2003.
Lipgens, W. (ed.). *Documents on the History of European Integration*, vol. 1: *Continental Plans for European Union, 1939–1945*, Berlin, 1985.
Livre blanc sur la défense 1994, Paris, 1994.
Ludlow, P. *The Making of the European Monetary System: A Case Study in the Politics of the European Community*, London, 1982.
Lynch, F.M.B. *France and the International Economy: From Vichy to the Treaty of Rome*, London, 1997.
Macmillan, H. *At the End of the Day, 1961–1963*, London, 1973.
Maelstaf, G. *Que faire de l'Allemagne? Les responsables français, le statut international de l'Allemagne et le problème de l'unité allemande (1945–1955)*, Paris, 1999.

Maillard, P. *De Gaulle et l'Allemagne. Le rêve inachevé*, Paris, 1990.
_____ *De Gaulle et l'Europe entre la nation et Maastricht*, Paris, 1995.
Mangold, P. *The Almost Impossible Ally: Harold Macmillan and Charles de Gaulle*, London, 2006.
Marjolin, R. *Le Travail d'une vie. Mémoires, 1911–1986*, Paris, 1986.*
Marsh, D. *The Bundesbank: The Bank that Rules Europe*, London, 1992.
Massigli, R. *Une comédie des erreurs, 1943–1956. Souvenirs et réflexions sur une étape de la construction européenne*, Paris, 1978.
Mauriac, F. *Bloc-notes*, 2nd edn, 5 vols, Paris, 1993.
Menon, A. *France, NATO and the Limits of Independence, 1981–97: The Politics of Ambivalence*, Basingstoke, 2000.
Messerlin, P.A. 'France and trade policy: is the "French exception" passée?', *International Affairs* 72(2), 1996, 293–309.
Michaud, Y. *Chirac dans le texte : la parole et l'impuissance*, Paris, 2004.
Milesi, G. *Le Roman de l'euro*, Paris, 1998.
Milward, A.S. *The Reconstruction of Western Europe, 1945–51*, London, 1987.
_____ *The European Rescue of the Nation-State*, 2nd edn, London, 2000.
Mitterrand, F. *Réflexions sur la politique extérieure de la France. Introduction à vingt-cinq discours (1981–1985)*, Paris, 1986.
_____ 'Lettre à tous les Français', *Le Monde*, 8 April 1988, and 9 April 1988.
_____ *De l'Allemagne, de la France*, Paris, 1996.
_____ *Onze discours sur l'Europe (1982–1995)*, Paris, 1996.
Monnet, J. *Mémoires*, Paris, 1976.* [Endnote references to the translation: *Memoirs*, London, 1978].
Montferrand, B. de. 'Stabilité européenne : le «plan Balladur»', *Politique internationale* 67, 1995, 238–48.
_____ *Défendre l'Europe. La tentation suisse*, Paris, 1999.
Moravcsik, A. *The Choice for Europe: Social Purpose and State Power from Messina to Maastricht*, Ithaca, 1998.
_____ 'De Gaulle between grain and *grandeur*: the political economy of French EC policy, 1958–1970 (part 1)', *Journal of Cold War Studies* 2(2), 2000, 3–43.
_____ 'De Gaulle between grain and *grandeur*: the political economy of French EC policy, 1958–1970 (part 2)', plus responses (S. Hoffmann, J.T.S. Keeler, A.S. Milward, J. Gillingham, J. Vanke, M. Trachtenberg) and a rejoinder, *Journal of Cold War Studies* 2(3), 2000, 4–142.
Nicholls, A.J. *Freedom with Responsibility: The Social Market Economy in Germany, 1918–1963*, Oxford, 1994.
Nixon, R. *The Memoirs of Richard Nixon*, New York, 1978.
Office for Official Publications of the European Communities. *Treaties Establishing the European Communities (ECSC, EEC, EAEC) – Single European Act – Other Basic Instruments*, Luxembourg, 1987.
_____ *Treaty on European Union*, Luxembourg, 1992.
_____ *European Union: Consolidated Versions of the Treaty on European Union and the Treaty Establishing the European Community*, Luxembourg, 1997.
_____ *Treaty of Nice Amending the Treaty on European Union, the Treaties Establishing the European Communities and Certain Related Acts*, Luxembourg, 2001.
_____ *Treaty Establishing a Constitution for Europe*, Luxembourg, 2005.
Organisation for Economic Cooperation and Development (OECD). *OECD Surveys: France*, periodical (published every one to two years).

Padoa-Schioppa, T. *The Road to Monetary Union in Europe: The Emperor, the Kings, and the Genies*, 2nd edn, Oxford, 2000.

Padoa-Schioppa, T. (ed.). *Efficiency, Stability and Equity: A Strategy for the Evolution of the Economic System of the European Community*, Oxford, 1987.

Pagedas, C.A. *Anglo-American Strategic Relations and the French Problem, 1960–1963: A Troubled Partnership*, London, 2000.

Pattison de Ménil, L. *Who Speaks for Europe? The Vision of Charles de Gaulle*, London, 1977.

Paxton, R.O. *Vichy France: Old Guard and New Order, 1940–1944*, 2nd edn, New York, 2001.

Pedersen, T. *Germany, France and the Integration of Europe: A Realist Interpretation*, London, 1998.

Perroux, F. *L'Europe sans rivages*, Paris, 1954.

Peyrefitte, A. *C'était de Gaulle*, 3 vols, Paris, 1994–2000.

Pflimlin, P. *Mémoires d'un Européen. De la IVe à la Ve République*, Paris, 1991.

Piettre, A. *L'Economie allemande contemporaine (Allemagne occidentale), 1945–1952*, Paris, 1952.

Pijpers, A., E. Regelsberger, and W. Wessels (eds). *European Political Cooperation in the 1980s: A Common Foreign Policy for Western Europe?* Dordrecht, 1988.

Pöhl, K.O. 'The further development of the European Monetary System', in Commission of the European Communities – Committee for the Study of Economic and Monetary Union, *Collection of Papers submitted to the Committee for the Study of Economic and Monetary Union*, Luxembourg, 1989, 129–84.

Poidevin, R. *Robert Schuman. Homme d'Etat, 1886–1963*, Paris, 1986.

Pomfret, R.W.T. *Mediterranean Policy of the European Community: A Study of Discrimination in Trade*, London, 1986.

_____ *Unequal Trade: The Economics of Discriminatory International Trade Policies*, Oxford, 1988.

Pompidou, G. *Pour rétablir une vérité*, Paris, 1982.

Quinlan, M. *European Defense Cooperation: Asset or Threat to NATO?* Washington, D.C., 2001.

Rathenau, W. *Tagebuch 1907–1922*, (ed.) H. Pogge von Strandmann, Düsseldorf, 1967.

Réau, E du. *L'Idée d'Europe au XXe siècle. Des mythes aux réalités*, Brussels, 1996.

Reuter, P. *Organisations européennes*, Paris, 1965.

Rioux, J.-P. *La France de la Quatrième République*, 2 vols, Paris, 1980–83.

Rouget, W. *Schwierige Nachbarschaft am Rhein. Frankreich-Deutschland*, Bonn, 1998.

Roussel, E. *Georges Pompidou, 1911–1974*, 2nd edn, Paris, 1994.

_____ *Jean Monnet, 1888–1979*, Paris, 1996.

Rueff, J. *Le Péché monétaire de l'Occident*, Paris, 1971.

Rupnik, J. 'La France de Mitterrand et les pays de l'Europe du Centre-Est', in S. Cohen (ed.), *Mitterrand et la sortie de la guerre froide*, Paris, 1998, 189–222.

Sakwa, R. and A. Stevens. *Contemporary Europe*, 2nd edn, Basingstoke, 2006.

Schabert, T. *Mitterrand et la réunification allemande. Une histoire secrète (1981–1995)*, Paris, 2005. [Revised and expanded edition of *Wie Weltgeschichte gemacht wird. Frankreich und die deutsche Einheit*, Stuttgart, 2002].

Schmidt, H. *Menschen und Mächte*, 2 vols, Berlin, 1987–90.*

Schoutheete de Tervarent, P. de. *La Coopération politique européenne*, 2nd edn, Brussels, 1986.

_____ 'The creation of the Common Foreign and Security Policy', in E. Regelsberger, P. de Schoutheete de Tervarent, and W. Wessels (eds), *Foreign Policy of the European Union: From EPC to CFSP and Beyond*, Boulder, 1997, 41–63.

Schumann, M. 'Témoignage sur l'identité européenne', in Association Georges Pompidou (ed.), *Georges Pompidou et l'Europe. Colloque—25 et 26 novembre 1993*, Brussels, 1995, 133–39.

Schwarz, H.-P. *Adenauer*, 2 vols, Stuttgart, 1986–91.* [Endnote references to the translation: *Konrad Adenauer: A German Politician and Statesman in a Period of War, Revolution and Construction*, 2 vols, Providence, 1995–97].

Séguin, P. *Discours pour la France*, Paris, 1992.

_____ *Itinéraire dans la France d'en bas, d'en haut et d'ailleurs*, Paris, 2003.

Seldon, A. *Major: A Political Life*, London, 1997.

Serfaty, S. *France, de Gaulle and Europe: The Policy of the Fourth and Fifth Republics toward the Continent*, Baltimore, 1968.

Seydoux, F. *Mémoires d'Outre-Rhin*, Paris, 1975.

Shevardnadze, E. *The Future Belongs to Freedom*, New York, 1991.

Simms, B. *Unfinest Hour: Britain and the Destruction of Bosnia*, London, 2001.

Simonian, H. *The Privileged Partnership: Franco-German Relations in the European Community, 1969–1984*, Oxford, 1985.

Soutou, G.-H. 'Georges Bidault et la construction européenne, 1944–1954', in S. Berstein, J.-M. Mayeur, and P. Milza (eds), *Le MRP et la construction européenne*, Brussels, 1993, 197–230.

_____ *L'Alliance incertaine. Les rapports politico-stratégiques franco-allemands, 1954–1996*, Paris, 1996.

_____ 'Le général de Gaulle et le plan Fouchet d'union politique européenne : un projet stratégique', *Revue d'Allemagne et des pays de langue allemande* 29(2), 1997, 211–20.

_____ 'Three rifts, two reconciliations: Franco-American relations during the Fifth Republic', in D.M. Andrews (ed.), *The Atlantic Alliance under Stress: US-European Relations after Iraq*, Cambridge, 2005, 102–27.

Soutou, G.-H. and J. Bérenger (eds). *L'Ordre européen du XVIe au XXe siècle*, Paris, 1998.

Strauss-Kahn, D. 'Une nation est née', *Le Monde*, 26 February 2003.

Sutton, M. *France to 2000: The Challenge of a Changing Europe*, EIU Economic Prospects Series, London, 1992.

_____ 'France and the European Union's enlargement eastwards', *The World Today* 50(8–9), 1994, 153–56.

_____ 'Euro-Maghreb Partnership: a new form of Association?', in The Economist Intelligence Unit, *European Trends*, 4th quarter 1994, 61–67.

Sutton, M. and J. Hellman. 'Distinguishing between anti-liberals' [debate], *Modern and Contemporary France* 7(4), 1999, 520–24.

Szász, A. *The Road to European Monetary Union*, Basingstoke, 1999.

Szulc, T. *Pope John Paul II: The Biography*, New York, 1995.

Teitgen, P.-H. *«Faites enter le témoin suivant». 1940–1958, de la Résistance à la Ve République*, Rennes, 1988.

Teltschik, H. *329 Tage. Innenansichten der Einigung*, Berlin, 1991.

Thatcher, M. *The Downing Street Years*, London, 1993.

Trachtenberg, M. *A Constructed Peace: The Making of the European Settlement, 1945–1963*, Princeton, 1999.

Tréan, C. 'La question de la frontière germano-polonaise a été «définitivement réglée»', *Le Monde*, 19 July 1990.

Tsoukalis, L. *The Politics and Economics of European Monetary Integration*, London, 1977.

———— *The New European Economy Revisited*, Oxford, 1997.

Ullman, R.H. 'The covert French connection', *Foreign Policy* 75, Summer 1989, 3–33.

Uri, P. *Penser pour l'action. Un fondateur de l'Europe*, Paris, 1991.

Urwin, D.W. *The Community of Europe: A History of European Integration since 1945*, 2nd edn, London, 1995.

Vaïsse, M. *La Grandeur. Politique étrangère du général de Gaulle, 1958–1969*, Paris, 1998.

Vaïsse, M., P. Mélandri, and F. Bozo (eds). *La France et l'OTAN, 1949–1996*, Brussels, 1996.

Vanke, J. 'Charles de Gaulle's uncertain idea of Europe', in D. Dinan (ed.), *Origins and Evolution of the European Union*, Oxford, 2006, 141–65.

Vanthoor, W.F.V. *European Monetary Union since 1848: A Political and Historical Analysis*, Cheltenham, 1996.

Védrine, H. *Les Mondes de François Mitterrand. A l'Elysée, 1981–1995*, Paris, 1996.

———— *France in an Age of Globalization*, with Dominique Moïsi, Washington, D.C., 2001. [Expanded edition of *Les Cartes de la France à l'heure de la mondialisation. Dialogue avec Dominique Moïsi*, Paris, 2000].

———— *Face á l'hyperpuissance. Textes et discours, 1995–2003*, Paris, 2003.

Vernet, D. 'Mitterrand, l'Europe et la réunification allemande', *Politique étrangère* 1, 2003, 165–79.

Villepin, D. de. *Le Cri de la gargouille*, Paris, 2002.

———— *Un autre monde*, Paris, 2003.

———— 'Diplomatie et action', *Politique internationale* 102, 2003–4, supplement, 5–62.

Wall, I.M. *The United States and the Making of Postwar France, 1945–1954*, Cambridge, 1991.

———— *France, the United States, and the Algerian War*, Berkeley, 2001.

Walter, A. *World Power and World Money: The Role of Hegemony and International Order*, 2nd edn, New York, 1993.

Watson, A. *The Evolution of International Society: A Comparative Historical Analysis*, London, 1992.

Weinberg, G.L. (ed.). *Hitler's Second Book: The Unpublished Sequel to Mein Kampf by Adolf Hitler*, New York, 2003.

Wight, M. *International Theory: The Three Traditions*, (eds) G. Wight and B. Porter, London, 1991.

Willis, F.R. *France, Germany, and the New Europe, 1945–1967*, 2nd edn, Stanford, 1968.

Wynaendts, H. *L'Engrenage. Chroniques yougoslaves, juillet 1991–août 1992*, Paris, 1993.

Yeager, L.B. *International Monetary Relations: Theory, History, and Policy*, New York, 1966.

Young, H. *This Blessed Plot: Britain and Europe from Churchill to Blair*, 2nd edn, London, 1999.

Young, J.W. *Britain, France and the Unity of Europe, 1945–1951*, Leicester, 1984.

_____ *France, the Cold War and the Western Alliance, 1944–49: French Foreign Policy and Post-War Europe*, Leicester, 1990.

Ypersele, J. van, and J.-C. Koeune. *The European Monetary System: Origins, Operation and Outlook*, Luxembourg, 1984.

Zaborowski, M. (ed.). *Friends Again? EU-US Relations after the Crisis*, Paris, 2006.

Zelikow, P. and C. Rice. *Germany Unified and Europe Transformed: A Study in Statecraft*, 2nd edn, Cambridge, Massachusetts, 1997.

Zielonka, J. *Europe as Empire: The Nature of the Enlarged European Union*, Oxford, 2006.

Zorgbibe, C. *Histoire de la construction européenne*, Paris, 1993.

Principal newspaper sources:
Agence Europe, Financial Times, Le Figaro, Le Monde, The Economist

INDEX